INDIA'S INTERNATIONAL RELATIONS

Volume 1

K.R. Gupta

ATLANTIC
PUBLISHERS & DISTRIBUTORS (P) LTD

Published by

ATLANTIC

PUBLISHERS & DISTRIBUTORS (P) LTD

7/22, Ansari Road, Darya Ganj,
New Delhi-110002
Phones : +91-11-23273880, 23275880, 23280451
Fax : +91-11-23285873
Web : www.atlanticbooks.com
E-mail : info@atlanticbooks.com

Branch Office
5, Nallathambi Street, Wallajah Road,
Chennai-600002
Phones : +91-44-64611085, 32413319
E-mail : chennai@atlanticbooks.com

Printed in India at Nice Printing Press, A-33/3A, Site-IV, Industrial Area, Sahibabad, Ghaziabad, U.P.

Preface

India's relations with the countries of the world have evolved considerably since the end of British rule in India. These relations reflect a traditional policy of non-alignment with its emphasis upon international peace, peaceful coexistence, integrity and independent foreign policy, which have been helpful for India in securing national interests as well as in building up its position in world politics. India's foreign policy since the time of Independence has essentially been to expand its strategic space. India's external relations have been characterized by the basic tenets of *Panchsheel.* Peace, disarmament, self-reliance, non-alignment, mutual respect and development are the bedrock of India's relations with other nations, and these principles determine its reactions to developments taking place in different parts of the world. India's foreign policy goals from 1947 until the late 1980s enabled it to achieve some success in carving out an independent international role.

The end of the bipolar world, with the disintegration of Soviet Union, ushered in an era of extraordinary flux and transition. At the turn of the century, world was still trying to cope with the ramifications of this paradigm shift, but even before we could come to terms with it, there was the tragic event of the gruesome terrorist attacks of World Trade Centre in New York which exposed the acute vulnerability of all nations to terrorist threats of unprecedented proportions. India too witnessed a terrorist attack on its Parliament in December 2001, which had a bearing on its foreign policy, particularly its relations with Pakistan—the nerve centre of terrorist activities.

India's foreign policy has to adapt to the rapidly changing global scenario, and at the same time, reconcile with the remarkable changes taking place within India itself. India has significantly expanded its network of international relationships and the country's political engagement and economic and technical cooperation with the world are greater today than ever before. India has also entered into strategic partnerships with the United States, Russia, UK, and the European Union and is pursuing strategic cooperation with China, and other South Asian countries, thus enlarging its bilateral relations and adding new dimensions to its policies and development options.

With the South Asian countries, India has accorded the highest priority to closer political, economic and cultural ties. It has a vision of South Asia as an integrated entity in which there is free flow of goods, people and ideas, unfettered by boundaries. There is a real opportunity today for shared prosperity between India and its neighbours.

The book *India's International Relations*, in two volumes, covers up all the important aspects of India's relations with major countries as well as its neighbours. The first volume contains six chapters with one chapter exclusively studying India's global perspective in terms of international relations. In the subsequent chapters, India's relations with the United States, Russia, China, the UK, and the European Union have been extensively studied. Each chapter focuses on a variety of topics ranging from historical relations to the current cooperation on socio-economic, political, military, science & technology, terrorism, and cultural issues, including latest treaties, agreements, pacts and other developments with exhaustive evaluation given at the end of each chapter.

Growing concerns about energy security have prompted India and the US to enter into a strategic partnership which culminated into Indo-US Civil Nuclear Deal that reflects the transformed relationship between the world's two largest democracies. The US-India strategic partnership is rooted in shared values and is broad in nature and scope, with two countries working together on global issues, including expanding economic freedom and democracy; ensuring plentiful sources of clean, safe, and reliable energy; protecting security; supporting innovation and technological advances; and promoting public health.

The second volume consists of four chapters. It studies India's relations with Pakistan, Bangladesh, Sri Lanka, and Nepal. It also focuses on its vital role in the whole of South Asia in pursuit of helping it emerge as a region of flourishing democracies.

I hope the vast coverage of the book will be of great help to the students, researchers and teachers of Indian politics and international relations. It would also be useful to the government executives and parliamentarians in India and several other countries concerned with the formulation and execution of the foreign policy.

Common readers interested in world politics would find the book useful, informative and interesting.

K.R. Gupta

Contents

1

India's International Relations: A Global Perspective

Commensurate with national interests and security, the improvement of bilateral relations is an important component of any foreign policy, and India has succeeded in establishing a network of mutually beneficial relations with all countries of the world.[1]

India's relations with the world have evolved considerably since the British colonial period. The foundation of India's foreign policy was laid during the freedom movement when our leaders, fighting for independence, were engaged with the great causes of the time. The principles of India's foreign policy, that emerged then, have stood the test of time: a belief in friendly relations with all countries of the world, the resolution of conflicts by peaceful means, the sovereign equality of all states, independence of thought and action as manifested in the principles of Non-alignment, and equity in the conduct of international relations.[2]

After India gained independence, it has maintained cordial relationship with most nations. India has a long history of collaboration with several countries. India is one of the founding members of the United Nations and it played a key role in establishing the Non-Aligned Movement (NAM) in 1961. India is also an active member of several international organizations.[3]

Jawaharlal Nehru, the first Prime Minister of India, who also served as foreign minister throughout his life, was the chief architect of India's foreign policy. According to Nehru, "India does not seek domination over others and our sole object is to be left in peace to ourselves to solve our own problems and where possible, to help and cooperate with others. In doing so, we try not to be swept by passion and anger and so maintain that temper of peaceful approach."

The basic object of India's foreign policy has been the maintenance of friendly relations with all nations of the world. Our policy is not to commit ourselves first to follow a certain line. Our policy is independence of action. If we say we are permanently neutral, it has no meaning except permanent retirement from public affairs in the national sense *Sannyas*. No country can do that and certainly we have no desire to retire from world affairs.

In the sphere of foreign affairs, India will follow an independent policy; keeping away from the power politics of groups aligned one against another. It will uphold the principle of freedom and will oppose racial discrimination, wherever, it may occur. It will work with the other peace-loving nations to promote international cooperation and goodwill without exploitation of one nation by another.

India's policy in regard to any matter is determined by the country itself and is, it may be said, pro-India with friendship towards other.

The use of the word 'neutral' to describe India's foreign policy is wrong except in terms of war. If you say there is a war on today, we are neutral. If you say there is a cold war, we are certainly neutral. The cold war is, in some ways, worse than a shooting war, worse not in disaster but in the sense that it is more degrading and it lowers the standards all the time. We do not propose to join that war. It does not matter who is wrong. We will not join in this exhibition of mutual abuse, because we do not serve anybody that way, certainly not the cause of peace. We want to befriend every country so that our circle of friendship may grow and become wide and cooperation and peace may thrive. What kind of friendship is that which envisages enmity with others? We should befriend all and stretch out our hands to all. For this reason our coming closer to the great country, Russia, is very important. But this does not mean that we have drifted away from any other country. This is neither the position now nor will it be at any time in the future. We have always wanted and we still want cooperation with the countries of the world to increase, and world peace to be strengthened.[4]

Any discussion on India's foreign policy has to begin with the contribution of Mahatma Gandhi, the father of the nation, who introduced an element of moral, value-based politics in our lives. It was not simply tactical in nature but a code of behaviour for the conduct of international relations by successive Indian governments. It is, therefore, no surprise that our external relations have been characterized by the basic tenets of *Panchsheel.* Peace, disarmament, self-reliance, non-alignment and development are the bedrock of India's relations with other nations, and they determine its reactions to external developments. Bedrock of Indian foreign policy is the element of consensus on vital foreign policy issues, transcending party affiliations, including political parties, diplomats, academics and opinion-makers alike.

While there is an undercurrent of continuity in India's foreign policy, its terms of reference have been undergoing a continuous change against the background of far-reaching, and sometimes, volatile changes in the global scenario.[5]

India's foreign policy, roughly extending from 1950 to 1980 may be called the '1st phase'—the phase of resistance, a process by which the Indian state along with the Indian bourgeoisie attempted to resist the forces of global capitalism and foster self-reliance. The second phase from 1980 onward is called the process of re-integration with the world economy.[6]

It is important to note a few significant changes that were made to adjust the foreign policy orientation to suit the changed circumstances. Apart from giving a greater economic orientation, it focused to re-tuning the non-alignment centred policy, attempts to which were made to mesh foreign policy priorities with security concerns.[7]

Some of the predicaments facing India are the challenges to the concept of the nation-state from linguistic, ethnic and religious groups, ongoing changes in the external equations and in the nature of global developmental and economic policies, trade and financial regimes, and the scourges of terrorism, often exported from other countries, as well as the menace of drugs and arms-trafficking and their links with terrorist and criminal outfits. Environmental conservation, protection and promotion of human rights, and disarmament have rightly assumed great importance in the world. While on some of these issues, India may have treaded a somewhat lonely path for sometime, gradually others are veering around to our approach. The vision of a world, free from inequities and violence, and devoted to economic and social uplift of humanity, so eloquently captured by the World Summit on Social Development, has to be realized. We are willing to cooperate with all in this endeavour, but will never tag ourselves in advance to others, or to a particular world-view. We retain the independent stance of our foreign policy, examining each issue on its merits, while being guided by our vital national interests and concerns.

A process of introspection is currently underway in our societal, economic and political structures, which will redefine a vibrant, dynamic and open India, at ease in its interactions with the world at large.

India's foreign policy has assumed a positive outward orientation with new policy initiatives aimed at consolidating traditional relationships, developing new relationships with countries and regions where India has vital strategic interests, a greater emphasis on economic dimensions in foreign policy, on the need to revitalize the NAM and to reform and restructure the United Nations to better reflect the aspirations of the developing countries.

India had never believed in the Cold War ethics. It resolutely opposed to those forces that sought to align the world into competing and adversarial camps. The end of Cold War and the disintegration of the Soviet Union, changing the relationship between the Russian Federation and the United States, changes of governments and the systems of governance in Eastern Europe and the positive interaction between Russia and China, have opened up new outlooks for India's foreign policy.[8]

During the 1990s, India's foreign policy has become reactive, defensive and obliging, because political parties have fractured the Indian society on the basis of caste *versus* caste, community *versus* community, region *versus* region, and language *versus* language. The consequence of this highly fragmented political process is that political parties have multiplied to promote their sectional and sectarian group interests.

Between 1989 and 1999, there have been five general elections—all of which have produced a fractured mandate. With no single party able to muster a clear majority on its own, India had entered the period of coalition politics in the last decade of the twentieth century. This has had effects on the foreign policy. Besides, in order to overcome the domestic economic crisis, India opted for aid from the International Monetary Fund (IMF) and the World Bank in the early nineties. As a result, the process of liberalisation and privatisation got underway, which in turn brought various pressures on the India's foreign policy.[9]

It is against these backgrounds, India has to restructure its policies to encompass changes, without losing continuity and balance, while firmly safeguarding the national interests.

India's size, population, and strategic location give it a prominent voice in international affairs, and its growing industrial base, military strength, and scientific and technical capacity give it added weight. The end of Cold War era dramatically affected India's foreign policy. It remains a leader of the developing world and the NAM. It is seeking to strengthen its political and commercial ties with the several countries, which include the United States, Russia, China, the United Kingdom, and the European Union. India also continues to play pivotal role in establishing a peaceful and progressive relationship with South Asian countries.[10]

India-US relations have remained complex and at times paradoxical. Historically, relations between India and the US were somewhat cold following Indian independence, as the first Indian Prime Minister Jawaharlal Nehru, was determined to keep away from the Cold War. Nehru chose a middle path, which subsequently came to be known as non-alignment. For most of the Cold War period, the US tended to have warmer relations with Pakistan, primarily as a way to contain

Soviet-friendly India and to use Pakistan to back the Afghan Mujahideen against the Soviet occupation of Afghanistan.

After the Sino-India War (1962) and the Indo-Pakistan War (1965), India had developed a close relationship with the Soviet Union. Consequently in 1971, the Indo-Soviet friendship treaty was signed that had an adverse effect on the Indo-US relations. The US saw Pakistan as a counter-weight to pro-Soviet India and started giving the former military and financial assistance. This created an atmosphere of suspicion between India and US.[11]

During 1970s, the US attitudes towards the Asian region, particularly India changed. In May 1974, India demonstrated its capabilities by testing a nuclear device. In 1976, it initiated a move towards normalization of relations with China and worked towards a rapprochement with the US. But it needs to be emphasized that despite these moves towards diversification of its relations, India maintained close relations with the Soviet Union.

In 1980s, it witnessed a gradual acceptance of India's growing pre-eminence in the region. This was reflected in India's (albeit unsuccessful) peacekeeping efforts in Sri Lanka despite its earlier involvement with the Tamil separatists, and during India's intervention in a coup attempt in the Maldives.

India and the US continued to have differences on various issues including the extension of the Non-Proliferation Treaty (NPT) and the Comprehensive Test Ban Treaty (CTBT).

The end of the Cold War and the disintegration of the Soviet Union accompanied by India's economic reforms initiated a process of gradual shift in the way the two countries perceived each other. India's nuclear tests in May 1998 brought the gradual process of the warming up of bilateral relations to an abrupt halt as the US also withheld spares for the Indian Navy's Sea King helicopters and Sea Harrier aircraft then undergoing repairs and overhaul in the UK.

The freeze did not last very long and improvement in relations was evident in the visit of US President Bill Clinton to India in March 2000, the first presidential visit in over 20 years. Since then relations between the two countries have swiftly evolved into what has been termed as a policy of comprehensive engagement.[12]

Recognizing India as a key to strategic US interests, the US has sought to strengthen its relationship with India. The two countries are the world's largest democracies, both committed to political freedom protected by representative government. India is also moving gradually toward greater economic freedom. The US and India have a common interest in the free flow of commerce and resources, including through the vital sea lanes of the Indian Ocean. They also share an interest in fighting terrorism and in creating a strategically stable Asia.

Differences remain, however, including over India's nuclear weapons program and the pace of India's economic reforms. In the past, these concerns may have dominated US thinking about India, but today the US views India as a growing world power with which it shares common strategic interests. A strong partnership between the two countries will continue to address differences and shape a dynamic and collaborative future.

In late September 2001, the US President George Bush lifted sanctions imposed under the terms of the 1994 Nuclear Proliferation Prevention Act following India's nuclear tests in May 1998. The non-proliferation dialogue initiated after the 1998 nuclear tests has bridged many of the gaps in understanding between the countries. In a meeting between President Bush and Indian Prime Minister A.B. Vajpayee in November 2001, the two leaders expressed a strong interest in transforming the US-India bilateral relationship. High level meetings and concrete cooperation between the two countries increased during 2002 and 2003. In January 2004, the US and India launched the Next Steps in Strategic Partnership (NSSP), which was both a milestone in the transformation of the bilateral relationship and a blueprint for its further progress.

In July 2005, President Bush hosted Prime Minister Dr. Manmohan Singh in Washington, DC. The two leaders announced the successful completion of the NSSP, as well as other agreements which further enhance cooperation in the areas of civil nuclear, civil space, and high technology commerce. Other initiatives announced at this meeting include a US-India

Economic Dialogue, Fight Against HIV/AIDS, Disaster Relief, Technology Cooperation, Democracy Initiative, Agriculture Knowledge Initiative, Trade Policy Forum, Energy Dialogue and CEO Forum. President Bush made a reciprocal visit to India in March 2006, during which the progress of these initiatives were reviewed, and new initiatives were launched.

In December 2006, the Congress passed the historic Henry J. Hyde United States-India Peaceful Atomic Cooperation Act, which allows direct civilian nuclear commerce with India for the first time in 30 years. The US policy had in the past opposed nuclear cooperation with India because the country had developed nuclear weapons in contravention of international conventions and never signed the Nuclear Non-Proliferation Treaty. The legislation clears the way for India to buy US nuclear reactors and fuel for civilian use.

The US and India further elevated the strategic partnership in 2007 to include cooperation in counter-terrorism, defense cooperation, education, and joint democracy promotion.[13]

India-Russia relations maintain a basic continuity from their accumulated inheritance stretching back to about 40 years after India gained independence. Both the countries enjoyed a close strategic relationship for the major portion of the Cold War era. In relation to what was the cornerstone of the India-Russia strategic relationship, both countries renewed the Treaty of Peace and Friendship, which was an extension of the previous Indo-Soviet Treaty of Peace and Friendship of 1971, that was extended for another 20 years in 1991.

The end of Cold War and the disintegration of the Soviet Union have, however, transformed that rivalry into Washington/Moscow policy coordination and have in their wake brought about a grand shift from alliance to re-alignment in South Asia. During the time of Yeltsin, President of Russian Federation, it was a period of exploratory interaction given the context of the Russian Federation engaged in re-structuring new global equations in the post-Soviet era.

The two countries have the mechanism of holding annual summit from the year 2000. A major breakthrough was achieved when the President of Russian Federation, Vladimir Putin visited

India in October 2000, December 2002 and 2004, and again in January 2007.

Russia is one of the most important military powers in the world after the United States of America. Russia gives a higher priority to India in its foreign policy and strategic calculations than America or other countries of the world in spite of the latter acknowledging India's importance incrementally. Realism requires that Russia remains a country of top priority in India's foreign policy.

India's relations with the Russian Federation are characterized by friendship and cooperation, based on trust and confidence. Our effort is directed towards retaining the positive elements of the old relationship while making adjustments as necessary, in a dynamic and forward-looking manner to the changed situation in both countries.[14]

The compatibility in the national interests of both nations and their commonly shared perceptions in respect of various issues give rise to the expectation and hope that Indo-Russia relations are destined to develop further, more mature, and warm and friendly cooperation in the future. It should also be remembered that China and India are the two most populous nations in Asia and together with Japan, constitute the three most powerful nations in Asia.

India's relations with China have been characterized by a series of tension and cooperation. It has gone through a tortuous process — from friendship to confrontation, from confrontation to *détente* and then to normalization. India has consistently viewed bilateral relations with China in a positive spirit. It seeks friendly, cooperative, good-neighborly and mutually beneficial relations with China on the basis of the five principles of peaceful co-existence, mutual sensitivity to each other's concerns and equality. It also remains committed to the process of dialogue to resolve outstanding differences and to build a strategic and cooperative partnership for peace and prosperity.

Indian Prime Minister Rajiv Gandhi's historic visit to Beijing in 1988 marked the resumption of political dialogue at the highest level. Both sides agreed to develop and expand bilateral relations in all fields, while continuing to address the outstanding differences. Premier Li Peng's visit to India in December 1991 further developed the relationship and fostered mutual understanding. His Indian counterpart Prime Minister P.V. Narashima Rao visited China in September 1993 during which the Agreement on the Maintenance of Peace and Tranquility along the Line of Actual Control (LAC) in the India-China Border Area was signed and the India-China Expert Group of Diplomatic and Military Officers to assist the JWG was set up.

During President Jiang Zemin's state visit to India in November 1996, the first visit of a Chinese Head of State, the two countries agreed to work towards a constructive and cooperative relationship while continuing to address outstanding differences.

Bilateral relations suffered a setback after the India's nuclear tests in May 1998, but soon, in early 1999, both countries made efforts to resume official level dialogue, with both Foreign Ministries holding talks in February 1999. Both sides reiterated that neither country is a threat to the other. High-level exchanges were renewed with the visit of President K.R. Narayanan in May-June 2000. This was the second visit to China by an Indian Head of State in the last 50 years and it marked a return to normalcy in bilateral relations.

During Prime Minister A.B. Vajpayee's visit to China in June 2003, a Joint Declaration on Principles for Relations and Comprehensive Cooperation and ten agreements were signed. When the Chinese Premier Wen Jiabao visited India in April 2005, the two Prime Ministers signed a joint statement, which established a strategic cooperative partnership for peace and prosperity between the two countries.

Every visit by the top leadership of the two countries has yielded in the setting up of new milestones in India-China relations.

Mr. Hu Jintao, President of China, visited India from 20 to 23 November 2006, which signifies another important milestone in bilateral relations. It was only the second visit to India by any Chinese President. The President visit showed that there is a mutual willingness to keep the irritants aside and move forward. The timing was appropriate since it also marked the high tide of "Sino-Indian Year of Friendship". A number of commitments were made in 2005 when Wen Jiabao, the Chinese Premier was in India and Hu was here mainly to consolidate those gains. The various agreements signed in New Delhi, to upgrade India-China relations, to further substantiate and reinforce their Strategic and Cooperative Partnership, committed them to pursuing the "Ten-Pronged Strategy" which embodied in the Joint Declaration. Indeed, it was a 'road map' for comprehensive development of bilateral relations.

China seems anxious to maintain good relations with India. President Hu's during his visit to India, speaking of *Panchsheel*, said that China and India are "true friends", not rivals but partners, even on the nuclear issue, it doesn't have too many reservations.

It is quite significant that in spite of many drawbacks in the bilateral relations, the two nations have upgraded their diplomatic relations to the current level of "strategic comprehensive partnership for peace and prosperity". Looking at the emerging world order in terms of the developments especially since 9/11, combating terrorism, the nuclear crisis in North Korea and President Hu Jintao's South Asia tour, one can be of more optimistic view of the future India-China bilateral relations. India and China are the two most important emerging economies in the world, their cooperation can, indeed, reap rich dividends for their progress.

However, India-China partnership cannot be achieved unless China walks a step ahead. At the same time, India has to rise above its personal gains and past experiences and accommodating a bit of China and Pakistan's concerns.

India has a very cordial relation with the United Kingdom (UK) and this is so in spite of the fact that there was lots of resentment against the British during their rule in India. The relationship between the two countries is warm and based on deep cultural, historical and, above all, personal roots. India's multi-faceted bilateral relationship with the UK has developed substantially over the past few years. There have been regular and close consultations at the highest levels. Strong ties with the UK are a priority for India given the political and civilization ties, substantial economic linkages and the large community of people of Indian origin living in the UK.

On foreign policy and defense, too, India and UK are cooperating more than ever before. Both the countries also extend cooperation on the issues such as security and terrorism which have an impact on both global and domestic agendas. Indian Prime Minister Dr. Manmohan Singh visited the UK during 19-20 September 2004. The bilateral summit was followed up to in September 2004 when the two Prime Ministers had adopted a joint declaration titled: "India-UK: Towards a New and Dynamic Partnership", setting out plans for a comprehensive strategic partnership. The joint declaration envisaged annual summits as well as meetings between Foreign Ministers and outlined areas for future cooperation in civil nuclear energy cooperation, space, defence, combating terrorism, economic ties, science and technology, education and culture.

The two leaders exchanged views on a range of bilateral, regional and multilateral issues including UN reform, cooperation against terrorism, the Millennium Development Goals, climate change including technology transfers for sustainable development and education exchanges. The two sides agreed to move forward their cooperation in the civilian nuclear energy sector. The UK had reviewed its policy with regard to civilian nuclear technology cooperation and scientific contacts with India a few weeks prior to the visit. At the Summit it recognized the need for a supportive international environment for meeting India's pressing energy requirements.

The UK strongly supports India's candidature for a permanent seat in the UN Security Council. India is a strategic partner for the European Union (EU). The UK is looking to develop this relationship in various fields, including in the area of counter-terrorism, on which the EU and India will work closely together. Promoting an effective EU in India complements the activity in promoting the UK. The UK wants India to take part in the work of G-8, therefore, invited for the first time Indian Prime Minister Dr. Manmohan Singh to the G-8 Summit at Gleneagles in July 2006.

Regarding bilateral military relationship, both countries armed forces share a common ethos, organisation and approach.

Today, both India and UK increasingly have shared goals too, and a common will to achieve them by active engagement in the world. Britain and India can do more together than which have already been done—bilaterally on education, business or culture, and internationally on tackling issues which confront us all such as the fight against terrorism, trade, global warming, poverty, sustainable development, etc.

The relations between India and the Member States of EU have a long history. But EU-India relations really took roots in their present form in 1963, when India was amongst the first developing countries to establish diplomatic relations with the then six-nation European Economic Community (EEC). India and EU states share a common commitment to democracy, pluralism, human rights and the rule of law and seek to pursue economic progress and prosperity for the people in a peaceful, stable and secure global environment.

The EU-India relations have developed at a remarkable speed over the past few years that include key areas such as political relations, trade and investment, economic and development cooperation as well as cultural exchanges. A strong impetus came from the Cooperation Agreement on Partnership and Development, which was signed between the EU and India in December 1993 and came into force in August 1994.

In July 1996, the European Commission presented a strategy called "Communication: 'EU-India Enhanced Partnership'," which suggested a number of steps to reinforce this relationship. The Council as well as the European Parliament subsequently endorsed the recommendations of the Commission.

With the first ever EU-India Summit, which was held in Lisbon in June 2000, a new chapter has opened in EU-India relations. The Summit Declaration was a visionary document which covers every aspect of the EU-India relationship and provides an action plan for upgrading this to a qualitatively higher level. It also reflects the commonality of views between India and EU on many issues, both political and economic, including shared convictions that need to build up a new strategic partnership in the new emerging world order.

The sixth EU-India Summit, held in September 2005, in New Delhi, was the culmination of a gradual upgrading of EU-India relations which started at The Hague Summit, in 2004, with the upgrading of EU-India relations to a "Strategic Partnership", as recommended by a 2004 Commission Communication on EU-India Relations.

The seventh EU-India Summit was held in Helsinki on 13 October 2006. A key outcome of the summit was an agreement on the establishment of a high-level trade group to study and explore ways to deepen the relationship in the field of trade and investment.

The outcome of the EU-India Summits has so far stressed the importance of maintaining the momentum towards further trade liberalization and strengthening the WTO, based on the agenda that adequately reflects the interest of all members of the multilateral trading system. Both sides agreed that their bilateral cooperation on WTO matters should be put on a more solid and structured basis. Besides that, it focuses on to deepen political dialogue and join forces on the international stage to address global challenges—violation of human rights, strengthening the UN's peacekeeping forces, fight against terrorism, strengthen dialogue on migration and consular issues, reinforced parliamentary exchanges, etc. The EU-India relations have grown exponentially from what used to be a purely trade and business driven relationship to one covering many other potential areas of mutual interest.

India's approach to friendship and good neighbourly relations was enunciated soon after its independence through the five principles of *Panchsheel*, namely mutual respect for each other's territory, non-aggression, non-interference, equality and mutual benefit and above all peaceful co-existence. While democracy remains India's abiding conviction, India has remained engaged with all governments and all countries in our neighborhoods.[15]

India's foreign policy has always regarded the concept of neighborhood as one of widening concentric circles, around a central axis of historical and cultural commonalities.[16]

From this point of view, India attaches the highest importance to developing cordial and friendly relations with her neighbors with a view to promoting peace, stability, mutual confidence in the region, and for developing strongly economic and commercial relations for all-round prosperity.[17]

With Pakistan, India has consistently pursued a policy seeking to improve relations under the framework of the Simla Agreement, signed in 1972, which provided for the solution of outstanding issues peacefully and bilaterally and for establishing durable peace in the subcontinent.[18]

India continues to reach out to Pakistan for dialogue and have made steady progress in enhancing economic cooperation and people-to-people contact, which led to change the relationships. The composite dialogue, the Joint Commission and the Joint Anti-terrorism Mechanism have provided a structured framework within which major issues are discussed. For India, terrorism remains an issue of particular concern. Infiltration continues from across the border. India has stressed to Pakistan that the success of the dialogue process is predicated on Pakistan fulfilling its commitment not to permit any territory under its control to be used to support terrorism in any manner.[19]

Instead of looking at each other as adversaries, both governments have had the courage to go beyond the misgivings of the past and to move ahead together in the interests of a better future for our people.[20]

India's links with Bangladesh, like with its other South Asian neighbors, are civilisational, cultural, social and economic. However, Bangladesh occupies a special place because India played a historic and unique role in the liberation of Bangladesh which emerged as a sovereign nation in 1971. Today, the bilateral relationship between India and Bangladesh is at levels far below its potential. Nonetheless, it remains our hope and endeavour to remain engaged on the entire spectrum of issues that would lend themselves to resolution in an atmosphere of goodwill, mutual trust and an open-minded approach.[21]

Relations between India and Nepal have been traditionally close and reflect the links of history, culture, language and religion. These relations continued to strengthen and symbolized by exchange of high-level visits.

Bilateral relations with Sri Lanka continued to be close, friendly and cooperative. Through the implementation of the 1964 and 1974 Agreements, the issues of the stateless people of Indian origin in Sri Lanka were resolved. High-level contacts were regularly maintained to strengthen bilateral cooperation in all fields of mutual interest. India has always stood for a peaceful political settlement of the ethnic issues.[22]

Recently, the government of India has taken initiatives to further strengthen ties with our neighbors, which have won international appreciation. These initiatives are based on five clear principles:

- First, with neighbors like Bangladesh, Bhutan, Maldives, Nepal and Sri Lanka, India does not ask for reciprocity but gives all that it can in good faith and trust.
- Secondly, no South Asian country should allow its territory to be used against the interests of another country of the region.
- Thirdly, none will interfere in the internal affairs of another.
- Fourthly, all South Asian countries must respect each other's territorial integrity and sovereignty.
- And finally, they should settle all their disputes through peaceful bilateral negotiations.

These tenets have paid rich dividends. A landmark treaty has been signed with Bangladesh on the sharing of waters of the Ganga. With Bhutan and Nepal, major projects of economic collaboration have been advanced. Our relations with Sri Lanka have shown steady improvement.[23]

India offers to all South Asian Association for Regional Cooperation (SAARC) member states a vast productive hinterland that would provide to them far greater opportunities for growth than if they were to rely exclusively either on their domestic markets or on markets much further away.[24]

India readily accepts that as the largest country in the South Asia region with the strongest economy, it has a greater responsibility in developing bilateral relationship with our neighbours.

As the larger neighbor, we are prepared to give much more than we can ever hope to get. This has been amply demonstrated through the free markets that India has already established with Sri Lanka, Nepal and Bhutan and in the bilateral Free Trade Agreement that we have offered to Bangladesh. India is keenly aware that its own peace and prosperity is inextricably linked with that of its neighbors. We are as committed to our own sustained economic development and welfare of our people as we are to partnering our neighbors on a mutually agreed basis in their economic development.[25]

In our immediate neighborhood, India's foreign policy has often been misconstrued as a search for hegemony. It has also often been accused of treating South Asia as an Indian sphere of influence. India's primacy in South Asia is based on demography and geography. We have borders with all the other South Asian countries, while only Pakistan and Afghanistan among the SAARC states share a frontier with each other. That reality will not change. India's commitment to develop political relations with its South Asian neighbors on the basis of sovereign equality and mutual respect is underlined by our recent decision to upgrade the 1949 friendship treaty with Bhutan and our willingness to review the 1950 treaty with Nepal. Amidst the increasing globalisation of South Asian economies and polities, there is no question of India pursuing the outdated idea of an exclusive sphere of influence. India's strong support to the entry of China and Japan into the SAARC as observers underlines India's commitment to open regionalism in the subcontinent.

The real opportunity in South Asia today is the prospect for shared prosperity between India and its neighbors. For too long we in South Asia had little to share but poverty. Today, amidst high growth rates across the subcontinent, we are in a position to advance together through free trade, open borders, and regional economic integration. Trans-border transport and energy corridors would not only link the subcontinent within itself but also with the abutting regions of South East Asia, Central Asia and the Persian Gulf.

India is conscious that no South Asian nation can succeed on its own. We must create a stake for every nation in the economic success of the other.[26] As India is an active member of the SAARC, with India's full support, SAARC has recently taken significant steps in accelerating the pace of economic cooperation.[27] India will continue to work and take the initiative in accelerating regional economic and political cooperation. India will also play a positive role in the deepening of South Asian economic integration as well as the establishment of new trans-border transport networks and energy pipelines with the eastern neighbors.[28]

NOTES

1. "India's Foreign Policy — 50 Years of Achievement" http://www.indianembassy.org/policy/Foreign Policy/fp(intro).htm
2. *Ibid.*
3. "Foreign Relations of India"—Wikipedia, the free encyclopedia en.wikipedia.org/wiki/Foreign relations of India — 126k
4. N. Jayapalan, *Foreign Policy of India*, Atlantic Publishers and Distributors (P) Ltd, New Delhi (2003), pp. 36-37.
5. "Continuity and Change within the Global Scenario", Address by I.K. Gujral, Minister of External Affairs, Government of India at the Council for Foreign Relations, New York, 3 October 1996. http://www.indianembassy.org/policy/Foreign Policy/global(gujral).htm
6. V. Shukla, *India's Foreign Policy in the New Millennium*, Atlantic Publishers and Distributors (P) Ltd, New Delhi (2005), pp. xvi-xvii.
7. "A Prominent Foreign Policy Initiative" www.idsa.in/publications/strategic-analysis/2004/april/Naidu.pdf
8. *Ibid.*, p. 5.
9. *Ibid.*, p. 6.
10. "Background Note: India" http://www.state.gov/r/pa/ei/bgn/3454.htm
11. *Ibid.*, p. 3.
12. "India-US Relations" http://www.aph.gov.au/library/pubs/rp/2001-02/02rp20.htm
13. *Ibid.*, p. 10.

14. *Ibid.*, p. 5.
15. Third Department of Peace and Conflict Studies Foundation Day Lecture, Address by Ms. Veena Sikri, High Commissioner of India to Bangladesh, at Dhaka University on June 9, 2006 http://www.hcidhaka.org/Speeches/june_09_06.html
16. *Ibid.*, p. 1.
17. *Ibid.*, p. 5.
18. *Ibid.*, p. 1.
19. "The Challenges Ahead for India's Foreign Policy", Speech by Foreign Secretary, Shri Shivshankar Menon at the Observer Research Foundation, New Delhi http://meaindia.nic.in/cgi-bin/db2www/meaxpsite/coverpage.d2w/coverpg?sec=ss&filename=speech/2007/04/11ss01.htm
20. *Ibid.*, p. 15.
21. *Ibid.*
22. "India's Neighbours" http://www.indianembassy.org/policy/Foreign_Policy/sasia.htm
23. *Ibid.*, p. 1.
24. *Ibid.*, p. 15.
25. *Ibid.*
26. Address by External Affairs Minister on the occasion of National Launch of Global India Foundation — "India and the Global Balance of Power" http://www.indianembassy.org.ua/english/speech7.htm
27. *Ibid.*, p. 1.
28. *Ibid.*, p. 26.

2

Indo-US Relations

BACKGROUND

The relationship between India and US since 1947 shows that though their relation has been friendly and cooperative yet this lacks warmth and cordiality.[1] The US sees its relations with India as central to maintaining long-term stability in Asia. The US interest in India was evident as early as five years before India got independence when President Franklin D. Roosevelt suggested to Winston Churchill that he supported India's freedom struggle movement. This support soon evaporated after the Indian National Congress decided not to support the World War II effort and launched the Quit India Movement. This move was not critical to the independence movement since its lobbying efforts were directed at the British government. In any event contacts between Indian leaders and the United States had been minimal and most of them including Mahatma Gandhi and Jawaharlal Nehru had been educated in Britain.

The first Indian Prime Minister Jawaharlal Nehru, who was the prime architect of India's foreign policy, was determined to keep away from the Cold War. Nehru chose a middle path, which subsequently came to be known as non-alignment. As early as 1947, in a note to India's Ambassador designate to China, K.P.S. Menon he wrote: "Our general policy is to avoid entanglement in power politics and not join any group of powers as against any other group. The two leading groups today are the Russian bloc and the Anglo-American bloc. We must be friendly to both and yet not join either. Both America and Russia are extraordinarily suspicious of each other as well as of other countries. This makes our path difficult and we may well be suspected by each of leaning towards the other. This cannot be helped. The Soviet Union, being our neighbor, we shall inevitably develop close relations with it. We cannot afford to antagonize Russia merely because we think that this may irritate someone else. Nor indeed can we antagonize the USA."

Consequently, India under Nehru pursued a globally oriented foreign policy while trying to maintain a careful distance between the power blocs of the East and the West. Its stand on disarmament, anti-colonialism and world peace won for India the respect of the newly independent countries of Asia and Africa, gratified that one of them could speak on equal terms with the two great powers. It was also a source of satisfaction for Indian nationalists who viewed it as final proof that Independence had truly been won.

However, India's policy of non-alignment suffered from two inherent weaknesses. While the policy of globalism and Asianism (a vision of United Asia) secured for India a politically high profile in spite of its military and economic weaknesses, success was dependent on the requirements (of the great powers) of the support and goodwill of the newly emerging nations which India claimed to have influence over. Secondly, Nehru ignored the need to evolve a concept of regional security. Political influence at the global level was considered to more than offset the need for diplomacy and military power to protect Indian interests (including territorial integrity) in South Asia. This policy was finally tested in the India-China border conflict in 1962 and found to be seriously deficient.

It is against this background that the development of India-US relations that had a shaky start, a history of disagreements over a wide range of issues, and instances of cooperation, albeit rare, took shape. Pakistan and China's relations with the US had also influenced the bilateral relationship. The result was a prismatic nature of India-US relations, which tended to be affected by the dynamics of the US ties with India's neighbors. The end of the Cold War and the collapse of the Soviet Union accompanied by India's economic reforms initiated a process of gradual shift in the way the two countries perceived each other.

This gradual process of the warming up of bilateral relations came to an abrupt halt after India's nuclear tests in May 1998. The freeze did not last very long and improvement in relations was evident with the visit of President Clinton to India in March 2000, the first presidential visit in over 20 years. Since then relations between the two countries have swiftly evolved into what has been termed as a policy of comprehensive engagement.

THE EARLY YEARS

As has been observed, after the end of the Second World War, there existed in the US a profound ignorance of Asia in general and India in particular. The US Secretary of State Dean Acheson's illusion that if the world is round, the Indians must be standing on their heads, represented the vagueness prevailing even among the educated Americans. Neither the Truman nor the Eisenhower administrations had people who were familiar with India. Eisenhower, despite being the first President to visit India, still viewed Asia in terms of a power vacuum ripe for communist expansion. The Korean War (1950-53) would certainly have reinforced his conviction. India's actions during and after the war were also a demonstration of its policy of non-alignment. As a member of the UN Commission on Korea and a non-permanent member of the Security Council, India voted for the 25 June 1950 resolution naming North Korea as aggressor and calling for the withdrawal of its troops to the 38th Parallel. It opposed or abstained from voting for subsequent US sponsored resolutions including one naming China as the aggressor and the Uniting for Peace resolution of September 1950. It also established an informal grouping of Asian and Arab delegations for purposes of mediation. It was the Indian draft resolution on the question of repatriation of prisoners of war that was ultimately passed. The five-nation Neutral Nations Repatriation Commission (NNPR) nominated India's General K.S. Thimmaiya as chairman. While India had established its non-aligned credentials by balancing US interests with those of the Soviet Union and China, the US was not only unhappy with the loss of support but also perceived India as moving away from the west but not from the communist countries. Another question to which India and the US consistently disagreed was that of China's membership of the United Nations.

India also opposed the US acts of establishing bases in Asia as part of its containment policy as well as its military aid to Pakistan from 1954 onwards while denying such assistance to India. Also, it was with the US support that Pakistan could raise the Kashmir issue in the Security Council (1957, 1962 and 1964). In terms of perception, while India's world view was that of members of military alliances and non-aligned nations, the US perception was that of allies and others.

These differences did not preclude occasional cooperation between the two countries when their interests converged. This was evident in Indian participation in the UN backed solution of the Suez crisis (1956), the agreement on the neutralization of Laos (1962) and the UN operations in Congo after 1961.

Economic relations between the two countries provided an interesting contrast to their political relations. American investment in India was substantial compared to that of other countries. The US aid program has been described as having 'motivations ranging from pure humanitarianism to crass materialism'. Between 1950 and 1965 the US provided 50 per cent of foreign aid received by India. However, more than half of this was in the form of food aid under Public Law 480 (1954). For the US it was a politically convenient way of disposing its food surplus. In 1957 the US established a Development Loan Fund to provide loans to enable India to procure capital goods from the former. It was also on the US initiative that the World Bank established an Aid-India Consortium, which provided substantial funds to India's Third Five-Year Plan. An agreement on the construction of nuclear power plants was signed in 1963 beginning with the one at Tarapur near Bombay. A contentious aspect of economic relations was that with very few exceptions, the US declined to invest in or assist Indian heavy industry. This could be perceived as an attempt to prevent India from achieving self-sufficiency in this sector as well as to ensure a market for US products. For this, as well as the supply of military equipment, India turned to the Soviet Union.

POST-INDIA-CHINA WAR

In the aftermath of the India-China border conflict of 1962, India requested, and received, military assistance not only from the Soviet Union but also from the US and Britain. Although much has been made of this gesture by the latter two countries, circumstances soon allowed the reduction of this commitment. There are two points to be made in this context. Firstly, only a small amount of 'emergency' assistance was actually committed. There was no offer of long-term military aid. Secondly, the US-UK offer was conditional on the successful resolution of the Kashmir dispute in which India was expected to make substantial concessions. The US-UK-brokered negotiations did take place in 1962-63 but were unsuccessful. Also, US military aid was provided on the condition that it would in no circumstances be used against any adversaries but China. This was in total contrast to the unconditional military assistance by the US to Pakistan. According to the then US Ambassador to India, Chester Bowles, "the Indians to conclude that we attribute to the People's Republic of China lion-like qualities in Southeast Asia and sheep-like qualities along India's 2200 mile border". In any event the very limited military assistance came to an end in September 1965 when Pakistan attacked India across the ceasefire line in Kashmir and India retaliated by attacking Pakistan across the border in Punjab. India was also less than impressed by the relatively less critical reaction by the US and UK to Pakistan's attack than to India's counter-attack as well as the use of US supplied military hardware by Pakistan.

The war also revealed a new correlation of forces in the region. China openly supported Pakistan while the Soviet Union was somewhat more neutral as compared to its earlier partisan support of India. Presumably with the tacit agreement of the US, the Soviet Union played a mediator role at the Tashkent talks between India and Pakistan and, for a while seemed to emerge as a security manager for the subcontinent. It even provided limited military supplies to Pakistan (already receiving arms from the US and China) between 1967-69, a move that angered India but had little effect, considering India's dependence on the Soviet Union for military and economic assistance.

Also during this period India was undergoing an economic and food crisis and the newly elected Prime Minister, Mrs. Indira Gandhi, was discovering the limitations that dependence imposed on India's desire for autonomy. The issue was micro-managed and ineptly handled by President Johnson. The US pressured India into devaluing the rupee in 1966 and, during the food crisis, used supply pressures in order to have India relent on international issues, especially Vietnam. According to the then US Ambassador to India: "Cables from Washington burned with comments about 'those ungrateful Indians', and the shipments of wheat were further delayed. Our official logic in regard to India seemed to run as follows: If India cannot support US policy, it should at least refrain from criticizing it, or accept the consequences." This spirit at its worst was reflected in a remark a White House official made to me. "Mrs. Gandhi," I asserted, "was only saying what UN Secretary General, U Thant and the Pope had said over and over again." "But", replied the official, "the Pope and U Thant don't need our wheat."

Prime Minister Indira Gandhi's mistrust of US policies in later years probably had its origin in these series of humiliations and, while India refused to compromise, the Prime Minister reportedly determined never again to be put in such a plight.

India-US relations further deteriorated after Richard Nixon assumed the presidency and moved towards a rapprochement with China, thereby eliminating the last argument in favor of support for India as part of a policy of containing China. Brought about with the help of Pakistan, the establishment of US-China relations resulted in what was a convergence of US-Pakistan-China interests, a move that could not but be perceived by India to be threatening. The crisis in East Pakistan (later Bangladesh) that led to a war in 1971 resulted in the first steps towards what would emerge as an Indo-centric power structure in South Asia. India decided to defy the US and its 'tilt' towards Pakistan and signed the Treaty of Peace, Friendship and Cooperation with the Soviet Union, thereby assuring India of material and diplomatic support in case of a war with Pakistan which, by then, seemed inevitable.

POST-BANGLADESH WAR

India's victory in the 1971 war with Pakistan and the creation of Bangladesh owed their success to Prime Minister Gandhi's primary policy objective: that India's security goals ranked foremost in its foreign policy. It was also an indication as to how far India's foreign policy goals had changed since the days of her father, Prime Minister Nehru. India had now emerged as South Asia's pre-eminent regional power. This was further demonstrated by the fact that the Simla Agreement of July 1972, with Pakistan was arrived at without the involvement of any external powers. Further, the two countries agreed to resolve any future problems bilaterally and work towards the development of friendly relations. This trend towards bilateralism became fairly well entrenched in the 1970s. As an analyst has observed: "From the Bangladesh war of 1971 till the Iranian Revolution of 1979 and the Soviet intervention in Afghanistan later that year, the development of Indo-Pakistan relations had been to a large extent been insulated from the course of superpower rivalry. Trends and events that helped or hindered the evolution of a regional détente in South Asia were largely, if not exclusively, sub-continental in origin."

Indeed, the US attitudes towards the region had changed. The US policy on the eve of the Soviet intervention did "recognize as a fact of life that no matter what measuring stick one uses", as State Department South Asian expert Howard Schaffer explained, "India is the most important power in the region". This was not a realization that came about spontaneously. In May 1974, India had demonstrated its capabilities by testing a nuclear device. In 1976, it initiated a move towards normalization of relations with China and worked towards a rapprochement with the United States. But it should be emphasized that despite these moves towards diversification of its relations, India maintained close relations with the Soviet Union.

In 1975, President Ford lifted the embargo on arms sales to India and Pakistan. In theory both countries could seek to buy arms, which would be considered on a case-by-case basis. During the subsequent Carter Administration India did enter into negotiations with the US for the purchase of TOW anti-tank missiles and light howitzers. The US agreed to sell anti-tank missiles worth $32 million (all figures are in dollars US unless otherwise mentioned) in 1980 but the deal fell through because the US would not allow their manufacture under license in India. The howitzer deal also failed to materialize on the issues of license manufacture, supply of spares and ammunition with the

US refusing to guarantee more than a twenty day supply of ammunition at a time. India clearly did not want to be put in a situation where its military capabilities would be reliant on US policies.

On the nuclear front, while the US had imposed sanctions on the transfer of nuclear technology after the 1974 test, it had continued to supply fuel for the Tarapur nuclear plant. In March 1978 the US Congress passed an act, with a two-year grace period, that prohibited nuclear exports to countries that did not accept safeguards. In 1980 President Carter approved a temporary waiver that allowed the export of 32 tons of fuel and in 1982 an agreement allowed France to supply fuel in return for India's acceptance of safeguards for the facility. With the advent of the Missile Technology Control Regime (MTCR) in 1987, India also faced embargoes on missile related technology. In 1992-94 the United States allowed India to buy cryogenic rocket engines from Russia but blocked the transfer of related technology.

The 1980s also witnessed a gradual acceptance of India's growing pre-eminence in the region. This was reflected in India's (albeit unsuccessful) peacekeeping efforts in Sri Lanka despite India's earlier involvement with the Tamil separatists, and during India's intervention in a coup attempt in the Maldives. In a letter to Prime Minister Rajiv Gandhi, President Reagan said: "I am impressed by your willingness to restore order without unnecessary bloodshed. I have no doubt that your action will be remembered as a valuable contribution to regional stability." Economic and trade relationships improved. Cooperation in the fields of defence and technology transfer also increased. Symbolic of this was the visit to the US by Defence Minister K.C. Pant in July 1989, the first visit by an Indian Defence Minister in over 25 years. This followed the visit of the US Secretary of State Caspar Weinburger in 1987 followed by his successor Frank Carlucci in 1988. President Reagan also issued a directive (1984) instructing government agencies to seek improved relations with India and accommodate its requests for dual-use technology. In 1986, the US agreed to supply a number of General Electric F 404 engines and avionics for India's Light Combat Aircraft (LCA). Later, the US also agreed to sell a Cray XMP14 supercomputer, the first such sale to a country outside the western alliance.

India-US bilateral relations began to warm up after the fall of the Berlin Wall and the disintegration of the Soviet Union. With the emergence of new world order, no one really knew how to adjust to this new reality. After the end of the Cold War, India-US relations in the first half of the 1990s have been described as one of "missed opportunities and contradictory policies". This could be attributed to a slow acknowledgment of the changed international order both at the political and bureaucratic levels. India and the US continued to have differences on various issues including the extension of the Non-Proliferation Treaty (NPT) and the Comprehensive Test Ban Treaty (CTBT). Another action that caused friction between India and the US was the passage of the Brown Amendment (November 1995) through Congress which allowed the US to supply Pakistan with military equipment worth $658 million and included maritime reconnaissance aircraft and missiles. President Clinton supported this move on the grounds that Pakistan had already paid for the equipment but refused to release the 26 F-16s. As has been observed: "Indian policymakers responded as much to the symbolism as the substance of the decision. Above all, the Brown Amendment indicated that the United States did not have an India policy but rather a South Asia policy, and that Congress and the president would continue to equate India and Pakistan".

The situation was further complicated when it was revealed that China had supplied M11 missiles to Pakistan and the US did not apply sanctions on China for violating the MTCR. On the other hand, there was a degree of India-US military cooperation. In 1991, US Air Force General Claude M. Kickleighter visited India and proposed extensive training and exchanges between the two militaries. The government's view of these exchanges was articulated by Prime Minister Narasimha Rao who noted how the professional-to-professional relations had achieved much more than politicians had been able to do in decades. In the 1990s, especially after India's declared policy of economic liberalization, it came to be viewed as an attractive market for the US business. Despite the lack of an overall policy framework, security cooperation also increased during this period. During the Gulf War, the Indian Government granted refueling rights to the US military aircraft en route from the Pacific to the Middle East. In 1996 and 1997, the Indian and the US navies held joint exercises (the Malabar series) in the Indian Ocean. A Defence Policy Group was established in the mid-1990s. Its activities included high-level exchanges, periodic policy reviews and reciprocal visits by senior commanders.

India's nuclear tests in May 1998 brought this cooperation to a complete halt as the US also withheld spares for the Indian Navy's Sea King helicopters and Sea Harrier aircraft then undergoing repairs and overhaul in the UK.

INDIA'S NEIGHBORS IMPACT

A major hurdle in the development of India-US relations in the past has been what could be termed the 'third country prism'. For a long time US-Pakistan relations had an adverse effect on US-India relations. Development of US-China relations had the same impact.

India's relations with the US were heavily influenced by the politics of the Cold War and India's policy of non-alignment as well as US perception that Pakistan was a trusted ally in its fight to contain communism. At no time was this more evident than during the period of Soviet intervention in Afghanistan when Pakistan became a front line state in the war against communism as well as a conduit for the supply of arms and other support to the Afghan resistance. Enthusiastic support by the US declined after the Soviet withdrawal from Afghanistan and the refusal of President Bush Sr. to certify that Pakistan did not possess nuclear weapons (1990). Subsequent cooling of US-Pakistan relations has ensured that Pakistan is no longer a major factor in the improvement of India-US relations.

China became a factor in India-US relations following the normalization of its ties with the US in 1971 and the subsequent 'tilt' of both countries towards Pakistan during its war with India that year. It is only during the last decade or so relations with China have not influenced the India-US relation.

INDIA-EAST ASIAN RELATIONS

Not only is India the largest power in the Indian Ocean, it also has the largest navy and coastguard of any state between the two most commercial straits in the world—Hormuz and

Malacca. In addition, not only are the Straits of Malacca and the Strait of Lombok acknowledged to be two of the most crucial strategic straits in the world, more than half of the world's maritime trade passes through them. In this region, more than a thousand miles from India's mainland lay its Andaman and Nicobar group of islands, the southmost of which is barely 90 nautical miles from the Indonesian province of Aceh. Of the 600-island cluster, over 300 are inhabited and are suspected of being used as transit points by gun runners, smugglers (including drug smugglers) and poachers. The region is also notorious for acts of piracy. Recognizing this, in 1985 India established a joint-services base at Port Blair (FORTAN, Fortress Andaman and Nicobar Islands). India's action initially caused a certain degree of disquiet among its ASEAN neighbors because of the size of its navy and its perceived closeness to the Soviet Union. But this reaction was shortlived as India became more open about its motives and the Indian Navy was soon paying ports of call to and conducting exercises with the navies of Indonesia, Singapore, Malaysia and Thailand.

The end of the Cold War also removed the hurdles to close India-ASEAN cooperation. During the 1990s, India-ASEAN relations improved steadily. India became a sectoral dialogue partner in 1992, full dialogue partner in 1995, and joined the ASEAN Regional Forum (ARF) in 1996. The first India-ASEAN summit took place on November 2002 in Cambodia.

In August 2001, India decided to upgrade its presence in the Andamans and set up its first tri-services command—the Strategic Forces Command. Its military presence already includes air force helicopters, three naval Fast Attack Craft (FAC) and offshore patrol vessels. Eventually, India is expected to have a full strength army component and an air base in the Andamans. This will give India strategic depth to compliment its ability to protect maritime traffic bound for the South China Sea and Australia. Malaysia's Defence Minister Datuk Seri Najib Tun Razak said, "We also conduct monitoring in our waters in the Straits and will offer assistance to anyone. They (users of the Straits) need not rely on the patrolling team only." He went on to say that any nation had the right to escort their ships to ensure security without the need to seek permission from Malaysia or Indonesia, as this did not violate international law.

India has not only been coordinating its efforts to combat maritime threats with countries in the region but with countries as far away as Japan. A joint India-Japan Coast Guard Exercise took place for the first time in Indian waters in November 2000 and a second joint exercise was conducted off the coast of Japan in 2001. In an interview with *The Hindu*, Japan's Ambassador to India Hiroshi Hirabayshi stated that Japan welcomed the new security arrangement between India and the US that would make shipping through the Malacca Straits safer. He added that India-Japan relations were poised for a quantum leap in the security, economic and political spheres. In the past, there had been no systematic security dialogue between India and Japan although there had been informal contacts between military officials of the two countries.

During a visit to Singapore in April 2002, Prime Minister Atal Bihari Vajpayee spoke of India's interest in the region. Delivering the Annual Singapore Lecture 2002, he observed: "We have crucial stakes in protecting our common sea-lanes, combating piracy, choking off narco-trade and curbing gunrunning. We need to tackle this jointly in a determined manner, through regular exchange of experiences, information and intelligence."

He once again emphasized India's interest in the wider Asia-Pacific region: "India has to be integral to any regional process pertaining to the Asia Pacific. We have a constructive and multi-faceted relationship with every major country of the region. This is also true of India's relations with ASEAN's East Asian neighbors."

Consequently, it can be argued that given its historical military relations with Vietnam and its growing strategic ties with Japan, India will have a role in the evolving security structure in the wider Asia-Pacific region. The growing strategic and military ties with the US Pacific Command would underscore this trend. It is an irony of sorts that India is within the geographical area covered by the US Pacific Command while Pakistan comes under the jurisdiction of the US Central Command.[2]

RELATIONS SINCE 2000

President Clinton's India Visit

It has been observed by some that President Clinton's India visit was a recognition of India's new-found status after its nuclear tests, that is, India as a major power because of its nuclear capability. A more plausible explanation is that it was a consequence of the realization that India's nuclear capability could not be reversed. The US is India's largest market and its largest foreign investor. As Karl Inderfurth, Assistant Secretary of State for South Asian Affairs, observed: "This trip should have taken place almost three years ago, in 1997 at the time of the 50th anniversary of India's independence when Clinton was going to go, the government fell. Shortly after that, there were the nuclear tests. Then we started thinking again about going. The government fell. So it has been a combination of domestic politics and world events that has delayed this. It's long overdue."

There were going to be no surprises and it was made clear by statements by senior officials in the US in the days preceding the visit. Speaking at the US Institute of Peace on 9 March 2000, Karl Inderfurth said that US-India relations would not be hostage to US relations with any other country and that India was viewed as a "key player in global affairs in the 21st century, and as a vital contributor to overall Asian regional peace and stability". A few days later Secretary of State Madeleine Albright in her remarks to the Asia Society in New York also referred to the fact that, while there were differing views between India and the US on nuclear and other strategic issues, they would not be allowed to stand in the way of the development of the overall bilateral relationship.

Subsequently, during his visit to India, President Clinton and India's Prime Minister Atal Bihari Vajpayee on 21 March 2000 resolved to "create a closer and qualitatively new relationship between the United States and India" and signed a joint statement on bilateral relations entitled "US-India Relations: A Vision for the 21st Century", which stated *inter alia:* "The United States believes India should forego nuclear weapons. India believes that it needs to maintain a credible minimum nuclear deterrent in keeping with its own assessment of its security needs. Nonetheless, India and the US are prepared to work together to prevent the proliferation of nuclear weapons and their means of delivery. To this end, we will persist with and build upon the productive bilateral dialogue already underway."

The "agreed principles" on institutional dialogue included:

- Regular India-US "summit" meetings;
- An annual foreign policy dialogue between the Secretary of State and the Minister for External Affairs;
- Continuation of the ongoing Dialogue on Security and Non-Proliferation between the Deputy Secretary of State and the External Affairs Minister;
- The Joint Working Group on Counter-terrorism would continue to meet regularly;
- The institutionalisation of a bilateral economic dialogue; and
- The creation of a Joint Consultative Group on Clean Energy and Environment and the setting up of the US India Science and Technology Forum to promote research and development and the transfer of technology.

In his address to the joint sitting of the Indian Parliament on 22 March 2000, President Clinton spoke of the commitment by both countries to forego nuclear testing and said that India could pursue defence policies in keeping with its commitment not to pursue a nuclear or missile arms race "which the Prime Minister has forcefully reaffirmed just in these last couple of days". On the question of India-Pakistan relations, he praised the Prime Minister for "his courageous journey to Lahore". He made it clear that he had not come to South Asia to mediate the dispute over Kashmir, and that this was a matter for resolution between them.

This was reflected in an interview with the American ABC (Television Channel) on 21 March 2000 when President Clinton enunciated US policy on the Kashmir dispute: respect for the line of control, resumption of dialogue between India and Pakistan and renunciation of violence as a means of solving the dispute (the three Rs). He further went on to add that he believed that there were "elements within the Pakistani government that have supported those who engaged in violence in Kashmir". However, he also maintained that there was no military solution to Kashmir's problems by India either, and that they "deserve to have their own concerns addressed on the merits".

Nonetheless, his remarks were significant from the Indian perspective. At a joint press conference earlier that day, Prime Minister Vajpayee had said that if Pakistan reaffirmed the principles of the Lahore Declaration, respected the Line of Control (the Simla Agreement of 1972 renamed the 1948 ceasefire line as Line of Control) and did not promote or support violence across it, he thought a dialogue could be resumed.

Despite the similarity of views between the two countries on the Kashmir problem, Pakistan's role and preconditions for peace in the region, President Clinton was reminded of his "dangerous place" comment at the state dinner in New Delhi. During the exchange of toasts, Indian President Narayanan commented: "It has been suggested that the Indian subcontinent is the most dangerous place in the world today, and Kashmir is a nuclear flashpoint. These alarmist descriptions will only encourage those who want to break the peace and indulge in terrorism and violence. The danger is not from us who have declared solemnly that we will not be the first to use nuclear weapons, but rather it is from those who refuse to make any such commitment." This was a pointed comment aimed at Pakistan, which has refused to give such an undertaking.

The trade part of the visit went off successfully with some US$ 2 billion worth of commercial agreements and US$ 1 billion in US Export-Import financing being finalized. Most of the agreements related to the information technology sector in which India's exports were growing at a rate of 50 per cent a year, with about two-thirds of them going to the US.

In all, this was probably the most extensive and successful visit to India by a US President, made more so by a decision by both sides to avoid the proliferation roadblock and concentrate on the expansion of the broader relationship. Even on proliferation issues the US appeared convinced by India's commitment to no more tests, no first use of nuclear weapons, and controls on the transfer of sensitive technology. In the words of Secretary Albright, "It was the beginning of a new chapter or, as a senior administration official put it what we've heard this week is the sound of ice melting a relationship that for 50 years was frozen in the contours of the Cold War."

President Bush Administration

Under the Bush administration India-US relations have developed at a pace that few could have foreseen. In his confirmation hearings before the Senate Foreign Relations Committee, the then Secretary of State designate Colin Powell stated, "India has the potential to help keep the peace in the vast Indian Ocean area and its periphery. We need to work harder and more consistently to help them in this endeavor." During his meeting with the National Security Adviser, Condoleezza Rice in April in Washington the Indian Minister for External Affairs and Defence, Jaswant Singh was 'interrupted' by President Bush who then proceeded to have a 40-minute ostensibly unscheduled private dialogue with him.

It was a reflection of the improvement in bilateral relations under the new US administration that India was one of the few countries that were informed of President Bush's forthcoming speech on his proposals regarding Nuclear Missile Defence (NMD). A day before, Condoleezza Rice phoned Jaswant Singh to advise him about the policy statement.

India's swift albeit carefully ambiguous response to the proposals was followed by a visit of the US Deputy of State Richard Armitage to New Delhi on 11 May 2001. This appeared to have been successful, with the Indian Government appreciating his presentation and looking forward to 'further exchanges'. He also carried a letter from President Bush in which he accepted an invitation to visit India.

These moves are part of evolving Indo-US relations. In a wide-ranging interview in May 2001 the Indian Ambassador to Washington, Lalit Mansingh, made the following points: Firstly, the nuclear genie could not be put back in the bottle, the two countries had to go beyond and look at common strategic interests. Secondly, contrary to the perception that the missile plan would impel China to expand its nuclear missile stockpiles, at present India did not fear such an outcome. But he refused to say whether growing cooperation was aimed at deterring China.

The appointment of Dr. Robert Blackwill, "a confidante of the President and his National Security Adviser, Dr. Condoleezza Rice", as US ambassador to India was an indicator of the importance that the Bush administration had placed on its relations with India.

However, it should be pointed out that while politico-military ties have continued to grow, the trade and investment relationship, despite its enormous potential, has continued to flounder, if not stagnate. India, after successfully implementing its first round of economic reforms in the early 1990s, failed to maintain the momentum. Many bureaucratic hurdles remain and progress on privatisation has slowed. Structural reforms appear to have stalled and the economy is now in its fourth year of slowdown. As the US Trade Representative Robert B. Zoellick has pointed out, India's tariffs and regulatory barriers remain high. Although the average tariff rate has fallen to about 30 per cent, it is still twice as high as China's average rate and 10 times as high as that of the United States. Consequently, while India's exports to the United States have steadily expanded since the mid-1990s (from $5.7 billion in 1995 to $10.7 billion in 2000), US trade flows to India since 1995 have stagnated, averaging $3.5 billion during the same period. The US investment in India has not had a very successful track record either. Ambassador Blackwill, in a speech delivered to the Indo-American Chamber of Commerce on 28 January 2002 observed: "Current performance is disheartening. In the calendar year 1995, US investment in India was $192 million; in 1996, $255 million; in 1997, $737 million; in 1998, 347 million; in 1998, $347 million; in 1999, $431 million; and in 2000, US investment in India totaled $336 million. Perhaps even more telling is that US firms ended up investing only 38 per cent of that approved by the Government of India. In certain quarters there still seems to be an elemental distrust of foreign investment." (This is in sharp contrast to US investment in China, which amounted to $4.4 billion in 2000).

However, the US continues to be India's largest partner and a leading foreign investor. It continues to be one of the largest foreign direct investors in India. The cumulative FDI flows from US from August 1991 to July 2007 stood at US$ 6215 million. FDI inflows from the US constitute about 12 per cent of total actual FDI inflows into India. The US is the leading portfolio investor in India. During 2006-07, portfolio investments by US were US$ 2240 million. The US is also the most important destination of Indian investment abroad. Between 1996 and March 2007, Indian companies invested US$ 2727 million in the US.

After September 2001

While the India-US engagement had been proceeding at a fairly fast pace right from the beginning of the Bush administration, it gained a new sense of immediacy after September 2001. In a speech delivered in New Delhi on 2 September the US Ambassador to India, Robert Blackwill, reiterated the earlier US position saying that "President Bush has a global approach to US-India relations, consistent with the rise of India as a world power" adding that this was because no nation can promote its values and advance its interests without the help of allies and friends.

In a Presidential Determination signed on 22 September, President George W. Bush waived all nuclear related sanctions on India and Pakistan. These included those under the Glenn Amendment, which bars licenses for items on the US Munitions list and prohibits defence sales under Foreign Military Sales and Foreign Military Financing. It was also revealed that the Commerce Department's "Entity List" (which deals with the transfer/sale of dual-use technologies) continued to be reviewed.

In a Joint Statement issued during Prime Minister Vajpayee's visit to Washington in November 2001, the two sides:

- Reaffirmed the enduring ties between the two countries and the importance of further transforming the relationship;
- Noted that both countries were targets of terrorism "as seen in the barbaric attacks" on 11 September in the US and on 1 October in Kashmir. (This point is significant in that it equated the events in the US to the attack on Jammu and Kashmir Legislative Assembly building in Srinagar, allegedly by Pakistan-based terrorists.);
- Expressed satisfaction with the progress made in India-US cooperation on counter-terrorism;
- Announced the establishment of a Joint Cyber-Terrorism Initiative;
- Agreed to begin a dialogue between the two governments to evaluate the processes by which we transfer dual-use

and military items, with a view towards greater transparency and efficiency; and

- Agreed to initiate discussions on civil space cooperation.

The intensity of India-US engagement can also be gauged from the fact that in the month of January 2002 alone Secretary of State Powell, Environmental Protection Agency Director Governor Christine Todd Whitman, FBI Director Robert Mueller, Defence Intelligence Agency head Admiral Thomas Wilson, and the State Department's Counter-Terrorism chief Francis Taylor visited New Delhi. In turn, Defence Minister George Fernandes and Home Minister Lal Krishna Advani travelled to Washington. In addition, in late April the Assistant Secretary of State for Political Military Affairs Lincoln Bloomfield Jr. visited India for the first India-US Political Military Dialogue to set the stage for a closer and even more productive bilateral security relationship, and in May the India-US Cyber Security Forum was also launched to discuss Critical Infrastructure Protection (CIP).

Following the event of September 2001, probably reflecting the strategic realities of the post-Cold War world and subsequently there has been a drastic change in US military cooperation with India. At a meeting of the US-India Defence Policy Group (DPG) in December 2001, the two sides committed themselves to substantially increase the pace of high-level policy dialogue, military-to-military exchanges and other joint activities.

As part of the growing India-US military links, the Indian Defence Minister George Fernandes visited Washington in January 2002 and held substantial talks with Defence Secretary Donald Rumsfeld and National Security Adviser Condoleezza Rice. Issues covered included terrorism as well as sharing of military intelligence. Defence Minister Fernandes took the opportunity to reassure the US that India's military stand-off with Pakistan could be resolved, easing concerns that the situation could escalate into a major war. The two sides also signed a General Security of Military Information Agreement (GSOMIA), which essentially guarantees that they would protect any classified technology shared between them. It also paves the way for the future sale of US weapons to India.

Clearly the events of 9/11 changed the dynamics of US-India defence relations. This was reflected in an interview with *The Hindu* on 3 May 2002 by the US Deputy Secretary of State Richard Armitage who once again emphasized the growing defence relationship saying that India had been very helpful in assisting with logistics and flights and what was significant was that the relationship was now drastically different from what it had been a year ago. "We love the idea of being able to call on occasion on Indian ports, naval ships we hope it will be good for US-India relations," he said. On the other hand, allaying apprehensions from some sections of Indian politicians, Ambassador Blackwill has made it clear that the US has no intention of stationing US troops permanently in India. Regarding Indian military acquisitions from Russia, the US attitude is that India was a free country and as such it was free to acquire defence systems from any country. Further, given the changed international situation, good relations between India and Russia were now in the interests of the US. This statement indeed is a measure of the changed quality of US-India relations.

In a move, which caused concern to Pakistan and China, was the joint exercises involving specialized mountain warfare troops that took place in Alaska in September 2002. It should be pointed out that the DPG meeting took place at a time when tensions between India and Pakistan were very high. As *The Times of India* observed, "...in what may count as one of the more remarkable chapters in the checkered history of Indo-US relations, New Delhi and Washington are engaged in a serious long-term military tie-up in the shadow of an immediate war in the sub-continent that the Bush administration is trying to prevent".[3]

Frequent bilateral engagements at political as well as official levels and the regular bilateral dialogues on a wide range of issues of mutual interest are reflective of the qualitative transformation in bilateral ties.

Recent Interaction of Ministers

US Secretary of State Dr. Condoleezza Rice visited India on 15-16 March 2005 as a first stop on her 6-nation Asian tour. She held meetings with the Prime Minister Dr. Manmohan Singh and UPA Chairperson Sonia Gandhi.

Discussions were held on various aspects of multi-faceted cooperative relationship. There was forward movement on starting an energy dialogue in all its dimensions, on advancing the defence relationships, and in importing the relationship to a larger strategic framework. Shri Natwar Singh, the then External Affairs Minister visited the USA on April 13-14, 2005 at the invitation of the President Bush, who reiterated his commitment to use his second term to take India-US relations to a substantially higher level. The US President referred to his administration's resolve to work very closely with India for international peace and security and for mutual economic benefit. The External Affairs Minister and the US Secretary of State explored ways to intensify cooperation, to accelerate work on the India-US Next Steps in Strategic Partnership Initiative and launched an Energy Dialogue that led on the US side by their Energy Secretary and on India's side by the Deputy Chairman of the Planning Commission Dr. Montek Singh Ahluwalia.

The main components of this dialogue include civil nuclear energy, hydrocarbons and cleaner technologies. Both sides also established a Joint Working Group on Space Cooperation and have agreed on its terms of reference.

Foreign Secretary Shri Shyam Saran visited the US from 16-19 May 2005 for a meeting of the India-US Global Issues Forum. He also held discussions with the US Under Secretary of State for Political Affairs, Nicholas Burns and other officials on bilateral as well as regional and global issues under the Asian Security Dialogue framework.[4]

Defence Minister Shri Pranab Mukherjee visited the US from 27-30 June 2005 at the invitation of the US Secretary of Defence Donald Rumsfeld. During the visit, he held meetings with Vice-President Richard Cheney, Secretary of State, Condoleezza Rice, National Security advisor, Stephen J. Hadley, etc. The US Secretary of Defence Donald Rumsfeld and Defence Minister Pranab Mukherjee signed a document entitled "New Framework for India-US Defence Relations", which visualizes an enhanced level of cooperation over the next ten years. They agreed to constitute a new "Defence Procurement and Production Group" broadening the scope of the existing "Security Cooperation Group" under the India-US Defence Policy Group (DPG) and to intensify interaction in the context of the DPG.[5]

Prime Minister Manmohan Singh's USA Visit

At the invitation of President George W. Bush, Prime Minister Dr. Manmohan Singh and his delegation paid a visit to the United States during July 18-20, 2005. In the Joint Statement the two leaders declared their resolve to transform the relationship and establish a global partnership. Discussions were held on various aspects that included potential for cooperation in the fields such as economic and trade relations, revitalizing the India-US Economic Dialogue and launching a bilateral CEOs Forum, energy, environment, democracy and development, combating terrorism, non-proliferation and security, completion of the Next Steps in Strategic Partnership (NSSP) initiative, high technology, space, civil nuclear technology, science and technology, agricultural education, fight against HIV/AIDS and disaster relief operations.

Prime Minister addressed a joint session of the US Congress on 19 July 2005. He had an interactive session with the Indian-American community and also with the US media at the National Press Club.

The Prime Minister met the US President again on 13 September 2005 during his visit to New York for the 60th United Nations General Assembly (UNGA) session. The Prime Minister and the US President, along with the United Nations (UN) Secretary General Kofi Annan, participated in the launch of the United Nations Democracy Fund on 14 September 2005. India made a contribution of US$ 10 million to the Democracy Fund.[6]

There has been steady progress in relations between India and the United States of America in recent times. India and the United States (US) made a strong commitment to transform their bilateral ties into strategic partnership, marked by frequent contacts at political and official levels and a growing convergence of views on global, regional and bilateral issues of common concern. India and the US interaction focused on strategic and security issues, defence, counter-terrorism, counter-proliferation, trade and investment, science and technology, space, health, energy and environment.

President George W. Bush Visits to India

At the invitation of Indian Prime Minister Dr. Manmohan Singh, the US President George W. Bush visited India during

March 1-3, 2006. President Bush's visit to India is the fifth by a US President. Earlier visits were by presidents Dwight Eisenhower (1959), Richard Nixon (1969), Jimmy Carter (1978) and William J. Clinton (2000). During his visit to India, the US President George W. Bush expressed satisfaction with the great progress the United States and India have made in advancing "Strategic Partnership" to meet the global challenges of the 21st century.

The US President George W. Bush said, "The successful transformation of the US-India relationship will have a decisive and positive influence on the future international system as it evolves in this new century." Reviewing the progress made in deepening the global partnership between the United States and India since their Joint Statement of July 18, 2005, the President Bush and the Prime Minister Singh reaffirmed their commitment to expand even further the growing ties between the two countries. Consistent with this objective, the two leaders highlight efforts the United States and India are making together in the following areas:

Economic Prosperity and Trade

1. India and US agreed to intensify efforts to develop a bilateral business climate supportive of trade and investment by:

(i) Welcoming the report of the US-India CEO Forum, agreeing to consider its recommendations aimed at substantially broadening our bilateral economic relations, and directing the Chairs of the Indo-US Economic Dialogue to follow up expeditiously with the CEO Forum.

(ii) Endorsing the efforts of the US-India Trade Policy Forum to reduce barriers to trade and investment with the goal of doubling bilateral trade in three years.

(iii) Agreeing to advance mutually beneficial bilateral trade and investment flows by holding a high-level public-private investment summit in 2006, continuing efforts to facilitate and promote foreign direct investment and eliminate impediments to it, and enhancing bilateral consultations on various issues including tariff and non-tariff barriers to trade in goods and services, and preventing the illicit use of the financial system.

2. The two countries sought to expand cooperation in agriculture by:

(i) Launching the Knowledge Initiative on Agriculture with a three-year financial commitment to link our universities, technical institutions, and businesses to support agriculture education, joint research, and capacity-building projects including in the area of biotechnology.

(ii) Endorsing an agreed work plan to promote bilateral trade in agriculture through agreements that lay out a path to open the US market to Indian mangoes, recognize India as having the authority to certify that shipments of Indian products to the United States meet USDA organic standards, and provide for discussions on current regulations affecting trade in fresh fruits and vegetables, poultry and dairy, and almonds.

(iii) Reaffirmed their shared commitment to completing the WTO Doha Development Agenda (DDA) before the end of 2006, and agreed to work together to help achieve this outcome.

Energy Security and a Clean Environment

1. Welcomed the successful completion of discussions on India's separation plan and looked forward to the full implementation of the commitments in the July 18, 2005 Joint Statement on nuclear cooperation. This historic accomplishment will permit the two countries to move forward towards the common objective of full civil nuclear energy cooperation between India and the United States and between India and the international community as a whole.

2. Welcomed the participation of India in the ITER initiative on fusion energy as an important further step towards the common goal of full nuclear energy cooperation.

3. Agreed on India's participation in Future Gen, an international public-private partnership to develop new, commercially viable technology for a clean coal near-zero emission power project. India will contribute funding to the project and participate in the Government Steering Committee of this initiative.

4. Welcomed the creation of the Asia Pacific Partnership on Clean Development and Climate, which will enable India and

the US to work together with other countries in the region to pursue sustainable development and meet increased energy needs while addressing concerns of energy security and climate change. The Partnership will collaborate to promote the development, diffusion, deployment and transfer of cleaner, cost-effective and more efficient technologies and practices.

5. Welcomed India's interest in the Integrated Ocean Drilling Program, an international marine research endeavor that will contribute to long-term energy solutions such as gas hydrates.

6. Noting the positive cooperation under the Indo-US Energy Dialogue, highlighted plans to hold joint conferences on topics such as "energy efficiency" and "natural gas", to conduct study missions on renewable energy, to establish a clearing house in India for coal-bed methane/coal-mine methane, and to exchange energy market information.

Innovation and the Knowledge Economy

1. Emphasizing the importance of knowledge partnerships, they announced the establishment of a Bi-National Science and Technology Commission, which the US and India will co-fund. It will generate collaborative partnerships in science and technology and promote industrial research and development.

2. Agreed that the United States and India would work together to promote innovation, creativity and technological advancement by providing a vibrant intellectual property rights regime, and to cooperate in the field of intellectual property rights to include capacity-building activities, human resource development and public awareness programs.

3. Agreed to continue exploring further cooperation in civil space, including areas such as space exploration, satellite navigation, and earth science. The United States and India committed to move forward with agreements that will permit the launch of US satellites and satellites containing US components by Indian space launch vehicles, opening up new opportunities for commercial space cooperation between the two countries.

4. Welcomed the inclusion of two US instruments in the Indian lunar mission Chandrayaan-1. They noted that

memoranda of understanding to be signed between ISRO and NASA would be significant steps forward in this area.

5. Welcomed the US Department of Commerce's plan to create a license exception for items that would otherwise require an export license to end-users in India engaged solely in civilian activities.

Global Safety and Security

1. Noted the enhanced counter-terrorism cooperation between the two countries and stressed that terrorism is a global scourge that must be fought and rooted out in every part of the world.

2. Welcomed the increased cooperation between the United States and India in the defense area, since the New Framework for the US-India Defence Relationship was signed on June 28, 2005, as evidenced by successful joint exercises, expanded defence cooperation and information sharing, and greater opportunities to jointly develop technologies and address security and humanitarian issues.

3. Reaffirmed their commitment to the protection of the free flow of commerce and to the safety of navigation, and agreed to the conclusion of a Maritime Cooperation Framework to enhance security in the maritime domain, to prevent piracy and other transnational crimes at sea, carry out search and rescue operations, combat marine pollution, respond to natural disasters, address emergent threats and enhance cooperative capabilities, including through logistics support. Both sides are working to finalize a Logistics Support Agreement at the earliest.

4. Welcomed India's intention to join the Container Security Initiative aimed at making global maritime trade and infrastructure more secure and reducing the risk of shipping containers being used to conceal weapons of mass destruction.

5. Reiterated their commitment to international efforts to prevent the proliferation of weapons of mass destruction.

6. Building on the July 2005 Disaster Relief Initiative, noted the important disaster management cooperation and their improved capabilities to respond to disaster situations.

7. Recognized the importance of capacity-building in cyber security and greater cooperation to secure their growing electronic

interdependencies, including protecting electronic transactions and critical infrastructure from cyber crime, terrorism and other malicious threats.

Deepening Democracy and Meeting International Challenges

1. Recalled their joint launch of the UN Democracy Fund in September 2005 and offered the experience and expertise of both Governments for capacity-building, training and exchanges to third countries that request such assistance to strengthen democratic institutions.

2. Welcomed the decision of India and the United States to designate a representative to the Government Advisory Board of the International Centre for Democratic Transition (ICDT) located in Budapest to facilitate cooperative activities with ICDT.

3. Agreed that the Virtual Coordination and Information Centres, set up in September 2005, should be further strengthened and a bilateral meeting aimed at developing a practical programme for utilization of its services be held soon.

4. Expressed satisfaction at the expedited USFDA drug approval processes that strengthen the combat against HIV/AIDS at the global level and encourage greater corporate participation to meet this challenge, including the establishment of the Indo-US Corporate Fund for HIV/AIDS.

5. Agreed to expand bilateral efforts and continue cooperation in the area of medical research and strengthen technical capacity in food and drug regulation in India as well as address the concern on avian influenza, including agreement to reach out to the private sector, develop regional communications strategies, and plan an in-region containment and response exercise. The President welcomed India's offer to host the International Partnership on Avian and Pandemic Influenza Meeting in 2007.

6. Welcomed India's membership in the Coalition Against Wildlife Trafficking, a partnership through which we will collaborate in the fight against illegal trade in wildlife and wildlife parts; we also welcome the opportunity to strengthen long-standing work together on the conservation of wildlife through cooperation on park management and eco tourism.[7]

India-US Relations under Barack Obama

Indo-US relations were all time high under the Bush administration. In fact several scholars point out that, while President Bush was not so successful across the globe, but with India, he seemed to have done the right things. The coming to power of Barack Obama has on the one hand, fuelled a lot of euphoria in India, on the other hand it has also raised certain concerns. Obama's professed policy towards Afghanistan, viz. the shifting of troops from Iraq marks the regaining of importance of Pakistan for the US. The US President's comments on Kashmir have raised worries on the Indian front. Indications coming from top officials of the Obama administration suggest the relationship with India is, however, expected to continue on the same path as it was during the Bush administration. In an interview with the *Time* magazine, Obama said that one of his critical foreign policy matters will be to help India and Pakistan resolve the Kashmir issue to make South Asia a safer place. The appointment of Hillary Clinton, who has been a good friend of India as the Secretary of State, is a positive signal. Obama would obviously have to take her opinion very seriously when it comes to dealing with the region. Again, the new Vice President, Joe Biden, who is known to be a friend of India, has said that it was his dream to make the two countries closest partners by 2020. Lawrence Summers, the chief White House Economic Advisor, is known to have great regard for Dr. Manmohan Singh. These are positive indications for India.

India is confident of its relationship with the US and expects that it would move forward rapidly to the next level under President Barack Obama, taking off from his predecessor George W. Bush left. "I have confidence that we will be able to move forward with the new US administration," Foreign Secretary of India, Shivshankar Menon said at a press conference here after the first high-level dialogue with the Obama administration. Noting that India-US relations have been undergoing a transformation since the 1990s, Menon said he was overall satisfied that they had more than met the objectives the two sides had set. Describing the relationship as a "work in progress", he said, "Both sides want to do much more, moving forward rapidly." Foreign Secretary Shivshankar Menon, who was on an official visit to the USA on a three days hectic diplomacy, met Secretary of State Hillary Clinton, Obama's National Security Advisor General James Jones and other senior officials besides leading lawmakers and representatives of Washington think tanks. The Mumbai attacks figured prominently during the discussion with Hillary Clinton and National Security Advisor General James Jones. In addition there were wide range of issues discussed during the meeting which include Mumbai attacks, counter-terrorism, situation in Afghanistan, Pakistan and Sri Lanka besides reviewing Indo-US bilateral ties. Menon said that during his talks he was "reassured" by the US of its determination to go through with the Indo-US nuclear deal, signed during the previous Bush administration. Referring to the meeting he had in Washington, Shivshankar Menon said, "In all the meetings with the administration, and in Congress, I found a very strong sense of satisfaction of the growth and the transformation of the Indo-US relations in the last few years and a very strong support for carrying these relations forward and building on the successes that we have achieved."[8]

IMPOSED SANCTIONS ON INDIA

In the wake of nuclear tests, conducted by India in 1998, the US imposed sanctions on India. Two extreme viewpoints emerged in the US administration. Gilman Benjamin, Chairman of the House of International Committee, said: "The strongest possible deterrents short of military action, are needed in South Asia to ensure against any move from weapon testing to weapon deployment." But Stuart E. Eizenstat, Under Secretary of State for Economic, Business and Agricultural Affairs, pointed out: "Sanctions are not a panacea and they are not cost free." He stated that frequency of imposing sanctions have increased. The US has applied sanctions for foreign policy purposes a total of 15 times since World War I, 104 times since World War II and 61 times since 1993.

The US justifies the imposition of sanctions on India as follows: "The US government shall terminate assistance to that country under the Foreign Assistance Act of 1961, except for humanitarian assistance or food or other agricultural commodities" [Sec. 102 (b) (2) (A)]. The United States has been extending economic assistance to India since 1951. But its contribution has declined substantially in recent period. Indeed, if debt-servicing payments are taken into account, there is a net flow of funds from India to US account of development loans. While US estimates the loss on account of termination of development assistance of $142.3 million, the government of India figures of utilization of aid from the US put it at lower figure. Under this Act, the US imposed seven different types of sanctions on India.

The sanctions, under these seven categories, had minimal impact on India in a short run. Moreover, the very nature of law, common to many of the US anti-non proliferation legislation is self-defeating. Once instituted it can only aggravate the situation without leaving any recourse to negotiation. Any remedy of the situation requires a fresh legislation by the US Congress. Once Symington Amendment was involved to put sanctions against Pakistan, the only way the US could get around the sanctions, for whatever purposes, was to enact new acts and amendments. Still, as recent disclosures about China-Pakistan transfers have shown, the US has been unable to resolve the matter in a meaningful manner. This happens because US non-proliferation objectives are not clear and therefore the concerned laws contain ambiguity.

The role and the use of sanctions as an instrument of US foreign policy had already been discussed in the Congress. The commercial concerns have also played a role in the enactment of laws diluting the requirements of sanctions under the Arms Export Control Act to allow for use of US government funds to guarantee export of agricultural products. This was the direct consequence of the Pakistani decision to open tenders for white wheat. Since the tenders were to close on July 15, 1998 the US Congress rushed to pass the law before July 14, 1998.

There were other bills pending before the Congress that would limit all sanctions present and future, to a period of two years.

Extension of such sanctions would require separate Congressional approval. Furthermore, the President is required to file elaborate declarations and analysis explaining the rationale for the sanctions as also the setting forth the costs and benefits of such sanctions. All these efforts, however, should not be construed as a prelude to the lifting of sanctions against India.

It is a long drawn process. There must be give and take from both sides. Any attempt by the US to dictate unconditional acceptance of its terms will only result in failure. While all efforts should take into account some of the US concerns such as proliferation of weapons of mass destruction (WMD), there is no way Indian security concerns can be compromised to please the US. The task of restoring good relations between India and the US will be difficult but not impossible if both sides are willing to address each other's concerns.

According to Brahma Chellaney, "India's economy has performed better under economic sanctions imposed after 'Shakti Tests' than in the previous 18 months." Sanctions are, however, a potential political instrument to mount pressure on weak-willed states as India's case exemplified. Rigid sanctions spur "fudging", a classic case being the inaction as Chinese nuclear and missile transfer to Pakistan. The US President Clinton gained executive flexibility in relation to US Arms Export Control Act under which economic sanctions were imposed on India and Pakistan. This flexibility provided the choice to dangle carrots and reward "good behaviour". Despite being armed with blanket authority by Congress to waive punitive actions, Clinton has kept India under pressure by maintaining the most biting sanctions—World Bank lending curbs—but extending waivers on sanctions hurting US companies' interests.

The World Bank related curbs, as stated, are estimated to cost India few hundred million dollars annually in higher, interest rates from increased commercial borrowing. By imposing this additional burden on Indian economy, even though manageable and free from strings attacked to World Bank loans, the Americans have strengthened their political leverage. A second set of sanctions related to technology control and denial predates the Shakti Tests. In this respect there is no hope of liberally interpreting the export control laws. The Entities Lists is the third type of sanctions for applying pointed pressure on specific firms. In contrast to Export Controls targeting specific technologies, entity related sanctions blacklisted particular companies, not for breaking US or international law, but for contributing to their home country's strategic programmes. The US blackballed 200 large Indian private and State-run enterprises; months after the Jaswant Singh-Strobe

Talbott talks began. It also helped ease International Financial Institution (IFI) bending curbs against Pakistan but not against India. Both actions were motivated by a desire to strengthen negotiating beverage against India.

R. Ramachandran pointed out that the US administration canceled $ 27 million aid to India. The American companies dealing with India will lose $300 million from OPIC, and $ 500 million in EXIM financing. Though the law requires the US banks to close their operation in India, the administration has not requested them to do so. The US exported $ 3.6 billion in goods to India to which dual-use technology exports (banned to sanctioned state under law) were $ 300 million. Under the decision of case-by-case review policy only 20 per cent of such restrictions could be affected; it works out $ 60 million. Voting against Indian loans at IMF and World Bank is not clear; so far pipeline loans have not been affected. The Farmer's Export Relief Act amended an arms export control law to exempt government loans and credit guarantee programmes that support the sale of food and other agricultural products including fertilizers. In fact this Act was being rushed lest Pakistan buy its wheat from elsewhere. For India's economy, these restrictions were peanuts; in due course they got further clipped.

Despite meagre impact or easing of the stringent effect, sanctions, besides being the political instrument of pressure, did inflict some difficulties in real terms. For instance, owing to the sanctions, the British manufacturer could not export the American components needed for Indian Navy's Sea-King helicopters as the transaction was deemed to be violative of US's Arms Export Control Act. Indian Navy's Sea-King 42-B anti-submarine warfare helicopters had been virtually grounded after US imposed sanctions on India following nuclear tests at Pokhran in May 1998. India had purchased these helicopters from UK based Westland Helicopters with US based Sirkorsky company. As a number of critical components in the Sea-King helicopters were of US origin, its British manufacturers could not supply these parts or service them till the US sanctions were lifted. This has left large number of "servo-packs" and "gear-boxes" of Sea-King helicopters lying unserviced in Britain due to lack of US spares.

While the navy was facing similar problem of spare parts for its Sea Harrier jump jet fighters, the matter was apparently resolved with the Hindustan Aeronautics Limited (HAL), being able to manufacture these parts indigenously. The Sea-King fleet, on the other hand, had been hamstrung and was operating at around 25 per cent of its capability with severe flying restrictions for about two years. The Navy has around three squadrons of Sea-King 42-B helicopters, which along with Sea Harrier fighters form the backbone of India's forces.

Thus, the US sanctions have forced the Indian Navy to restrict the flying hours of its anti-submarine warfare and fighter aircraft by over 25 per cent. Unofficially, naval sources concede that the curtailment is even higher. Expert describes the cutback in flying as a serious setback on the navy's operational readiness. Repair and servicing of the British assembled Sea-King anti-submarine warfare (ASW) helicopters and Sea Harrier fighter-cum-maritime reconnaissance jets have been put on hold because several crucial parts requiring replacement were American. The US manufacturers could not supply the parts because of sanctions. The UK was also constrained by its commitment to the US-led NATO arrangement.

Besides impact on defence, particularly Navy, more than three years after the echo of nuclear explosions died down in Pokhran, the "developmental activities" came to a grinding halt as a result of sanctions. The forest department was feeling the tremors because this had an adverse impact on the employment. Two of the major projects that were being carried out with Japanese financial assistance were withdrawn since they were unlikely to get further extensions. These included the Afforestation and Pasture Development Project (APDP) targeted at the Indira Gandhi Canal area and the Forestry Development Project (FDP) aimed at development of 14 non-desert districts of Rajasthan. These two projects together employ nearly 4500 people.

Thus, sanctions imposed on India may be ineffective in the short run. But they were adversely affecting the defence and economy in the long run as exemplified by implied consequences on Navy and direct financial crunch on a forestation projects of Rajasthan.

The partial lifting of sanctions in the last week of October 1999 served two-fold purposes: (a) to create a positive atmosphere in India-US relations in preparation for the visit of President Clinton to India and Bangladesh, and (b) it is a gesture to encourage India to fall in line with the US agenda on non-proliferation, which remains intact despite US Senate's vote against the ratification of the CTBT. Such removal of sanctions signifies the US desire to engage India constructively on important issues about which there are differences of opinion between the two countries whether they are related to non-proliferation or WTO. Secondly, the removal of sanctions implies an acknowledgement by the US that India is not likely to succumb to punitive attitude or economic pressure at the cost of its basic national interests. Thirdly, sanctions, which have been removed in their specificity, imply a willingness to expand bilateral economic and commercial relations and to slowly cooperate in the field of defence cooperation, wherever possible.

Easing sanctions is merely the extension of the waivers that expired on October 21, 1999. In exercising the authority given to President Clinton by Congress, he waived the same set of sanctions he had lifted on December 1, 1998. Those sanctions had been hurting US commercial interests more than India's economy. President maintained the one punitive action that really affects India—the prohibition on credit lending by international financial institutions (IFIs). Equally important is the fact that the US still maintains rigorous technology sanctions. These include not only the technology controls predating the May 1998 Indian nuclear-weapon tests but the additional duel-use export barriers that were imposed in the months following Operation Shakti.

The essential message that came out from the partial easing of sanctions against India was that the US was seeking to protect its commercial interests while maintaining political leverage. For the first time US invoked section 102 (b) of its Arms Control Act, which had no implementing regulations. But since then, the administration and Congress worked together to evolve regulations that seek to arm Washington with leverage but ensure that the US business do not get hurt in the process.

Sometimes sanctions relaxation from time to time serves either to protect the commercial interests (as happened when, within months, many post-Shakti economic sanctions were lifted) or to give the illusion of a softening in the attitude (illustrated by the removal of some Indian enterprises from the Entity List). Sanctions relaxation in one area, sometimes has been followed by new punitive measures in another.

The Bush administration in US gradually developed a perception that sanctions were no more beneficial; quite contrary they were creating hurdle in the required India-US relations. Christina Rocca, President Bush nominee to run South Asian Affairs, publicly stated, "The US post-Pokhran-II sanctions against both India and Pakistan must go as they have outlived their usefulness." Senate Foreign Relations Committee Chairman, Joseph Biden urged Bush: "to act speedily by exercising his authority to waive sanctions until the Congress takes action." Another influential Democrat, Tom Lantos said: "I am planning to introduce a legislation in the House of Representative for lifting the sanctions against India that these restrictions have outlived their usefulness and are no longer in the interests of the United States that economic sanctions apart, the non-proliferation issue should not be allowed to stand in the way of engaging India in greater scientific and defence cooperation either. The US is likely to get further commitments and compliance from India on non-proliferation and test ban agreements by lifting sanctions and engaging in greater scientific and defence cooperation."

Even excesses, inadvertently committed during sanctions were acknowledged and apologized. For instance the US ambassador to India, Richard Celeste said: "Sanctions on science and technology institutions, not involved in research in nuclear warheads and delivery systems was wrong. It was a mistake on our part. As a result of blanket sanctions some 'crystallography' projects, most importantly the one carried out by Atomic Energy Commission's Chairman, R. Chidambram was also affected. Chidambram was even refused a visa to the US, where he was to attend a conference relating to his research in the field. It was a mistake to discourage him to participate in the meeting related to his work in 'crystallography', which had nothing to do with nuclear research. Since he was a nuclear scientist, he was affected by sanctions. We need to rise our scientific collaboration so that future misunderstanding do not spill in this area."

Under such growing support for the Bush administration's plan, the United States lifted the 1998 economic and military sanctions against both India and Pakistan. Lifting of sanctions may not be of much consequence to India as punitive provisions were already nullified by the Clinton administration. Two major areas where there were relief to India—dual-use technology and international lending by multilateral agencies like World Bank and Asia Development Bank (ADB). With regard to defence supplies, lifting sanctions helped in shopping for "mission critical high tech components" especially in missile development projects and spares for the existing hardware.

Psychologically, no doubt, India has an advantage in export markets. Lifting of sanctions also made research in space, biotechnology and chemicals with dual-uses easier with free exchange of information and data worldwide. In the case of foreign lending, the US-exam and other American lending agencies had already diluted the impact of sanctions on exposure in Indian projects. But definitely it is easier for these lending agencies to take exposure in Indian projects on principles of commercial jurisprudence.

On the whole impression about lifting of sanctions is that those, which the US had imposed on India after Pokhran-I in 1974 still remained; they were far more stringent. Since the sanctions have been deemed by the US to be no longer in keeping with the national interests, they have been withdrawn. As an immediate effect, what it earns is that the status of India and Pakistan as nascent nuclear powers has been recognized. And also the removal of sanctions signaled that the US has little choice but to accept that India (and Pakistan) have moved into the nuclear club.[9]

ECONOMIC RELATIONS

India and the US have multi-faceted relations ranging from political, strategic to economic and commercial. India-US economic relations in the form of bilateral investments and trade constitute an important element in India-US bilateral relations particularly because India is now the second fastest growing economy in the world and USA is the world's largest economy.

Economic reforms introduced since 1991 have radically changed the course of the Indian economy and led to its gradual integration with the global economy. Benefits of the reform process are visible in the form of better growth rates, higher investment and trade flows and accelerated decline in income poverty. The effects of these reforms on trade and investment relations with the United States have been profound. The US is the largest investing country in India in terms of FDI approvals, actual inflows, and portfolio investment. The US investments cover almost every sector in India, which is open for private participants. India's investments in US are picking up. The US is also India's largest trading partner. By 2003, India became the 24th largest export destination for the US. At present, the US accounts for 14.93 per cent of India's exports and around 6.32 per cent of India's imports. India accounts for 0.75 per cent of the US's total exports and imports. India's exports to the US during 2006-07 registered a growth of 8.63 per cent over the previous year while India's imports from US registered a growth of 24.03 per cent over the previous year. In terms of exports to the US, India now ranks eighteenth largest country. Since 2000, the two countries have been making efforts to strengthen institutional structure of bilateral economic relations by means of the "India-US Economic Dialogue" that aims at deepening the Indo-American partnership through regular dialogue and engagement.

US Investments In India

Foreign Direct Investment (FDI): the US is one of the largest foreign direct investors in India. The stock of actual FDI inflow increased from US$ 11.3 million in 1991 to US$ 4132.8 million as on August 2004 recording an increase at a compound rate of 57.5 per cent per annum. The cumulative FDI flows from US during 1991-2007 stood at US$ 6215 million. The FDI inflows from the US constitute about 12 per cent of the total actual FDI inflows into India. The overall foreign direct investment (FDI) equity flow into India from the US during April 2000-June 2008 was US$ 5.4 billion. During April-August 2008, FDI inflow from the US was US$ 1.15 billion.

area to the US investors. India's telecom sector has been growing at a rate of about 20 per cent per annum for the past two years. In this sector there exists huge vast untapped rural potential. India is the second largest US market in the world. At present, nearly two in five of the Fortune 500 companies outsource their software requirements to India. Abundant investment opportunities exist for further strengthening Indo-US economic ties in the IT sector, especially in areas like telecommunication infrastructure, optic fibre cable, satellite base communication wireless, IT-enabled services, IT-enabled education, data centres and server farms, and software development. Besides, pharmaceuticals, biotechnology and chemical industries also provide great opportunities for closer cooperation.

Top sectors attracting FDI from USA are: Fuels (power & oil ref.) (35.93%); Telecommunications (radio paging, cellular mobile & basic telephone services (10.56%); Electrical Equipment (including computer software & electronics) (9.50%); Food Processing Industries (food products & marine products) (9.43%); and Service Sector (fin. & non-fin. services) (8.28%).

The US is one of the largest foreign direct investors in India. Cumulative FDI inflows from US till July 2008 was $ 7.96 billion. FDI inflows from US constitute about 8 per cent of actual FDI inflows into India in rupee terms. FDI by US during the year 2000-01 to February 2008 stood at $ 4464 million which was 8.03 per cent of total FDI inflows in terms of rupees.

Portfolio Investment: In portfolio investment also, the US is the leading investor. There are 234 US based FIIs and 169 US based sub-accounts registered with SEBI. As of June 30, 2004, US based FIIs have made a net investment of nearly $ 10.2 billion out of a total of $ 25.3 billion as on that date in the Indian capital markets, which accounts for about 40.5 per cent of the net investments made by the FIIs since 1993.

The US companies in India are involved in a broad spectrum of economic activities. From infrastructure to consumer goods, and from information technology to consultancy services, American companies are represented in India as never before.

Table 2.2: Year-Wise Foreign Institutional Investments

Years	Total FII ($ Mn)	FII from USA ($ Mn)	US Share (%)
1993-94	1634	781	47.80
1994-95	1528	894	58.51
1995-96	2036	856	42.04
1996-97	2424	1019	42.04
1997-98	1463	1005	68.69
1998-99	-176	-9	5.11
1999-2000	2235	841	37.63
2000-01	2222	1174	52.84
2001-02	1702	533	31.32
2002-03	525	174	33.14
2003-04	8630	2863	33.17
2004-05	10172	2065	20.30
2005-06	9332	3266	34.99
2006-07	7100	2240	31.55
Total	**50827**	**17702**	**539.13**

Source: Securities and Exchange Board of India.

India's Investments in USA

The policy for Indian direct investment abroad was initiated in 1992. Streamlining of the procedures and substantial liberalization has been done since 1995. As of now, Indian corporates/registered partnership firms are allowed to invest in entities abroad up to 100 per cent of their net worth and are permitted to make overseas investment in any bona fide business activity. The overall annual ceiling on overseas investment and also the requirement of prior approval of RBI for diversification of activity and for transfer by way of sales of shares have been done away with. The basic rationale for opening up the regime of Indian investment overseas has been the need to provide Indian industry access to new markets and technologies with a view to increasing their competitiveness globally and help the country's export efforts.

Since 1996 and up to September 2004, the total approved Indian investment abroad amounts to US$ 11083.11 million of which 60.9 per cent has been the actual outflow. The US share ($ 2080.367 million) constitutes 18.77 per cent of the total approval. Since 1996, the US attracted highest Indian direct investments (US$ 2080.367 million) followed by Russia (US$ 1751.39 million), Mauritius (US$ 948.864 million) and Sudan (US$ 912.03 million). India's outgoing investments has been largest in the field of manufacturing (54.8%) followed by non-financial services including software development (35.4%).

Indian investments in the US have been growing significantly since 2002, by around 75 per cent per year. Investments in 2006 was estimated at around US$ 2 billion which rose sharply in 2007 to touch US$ 13 billion. In 2007-08 alone, an estimated US$ 10.25 billion was invested by Indian companies in the US. In 2008, investments were in excess of US$ 8 billion as on May 2008. The United States is India's largest trading partner with a 13 per cent share.

In the financial year 2004-05 (April-August, 2004) actual outflows from India on account of overseas investment was US$ 575.14 million as compared to US$ 384.49 million in the corresponding period of last year. In the year 2004-05, the US attracted highest Indian direct investments (US$ 125.4 million) followed by Australia (US$ 116.33 million), Kazakhstan (US$ 39.05 million) and Hong Kong (US$ 28.49 million). India's outgoing investments was largest in the field of manufacturing at US$ 279.07 million followed by non-financial services (including software development) at US$ 75.27 million, others at US$ 61.27 million and trading sector at US$ 30.3 million. The returns on account of repatriation of dividend, royalty, consultancy fee, etc. from overseas JV/WOS during April-August, 2004 amounted to US$ 40.87 million.

Several of India's IT companies have offices in US. In addition, Indian companies have also begun to make investments in other areas including in the manufacture of tractors (Mahindras), pharmaceuticals (Ranbaxy, Dr. Reddy's, etc.), laminated tubes (Essel Propack), Tea (Tata tea), etc.

Institutional Framework for India-US Economic Cooperation

The institutional framework for bilateral economic relations has two streams. One is at government-to-government level and the other is at business-to-business level. Both these streams have regular interactions with eachother to promote and strengthen the trade and economic interactions between the two countries.

US-India Economic Dialogue: During the visit of US President Clinton to India in March 2000, a joint statement "US-India Relations: A Vision for the 21st Century" was issued by the then Prime Minister Vajpayee and President Clinton which pledged to deepen the Indo-American partnership through dialogue and engagement. It also outlined an architecture of several high level consultations which would institutionalize this dialogue in a separate document "Agreed Principles: Institutional Dialogue between the United States and India". This architecture laid out the following framework for the bilateral economic dialogue.

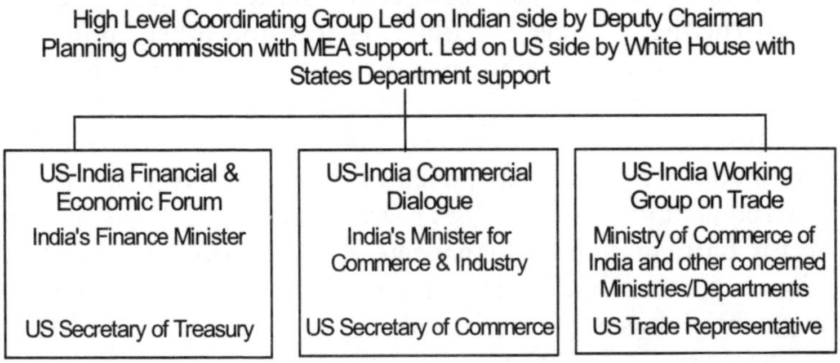

In addition to the above, the "Agreed Principles" provided for (a) setting up of a Joint Consultative Group on Clean Energy and Environment; and (b) establishing US-India Science and Technology Forum, both of which were strictly not under the rubric of the Economic Dialogue.

Subsequently in 2001, in addition to the three forums under the Economic Dialogue, two additional forums were created to address environment and energy issues under the Economic Dialogue itself. Besides, following meetings at the level of Prime Minister Vajpayee and President Bush in November 2002, efforts began to develop a "Statement of Principles" on High Technology trade including trade in "dual use" goods and technologies. On February 5, 2003 a "Statement of Principles for India-US High Technology Commerce" was signed in Washington, DC. The basic objectives of HTCG are: (a) to further the objectives specified in the "Statement of Principles" of November 2002, (b) to develop a schedule of meetings and activities for promotion of High Technology commerce, (c) to take steps to remove systemic tariff and non-tariff barriers, (d) to identify and generate awareness of market opportunities recognizing the importance of private sector in this endeavour, (e) to create appropriate environment for successful High Technology commerce in partnership with private sector, and (f) to maintain regular information flow on the changes on respective export control laws, regulations and policies and establishment of mechanism for prompt discussion on any bilateral "dual use" export control issues.

Prospect for Further India-US Economic Cooperation

There are several areas where economic cooperation between India and the US can progress further. These include infrastructure, IT, telecom sector, energy and other knowledge industries such as pharmaceuticals and biotechnology. Closer economic ties in infrastructure sector can yield mutual benefits to both the countries. The Government of India is continuously reviewing its policies to create an investor-friendly environment in sectors such as roads, ports and airports. Private sector participation in management, BOT projects, greenfield airports, terminals and shipping berths and capacity augmentation has been initiated.

The IT sector is India's one of the fastest growing sectors with over 50 per cent average annual compounded growth since 1991. Today, nearly two in five of the Fortune 500 companies outsource their software requirements to India. Abundant investment opportunities exist for further strengthening Indo-US economic ties in the IT sector, especially, in areas like communication infrastructure, optic fiber cable, gateways, satellite-based communication wireless, IT-enabled services, IT-enable education, data centers and server farms, and software development.

India's telecommunication sector, already a major recipient of US investment, is expected to continue to provide substantial opportunities to US investors. India's telecom sector has been growing at a rate of about 20 per cent per annum for the past few years. The tele-density has increased from 1.94 per cent in 1999 to 7.02 per cent in 2004. It rose sharply at 30.64 per cent as on September 2008. India is looking forward to increase the tele-density to 20 by 2008. India's wireless market by far is the fastest growing market in the world. The number of cellular subscribers has increased from 1 million in 1998 to 41 million in 2004. India is looking forward to achieve an annual growth rate of 13 per cent in cable TV subscribers, 18 per cent in TV set owners, 27 per cent in PC penetration, 28 per cent in cell phones, 30 per cent in telephones and 58 per cent in internet subscribers in the next four years. The proportion of households moving towards richer and well-to-do category is going up in India. There also exists huge untapped rural potential.

The Government of India is keen on foreign investment in manufacturing telecom equipment and handsets. Approximately 16 million handsets were sold in India in 2003 and for 2004 it is 30 million. In order to provide telecom services to 200 million telephone users by 2007, 40 million Internet users by 2010, and 20 million broadband users by 2010, we need an investment of more than US$ 20 billion. Most of these investments are expected to come from foreign investment source. Some of the key changes include increase in foreign ownership limit, reduction of regulatory charges, moving to unified licensing and spectrum policy, bringing about comprehensive broadband policy and revamping of national telecom policy. Keeping in view the comparative advantages of the two countries, there is a tremendous scope for further strengthening the business ties between the two countries in this sphere.

India's energy sector has been an important destination for the US investment. The sector offers for exploitation a vast untapped potential to investors in hydroelectricity, oil & natural gas and coal. Although several US companies have been looking at the Indian energy market closely, progress has so far been limited. With the introduction of Central Electricity Act 2003, the government of India has now liberalized the power sector. Private sector participation is now allowed in generation, distribution and transmission. Considering the vast present and projected demand-supply gap, there is tremendous potential for economic cooperation between the two countries in this area. Pharmaceuticals, biotechnology and chemical industries also provide great opportunities for closer cooperation. India is one of the largest manufacturers and exporters of pharmaceuticals. It also holds the key for genotype drug design and is widely acclaimed for its large pool of trained doctors and cost-effective research & development (R&D) activities.

Table 2.3: Details of Top Investing Companies of US

(in million)

Nos.	Name of the collaborator	Sector	State	Amount of FDI approved - Rupees/(US$) - % of FDI
1	Coca-Cola South Asia Holdings Inc., Atlanta.	Food Products	Not indicated	Rs.23,870.00 (US$ 694.10) 100%
2	Mission Energy Company, USA	Power	Tamil Nadu	Rs. 15,414.89 (US $ 358.49) 99.40%
3	Fluor Damiel Inc.	Power	Andhra Pradesh	Rs. 11,394.00 (US $ 317.65) 49%
4	CMS Generation	Power	West Bengal	Rs. 9,465.00 (US $ 301.72) 75%
5	Ford Motor Company	Passenger Cars	Maharashtra	Rs. 8,635.00 (US $ 275.00) 50%
6	Hughes Electronics Corp	Cellular Mobile/Basic Telephone Service	Not indicated	Rs. 7,999.90 (US $ 254.77) 40%
7	Public Power International Ltd, British Virgin Island	Power	Orissa	Rs. 7,440.00 (US $ 207.42) 100%
8	Soros Fund Management, New York	Power	Madhya Pradesh	Rs. 7,000.00 (US $ 195.15) 100%
9	Panda Energy Corpn USA & Its Associates, Texas.	Power	Orissa	Rs. 5,950.00 (US $ 165.88) 100%

In order to promote bilateral trade and investment in the knowledge-based industries, the US-India Business Council (USIBC), along with FICCI, had launched a Knowledge Trade Initiative (KTI). The KTI is a bilateral forum between India and the US to discuss key issues affecting the trade of knowledge-based products and services between the two countries. The KTI aims to solidify the Indo-US leadership in the knowledge economy by harmonizing bilateral positions on key issues affecting knowledge trade.

The US investor community is today increasingly sharing confidence in the future of the Indian economy. The growing synergy between the two countries in the technology sector and mutually shared respect for democracy, rule of law and well established business practices make the two countries natural business partners.

US Fortune-500 Investors in India

Abbott Laboratories
AlliedSignal Incorporated
American Express Company
American Home Products Corporation
AMP Incorporated
Apple Computer, Incorporated
Asarco, Incorporated
Associates First Capital
AT&T
Avery Dennison Corporation
Bank of America Corporation
The Bank of New York
Bankers Trust New York Corporate
The Black & Decker Corporation
Brunswick Corporation
Caterpillar, Incorporated
The Chase Manhattan Corporation
Chevron Corporation
Citicorp
CMS Energy
The Coca-Cola Company
Colgate-Palmolive Company
COMPAQ Computer Corporation
ConAgra, Incorporated

Ingersoll-Rand Company
Intel Corporation
International Business Machines Corp.
Johnson Controls Incorporated
Johnson & Johnson
Kellogg Company
McDonald's Corporation
The McGraw-Hill Co., Incorporated
Merck & Company, Incorporated
Merrill Lynch & Company, Inc.
Microsoft Corporation
Minnesota Mining & Manufacturers
Mobil Corporation
Monsanto Company
J.P. Morgan & Company
Morgan Stanley Group
Motorola Incorporated
NYNEX Corporation
Oracle Corporation
Parker Hannifin Corporation
PepsiCo Incorporated
Pfizer Incorporated

Cooper Industries, Incorporated
Corning Incorporated
CPC International Incorporated
Cummins Engine Company, Incorporated
Dana Corporation
Digital Equipment
The Dow Chemical Company
E.I. DuPont de Nemours & Company
Eastman Kodak Company
Emerson Electric Company
Enron Corporation
The Estee Lauder Co., Incorporated
Exxon/Esso
Farmland Industries, Incorporated
Federal Express
Fluor
Ford Motor Company
General Electric Company
General Motors Corporation
The Gillette Company
The Goodyear Tyre & Rubber Company
W.R. Grace & Company
Harris Corporation
Hasbro Incorporated
Hewlett-Packard Company
Honeywell, Incorporated
Phelps Dodge Corporation
Phillip Morris Companies Inc.
Phillips Petroleum Company
PPG Industries, Incorporated
The Procter & Gamble Company
Qualcomm
Raytheon Company
Rockwell International Corporation
Rohm & Haas Company
Sara Lee Corporation
Shering-Plough Corporation
Silicon Graphics
Sprint Corporation
Sun Microsystems
Tenneco Incorporated
Textron Incorporated
TRW Incorporated
Union Carbide Corporation
United Parcel Service of America
United Technologies Corporation
UNISYS Corporation
US WEST, Incorporated
USX Corporation
The Walt Disney Company
Warner-Lambert Company

Trade Relations

Trade and commerce form a crucial component in the rapidly expanding and multi-faceted relations between India and US. From modest $ 5.6 billions in 1990, the bilateral trade in merchandise goods has increased to $ 26.76 billion in 2005 representing an impressive 378 per cent growth in a span of 15 years. India's merchandise exports to the US grew at 20.78 per cent from US$ 15.57 billion in 2004 to US$ 18.81 billion in 2005. The US exports of merchandise to India increased from US$ 6.11 billion in 2004 to US$ 7.99 billion in 2005, an increase of 30.77 per cent. Trade and commerce between India and US has increased manifolds in recent years. From a modest $ 5.6 billion in 1990, the bilateral trade in merchandise goods has increased to $ 41.62 billion in 2007 representing an impressive 743 per cent growth in a span of 17 years. The total bilateral trade between India and the US is likely to exceed $ 50 billion by the year 2008 against $ 41.6 billion last year. A tabular profile of the bilateral trade during the recent period is given below:

Table 2.4: Trade with the USA

(US $ million)

Year	Exports	Growth%	Imports	Growth%	Balance of Trade
2004-05	13765.75	19.81	7001.35	39.06	(+) 6764.40
2005-06	17353.06	26.06	9464.74	35.04	(+) 7898.32
2006-07	18851.42	8.63	11726.96	24.03	(+) 7124.46
2006-07 (Apr-Oct)	11030.52	-	5953.70	-	(+) 5076.82
2007-08 (Apr-Oct)	11914.86	8.02	7825.04	31.43	(+) 4089.82

Source: US Department of Commerce.

A profile of growth trends of some major items of bilateral trade in merchandise in the recent period is given below:

Bilateral Trade between India and the US

Table 2.5: Bilateral Merchandise Trade (2001 to 2008)

(US$ millions)

	Years				
Item	2004	2005	2006	2007	2008
India's export to US	15572	18808	21826	24024	8806
US exports to India	6109	7958	10091	17592	5334
Total Bilateral Trade	21681	26766	31917	41616	14140

Source: US Department of Commerce.

India mostly exports gems and jewellery, organic chemicals and engineering goods and textiles to the US. India's IT, ITEs services exports, research and development and engineering services exports to the US amounted to around US$ 24 billion in 2007.

India's merchandise exports to the US grew by 8.63 per cent, going up to US$ 18.85 billion in 2006-07 from US$ 17.35 billion in 2005-06. During 2007-08, merchandise exports from India to US went up by 9.81 per cent to reach US$ 20.72 billion against US$ 18.85 billion in 2006-07. For the first quarter of 2008-09, India exported goods worth US$ 5.023 billion to the US.

US export to India mainly consists of aircraft and aviation machinery, nuclear reactors other machinery, optical and medical instruments, precious stones and metals, fertilizers and organic chemicals. US export to India grew by an astonishing 79.33 per cent to reach US$ 21.02 billion in 2007-08 against US$ 11.72 billion in 2006-07. For the first quarter of 2008-09, US exported goods worth US$ 3.96 billion to India. Of the US$ 17.6 billion exports to India in 2007, aviation accounts to about $ 6 billion which is 34.4 per cent. The growth has been quite rapid from $ 2 billion in 2006 to $ 6 billion is 2007.

India's Exports to US

- Cut and polished diamonds and jewelry is a major item of India's exports to the US, accounting for 25.7%. Exports of this item declined from $ 6.19 billion in 2007 to $ 5.6 billion in 2008.
- Textiles exports to the US, which account for 21.1%, fell from $ 5.45 billion in 2007 to $ 5.42 billion in 2008.
- Iron & steel products which account for 7% to India's exports to the US, grew from $ 1.23 billion in 2007 to $ 1.68 billion in 2008.
- Exports of pharmaceutical products grew from $ 896 million in 2007 to $ 1480 million in 2008.

US Exports to India

- Export of fertilizers which accounts for 14.9% of US exports to India, grew from $ 778 million in 2007 to $ 2.79 billion in 2008.

- Export of aircraft, aviation machinery and parts, which accounts for 14.4%, declined from $ 6.06 billion in 2007 to $ 2.69 billion in 2008.
- Export of precious stones and metals from US to India which accounts for 13.6%, grew from $ 1.89 billion in 2007 to $ 2.55 billion in 2008.
- Machinery exports fell from $ 2.27 billion in 2007 to $ 2.44 billion in 2008.

Trade During the Period January to March 2006

During the period April-October 2007, India's exports to the US were US$ 11,914.86 million registering a positive growth of 8.02 per cent over corresponding period of the previous year. During the same period India's imports from the US were US$ 7,825.04 million registering a growth of 31.43 per cent over the corresponding period of the previous year.

Major Items of Export from India to US

For the year 2007, merchandise exports from India to US grew at 7.01 per cent from $ 24.07 billion in 2007 to $ 25.76 billion in 2008.

(a) Diamonds & precious stones (21.7%).

(b) Textiles (21.1%).

(c) Iron & steel (6.5%).

(d) Organic chemicals (5.7%).

(e) Machinery (5.6%).

(f) Electrical machinery (5.3%).

(g) Pharmaceutical products (5.8%).

Major Items of Export from US to India

For the year 2007, merchandise exports from US to India increased from 17.59 billion in 2007 to $ 18.67 billion in 2008 which is a growth of 6.13 per cent.

Select major items with their percentage shares are given below:

(a) Machinery (13.1%).

(b) Precious stones & metals (13.6%).

(c) Fertilizers (14.9%).

(d) Optical instruments & equipment (5%).
(e) Aviation & aircraft (14.4%).[10]
(f) Electrical machinery (7.2%).
(g) Mineral fuel, oil, etc. (4.7%).

DEFENCE COOPERATION

Defence cooperation between the United States and India is in the early stages of development (unlike US-Pakistan military ties, which date back to the 1950s). Since September 2001, and despite a concurrent US rapprochement with Pakistan, US-India security cooperation has flourished. The India-US Defense Policy Group (DPG) — moribund since India's 1998 nuclear tests and ensuing the US sanctions — was revived in late 2001 and meets annually; US diplomats call military cooperation among the most important aspects of transformed bilateral relations.[11]

The US Secretary for Defense Ronald Rumsfeld and the Minister of Defence of India Mr. Pranab Mukherjee set in place a New Framework for the US-India Defense Relationship on June 28, 2005. The United States and India signed a ten-year defense pact outlining planned collaboration in multilateral operations, expanded two-way defense trade, increasing opportunities for technology transfers and co-production, expanded collaboration related to missile defense, and establishment of a bilateral Defense Procurement and Production Group. The United States views defense cooperation with India in the context of "common principles and shared national interests" such as defeating terrorism, preventing weapons proliferation, and maintaining regional stability. Many analysts laud increased US-India security ties as providing an alleged "counterbalance" to growing Chinese influence in Asia. Ten years ago, in January 1995, the two countries had signed the Agreed Minute on Defense Relations. Since then, changes in the international security environment and opportunities for cooperation unimaginable in 1995 led both countries to agree to the new Framework so as to build on past successes, seize new opportunities and chart a course for the India-US defense relationship for the next 10 years, a defence relationship in support of the broader India-US global partnership resolved to by Prime Minister and President Bush in the Joint Statement of July 18, 2005. During Prime Minister Dr. Manmohan Singh's visit to the United States in July 2005, the two countries had announced a "US–India Disaster Response Initiative" to build on the successful experience during the Tsunami Operations of 2004 and to establish an ongoing effort to prepare for and conduct relief operations in the Indian Ocean region and beyond. During President Bush's visit to India in March 2006, the two countries signed a "Maritime Cooperation Framework" agreement to enhance security in the maritime domain, to prevent piracy and other transnational crimes at sea, carry out search and rescue operations, combat marine pollution, respond to natural disasters, address emergence threats and enhance cooperative capabilities including logistics support.

In the bilateral context the Framework seeks to enable cooperation in the area of defense technology, continued joint and combined exercises and exchanges, achieve greater interaction between the two armed forces, increase opportunities for technology transfer, collaboration, co-production and research and development, etc. In the context of a global partnership, the Defense Framework sets out the common interest of both countries in maintaining security and stability, defeating terrorism and violent religious extremism, protecting the free flow of commerce via land, air and sea lanes and preventing the spread of weapons of mass destruction and associated materials, data and technologies.

The Defense Policy Group (DPG) continues to be the primary mechanism to guide the India-US defense relationship. It held its seventh meeting on November 21-23, 2005. The meeting was co-chaired by Under Secretary of Defense for Policy Mr. Eric. S. Edelman and Defence Secretary Government of India, Mr. Shekhar Dutt. The DPG included an intensive exchange of views on the international strategic and security situation and on the further development of bilateral defense cooperation as envisaged under the June 28 Defense Framework. The DPG reviewed the reports of the four sub-groups — Military Cooperation Group, Joint Technology Group, Senior Security Technology Group and Senior Technology Security Group and the Defense Procurement & Production Group (DPPG). The newly constituted DPPG held its first meeting in Washington, DC on November 18-21, 2005 and discussed ways to strengthen cooperation in the field of defense supplies as well as industrial and technological cooperation between USA and India.

Under the India-US Defence Policy Group, which is the apex institutional dialogue mechanism for defence cooperation, the Joint Technology Group held its 9th meeting on April 10, 2007 in Washington, the Defence Procurement and Production Group held its fourth meeting in New Delhi on 26 November 2007 and the 8th meeting of Military Cooperation Group met in Hawaii on 11-13 December 2007.

The armed forces of the two countries have been holding joint exercises since the resumption of defense cooperation between them. Indian and US Special Forces had conducted airborne joint exercises "Balance Iroquois" in Agra in May 2002, and "Geronimo Thrust" in Alaska in September-October 2002. A joint air transport exercise "Cope India" was conducted in Agra in October 2002. The Navies of the two countries have undertaken joint patrolling to secure the maritime trade routes in the Strait of Malacca. The largest ever India-US naval exercise "Malabar" was held at Kochi from September 26 to October 3, 2002 featuring over 1,500 Indian and American naval personnel conducting flying operations, anti-submarine warfare exercises and replenishment at sea.

A peacekeeping command post exercise was held jointly in New Delhi in April 2003 and Special Forces of the two countries conducted joint counter insurgency exercises "Vajra Prahar" in Mizoram in April 2003. A counter-insurgency and Jungle Warfare exercise "Yudha Abhyas" was held in Mizoram in March-April, 2004. "Cope Thunder" multi-lateral exercises held in Alaska in July-August 2004 had Indian Air Force units including 200 personnel and six Jaguar fighters. About 2,000 Indian and US Navy personnel took part in "Malabar 04", a training exercise off the southwest coast of India on October 1-9, 2004. A major IAF-USAF dissimilar air combat training Exercise "Cope India 2005" took place at Air Force Station Kalaikunda on 7-17 November 2005. The USAF participation comprised twelve F-16, based at Misawa Air Base, Japan, and one E-3 AWACS based at Kadena Air Base, Okinawa. IAF participation comprised MiG-21 Bison, MiG-27, Mirage-2000, MiG 29 and Su-30 K. Besides, few sorties on Su-30 MKI were included for the first time.

In 2007, India-US Defence Joint Working Group held two meetings—first in April in New Delhi and second in November in Washington. In the first, ship acquisition by India from the US, US$ Trenton was handed over to Indian Navy on 17 January 2007. It has been commissioned as INS Jalashwa. The defence forces of the two countries engaged in bilateral exercises. US companies participated in the Aero India show held in Bangalore from 9 to 13 February 2007. India-US joint military exercises were held in Alaska from 8-26 September 2007.

The US and Indian Special Forces soldiers have held joint exercises near the India-China border, and major annual "Malabar" joint naval exercises were held at the Indian coast in October 2006. Despite these developments, there remain indications that the perceptions and expectations of top US and Indian military leaders are divergent on several key issues, including India's regional role, approaches to countering terrorism, and US-Pakistan relations. Along with increasing military-to-military ties, the issue of US arms sales to India has taken a higher profile. In 2002, the Pentagon negotiated a sale to India of 12 counter-battery radar (or "Fire finder" radars) worth a total of $190 million. India also purchased $29 million worth of counter-terrorism equipment for its special forces and has received sophisticated US made electronic ground sensors to help stem the tide of militant infiltration in the Kashmir region. In July 2004, Congress was notified of a possible sale to India involving up to $40 million worth of aircraft self-protection systems to be mounted on the Boeing 737s that carry the Indian head of state. The State Department has authorized Israel to sell to India the jointly developed US-Israeli Phalcon airborne early warning system; an expensive asset that some analysts believe may tilt the regional strategic balance even further in India's favor. In August 2006, New Delhi approved a $44 million plan to purchase the USS Trenton, a decommissioned American amphibious transport dock. The ship, which will become the second largest in the Indian navy, is set to fly the Indian flag in early 2007.

The Indian government reportedly possesses an extensive list of desired US made weapons, including PAC-3 anti-missile systems, electronic warfare systems, and possibly even fighter aircraft. The March 2005 unveiling of the Bush Administration's "new strategy for South Asia" included assertions that the United States welcomed Indian requests for information on the possible purchase of F-16 or F/A-18 multi-role fighters, and indicated that Washington is "ready to discuss the sale of transformative systems in areas such as command and control, early warning, and missile defense". Still, some top Indian officials express concern that the United States is a "fickle" partner that may not always be relied upon to provide the reciprocity, sensitivity, and high-technology transfers sought by New Delhi. In February 2006, the Indian Navy declined an offer to lease two US P-3C maritime reconnaissance aircraft, calling the arrangements "expensive": In a controversial turn, the Indian government has sought to purchase a sophisticated anti-missile platform, the Arrow Weapon System, from Israel. Because the United States took the lead in the system's development, the US government has veto power over any Israeli exports of the Arrow. Although Defense Department officials are seen to support the sale as meshing with President Bush's policy of cooperating with friendly countries on missile defense, State Department officials are reported to oppose the transfer, believing that it would send the wrong signal to other weapon-exporting states at a time when the US is seeking to discourage international weapons proliferation. Indications are that a US interest in maintaining a strategic balance on the subcontinent, along with US obligations under the Missile Technology Control Regime, may preclude any approval of the Arrow sale.

Joint US-India military exercises and arms sales negotiations can cause disquiet in Pakistan, where there is concern that induction of advanced weapons systems into the region could disrupt the "strategic balance" there. Islamabad worries that its already disadvantageous conventional military status *vis-à-vis* New Delhi will be further eroded by India's acquisition of sophisticated "force multipliers". In fact, numerous observers identify a pro-India drift in the US government's strategic orientation in South Asia. Yet Washington regularly lauds

Islamabad's role as a key ally in the US-led counter-terrorism coalition and assures Pakistan that it will take no actions to disrupt strategic balance in the subcontinent.[12]

Security Assistance

The US has provided about $157 million in military assistance to India since 1947, more than 90 per cent of it distributed from 1962-1966. In recent years, modest security-related assistance has emphasized export control enhancements and military training. Earlier Bush Administration requests for Foreign Military Financing were withdrawn, with the two countries agreeing to pursue commercial sales programs. The Pentagon reports military sales agreements with India worth $202 million during FY 2002-05.[13]

Boxer Expeditionary Strike Group and Indian Navy in Malabar

The USS Boxer (LHD 4) Expeditionary Strike Group (BOXESG) and the Indian Navy's Western Fleet "Exercise Malabar" was held from 25 October to 5 November 2006 in the Southwest coast of India. The purpose of the multinational exercise, which focuses on a number of naval mission areas, is to strengthen ties between American, Canadian and Indian forces as well as enhance the cooperative security relationship between the nations involved.

More than 6,500 US Navy personnel took part in "Exercise Malabar". "The United States and India share democratic traditions, and we share sea faring traditions," said Capt. David Angood, commander of BOXESG and Amphibious Squadron (PHIBRON) 5. "We are natural partners and friends, and look forward to continuing to strengthen the bonds and personal relationships between our two navies and advancing into more complex operational and strategic areas that go beyond tactical exercises," he added. The Indian Western Fleet commander, noting that each Malabar exercise increases bonds and readiness between the forces, echoed these thoughts, "During each Malabar exercise, we try to take it up a notch from the previous," said the Flag Officer Commanding the Indian Western Fleet, Rear Adm. Anup Singh. He added that safety is the top priority and open lines of communication are vital.

During the exercise, the three nations' ships worked together in a variety of functional skill areas, including force protection drills, visit, boarding search and seizure (VBSS), formation steaming, coordinated surface fire support, amphibious landing, live-fire events for attached aircraft, torpedo firing events and anti-submarine warfare training.

Thirteen naval assets involved in the exercise from the three nations as well as Marines from the 15th Marine Expeditionary Unit (MEU), Special Operations Capable (SOC). This is the first time that a US Expeditionary Strike Group (ESG) participated and led the exercise. The exercise, in general, focused on expeditionary warfare.

Several different personnel exchange occurred throughout the exercises. Thirty-one Indian Navy Sailors had trained aboard Boxer with the 2/4 Weapons Company of the 15th MEU (SOC) on weapons tactics, physical training and vehicle integration.

Malabar 2006 also incorporates the Canadian Navy for the first time with the frigate HMCS Ottawa (FFH 341), and US Coast Guard with the USCGC Midgett (WHEC 726), which are both part of BOXESG.[14]

COOPERATION ON COUNTER-TERRORISM

India and the United States have institutionalized their cooperation to combat international terrorism through a Joint Working Group on Counter Terrorism. The first meeting of the joint working group on counter-terrorism was held on February 7-8, 2000 in Washington. This joint working group is also a part of the wide-ranging architecture of institutional dialogue established by the two sides during the visit of President Clinton to India in March 2000.

During the visit of Prime Minister Vajpayee to the United States, Prime Minister and President Clinton reaffirmed the importance of this working group for intensifying co-operation between the two countries to combat international terrorism. The two leaders also decided to expand the mandate of the Joint Working Group to include discussion on such issues as narco-terrorism and Afghanistan.

The second meeting of the Joint Working Group was held on September 25-26, 2000 in New Delhi. Mr. Alok Prasad,

Joint Secretary in the Ministry of External Affairs led the Indian delegation. Ambassador Michael A. Sheehan, US Coordinator for Counter-terrorism led the US delegation. Both delegations included an inter-agency group of counter-terrorism and narco-terrorism law enforcement officials. Ambassador Sheehan also called on the Foreign Secretary, the Home Secretary and other senior officials.

The two sides expressed concern over the growing menace of international terrorism, extremism and drug trafficking. The two sides unequivocally condemned all acts, methods and practices of terrorism as criminal and unjustifiable whatever the considerations—political, philosophical, ideological, racial, ethnic, religious or any other—that may be invoked to justify them. The Indian government welcomed further anti-terrorism assistance programmes from the US. The Group expressed support for a comprehensive UN Convention on terrorism.

Inter-agency teams from the two countries agreed on a range of measures to enhance cooperation between the two countries to combat international terrorism. The two sides would share experience, exchange information and coordinate approaches and action.

Both India and the United States have shared interests in strengthening a regime to counter international terrorism. The Joint Working Group is intended to enhance the effectiveness of the bilateral co-operation and the international efforts to counter terrorism worldwide.

The third meeting of the US-India Counter-Terrorist Working Group was held on June 26, 2001 in Washington, DC. Acting Coordinator for Counter-terrorism, Edmund Hull, hosted the meeting at the Department of State. Joint Secretary Jayant Prasad, the Ministry of External Affairs, headed the Indian delegation. Both delegations included an inter-agency group of counter-terrorism and law enforcement officials.

Both sides agreed that the policies of the Taliban continue to foster terrorism that threatens the interest of both countries, as well as regional and international stability. They affirmed their support for United Nations Security Council Resolutions 1267 and 1333 imposed on the Taliban for supporting terrorism, harboring Osama bin Laden and failing to close down terrorist training camps in Afghanistan. They agreed on the critical importance of the effective implementation of these resolutions, including through an appropriate monitoring mechanism. In addition, the two sides continued consultations on the India-proposed Comprehensive Convention against International terrorism being discussed in the Sixth Committee of the UNGA, and reiterated support for its early finalization.

The Indian side welcomed the US decision to qualitatively upgrade and widen the scope of the Anti-terrorism Training Assistance Program. The Indian side welcomed the US offer to share experience and expertise in strengthening counter-terrorism institutional structures in India. The Indian government accepted the US offer for a seminar to counter chemical, biological, radiological, and nuclear (CBRN) terrorist threats. Inter-agency teams from the two countries decided to enhance exchange of information and strengthen coordination of approaches and actions in combating international terrorism.

The two sides welcomed the fact that their governments had reached a referendum agreement on the text of a mutual legal assistance treaty, and agreed to recommend to their respective governments.

The fourth meeting of the India-US Joint Working Group on Counter-terrorism was held on 21-22 January 2002 in New Delhi. Mr. Jayant Prasad, Joint Secretary in the Ministry of External Affairs, led the Indian delegation and Ambassador Francis X. Taylor, US State Department Coordinator, headed the US delegation on counter-terrorism. Both delegations included an inter-agency group on counter-terrorism, law enforcement, defense, and finance officials.

The two delegations recalled that India and the United States have been victims of terrible acts of terrorism since their last meeting in June 2001.

They welcomed the new international resolve, commitment, and partnership in combating the menace of terrorism. They expressed satisfaction with the progress in the global war against terrorism, but recognized that the campaign will be long-drawn and multi-faceted, involving political, diplomatic, military, intelligence, and financial measures. The two sides emphasized

Though there is a gap between the approval and actual inflow, the ratio of cumulative US FDI inflow to approval has accelerated in the recent years indicating that FDI approved in the past years are materializing now.

Table 2.1: Share of US FDI in Total – Actual Inflow

Years	Total FDI ($ Mn)	US FDI ($ Mn)	US Share (%)
1991	143.6	11.3	7.87
1992	258.0	43.9	17.02
1993	582.9	147.7	25.34
1994	1048.5	118.9	11.34
1995	2172.0	215.6	9.93
1996	3021.0	271.0	8.97
1997	4579.1	736.6	16.09
1998	3377.2	347.1	10.28
1999	4016.1	431.2	10.74
2000	4498.1	418.4	9.30
2001	4281.1	367.6	8.59
2002	4434.5	282.8	6.38
2003	3109.0	396.3	12.75
2004	3753.6	647.65	9.93
2005	4353.8	472.07	10.00
2006	11,122	732.34	6.59
2007	21,797	875.50	4.02
Total	**76547.50**	**6515.96**	**185.14**

Source: Data Compiled from SIA Newsletter, Department of Industrial Policy & Promotion, Govt. of India.

The US companies in India are involved in a broad spectrum of economic activities. From infrastructure to consumer goods, and from information technology to consultancy services, American companies are represented in India as never before.

Energy sector in India has been an important destination for the US investment. The sector offers a vast untapped potential to investors in hydroelectricity, oil and natural gas and coal. In the context of vast present and projected demand-supply gap, there is tremendous potential for economic cooperation between the two countries in this area.

India's telecommunication sector has been a major recipient of US investment and is expected to continue to be an attractive that success in the war against terrorism depended heavily on international cooperation as well as national commitment to renounce use of or support to terrorism. They unequivocally condemned all acts of terrorism, whatever the considerations that may be invoked to justify them, and reaffirmed their nations' commitment to cooperate to prevent acts of terrorism and to eradicate terrorist organizations, which are a threat to international peace and security.

The delegations expressed satisfaction of the cooperation extended in response to the terrorist attacks in the United States on 11 September and on the Indian Parliament on 13 December 2001. They reaffirmed their commitment to strengthen this cooperation and also noted that all countries have the obligation to cooperate in bringing terrorists to justice. They condemned the attack at the US Consulate in Calcutta and conveyed their condolences to the families of the victims.

The two delegations expressed their strong support for the full implementation of UNSC Resolution 1373 of September 2001, which provides a comprehensive approach for sustained global and regional cooperation, national responsibility and building domestic capabilities in combating terrorism. In addition, the two sides continued consultations on the India-proposed Comprehensive Convention against International Terrorism being discussed in the Sixth Committee of the UNGA, and reiterated support for its finalization and adoption.

The delegations reviewed the international terrorism situation, including in South Asia, Central Asia, and Southeast Asia. They shared their assessment of the impact of the military, financial, and other measures taken against terrorist groups and networks after September 11 and December 13, 2000. They also exchanged information on legislative, institutional and law enforcement steps that the two governments are taking to strengthen homeland/internal security and agreed to further share experience in this regard at the next meeting of the Joint Working Group. Experts on the two sides had detailed discussions on financing of terrorist activities and agreed that the widespread use of informal channels for financial flows presents a special challenge to governments.

They agreed that closer cooperation and strengthening mutual capabilities in cutting off financial flows to terrorist organizations would constitute an important component of their counter terrorism cooperation. Counter-terrorism officials on the two sides reviewed the anti-terrorism training and capacity building programs conducted by the United States. The Indian side welcomed the US offer to further expand the program, covering preventive, protective, and consequence management capabilities in both conventional and WMD terrorism. The Indian delegation also welcomed the US pilot project involving equipment and technology to strengthen border management and surveillance. The delegations also discussed forensic cooperation. In addition, the two sides added aviation security to their expanding counter-terrorism agenda. Indian and US officials discussed ways to further strengthen their intelligence and investigative cooperation, including the possibility of access to each other's databases on terrorists.

The delegations welcomed the launch of the Joint Initiative on Cyber Terrorism, agreed on by Prime Minister Vajpayee and President Bush during their meeting in November 2001 in Washington, DC.

The delegations also welcomed the decision of the India-US Defense Policy Group in December 2001 to add a new emphasis in their defense cooperation on counter-terrorism initiatives, including expanding mutual support in this area. The delegations reaffirmed their commitment to further deepen and expand counter-terrorism cooperation.

The fifth meeting of the India-US Joint Working Group on Counter-terrorism was held on July 11-12, 2002 in Washington, DC. Coordinator for Counter-terrorism, Francis X. Taylor hosted the meeting at the Department of State. Joint Secretary Jayant Prasad of the Ministry of External Affairs headed the Indian delegation. Both delegations included officials and experts from their respective governments in line with the multidisciplinary approach needed to successfully fight terrorism. The India-US Joint Working Group on Counter-terrorism was established in January 2000. The Joint Working Group met three times in twelve months, reflecting the importance that the two sides attach to international cooperation in combating terrorism.

During this period, India and the United States have accomplished much in their counter-terrorism cooperation. They have, *inter alia*:

- Broadened their exchange of information and assessments on the international and regional terrorist situation;
- Strengthened intelligence and investigative cooperation;
- Qualitatively upgraded and expanded anti-terrorism training programs for Indian law enforcement officials;
- Signed a Mutual Legal Assistance Treaty;
- Launched a bilateral Cyber Security Forum, with a wide-ranging program of action to address cyber terrorism and information security;
- Introduced military-to-military cooperation on counter-terrorism to supplement the initiatives of the India-US Defence Policy Group in this area;
- Worked together closely on multilateral initiatives on terrorism, including on the implementation of UNSC Resolution 1373;
- Initiated dialogue and cooperation in homeland/internal security, terrorist financing, forensic science transportation security and border management; and
- Taken concrete steps to detect and counter the activities of individual terrorists and organisations of concern to the two countries.

The two delegations reviewed the international terrorist situation, including in South Asia, Central Asia and Southeast Asia. They shared their assessment of the impact of the military, law enforcement, financial and other measures taken against terrorists and their networks over the last six months. They expressed satisfaction at the progress made in the campaign against Al-Qaeda, but also recognised that the efforts of Al-Qaeda cadres and associates to regroup in other countries and to form coalitions within other groups continue to pose a serious threat. The two sides agreed to further intensify intelligence sharing and coordinate action in pursuit of the remains of Al-

Qaeda members and associated terrorist groups. The delegations also discussed the nexus between weapons of mass destruction, proliferation and terrorism.

The delegations reviewed their cooperation in the areas of anti-terrorism assistance and capacity building programmes conducted by the United States, border monitoring, military-to-military cooperation, law enforcement exchanges and legal assistance, internal/homeland security, counter-terrorism finance and money laundering operation, transportation and aviation security and cyber terrorism.

The delegations expressed their strong support for the full and effective implementation of UNSC Resolution 1373 and the work of the UN Security Council's Counter-terrorism Committee. The UNSCR 1373 provides a comprehensive and mandatory framework for sustained global action against terrorism. In addition, both sides consulted on the possibility of an early finalization of an effective Comprehensive Convention on International Terrorism.

The two delegations reviewed cooperation in the areas of extradition and mutual legal assistance with a view to deepening and broadening that cooperation. Both sides agreed to continue full cooperation in the investigation of the hijacking of Indian Airlines flight 814.

Recognizing the importance of equipment and technology in strengthening counter-terrorism capability, the US Technology Support Working Group will meet with its Indian counterpart before the next JWG. Discussions on counter-terrorism equipment between the US Department of Defence and India's Ministry of Defence will continue under the aegis of the Defence Policy Group. Both sides also agreed to continue their dialogue on technology tools for enhancing border management.

India and the United States unequivocally condemned all acts of terrorism, whatever the supposed justification, and reaffirmed their nations' commitments to cooperate in preventing acts of terrorism and neutralizing terrorist organisations, which are a threat to international peace and security.

The resolve of India and the United States to fight terrorism has never been stronger, and their commitment to intensify bilateral cooperation in this endeavor is deeper than ever before. Nowhere is this more evident than in the mutual support rendered in response to terrorist attacks in the two countries.

The sixth meeting of the India-US Joint Working Group on Counter-terrorism was held on August 31-September 1, 2004 in New Delhi. The Indian delegation was led by Ms. Meera Shankar, Additional Secretary (International Security) in the Ministry of External Affairs. Ambassador J. Cofer Black led the US delegation. Both delegations included an inter-agency/inter-ministerial group of officials dealing with counter-terrorism and law enforcement.

The discussions included an assessment of the current international terrorism situation, a review of the US-led operations in Afghanistan and a review of the trends and concerns about the situation in South Asia, including cross border terrorism. The two sides shared assessments about the increase in arms and narcotics trafficking in the region and the linkages between trafficking in narcotics and financing of terrorism. The destabilizing impact of these linkages was a matter of growing concern to both countries. Both sides agreed that, even as the challenge posed by international terrorism continues to mutate, it is important for the international community to strengthen counter-terrorism cooperation to effectively meet this challenge.

The two sides exchanged information on law enforcement, legislative, financial and other measures taken in the field of counter-terrorism. The US side reiterated support for India's early membership to the International Financial Regulatory Institutions (FATF/EGMONT Group). Training and capacity-building programmes were discussed and both sides agreed to continue their ongoing cooperation in this field and also explore the possibility of cooperation in new areas of mutual interest. It was agreed to look for ways to further ongoing cooperation against narcotics trafficking and financing of terrorism and work towards early ratification and implementation of the Treaty on Mutual Legal Assistance.

Perspectives were exchanged on multilateral efforts to counter terrorism. Both sides agreed that the institutional mechanisms, set up by the UN Security Council, should continue to be strengthened. The two sides unequivocally condemned all acts, methods and practices of terrorism and agreed that measures in the multilateral context should be comprehensive, sustained and responsive to different regional situations.

Set up in 2000, the Joint Working Group is seen as a useful mechanism by both sides to get a first-hand understanding of each other's specific concerns. The importance attached by respective Governments to the ongoing cooperation in counter-terrorism was reiterated, in particular in areas of capacity building, exchange of information and intelligence and regular sharing of assessments of emerging trends and concerns relating to international terrorism.

The seventh meeting of the India-US Joint Working Group on Counter-terrorism was held in Washington on April 19-20, 2006. Ambassador K.C. Singh, Additional Secretary (International Organizations), Ministry of External Affairs, Government of India, led the Indian delegation. Ambassador Henry Crumpton, Coordinator for Counter-terrorism, Department of State, led the US delegation. The discussions advanced US-India cooperation in areas of common concern such as bio-terrorism, aviation security, advancements in biometrics, cyber-security and terrorism, WMD-terrorism, terrorist finance and money laundering and violent extremism. Both sides agreed to share information on a real time basis, respond to counter-terrorism assistance requests expeditiously and collaborate to upgrade preparedness and capability to deal with acts of terrorism. The delegations also focused on improving the current mechanisms for extradition and legal cooperation.[15]

The ninth meeting of India-US Joint Working Group on Counter-terrorism was held in Washington on 29-30 November 2007 to discuss bilateral cooperation in combating terrorism.

STRATEGIC PARTNERSHIP

Civil Nuclear Cooperation

The United States and India reached a historic agreement on civil nuclear cooperation on March 2, 2006. The agreement addresses India's surging energy needs for its growing economy. This will also ease the burden on other countries as the world's energy needs continue to rise:

- The US and India have agreed to pursue civil nuclear cooperation to allow India to cooperate and trade in this key area.
- India has agreed to take steps that will bring it into the international non-proliferation mainstream, including placing its civilian nuclear facilities and programs under IAEA safeguards and adhering to the guidelines of the Nuclear Suppliers Group and the Missile Technology Control Regime.

The US-India strategic partnership is rooted in shared values and is broad in nature and scope, with two countries working together on global issues, including expanding economic freedom and democracy; ensuring plentiful sources of clean, safe, and reliable energy; protecting security; supporting innovation and technological advances; and promoting public health.

Economy

The United States and India are expanding cooperation to enhance job creation and economic growth; support economic reform and liberalization; develop a bilateral business climate supportive of trade and investment; and improve market access to goods and services.

- **Trade:** Over the last five years, the US exports to India have more than doubled, helping to create better-paying jobs in the United States. The United States and India agree that trade is essential to promoting global economic growth, development, freedom, and prosperity. Both countries are committed to completing the WTO Doha Development Agenda as soon as possible.
- **Investment:** The United States and India welcomed the report of the US-India CEO Forum and agreed to work on its recommendations through the Economic Dialogue; endorsed the efforts of the US-India Trade Policy Forum to reduce barriers to trade and investment; agreed to hold a high-level public-private investment summit in 2006; and are continuing the dialogue on various issues, including further liberalization of investment restrictions, regulatory transparency, dispute settlement, and reducing tariff and non-tariff barriers to trade.

- **Agriculture:** The United States and India have launched the Knowledge Initiative on Agriculture to link universities, technical institutions, and businesses to support high-priority joint agriculture education, research, and capacity-building projects including biotechnology.

Democracy

Building on their common values and interests, the United States and India affirmed their joint commitment to promote freedom and democracy and assist countries in transition. Effective democracies with governments accountable to the people are the best means of ensuring long-term stability and prosperity.

- The United States and India will work together to support the growth and development of vibrant civil societies, including independent media and non-governmental organizations, in countries that seek such assistance.

Energy and Environment

The United States and India are working together to help meet India's rising demand for energy by looking at new technologies to produce clean, safe, and reliable energy.

- **Future Gen:** India will join the Future Gen international partnership that will work to create a zero-emissions coal-fired power plant, enabling greater use of coal in an environmentally sustainable way.
- **International Thermonuclear Experimental Reactor (ITER):** India has joined the United States, Russia, the European Union, Japan, the Republic of Korea, and China as an ITER member.
- **Asia-Pacific Partnership on Clean Development and Climate:** The United States and India, together with Australia, China, Japan, and the Republic of Korea, will work on practical ways to improve energy security, air quality, and reduce greenhouse gas emissions in ways that foster economic growth.

Security

The United States and India are building the foundation of a durable defense relationship that will continue to support our common strategic and security interests.

- **Maritime Security Cooperation:** The United States and India are committed to a comprehensive cooperative effort to ensure a secure maritime domain.
- **Counter-terrorism:** The United States and India are jointly expanding the scope of our counter-terrorism cooperation, including work on bio-terrorism and cyber security.
- **Military Logistics Support:** The United States and India will soon sign an agreement to facilitate mutual logistic support during combined training, exercises, and disaster relief operations.
- **Defence Trade:** The United States reaffirmed its goal to help meet India's defence needs and to provide the important technologies and capabilities that India seeks.
- **Non-proliferation:** Both countries support efforts to limit the spread of enrichment and reprocessing technologies and also support the conclusion of a Fissile Material Cut-off Treaty.

Innovative and Advanced Technologies

The United States and India are working together to support the creation of innovative, dynamic, knowledge-based economies.

- **Intellectual Property Rights (IPRs):** The United States is funding IPRs training programs to strengthen enforcement and patent examination, as a vibrant IPRs regime is critical to the promotion of a creative, technologically advanced economy.
- **Science:** The United States and India established and co-fund the $30 million Bi-National Science and Technology Commission to generate collaborative partnerships in science and technology.
- **Space:** The United States and India have agreed to continue exploring further cooperation in civil space, including areas such as space exploration, satellite navigation, and earth science. In addition, agreements are being completed that will allow for the launch of US satellites and satellites containing US components by Indian launch vehicles.

Public Health

The United States and India are cooperating to expand efforts to combat and prevent Avian Influenza and HIV/AIDS.

- **Avian Influenza:** The United States and India agreed to expand bilateral efforts on avian influenza by, among other things, reaching out to the private sector, developing regional communication strategies, and planning an in-region containment and response exercise. India hosted the International Partnership on Avian and Pandemic Influenza Meeting in 2007.
- **HIV/AIDS:** In July 2005, President Bush and Prime Minister Singh agreed to further strengthen cooperation on HIV/AIDS by leveraging resources, knowledge, and expertise. Since then:
  - The United States increased funding in FY 2006 for HIV/AIDS prevention, care, and treatment programs to $29.3 million.
  - We have established an Indo-US Corporate Sector Fund for HIV/AIDS, which is a partnership among US and Indian businesses to fight AIDS. Six companies have already pledged a total of $1.2 million to the Fund.
  - The US Food and Drug Administration has given approval to 13 generic anti-retroviral drugs produced by Indian pharmaceutical companies. These drugs can now be purchased as part of the President's Emergency Plan for HIV/AIDS for use around the world.[16]

COOPERATION ON ENERGY

Growing concerns about energy security have prompted India and the US to launch a new Energy Dialogue that reflects the transformed strategic relationship between the world's two largest democracies. The US and India are becoming increasingly reliant upon oil and natural gas markets to satisfy their energy needs. Both countries recognize their mutual interests which are best served by working together in a collaborative fashion to ensure stability in global energy markets. India and the US launched a new Energy Dialogue in May 2005 which aimed at increased trade and investment in the energy sector by working with the public and private sectors to further identify areas of cooperation and collaboration. The co-chairs of this mechanism are Dr. Montek Singh Ahluwalia, Deputy Chairman, Planning Commission on the India side, and Mr. Samuel Bodman, Energy Secretary on the US side. A Steering Committee was also formed to supervise the work of the group headed by India's Foreign Secretary and the US Undersecretary for Energy Efficiency.

Five working groups have been formed covering the areas: (a) oil and natural gas, (b) electric power, (c) coal, (d) energy efficiency, renewable energy and new technologies, and (e) civil nuclear power. The working groups have finalized their terms of reference and are now moving to achieve their goals which include strengthening mutual energy security and promoting stable energy markets; advancing understanding of efficient generation, transmission, distribution and use of electricity; developing and deploying clean energy technologies and energy conservation practices; dialogue and action on issues associated with civilian uses of nuclear energy.

During Prime Minister Dr. Manmohan Singh's visit to Washington, DC in July 2005, President George Bush told the Prime Minister that he would work to achieve full civil nuclear energy cooperation.[17] Recognizing the significance of civilian nuclear energy, the two leaders discussed India's plans to develop its civilian nuclear energy program. President Bush conveyed his appreciation to the Prime Minister over India's strong commitment to preventing Weapons of Mass Destruction (WMD) proliferation and stated that as a responsible state with advanced nuclear technology, India should acquire the same benefits and advantages as other such states. The President told the Prime Minister that he would seek agreement from Congress to adjust US laws and policies, and the US would work with its friends and allies to adjust international regimes to enable full civil nuclear energy cooperation and trade with India.

The President also indicated that the US would encourage its partners to consider India's request for its inclusion in the International Thermonuclear Experimental Reactor (ITER) research project and generation IV International Forum. The

Prime Minister conveyed that for his part, India would reciprocally agree that it would be ready to assume the same responsibilities and practices and acquire the same benefits and advantages as other leading countries with advanced nuclear technology, such as the United States. These responsibilities included identifying and separating civilian and military nuclear facilities and filing a declaration regarding civilian facilities with International Atomic Energy Agency (IAEA); voluntary placing of civilian nuclear facilities under IAEA safeguards and signing an additional IAEA protocol with respect to these facilities; and harmonization and adherence to Missile Technology Control Regime (MTCR) and Nuclear Suppliers Group (NSG) guidelines.[18]

The two leaders also agreed to establish a working group to undertake necessary actions on a phased basis the to fulfill these commitments. The working group is co-chaired by the Foreign Secretary of India and the Undersecretary of State for Political Affairs of the US. The working group met in India in October 2005.

The US Energy Secretary Bodman visited India in March 2007. The Coal Energy Group under the India-US Energy Dialogue met in June 2007 at Washington, DC. External Affairs Minister Pranab Mukherjee led the delegation to the Major Economies Meeting on Energy Security and Climate Change convened by the US President George W. Bush held on 27 September 2007.

India has been invited to join the ITER project as a full-partner. The ITER is the experimental step between the latest studies in plasma physics and future electricity producing fusion power plants. This decision was taken in December 2005 at the ITER negotiations meeting at Jeju, South Korea. The US strongly supported India's application.

CIVIL NUCLEAR DEAL

On 26 June 2006, the US House International Relations Committee passed a Bill H.R. 5682 titled: "United States and India Nuclear Cooperation Promotion Act of 2006" with an overwhelming majority of 37-5. Later the US House of Representatives passed the bill with an overwhelming majority of 359-68 on 26 July 2006. Similarly, the US Senate Foreign Relations Committee approved by a vote of 16-2 its version of the Bill S.3709 entitled the "United States and India Peaceful Atomic Energy Cooperation Act" on June 29, 2006. On 16 November 2006, the US Senate in its lame duck session passed the Bill by an overwhelming majority of 85-12.

The nuclear understanding has been discussed with the US side in several meetings since July 18, 2005. Notable meetings, apart from the meetings discussed earlier, *inter alia*, include:

- Meeting between Prime Minister and President Bush in New York on September 25, 2005.
- Meeting between President Bush and Prime Minister Manmohan Singh on March 2, 2006 in New Delhi.
- Meeting between Foreign Secretary Shyam Saran and US Undersecretary Burns in Washington, DC in April 2006.
- Meeting between Foreign Secretary and US Undersecretary Burns in London on May 23, 2006.
- Meeting between Prime Minister and President Bush in St. Petersburg on July 17, 2006.
- Meeting between Foreign Secretary and US Undersecretary Burns in Paris in July 2006.
- Meeting between Foreign Secretary and US Undersecretary Burns in New York in September 2006.
- Meeting between Raksha Mantri Pranab Mukherji and US Secretary of State Condoleezza Rice in New York on September 21, 2006.

The above meetings were used to exchange views and take stock of the process underway to bring about full civil nuclear energy cooperation, and to convey India's concerns on some aspects of the legislation under consideration in the US Congress.

Earlier, an India-US Working Group was set up for implementation of the nuclear understanding which met four times: in Delhi from October 21-22, 2005, in Washington, DC from December 21-22, 2005, in Delhi from January 19-20, 2006 and again in Delhi from February 23-24, 2006.

India-US Bilateral Nuclear Cooperation Agreement

Both sides held one round of 123 negotiations from June 12-14, 2006 during which substantial progress was registered. Foreign Secretary also met Undersecretary Burns in July and September 2006 to discuss US legislation and the next steps on the 123 Agreement negotiations. Thereafter, an informal meeting between teams of the two countries took place in New Delhi from November 6-8, 2006 to discuss various concepts pertaining to the legislation and unresolved issues in the agreement.

Discussions with IAEA

Discussions with IAEA on the Safeguards Agreement were initiated when the Chairman of the Atomic Energy Commission, Dr. A. Kakodkar visited Vienna in early March 2006 for a meeting with the Director General of the IAEA. Subsequently, an IAEA team visited New Delhi for discussions with India on July 8, 2006.

Adjustment of NSG Guidelines

As part of its commitments, the US circulated a statement in the NSG in March 2006 proposing to adjust NSG Guidelines with respect to India to enable full civil nuclear cooperation. An Indian delegation made a presentation to the NSG meeting in Vienna in October 2006.

Prime Minister Dr. Manmohan Singh had made a statement during a Short Duration Discussion in Rajya Sabha on 17 August and in Lok Sabha on 23 August 2006. The statements made clear that anything that went beyond the parameters of July 18 Joint Statement would be unacceptable to India. There were elements of concerns with regard to what is in the current version of the Bills, and these had been conveyed to the US Government.

The India-US nuclear understanding is as laid out in the July 18, 2005 Joint Statement and the Separation Plan tabled in Parliament by the Prime Minister on March 7, 2006. There is no question of accepting any additional requirements beyond those contained in July 18, 2005 Joint Statement and March 2006 Separation Plan. This has been conveyed to the US. The US in its Statement of Administration Policy of July 26, 2006 issued after the passage of the House version of the Waiver Bill has clarified that any conditions imposed by the waiver bills to be passed by US Congress that goes beyond the July 18, 2005 Joint Statement would not be acceptable to the US Administration.

India finalized its Separation Plan in March 2006 and the Prime Minister tabled it in the Parliament on March 7, 2006. The full and complete version of this plan was once again laid on the table of the Parliament by Prime Minister on 11 May 2006. The Separation Plan has laid out the schedule of placing India's nuclear reactors under safeguards beginning from 2007. As, Prime Minister stated in the Parliament, on 17 August 2006, India would not place its nuclear facilities under safeguards till all restrictions on India are lifted.[19]

Henry J. Hyde India-US Civil Nuclear Cooperation Act

The US President George W. Bush signed on December 18, 2006 the Indo-US Nuclear Co-operation Bill dubbed the Henry J. Hyde India-US Civil Nuclear Cooperation Act into law at a special White House ceremony. "The deal will help keep America safe by paving the way for India to join the global efforts to stop the spread of nuclear weapons. After 30 years outside the system, India will now operate its civilian nuclear energy programme under internationally-accepted guidelines and the world is going to be safer as a result," the US president said.

Indian-American community leaders and activists were present at the historic signing, along with several senior Bush administration officers and Congressional aides including Nick Burns, the chief negotiating officer, Assistant Secretary of State for South Asian Affairs Richard Boucher, and several lobbyists. Deputy Chief of Mission Raminder Jassal represented the Indian government. But the Bill's biggest supporters were absent due to ill-health and other personal reasons. They were retiring Congressman Henry Hyde, after whom the Bill was named, Senator Joseph Biden, Senate Minority Leader Harry Reed and Congressman Tom Lantos.

"Another important stage in this process has now been reached with the passage of legislation by the US Congress, with substantial bipartisan support, in pursuance of the undertakings of the United States in the July Joint Statement that it would seek to adjust US laws and policies to achieve full civil nuclear cooperation with India. This Act is necessary for the United States to resume civil nuclear cooperation with India and also an important step leading to the lifting of international restrictions currently applicable to India," Prime Minister Dr. Manmohan Singh said in the Lok Sabha during discussion on India-US Civil Nuclear Cooperation on December 18, 2006. "We appreciate the efforts made by the US Administration and the bipartisan support in the US Congress, which has led to the passage of this legislation. This law has several positive features, which take into account our concerns. However, there are areas, which continue to be a cause for concern, and we will need to discuss them with the US Administration before the bilateral cooperation agreement can be finalized. The House can rest assured that in these negotiations, the commitments and assurances I gave to Parliament on August 17, 2006 will constitute our guidelines," Singh added.

The passage of the legislation enables the US Administration to follow up on another commitment made by the US in the July 18 Joint Statement, viz. approaching its international partners, particularly in the NSG, to lift restrictions to allow full civil nuclear cooperation with India.

"It is an honour to sign this bill that will strengthen the relationship between the two largest democracies in the world. The relationship between the US and India has never been so vital," Bush said. "We recognize that clean energy is going to be important for the advancement of our economies. During my visit to India, we concluded this historic agreement that will allow us to share civilian nuclear technology and bring India's civilian nuclear program under the safeguards of IAEA. As part of the agreement, the US and India have committed to take a series of steps to make nuclear cooperation a reality and we are going to fulfill these commitments," Bush added.

The India-US Civil Nuclear Cooperation Act will help America achieve four key goals:

1. This Act will help strengthen cooperation between India and the United States on energy, one of the most important challenges of the 21st century. India is now the world's

fifth largest consumer of energy, and its demand for electricity is expected almost to double by 2015. The United States has a clear interest in helping India meet this demand with nuclear energy. By helping India expand its use of safe, clean nuclear energy, this Act lays the foundation for a new strategic partnership between our two nations that will help ease India's demands for fossil fuels and ease pressure on global markets.

2. This Act will help promote economic growth. This Act helps open an important new market for American businesses by paving the way for investment in India's civilian nuclear industry for the first time. This new trade will help American companies gain new customers abroad and create new jobs here at home.
3. This Act will help make it possible for India to reduce emissions and improve its environment. Today, India produces nearly 70 per cent of its electricity from coal. Burning coal produces air pollution and greenhouse gases, but nuclear power can generate massive amounts of electricity without producing any air pollution or greenhouse gases. By sharing advanced civilian nuclear technology, we will help India meet its growing demand for energy and lower emissions at the same time.
4. This Act will strengthen the partnership between the world's two largest democracies and help both countries to meet the energy and security challenges of the 21st century. America and India are allies in the war on terror, partners in global trade, and stewards of our environment. India is a democracy that protects the rule of law and is accountable to its people, and an open society that defends freedom of speech and freedom of religion. Both countries are working together to expand economic opportunities in both countries. India's economy has more than doubled in size since 1991, and it is one of the fastest-growing markets for American exports. This trade is creating new jobs in America and raising the standard of living of millions throughout India. This Act is also an important step that will help in sharing civilian nuclear technology and bring India's civilian nuclear

> program under the safeguards of the international atomic energy agency. The nuclear cooperation will not only help the people of India produce more of their energy from clean, safe civilian nuclear power, but also help both countries' economy grow, and make America more secure.

India is interested in long-term, stable and predictable cooperation in civil nuclear energy with the United States and other members of the international community. Such a partnership with the United States can be facilitated if the legislation—its scope, content and implementation—were to strengthen the hands of the Administration to fulfill all the commitments agreed to by the US in the July 18 Joint Statement and the March 2 Separation Plan.[20]

On the other hand, this objective can be hindered by extraneous issues that were not part of the understandings in the July 18 Joint Statement and the March 2 Separation Plan.

With regard to the recently enacted US law on civil nuclear cooperation, India made it clear on January 10, 2007 that it will 'walk out' of the deal if at any point it seems to undermine its national interest. "There are concerns, of course.... If at any point, it becomes apparent that it (deal) is something which would undermine India's national interest, we will walk out, no matter how much political investment has been made," the Prime Minister's special envoy on nuclear issue Shyam Saran said while delivering a lecture on "India-US Understanding on Civil Nuclear Cooperation and Future".

However, New Delhi expressed confidence that the elements over which it has "genuine" reason for concern, including conditional access to reprocessing technology and reprocessing of spent fuel, would be addressed in the 123 Agreement being negotiated to operationalise the deal.

"The civil nuclear deal", Saran pointed out, "will become a reality only after the 45-nation NSG changes guidelines to allow civil nuclear cooperation with India and New Delhi concludes a safeguards agreement with the IAEA." Shyam Saran said, "India continued to lobby for support among the NSG countries and was now 'better placed' in the grouping. But that does not mean that problems are over and we need to work with all members."

On the provision that US will end the agreement if India were to conduct a nuclear test, he said, as India was not ready to give any legal commitment in this regard, Washington also was doing the same.

On what will happen to the agreement if the regime changes and forms a new administration in the US, he said the bipartisan support given to the bill on it augurs well.

Prime Minister Dr. Manmohan Singh returning from the India-ASEAN and East Asia Summits in the Philippines on January 16, 2007, told accompanying journalists that "there are issues, and concerns, we have to discuss (these) with the US administration". Manmohan Singh said, "Negotiations will commence 'very shortly' with the US on a bilateral agreement to operationalise the civil nuclear deal during which India will flag its concerns with regard to the law passed by the American Congress on the issue." New Delhi has made it clear that India will not accept any legally binding provision on future nuclear testing in the 123 Agreement and that it will "walk out" of the deal if it seems to undermine its national interest at any point.

ENVIRONMENT TRACK OF ECONOMIC DIALOGUE

The Environment Track of the US-India Economic Dialogue was established as a result of the Joint Statement issued by the White House following the meeting between the President of the United States and the Prime Minister of India on November 9, 2001. This prompted the visit to India by the Administrator of the US Environmental Protection Agency (EPA) in January 2002, where a Memorandum of Understanding (MoU) between the Environmental Protection Agency of the United States of America and The Ministry of Environment and Forests (MoEF) of the Government of India Concerning Cooperation in Environmental Protection was signed. This MoU established a framework for policy and technical cooperation between MoEF and EPA (with support from the US Agency for International Development) in four major areas: air quality management, water quality management, management of toxic chemicals and hazardous waste, and environmental governance. In 2005, EPA also entered into a Cooperative Agreement with the National Environmental Engineering Research Institute in India to also support activities under the MoU and Environment Track.

The leadership of the US-India Economic Dialogue is promoting greater integration of the US and Indian private sector of the Economic Dialogue. The Environment Track is similarly seeking avenues to promote increased private sector engagement, to supplement the emphasis to date of government-to-government cooperation. To accomplish this, the Environment Track has identified several focused government-industry environmental partnerships that it will champion. These partnerships address shared environmental priorities and promote activities with both local and global environmental benefits. They will provide a platform to engage the private sector in bilateral environmental cooperation activities, and will also seek to promote cross-Ministerial/Agency cooperation. They also demonstrate the collaboration envisioned for the new Asia Pacific Partnership for Clean Development and Climate Change. The three government-industry environmental partnerships to be promoted include:

Methane-to-Markets Partnership

India and the US are founding country partners of the Methane-to-Markets Partnership to reduce global methane emissions to enhance economic growth, improve the environment, promote energy security, and reduce greenhouse gases. Other benefits include improving mine safety, reducing waste, and improving local air quality. Initial bilateral cooperation is expected to focus on promoting methane recovery and use at landfills, coal mines, and in the petroleum and natural gas sector. The EPA and the US Trade Development Agency are working with the Government of India to develop a Coal bed Methane Clearing House to promote projects and private sector engagement in coal bed/coal mine methane opportunities. Workshops on Landfill Methane were held in New Delhi and Mumbai in March 2006.

Partnership for Clean Fuels and Vehicles

Initial activities under this partnership will bring together relevant government, industry, research organizations and other stakeholders to better characterize emissions from in-use vehicles, demonstrate technology options for reducing diesel emission from heavy-duty vehicles, and share US expertise and tools to encourage improved fuel quality, consistent with goals outlined in India's Auto Fuel Policy. A Diesel Retrofit Demonstration Project in Pune has been launched in April 2006.

Mercury Partnerships

Under this initiative the US and India will seek to promote best management practices to reduce environmental releases through training, demonstration, and technology transfer activities working with relevant US and Indian private sector partners. Key areas being pursued include improving monitoring and inventory of mercury emissions, exploring opportunities for reducing mercury in products where cost-effective alternatives exist, and encouraging efforts to reduce releases of mercury from key sector sources, such as those outlined in MoEF's Charter for Corporate Responsibility for Environmental Protection.

The US-India Environmental Cooperation will also be further developed under the four core activity areas of the EPA-MoEF Memorandum of Understanding Concerning Cooperation in Environmental Protection:

1. Air Quality Management

Urban Air Quality Management

This program provides training, demonstration and technology transfer to support adoption of science-based air pollution control strategies in Indian cities in order to (a) establish baseline data on ambient air quality and pollution sources; (b) define most cost-effective source reduction opportunities and investments; (c) assist policy makers to evaluate health and economic impacts; and (d) develop informed stakeholder groups to increase commitment and accountability for air quality improvements. This includes capacity-building in air monitoring, emissions inventory, modeling, source apportionment and control strategy development (with cost benefit analysis), as well as health benefits assessment.

Power Plant Emissions

This program builds on the results of a 2004 Central Pollution Control Board (CPCB) hosted workshop on air pollution monitoring and control from power plants, and a 2005 National Thermal Power Corporation hosted training course on

EPA's software tool used to assist power plants in optimizing performance of their electrostatic precipitators (ESP). The next phase will demonstrate the ESP optimization tool at a power plant to identify cost-effective alternatives to reduce PM emissions, as well as evaluate co-benefit mercury emissions reductions, including training and transfer of stack emissions monitoring technology. The EPA will also share expertise on cap-and-trade programs for reducing power plant emissions, and will provide consultative support to MoEF and CPCB as they develop NOx emission standards for power plants in India, as currently planned.

Indoor Air Pollution from Chulhas (cookstoves)

This program supports the goals of the Partnership for Clean Indoor Air to address the increased environmental health risk faced by a majority of Indians who burn traditional biomass and coal indoors for cooking and heating, resulting in an estimated 400,000 premature deaths annually – primarily women and children. Efforts are aimed at bringing together governments, non-governmental organizations, and industry to work on: improving the design and performance of cooking and heating technology; social awareness and marketing; business development; and monitoring indoor air pollution.

2. Water Quality Management (Focus on Urban Drinking Water Quality)

Drinking Water Laboratory Strengthening

The EPA will work with Indian partners and WHO in India to strengthen capacity of drinking water quality laboratories for effective monitoring and surveillance. This project will produce an Indian drinking water laboratory operations and methods manual, and training on lab management and chemical and microbiological test methods.

Water Safety Plan Demonstration

This project will include cooperative work with central, state, and municipal government, and with WHO in India, to demonstrate use of Water Safety Plans, a comprehensive risk assessment and management tool to enhance drinking water safety. The project seeks to address highest vulnerabilities in the drinking water system, and reduce water-borne disease through source water protection, a drinking water treatment plant optimization program, and improved distribution systems. A demonstration project planned for Hyderabad has been started in 2006.

3. Management of Toxic Chemicals and Hazardous Waste

Mercury Monitoring and Inventory

In addition to proposed government-industry mercury partnership activities highlighted above, MoEF has requested cooperation with EPA and UNEP in strengthening and enhancing mercury estimation capability for scientists, technocrats and policy formulators in Indian regulatory agencies and environment departments.

Lindane Risk Reduction

The EPA is sharing information and expertise with the Indian Ministry of Agriculture and MoEF/CPCB in support of their efforts to evaluate alternatives and risk reduction strategies to reduce releases and human exposure to lindane in the environment, in cooperation with the World Health Organization.

4. Environmental Governance

Improved Environmental Compliance and Enforcement

Environmental compliance and enforcement capacity building is a central focus of the EPA-MoEF MoU Environmental Governance agenda. The EPA has provided several training courses and conducted an institutional evaluation on compliance and enforcement issues in India. A report identified numerous recommendations, and proposals exist to follow up in key areas, including (1) enhanced application of civil judicial enforcement authorities in India, and (2) application of industry self-monitoring and citizen monitoring, including sharing lessons learned through the newly launched Asia Environmental Compliance and Enforcement Network. Numerous additional US-India bilateral climate change related activities are also being advanced under the auspices of a multi-agency US-India Bilateral Dialogue on Climate Change.[21]

JOINT PROMOTION OF ECONOMIC DEVELOPMENT

The Joint Promotion of Economic Development was the subject of a Cooperation Framework Agreement between the US Trade and Development Agency (USTDA) and India's Ministry of Finance that was signed on November 9, 2005. The agreement formalizes USTDA's program with public sector entities in India and covers activities such as project preparation, trade capacity-building, investment analysis, training, and sector development. Such activities will foster India's economic ties with the US public and private sectors and support key bilateral initiatives, such as the US-India Economic and Energy Dialogues.

The agreement was signed by the US-India Financial and Economic Forum, as part of US Treasury Secretary John Snow's visit to India. The US Ambassador to India David C. Mulford and India's Ministry of Finance Secretary Ashok Kumar Jha signed the framework agreement on behalf of the US and Indian governments, respectively. The USTDA Director for Policy and Program Geoffrey R. Jackson was present at the signing.

The Cooperation Framework Agreement will facilitate the coordination of USTDA activities with the Indian public sector, providing a mechanism for Ministry of Finance review and approval of new activities. Having the agreement in place is expected to speed up the Indian Government's review and approval process of proposed activities, thereby facilitating the start of new initiatives in a broad range of key sectors, including energy and power, water, environment, and transportation. Currently under review are technical cooperation projects with GAIL and Neyveli Lignite Corporation, Limited, involving gas transport and coal mining, respectively.

The US Trade and Development Agency advances economic development and US commercial interests in developing and middle-income countries. The agency funds various forms of technical assistance, feasibility studies, training, orientation visits and business workshops that support the development of a modern infrastructure and a fair and open trading environment. The USTDA's strategic use of foreign assistance funds to support sound investment policy and decision-making in host countries creates an enabling environment for trade, investment and sustainable economic development. In carrying out its mission, the USTDA gives emphasis to economic sectors that may benefit from the US exports of goods and services.[22]

COOPERATION ON EDUCATION

During the US visit of the Indian Prime Minister Dr. Manmohan Singh, a Memorandum of Understanding was signed for conclusion on July 20, 2005, between Indian Department of Space, Department of Science and Technology (DST), Amrita Vishwa Vidyapeetham (Amrita University) and the following US Universities—The University of California, at Berkeley and San Diego, Carnegie-Mellon University, Pittsburgh, The University at Buffalo, New York, Stanford University, California and research centers: California Institute for Telecommunications and Information Technology (Cal-IT2), Center for Information Technology Research in the Interest of Society (CITRIS) and corporate partners: Microsoft Corporation and Qualcomm Incorporated.

This agreement would offer Indo-US cooperation on e-learning to enhance technical education in India in cooperation with the US universities as Resource Partners. The Resource Partners would encourage their faculty to participate in this programme and allow them to share their teaching materials with the Indian counterparts. The Indian Space Research Organisation (ISRO) would provide the necessary transponder capacity and bandwidth on its satellite EDUSAT that is already dedicated to education. The ISRO will also provide VSAT Hubs/ teaching-end infrastructure and establish the ground infrastructure at participating educational institutions. Initially, around 25 selected educational institutions are expected to participate in the program. The Technology Information Forecasting and Assessment Council (TIFAC), an autonomous body under the Department of Science & Technology, will enable the creation of e-learning contents, capture them in multimedia rich course material and archive them for continued use. The Indo-US S&T Forum will facilitate implementation of this initiative. The Microsoft India has committed to defray the expenses of visiting faculty from the US institutions.

The proposed program holds great promise of taking advantage of the tremendous synergy between the United States and India, and makes it possible to build a truly ambitious education system in advanced technology areas. The program exploits efficient digital connectivity through satellite and interactive technologies developed by ISRO and Amrita University with a view to further enhance academic standard in educational institutions. The program also ensures quick and simultaneous delivery of lecture sessions to undergraduate (BS, B.Tech, B.E.) and postgraduate (MS, M.Tech, M.E. and Ph.D.) level college and university students and for teachers training all over India using the ISRO's satellite network, and the e-learning facilities at Amrita University. It also provides access to subject experts and repeatability of delivery of lectures from the archives. All the parties have agreed to work together for effectively imparting quality education and research covering the disciplines of Computer Science & Engineering, Information and Communication Technologies, Electronics & Communication, Manufacturing, Biotechnology and Bioinformatics, Healthcare, etc.[23]

COOPERATION ON AGRICULTURAL EDUCATION

More than 50 years ago, India and the United States signed agreements to improve agricultural education and research in India. The US also launched extension/outreach services aimed at providing advice to Indian farmers on new agricultural technologies. A key result of these initiatives was the establishment of five state agricultural universities in India with considerable advisory support from colleagues at American Land-Grant universities. This rich tradition of collaboration in knowledge exchange helped to launch India's Green Revolution, which itself led to the country's subsequent emergence from food insecurity. At the same time, through cooperation, American campuses were extensively enriched with international insights and networks.

Recent years have seen a host of changes. The private sector and foundations are also playing an increasingly active role. Agriculture has become global in its reach, much more complex in its trades and exchanges, more technologically grounded, and ever more challenged with balancing sustainability, productivity and social responsiveness.

The United States-India Knowledge Initiative on Agricultural Education, Teaching, Research, Service and Commercial Linkages, announced on July 18, 2005, provides the momentum needed to re-energize the longstanding tradition of knowledge exchange. Through this it will draw upon what we have learned to find new, creative and realistic ways to revitalize our partnership as such that agricultural programs at our colleges and universities are better able to respond to the current and future needs of our people, and to opportunities in today's vibrant private business environment.

Under the bilateral Knowledge Initiative on Agriculture (AKI), a work plan to focus on four areas of cooperation—university capacity building, food processing and marketing, biotechnology and water management—has been finalised and is being implemented. The 5th meeting of the Board constituted under the AKI met in Washington, DC in June 2007 to review the implementation of the work plan.

The Knowledge Initiative which developed a plan for the two governments by November 2005 that identifies priority areas for partnerships in teaching, research, and service. The plan also describes steps needed to initiate and develop those partnerships, and it will consider the following resource implications:

- **Teaching**—The Knowledge Initiative will consider new and existing mechanisms to strengthen curricular design, course content and delivery, and degree attainment in both countries so as to internationalize the student experience. It will also look for ways to enhance the structure and sustainability of agricultural programs at universities.
- **Research**—The Initiative will examine and prioritize key collaborative research approaches, topic areas and impact assessments. Possible areas of focus include improved bioproducts; more sustainable use of water and other resources; strengthened systems of pest management; and better understanding of economically viable and environmentally sustainable production systems.

- **Service**—The Initiative will identify effective, innovative and collaborative approaches that link research results to those who use them such as producers, processors, and marketers of farm goods. Public and private advisory services will be considered.
- **Commercial Linkages**—The Initiative will look for ways to include private sector suppliers and marketers as participants and funding partners.[24]

SCIENCE AND TECHNOLOGY COOPERATION

India and the United States signed an umbrella Science & Technology (S&T) agreement in Washington during the July 18, 2005 visit of Indian Prime Minister Manmohan Singh to the United States. The purpose of the agreement is to strengthen the science and technology capabilities of the US and India, expand relations between their extensive scientific and technological communities, and to promote technological and scientific cooperation in areas of mutual benefit.

The relationship between India and the US in the field of science and technology continues to strengthen. The 5th meeting of High Technology Cooperation, co-chaired by the foreign secretary, was held in Washington, DC in February 2007 in which a Working Group on nontechnology and a sub-group to discuss Medical devices were established.

This new agreement, for the first time establishes intellectual property right protocols and other provisions necessary to conduct active collaborative research. It will accelerate cooperation between Indian and US scientists in government agencies, private sector, and academia in such areas as: basic sciences, space, energy, nanotechnology, health, and information technology that will advance scientific understanding and benefit all our people.

Scientific and economic links between India and the United States have remained strong since the early 1960s, first in agriculture, and then spreading into a broad range of areas involving most of the US Government technical agencies. The United States and India established a $110 million Public Law 480 "Rupee Fund" in 1987 to promote and fund science and technology collaboration and educational and cultural exchanges.

The Rupee Fund Agreement, which stimulated a broad set of cooperative activity between the US and India, continued until 1998. The Indo-US Science and Technology Forum established in 2000, was created and endowed with a portion of the remaining Public Law 480 Rupee Funds.

The Forum makes a valuable contribution to strengthening the bilateral US-India relationship by exploring and identifying fruitful areas of cooperation through sponsoring workshops, scientist exchanges and meetings. It has sponsored major events like the India-United States Conference on Space Science, Applications and Commerce, activities in technology innovation, climate change, and fosters contact among young promising scientists. The new science and technology agreement will complement the activity of the Indo-US Science and Technology Forum by facilitating follow-on technical collaborations.

ECONOMIC DIALOGUE CEO FORUM

The significance for each country of India-US economic partnership cannot be overstated. Extending beyond trade, which is rapidly growing, the intensifying and increasingly complex economic links being forged between the two countries are having a profound impact on the joint and respective economic outlook in the 21st century. In recognition of that fact and to provide a useful context, the governments of the United States and India agreed to energize the wide-ranging Economic Dialogue (ED) covering key sectors in the economic partnership. The Co-conveners of the Economic Dialogue are assistant to the President for Economic Policy and Director of the National Economic Council Allan Hubbard (US) and Deputy Chairman of Planning Commission Dr. Montek Singh Ahluwalia (India).

The Economic Dialogue has four tracks: the Trade Policy Forum, the Financial and Economic Forum, the Environment Dialogue and the Commercial Dialogue. Each of these tracks is led by the respective US agency and Indian ministry. The Economic Dialogue has two cross-cutting themes in biotechnology and information technology. The IT theme is now expanded to become the Information and Communications Technology Working Group (ICT Working Group).

CHIEF EXECUTIVE OFFICERS (CEO) FORUM

Both governments have agreed to establish a high-level private sector forum to exchange business community views on key economic priorities. Input from the business community is an integral component of a successful bilateral economic dialogue. To harness that input, the United States and India have established a CEO Forum, composed of 10 chief executives from each country. The chief executive officers represent a cross-section of industrial sectors, particularly those that have a stake in improving the commercial climate between the two countries. This will also serve as a channel to provide senior-level private sector input into discussions and formulation of economic policy. Their input will help the United States and India make progress on key issues that will enhance economic growth and job creation and promote bilateral trade and investment by harnessing the energy and expertise of private sector leaders.

NEXT STEPS IN STRATEGIC PARTNERSHIP

India and United States have reached a milestone in their strategic relationship by completing the Next Steps in Strategic Partnership (NSSP). The successful completion of this initiative clears the way for even greater engagement in a number of key areas in which cooperation has previously been limited or non-existent.

The Next Steps in Strategic Partnership, announced in January 2004, was designed to increase cooperation in civilian nuclear activities, civilian space programs, high-technology trade, and missile defense.

Since January 2004, cooperation under the Next Steps in Strategic Partnership progressed through a series of reciprocal steps that built on each other. These steps included expanded engagement on nuclear regulatory and safety issues, enhanced cooperation in missile defense, peaceful uses of space technology, and steps to create the appropriate environment for increased high-technology commerce.

To combat the proliferation of weapons of mass destruction, relevant laws, regulations, and export-related procedures have been strengthened, and measures to increase bilateral and international cooperation in this area were instituted. These cooperative efforts were undertaken in accordance with our respective national laws and international obligations.

The successful completion of the Next Steps in Strategic Partnership is an important milestone in the transformation of the relationship between the United States and India. In particular, completion of the Next Steps in Strategic Partnership will enable the United States to expand the scope of bilateral commercial satellite cooperation, remove US export license requirements for unilaterally controlled nuclear items to most end users, and revise export license requirements for certain items going to safeguarded civil nuclear power facilities.

Completion of the Next Steps in Strategic Partnership demonstrates that President Bush's and Prime Minister Singh's vision of a US-India strategic partnership is becoming a reality, and paves the way for greater cooperation on strategic, energy security, and economic matters. Both nations are committed to building upon the progress made since January 2004 and working to identify new ways to expand the growing cooperative relationship.[25]

COOPERATION IN STRENGTHENING INFORMATION AND COMMUNICATION TECHNOLOGY

The extent and depth of India-US cooperation in the development and formulation of policy in the information and communications technology (ICT) sector has recently made significant progress. A key underpinning of the deepening bilateral economic partnership has been the demand for enhanced electronic connectivity between the two countries. India has become a key market for many information communication technology products made in the United States, while the United States is an important consumer of Indian IT-enabled services.

The launch of the United States-India Information and Communications Technology Working Group recognizes the impact that this sector has potential on the future of the bilateral economic partnership. It will focus the strong interest that exists on each side to enhance understanding and share perspectives on developments in the information and telecommunications sector, leading to tangible accomplishments and problem-solving. The participants will consist of appropriate representatives from each government who will work in close coordination with the private sector.

The dialogue will seek to address outstanding issues and create opportunities that can benefit through a more regular and structured dialogue process. These include explorations of further policy development, commercial opportunities and obstacles and matched goals in multilateral settings such as the World Summit on the Information Society, the International Telecommunication Union, and the World Trade Organization. In particular, the Working Group will explore ways that investment and regulatory regimes can be developed to maximize development of the sector, provide meaningful market access opportunities, and support robust competition.

Officials from India and the United States have participated in exchanges of high-level delegations, training opportunities, regional conferences and ongoing sharing of information and perspectives. The US Government, through the Department of State, the Department of Commerce, the US Trade Representative's Office and the Federal Communications Commission, has established productive working relationships with counterparts in India, including the Ministry of Information and Communications, the Telecom Regulatory Authority of India (TRAI), and the Ministry of External Affairs. The extent and quality of the discussions continue to grow, resulting in mutual understanding and concrete benefits.

As a cross-cutting theme, the Information and Communications Technology dialogue will aim to support the overall objectives of the Economic Dialogue which include: better coordination of discussions and activities between the two governments, soliciting the support of private sector stakeholders and incorporating their views into government decisions and actions concerning the bilateral economic relationship. The dialogue will complement the work of the existing High-Technology Cooperation Group and the Cybersecurity Forum.

The United States encourages liberalization of telecommunications markets worldwide and supports standards that are open, inter-operable, non-discriminatory, and demand-driven. The US-India Information and Communications

Technology Working Group promises to be a good example of how regulatory dialogue and increased transparency can benefit both countries and recognizes the role of information and communications technology in promoting sustained economic growth and strengthening the US-Indian economic partnership.[26]

TRADE POLICY FORUM

The US Ambassador Robert Portman and Indian Minister of Commerce and Industry Kamal Nath announced on July 18, 2005 that the establishment of a new consultative mechanism called "The United States-India Trade Policy Forum," to be chaired by themselves or their Deputies. Other relevant US Government agencies and Indian Ministries will also participate. The Forum will be part of the overall United States-India Economic Dialogue, replacing the Trade Policy Working Group. It will be convened on a regular basis.

The Forum will provide an opportunity to work together to expand trade between the two countries. Both governments will consider a wide range of issues of interest to both governments with the expectation of expanding bilateral trade and investment.

The agenda could cover the following subjects: tariff and non-tariff trade barriers, foreign direct investment, subsidies, customs procedures, standards, testing, labeling and certification, intellectual property rights protection, sanitary and phytosanitary measures, government procurement, and services. It also offers the opportunity for both governments to work together bilaterally toward a successful outcome of the Doha Round of multilateral trade negotiations.[27]

GLOBAL DEMOCRACY INITIATIVE

India and the United States share a fundamental commitment to democracy and believe that they have an obligation to the global community to strengthen values, ideals and practices of freedom, pluralism, and rule of law. With their solid democratic traditions and institutions, they have agreed to assist other societies in transition seeking to become more open and democratic. They recognize democracy as a universal aspiration that transcends social, cultural and religious boundaries.

Each has expressed at the highest levels their belief that democracy is central to economic prosperity and development and to building peaceful societies.

Possessing a wealth of knowledge and experience that can, and must, be shared with other emerging democracies, the United States and India will offer assistance when sought to build institutions and develop relevant human resources that make the workings of democracy credible. An independent judiciary, a credible election commission, an active human rights commission, and effective and transparent auditing process are some of the critical elements of that democratic ideal. The spread of parliamentary practices is also an important contribution to the process of democratic transition. Gender equality is an integral aspect of democratic societies, and support for programs promoting this objective is envisaged as a high priority.

Respect for diversity and pluralism is intrinsic to democracy. The US and India will support programs that will sustain and nurture the value of pluralism. They will encourage and support the United Nations in its electoral assistance programs, including through national capacity-building, constitution drafting and electoral expertise for transition democracies.

The United States and India welcomed the Democracy Fund under the United Nations and announced that they are taking steps to make a contribution of US$ 10 million each to the Fund in the year 2005. They invited other democratic nations to contribute generously to the Fund, which should assist societies in building the institutions of democracy.

Through the launch of their Global Democracy Initiative to promote democracy and development, they have agreed to:

- Reaffirm the Community of Democracies Santiago Commitment, and to work together to jointly implement the Santiago Commitment, including other states and civil society organizations, to promote democracy and development.
- Organize together training courses in India, the United States, or a third country where necessary, to enhance capabilities to strengthen democratic institutions and develop their human resources.

- Establish a virtual Coordination and Information Center to share best practices on democracy, identify opportunities for joint support, and highlight capacity-building training programs.
- Partnering at the UN General Assembly Summit on the Millennium Development Goals to ensure that the outcome advances the important link of democracy and development.[28]

FIGHT AGAINST HIV/AIDS

Recognizing that the HIV/AIDS pandemic constitutes one of the greatest challenges facing humankind in the 21st century, India and the United States declared their shared commitment to strengthening cooperation to combat the disease at the global level. Prime Minister Dr. Manmohan Singh and President Goerge Bush vowed to scale up current prevention and control initiatives in India and extend these efforts, where appropriate, to other vulnerable countries.

Expedited FDA review of Anti-Retroviral Drugs (ARVs) under the President's Emergency Plan and ongoing collaboration in the sciences regarding this partnership, the US will continue to expedite the review of applications for approval or tentative approval by the Food & Drug Administration (FDA) of generic anti-retrovirals (ARVs) received from Indian pharmaceutical companies under the President's Emergency Plan. Eight of ten generic anti-retrovirals approved so far are Indian products.

India and the US will continue to collaborate in basic sciences, product development, and clinical trials research, in the hopes that joint efforts may lead to the development of products with global relevance to Africa and other parts of Asia, particularly pediatric formulations of anti-retrovirals. The US and India will explore new opportunities for public-private collaboration on HIV/AIDS product development and increase capacity to conduct world-class clinical trials in India.

US-India HIV/AIDS Private Sector Corporate Initiative: With a large number of infections, India is at a critical point in its fight against HIV/AIDS. Following on India's recent scale up of resources and renewed political commitment to fight HIV/AIDS,

President Bush announced an additional US contribution of $7 million to expand resources available to fight HIV/AIDS in India. These new resources will catalyze an innovative partnership, the HIV/AIDS Private Sector Corporate Initiative. This initiative will build alliances between US and Indian companies and the governments of India and the United States in the fight against HIV/AIDS, and could be expanded to other countries. It has three components: Establishment of a Private Sector HIV/AIDS Capital Fund that will accept donations from both Indian and US companies; Expansion of HIV/AIDS Workplace Programs; and increased access to safe, effective, quality anti-retroviral drugs, particularly for pediatric treatment.[29]

Indo-US cooperation in the field of health and medicine continues to grow during the year 2007. The Indo-US Vaccine Action Programme has been extended for further five years. Indo-US cooperation for capacity-building is developed with US universities in order to acquire international clinical trial standards. India and the US are collaborating to set up two schools of public health in India.

DISASTER RELIEF INITIATIVE

India and the United States are committed to aiding those affected by the December 2004 Tsunami's devastation and, through the creation of the Tsunami Core Group, demonstrated their willingness and desire to be full-fledged partners in the relief operations. Recognizing that the combined efforts of the US and India significantly enhanced the world's response to the Tsunami disaster of December 26, 2004. The US President Goerge Bush and the Indian Prime Minister Dr. Manmohan Singh announced on July 18, 2005 the launch of the US-India Disaster Relief Initiative (DRI) to contribute to disaster preparedness and future relief operations.

The Disaster Relief Initiative will build upon the existent, strong civilian relationship between the two governments in disaster relief, involving the US Agency for International Development and the Indian Ministry of Home Affairs. Through the Initiative, the US and India seek to increase their ability to respond to disasters in an integrated fashion, partnering with other US, Indian and UN agencies, as well as international

Non-Governmental Organizations (NGOs) and other governments as appropriate. The US and India will continue to work together with the regional community on the development and implementation of early warning system programs.

As mandated by the new framework for the US-India defense relationship, the US and India will strengthen their military capabilities to respond effectively to future disasters by conducting joint military exercises. The US Pacific Command (USPACOM) and the Indian Integrated Defence Staff (IDS) will be the respective military leads in each country to establish a dialogue and identify additional military training needs, skill-development requirements, and other challenges to a speedy and effective disaster response.

As part of the Disaster Relief Initiative, the US and India agree to cooperate to help build disaster response capabilities in other countries. They would also share best practices and experiences with a view to strengthening a regional response to natural disasters.[30]

ESTABLISHMENT OF A BINATIONAL SCIENCE AND TECHNOLOGY COMMISSION

President George Bush and Prime Minister Manmohan Singh announced to establish a Binational Science and Technology Endowment Fund and a standing Science and Technology (S&T) Joint Commission. These initiatives aim to accelerate cooperation in many technical fields of mutual interest to India and the United States and benefit the economy and well-being of citizens of both countries. These initiatives build on the S&T Cooperation Agreement were signed on October 17, 2005.

India and the US have highly developed educational, research and development capacities. Scientific and economic links between India and the United States have remained strong since the early 1960s, first in agriculture, and then spreading into a broad range of areas involving mostly US government technical agencies.

The United States and India will each contribute to start the Binational S&T Endowment Fund. Additional contributions should be added from private sources. Income from the Fund will support the joint research and the development of India-US S&T projects selected through a competitive process. Projects considered for funding will span a broad spectrum of topics of mutual priority, particularly those with potential to jump from the laboratory into the private sector. Topics include: biotechnology; health and infectious diseases; advanced materials and nanotechnology science; climate science; clean energy technologies; clean water technologies, hydrology and watershed management; cyber security; natural resource and wildlife conservation management; basic space, atmospheric and earth sciences; and marine sciences.

Recognizing the unique and expanding role of Science and Technology in Indo-US relations, the Prime Minister and the President also agreed to form a Binational S&T Joint Commission that would provide a framework for a vigorous public-private partnership aimed at:

- Serving as a bridge and forum for dialogue between the government and science and technology agencies in both countries;
- Fostering R&D and scientific exchanges between governments, universities, research institutions, and the private sectors;
- Encouraging the joint research and development of fast and medium track S&T projects for commercial products for mutual benefit of both countries through mutually agreed mechanisms;
- Overseeing Indo-US cooperation in Science and Technology implemented through existing and emerging arrangements, including the Indo-US S&T Forum and the Binational S&T Endowment Fund; and
- Encouraging commercialization of new technologies and identifying and promoting reduction of regulatory and bureaucratic barriers in both countries.

The Joint Commission will be appointed and serviced by the Department of State of the Government of the United States of America and the Government of India, co-chaired by senior leaders from each country, and composed of representatives from the scientific community, government and industry. Taken together, these activities herald a new era in S&T cooperation between the two countries.[31]

COOPERATION ON CIVIL AVIATION

A Memorandum of Agreement (MoA) between the Federal Aviation Authority (FAA) of US and the Ministry of Civil Aviation in India was signed on November 13, 2006 in the presence of Shri Praful Patel, Minister of Civil Aviation. The Union Cabinet approved of this Agreement on 3rd May 2006. The Agreement provides for assistance by the FAA to the Civil Aviation sector in India in developing and modernizing the civil aviation infrastructure in the managerial, operational and technical areas. All assistance under this Agreement will be on the basis of reimbursement of costs. Similar Agreements have been signed by the US with more than 100 countries. The assistance essentially includes the following areas:

- Providing technical and managerial expertise in developing, improving and operation of civil aviation infrastructure, standards, procedures, policies, training and equipment;
- Providing training for civil aviation personnel;
- Inspection and calibration of our civil aviation equipment and air navigation facility;
- Providing resources, logistical support and equipment for air navigation facilities;
- Assistance in airport certification in India; and
- Assistance in the field of Helicopter Operational Safety initiative.

The Memorandum of Agreement is an umbrella agreement and would have many agreements signed with different agencies like Directorate General of Civil Aviation, Airports Authority of India, Hindustan Aeronautics Ltd., etc. The agreement is in the nature of a framework agreement, which would create enabling provisions for seeking specific assistances from FAA. Therefore, this agreement is an essential requirement for seeking/receiving assistance from FAA. Shri R.K. Singh, Joint Secretary, Ministry of Civil Aviation signed the MoA, from the Indian side. From the American side Ms. Marion Blakey, FAA Administrator, signed it.[32]

EVALUATION

The relationship between India and United States, since 1947 clearly illustrates observations that though India-US relations have been friendly and cooperative yet these have lacked warmth and cordiality. The relations between US and India have been marked by divergent worldviews that led both the countries not to develop the type of relations that the United States had with other major democracies, despite several instances of overlapping security interests. Initial suspicions started during the post-independence India, because India was unwilling to commit to the western alliance in the emerging Cold War, as well as India's adoption of a quasi-socialist economy. India under first Prime Minister Jawaharlal Nehru pursued a globally oriented foreign policy while trying to maintain a careful distance between the power blocs of the East and the West. It is against this background that the relationship between India-US had a shaky start. Besides, India's unfriendly neighbourly relations with Pakistan and China also influenced the India-US bilateral relationship.

Economic relations between the two countries were cordial. American investment in India was substantial compared to that of other countries. From 1950 to 1965 the US provided 50 per cent of foreign aid to India. In 1957 the US established a Development Loan Fund. The US took initiative that led the World Bank to establish an Aid-India Consortium, which provided substantial funds to India in Third Five-Year Plan. The two nations also reached an agreement on the construction of nuclear power plants in 1963 beginning with the one at Tarapur near Bombay (Presently Mumbai). A contentious aspect of economic relations was that with a very few exceptions, the US declined to invest in or assist Indian heavy industry.

In the aftermath of the India-China border conflict of 1962, India requested, and received, military assistance from the US and Britain. But there was no offer of long-term military aid; the US-UK offer was conditional on the successful resolution of the Kashmir dispute in which India was expected to make substantial concessions. The US military aid was provided on the condition that it would in no circumstances be used against any adversaries but China. This was in total contrast to the unconditional military assistance by the US to Pakistan. The bilateral relations of India-US further deteriorated after Richard Nixon assumed the presidency and moved towards a rapprochement with China and Pakistan.

In the Post-Bangladesh War senario, the US attitudes towards the South Asian countries changed. In 1975, the US President Ford lifted the embargo on arms sales to India and Pakistan. During the subsequent President Carter's administration India did enter into negotiations with the US for the purchase of TOW anti-tank missiles and light howitzers. In 1980, Mr. Ronald Reagan became the President of US; it brought certain changes in India-US relations. Indian Prime Minister Rajiv Gandhi was able to garner considerable goodwill in the United States, the rationale of the Cold War kept the two countries apart. It was during the Rajiv Gandhi period from 1984-89 that the first discussions about transferring defense related technology began. Rajiv Gandhi had done well in extending India's hand of friendship and cooperation to the US. Economic and trade relationships improved. Cooperation in the fields of defense and technology transfer also increased. Symbolic of this was the visit to the US of Defense Minister K.C. Pant in July 1989, the first visit by an Indian Defense Minister in over 25 years. This followed the visit of the US Secretary of State Caspar Weinburger in 1987 followed by his successor Frank Carlucci in 1988. President Reagan also issued a directive (1984) instructing government agencies to seek improved relations with India and accommodate its requests for dual-use technology. In 1986 the US agreed to supply a number of General Electric F404 engines and avionics for India's Light Combat Aircraft (LCA). Later, the US also agreed to sell a Cray XMP14 supercomputer, the first such sale to a country outside the western alliance.

India and US relation began to improve after the collapse of the Berlin Wall and the disintegration of the Soviet Union. But India and the US continued to have differences on various issues including the extension of the NPT and the CTBT. Another action that caused friction between India and the US was the passage through US Congress of the Brown Amendment (November 1995), which allowed the US to supply Pakistan with military equipment. The US President Clinton supported this move on the grounds that Pakistan had already paid for the equipment but refused to release the 26 F-16s. China had supplied M11 missiles to Pakistan, the US did not apply sanctions on China for violating the MTCR, and this made the situation further complicated. On the other hand, US Air Force General Claude M. Kickleighter visited India in 1991, and proposed extensive training and exchanges between the two countries' militaries. The government's view of these exchanges was articulated by Prime Minister Narasimha Rao who noted how the professional-to-professional relations had achieved much more than politicians had been able to do in decades.

From 1990 to 1997 the relationship between the two countries improved drastically after India declared policy of economic liberalization, and it came to be viewed as an attractive market for the US business; during the Gulf War, the Indian Government granted refueling rights to the US military aircraft *en route* from the Pacific to the Middle East; in 1996 and 1997, the Indian and the US navies held joint exercises (the Malabar series) in the Indian Ocean. Besides, a Defense Policy Group (DPG) was established, and its activities included high-level exchanges, periodic policy reviews and reciprocal visits by senior commanders. India's unannounced nuclear tests in May 1998 brought this cooperation to a complete halt as the US also withheld spares for the Indian Navy's Sea King helicopters and Sea Harrier aircraft then undergoing repairs and overhaul in the UK.

India's relations with the US were influenced by the politics of the neighboring countries. Major hurdles in the development of India-US relations have been seen in the past. For a long time US-Pakistan relations had an adverse effect on US-India relations. China became a factor in India-US relations following the normalization of its ties with the US in 1971 and the subsequent 'tilt' of both the countries towards Pakistan during its war with India that year. It is only during the last decade or so relations with China have not influenced the India-US relation.

The US President Clinton visited India on 21 March 2000. It was probably the most extensive and successful visit to India by a US President, made more so by a decision by both sides to avoid the proliferation road block and concentrate on the expansion of the broader relationship. President Clinton and Prime Minister Atal Bihari Vajpayee on 21 March 2000 resolved to create a closer and qualitatively new relationship between the United States and India and signed a joint statement on bilateral relations entitled: "US-India Relations: A Vision for the 21st Century". Under the Bush administration Indo-US relations developed at a pace that few could have foreseen. While the India-US engagement had been proceeding at a fairly fast pace right from the beginning of the Bush administration, it gained a new sense of immediacy after September 2001.

Following the shocking tragedy of September 2001 probably reflecting the strategic realities of the post-Cold War world and subsequently there has been a drastic change in US-India defense relations. Both countries committed themselves to substantially increase the pace of high-level policy dialogue, military-to-military exchanges and other joint activities.

Indian Prime Minister Dr. Manmohan Singh visited the United States in July 18-20, 2005. During the visit an agreement was reached between the two countries and issued a Joint Statement. The two leaders declared their resolve to transform the relationship and establish a global partnership. Discussions were held on various aspects that included potential for cooperation in the fields such as economic and trade relations, revitalizing the India-US Economic Dialogue and launching a bilateral CEOs Forum, energy, environment, democracy and development, combating terrorism, non-proliferation and security, completion of the Next Steps in Strategic Partnership (NSSP) initiative, high technology, space, civil nuclear technology, science and technology, agricultural education, fight against HIV/ AIDS and disaster relief operations.

The India-US relationship took a turn for the better with the advent of the second Bush administration. The US considered India as a key player in future for its foreign policy towards Asia. There has been a shift in the US foreign policy objectives towards India. President Bush's visit to India in 1-3 March 2006 was about redrawing the global order and it laid the foundation for cooperation in defense, trade in high technology, space projects, promoting democracy, nuclear energy, non-proliferation, anti-terrorism, regional stability and so on. President George Bush visit also reviewing the progress made in India since their Joint Statement of July 18, 2005. Bush and the Prime Minister

Singh reaffirm their commitment to expand even further the growing ties between the two countries. Consistent with this objective, the two leaders highlight efforts the United States and India are making together in various areas which include: (i) Economic Prosperity and Trade; (ii) Energy Security and a Clean Environment; (iii) Innovation and the Knowledge Economy; (iv) Global Safety and Security; and (v) Deepening Democracy and Meeting International Challenges.

India's test of five nuclear devices in May 1998 played a catalytic role in bringing the two countries (India and US) together. It was Shakti 1998, which changed the entire scenario and augmented for a changed US foreign policy towards South Asia, particularly towards India. The sanctions imposed on India may be ineffective in the short run. But they were adversely affecting the socio-economic, defense and political relations in the long-run; for instance as it is exemplified by implied consequences on Navy and direct financial crunch on a forestation projects of Rajasthan.

The Bush administration in US gradually developed a perception that sanctions were no more beneficial for both nations, quite contrary they were creating hurdles in the India-US bilateral relations. Lifting of these sanctions, among other things made research in space, biotechnology and chemicals with dual-uses easier with free exchange of information and data worldwide.

Many of these sanctions were gradually lifted through congressional-executive cooperation from 1998 to 2000. The remaining nuclear sanctions on India and Pakistan were removed in autumn 2001. Also, the May 1998 nuclear tests helped India stand firmly *vis-à-vis* its security concerns and threats as well as in its projection of a power to be reckoned with.

The current fundamental transformation in relations between the US and India has its roots in common values and interests as democratic societies committed to political freedom, tolerance and representative government. Both nations have suffered at the hands of terrorists and recognize the necessity of eliminating this inhuman threat to the people and other transnational threats such as the spread of weapons of mass destruction, the drug trade, HIV/AIDS and trafficking of women and children. Both countries seek a freer and more equitable international trading system. And both countries cooperate in military-to-military relationship as well as countless contacts in trade, business and education.

The present India-US exchanges are indicative of a constructive and healthy bilateral engagement, potentially directed towards partnership-building based on "increasingly overlapping national interests". The US foreign policy priorities shift from non-proliferation (the rhetoric that had hitherto shaped US policy towards South Asia, especially India) to trade and commerce, terrorism, energy security, regional security and stability, and promoting democracy, has helped bridge the gap between the two countries.

In the recent past, the US has started recognising India as a rising power aided by a *de facto* nuclear status coupled with its economic and political potential (e.g. possibility of a permanent seat on the UNSC) signals India's emergence as a power to be reckoned with. Henry Kissinger has assessed India's capability by saying that, "India can make a major contribution to Asia and the world if it is co-opted into the non-proliferation regime instead of being treated with hostility as an outsider". As Prime Minister Manmohan Singh himself once said, "the best is yet to come".

It seems that the Bush administration would continue to extend full cooperation to India in order to witness a more robust relationship with India, perhaps as a counterweight to China, in order to protect its long-term strategic interests in Asia and the Asia-Pacific. India, however, would prefer to be a neutral state. Also India's desire is to improve its relations with the US and China and not to be perceived as aligning itself against one or the other. Firm plans have been developed for closer engagement in the future. This is the surest indication yet that India-US relations are developing with a long-term perspective in mind and that the recent US-Pakistan re-engagement has had no discernible impact.

With regard to the recently enacted US law on civil nuclear deal, New Delhi made it clear on January 10, 2007 that it will 'walk out' of the deal, if at any point, it seems to undermine its national interest. However, it expressed confidence that the elements over which it has 'genuine' reason for concern, including conditional access to reprocessing technology and reprocessing of spent fuel, would be addressed in the 123 Agreement being negotiated to operationalise the deal. In sum, commitment and sensitivity towards each other's national security interests will go a long way in concretizing and giving a definitive shape to India-US bilateral relationship.

NOTES

1. N. Jayapalan, (2001). *Foreign Policy of India,* Atlantic Publishers and Distributers (P) Ltd., New Delhi, p.126.
2. "India-US Relations in a Changing Strategic Environment", Parliament of Australia - Department of the Parliamentary Library ... www.aph.gov.au/library/pubs/rp/2001-02/02rp20.htm
3. *Ibid.*
4. *Annual Report 2005-06*, Ministry of External Affairs, p. 89.
5. *Annual Report 2005-06*, Ministry of External Affairs, p. 90.
6. *Annual Report 2005-06*, Ministry of External Affairs, pp.89-90.
7. "India-US Joint Statement", Embassy of India, Washington, DC, March 2, 2006.
8. *Deccan Herald*, 12 March 2009. http://www.indianembassy.org/newsite/default.asp
9. S.J.R Bilgrami, (2004). *Dynamics of Sanctions in World Affairs,* Atlantic Publishers and Distributers (P) Ltd., New Delhi, pp.175-201.
10. "India-US Economic Relations: India-US Trade", Embassy of India, Washington, DC, March 2, 2006. http://www.indianembassy.org/newsite/default.asp
11. K. Alan Konstadt, "India-US Relations", Congress Research Services (CRS), The Library of Congress, updated Feb. 9, 2006 (CRS-9), p.12. fpc.state.gov/documents/organization/61525.pdf
12. "India-US Defense Cooperation", Embassy of India, Washington, DC, March 2, 2006. http://www.indianembassy.org/newsite/default.asp
13. *Ibid.*, p. 10.
14. Boxer Expeditionary Strike Group and Indian Navy Begin Malabar ... ABOARD USS BOXER, At Sea - USS Boxer (LHD 4) Expeditionary Strike Group (BOXESG) and the Indian Navy's Western Fleet began Exercise Malabar 2006 Oct. 25 off ... www.newdelhi.usembassy.gov/pr102706.html

15. Joint Working Group on Counter-terrorism And Its Productive First Meeting in February 2000. "Joint India-US Statement", March 21, 2000. www.indianembassy.org/indusrel/clinton india/joint india us statement mar 21 2000.htm (1st to 7th meetings)
16. "India-United States: Strategic Partnership", Fact Sheet/White House Office of the Press Secretary, New Delhi, March 2, 2006. www.whitehouse.gov/news/ releases/2006/03/20060302-13.html - 27k -
17. "India-US Cooperation on Energy", Embassy of India, Washington, DC March 2, 2006. http://www.indianembassy.org/newsite/default.asp
18. *Annual Report 2005-06*, Ministry of External Affairs, pp. 8-9.
19. Reply of the External Affairs Minister, Mr. Pranab Mukherjee in Lok Sabha to a Parliament Question on the current status of the India-US Nuclear Deal, November 23, 2006, New Delhi.
20. "India-US Relations", Fact Sheet/White House Office of the Press Secretary 19, December 2006, New Delhi. http://www.indianembassy.org/newsite/default.asp
21. "India-United States: Strategic Partnership", Fact Sheet/White House Office of the Press Secretary March 2, 2006, New Delhi. www.whitehouse.gov/news/ releases/2006/03/20060302-13.html - 27k -
22. "USTAD Signs Cooperation Framework Agreement with the Government of India", November 9, 2005, New Delhi. www.indianembassy.org/indusrel/indusrel.htm
23. "MoU between Department of Science and Technology, Department of Space and US Universities on E-Learning", Fact Sheet, Washington, DC, July 20, 2005. http://meaindia.nic.in/treatiesagreement/2005/20ta2007200501.htm
24. "India-US Knowledge Initiative on Agricultural Education, Teaching, Research, Service and Commercial Linkages", Washington, DC, July 18, 2005. http://meaindia.nic.in/treatiesagreement/2005/18ta1807200511.htm
25. "India and US Successfully Complete Next Steps in Strategic Partnership", Washington, DC, July 18, 2005. http://meaindia.nic.in/treatiesagreement/2005/18ta1807200504.htm
26. "India and US Economic Dialogue: Strengthening Information and Communication Technology Cooperation", Washington, DC, July 18, 2005. http://meaindia.nic.in/treatiesagreement/2005/18ta1807200503.htm
27. "India and US Trade Policy Forum", Washington, DC, July 18, 2005. http://meaindia.nic.in/treatiesagreement/2005/18ta1807200504.htm
28. "India and US Global Democracy Initiative", Washington, DC, July 18, 2005. http://meaindia.nic.in/treatiesagreement/2005/18ta1807200505.htm

29. "India and US: Partners in the Fight Against HIV/AIDS", Washington, DC, July 18, 2005.
http://meaindia.nic.in/treatiesagreement/2005/18ta1807200510.htm
30. "India-US Disasters Relief Initiative", Washington, DC, July 18, 2005.
http://meaindia.nic.in/treatiesagreement/2005/18ta1807200508.htm
31. "US-India to Establish a Bi-National Science and Technology Commission", Fact Sheet/White House Office of the Press Secretary New Delhi, India March 2, 2006.
www.whitehouse.gov/news/ releases/2006/03/20060302-13.html - 27k -
32. A Memorandum of Agreement (MoA) signed between USA and India in Civil Aviation Sector, (Press Information Bureau) Press Releases, New Delhi, November 13, 2006.

3

India-Russia Relations

BACKGROUND

India and Russia are the world's pre-eminent examples of pluralistic, multi-denominational societies with a deeply-rooted tradition of tolerance and constructive co-existence between different faiths and beliefs of great internal diversity, combined with a strong sense of national and cultural unity, operating in a federal political framework. This dimension has enriched the cultural heritage of both countries and helped cultural empathy. Another common element of fundamental importance is that both countries are democracies with a commitment to freedom of speech, assembly, free press and a strong parliament and judiciary. Besides, both these countries have large and rapidly growing economies with very substantial human and natural resources, augmented by new strengths generated through reform and liberalisation, emergence of active entrepreneurship and strong science and technology traditions and capabilities.[1]

The importance attached to them cuts across party lines in India and is not subject to political vicissitudes. Both countries have enjoyed close strategic relations during much of the Cold War era. The relations were all-encompassing, and were the result of various factors including the geostrategic and geopolitical alignments that dominated much of the Cold War period. The two countries signed the Treaty of Peace, Friendship and Cooperation in August 1971.

The signing of this Treaty opened a new era of Indo-Soviet friendship and cooperation. It marked an important milestone in the relations between the two countries and provided a legal and political basis for strengthening of Indo-Soviet cooperation in political, cultural, technical and scientific spheres.[2] Throughout the Cold War era, the former Soviet Union provided crucial political, economic, military and moral support to India. However, the military support remained the most prominent aspect of the two countries relations, with the former Soviet Union accounting for nearly 75 per cent of the military hardware possessed by India till the collapse of the Soviet Union in 1991.

After disintegration of the USSR, the Russian Federation, the successor of the former USSR was in a much weakened position having lost the status of a superpower, had to reorient its foreign policy in the context of its own altered status and the developing geostrategic environment. During this period of transition, the overall orientation of the Russian foreign policy was to establish a "Look West" policy with the United States as its top priority. Thus, during that period, the Russian Foreign Ministry published the *Concept of Russian Federation's Foreign Policy*, in which Asia in general and South Asia in particular was accorded a low priority in Moscow's restructuring process.

India recognised Russia as the successor-state to the former Soviet Union. The former Russian President, Boris Yelsin paid an official visit to India in January 1993, and both countries renewed the Treaty of Friendship and Cooperation, which was an extension of the previous Treaty of Peace, Friendship and Cooperation of 1971. The then Prime Minister of India, Shri Narasimha Rao, reciprocated Yelsin's visit in July 1994. The two leaders signed the Moscow Declaration on the Further Development and Intensification of Cooperation, and the Moscow Declaration on the Protection of Interests of Pluralistic States assuring international and bilateral goodwill and continuation of Russian arms and military equipment exports to India.

Besides, the bilateral relations between India and Russia improved as a result of eight agreements signed in December 1994 during the visit of Russian Prime Minister Victor Chernomyrdin to India. The agreements included military and technical cooperation from 1995 to 2000; merchant shipping; promotion and mutual protection of investments; and trade and outer space cooperation.[3]

There is a national consensus on the need for a strong and stable relationship with the Russian Federation. India's relations with the Russian Federation are multi-faceted and encompass different sectors including political consultations, economic and commercial relations and cooperation in trade and economy, science and technology, culture, education and defence. It is significant that India and Russia are the largest democracies—India in terms of the population and Russia in terms of its size.

RELATIONS SINCE 2000

In the new Foreign Policy Concept released by Russian Federation on July 10, 2000, it has been stated that one of the crucial directions in the Russian foreign policy in Asia will be to develop friendly relations with the leading Asian states including India. It further states that Russia intends to strengthen its traditional partnership with India, including in international affairs.[4]

The two countries have the mechanism of holding Annual Summits from the year 2000. A major breakthrough was achieved when the Russian President, Vladimir Putin visited India in October 2000. Both countries signed a Declaration on Strategic Partnership, and 10 (ten) agreements on various aspects of India and Russia bilateral relations. The strategic partnership is a dynamic and forward-looking principle which provides an anchor of certainty and dependability. The Declaration on Strategic Partnership spelt out in detail the long-term nature of Indo-Russian relations in all aspects of mutual cooperation, like political, defence, economic and trade, science and technological, and cultural spheres. Russia continues to occupy a very important place in our foreign policy and this approach is reciprocated by Russia.[5] The Joint Statement issued at the conclusion of the bilateral talks affirmed Indian and Russian positions on various bilateral, regional and international issues.

President Putin's visit was reciprocated by the Indian Prime Minister Atal Bihari Vajpayee to Russia in November 2001. During the second visit of President Putin to India in December 2002, both Russia and India signed a "Declaration on Further Consolidation of Strategic Partnership" between them.

President Putin visited India from 3-5 December 2004 for the fifth India-Russia Annual Summit. During the visit, a number of agreements were signed, which include the Joint Declaration signed by the President Putin and the Prime Minister Dr. Manmohan Singh and four inter-governmental agreements covering the areas of space, consular and regional cooperation, etc. The Joint Declaration emphasizes the Strategic Partnership between the two countries and also notes the transformation in the global environment in the recent past and stresses the need for a new international architecture based on a multi-polar world. A substantial and new emphasis on economic relations including energy, IT and banking was made. Five MoUs in Banking and Energy sectors were also signed during the visit.[6]

President Putin reiterated support for India's candidature as a permanent member in the expanded UN Security Council. Both the countries also underlined the importance of fighting terrorism by the international community jointly without adopting double standards. During the visit President Putin inaugurated the BRAHMOS Cruise missile complex in Delhi and visited Infosys and HAL in Bangalore.

Prime Minister Dr. Manmohan Singh visited Moscow from May 8-10, 2005 to participate in the 60th anniversary celebrations of the Victory Day. During the visit Prime Minister held bilateral talks with President Putin. President A.P.J. Abdul Kalam paid a state visit to the Russian Federation during 22-25 May 2005. He met President Putin to discuss entire range of bilateral and international issues of mutual concern. He visited a number of academic and industrial organizations. Smt. Sonia Gandhi, President of Indian National Congress and chairperson of United Progressive Alliance paid a visit to Russia as a guest of President Putin from June 12-16, 2005. In July 2005 the Prime Minister Dr. Manmohan Singh held a meeting with President Putin on the sidelines of the Gleneagles G-8 meeting, and then in September in New York on the sidelines of United Nations General Assembly (UNGA) session.

Prime Minister Dr. Manmohan Singh again visited Moscow from December 4-7, 2005 for the annual summit level meeting, a practice that has been instituted from the year 2000. On 6th December Prime Minister had detailed talks with President

Putin at a restricted meeting and subsequently at the delegation level meeting. He also received the Defence Minister and the Energy and Industry Minister of the Russian Federation for separate meetings.

The three agreements signed after summit level meetings with President Putin were: (i) Agreement on Reciprocal Protection of Intellectual Property Rights in the field of Military-Technical Cooperation; (ii) Agreement on Safeguard Technologies while implementing long-term cooperation in the areas of joint development, operation and use of the GLONASS System for peaceful purposes; and (iii) Agreement between the Indian Space Research Organisation and the Federal Space Agency of the Russian Federation on Cooperation in the field of solar physics and solar-terrestrial relationships within the framework of the Coronas-Photon Project.

Indian Prime Minister Dr. Manmohan Singh paid an official visit to Moscow during 11-12 November 2007 and held delegation level talks with the President of Russia, Vladimir Putin. He also met the Prime Minister of Russia, Viktor Zubkov. During his visit several documents were signed which mark sustained bilateral relations with these two countries.

RECENT INTERACTIONS

There have been a large number of important visits/bilateral contacts between India and Russian Federation in recent times. Russian Foreign Minister Mr. Sergei Lavrov visited India during October 8-10, 2004. This was his first visit after the UPA Government took office in New Delhi and also first after Mr. Lavrov's appointment as Foreign Minister. He called on Prime Minister Dr. Manmohan Singh and held meetings with External Affairs Minister and Defence Minister. Thereafter the two Foreign Ministers met regularly in different venues (including the trilateral India, Russia and China Foreign Minister's meeting in Vladivostok).

India and Russia hold regular foreign office consultations on several issues of mutual interest. These include East Asia, Middle East, Central Asia, Disarmament and Export Control, United Nations, Strategic Stability, Shanghai Cooperation Organisation, WTO, etc. Indian Foreign Secretary visited

Moscow during March 10-11, 2004 and held Foreign Office consultations with his counterpart, the first Deputy Foreign Minister of the Russian Federation. He also called on Foreign Minister Mr. Lavrov.

External Affairs Minister Mr. Natwar Singh visited Vladivostok in early June 2005 to participate in the trilateral (India-Russia-China) Foreign Minister level meeting. External Affairs Minister also held a bilateral meeting with Russian Foreign Minister Lavrov. External Affairs Minister visited Moscow again in October to co-chair the 11th Session of Indo-Russia Inter-Governmental Commission for Economic, Scientific, Technological and Cultural Cooperation. External Affairs Minister attended the Shanghai Cooperation Organization (SCO) Heads of Government meeting in Moscow.

Defence Minister paid an official visit to Russia in November 2005 for the meeting of Indo-Russian Inter-Governmental Commission on Military Technical Cooperation. Earlier in October 2005, Russian Defence Minister Sergei Lavrov visited India in connection with joint military exercises in India. Russian Energy and Industry Minister Victory Khristenko visited Delhi in November to attend a Round Table of North and Central Asia Oil Producers and Consumers. Shri Manishankar Aiyar, Minister of Petroleum and Natural Gas, visited Russia in February, and then again during September-October to take part in the ceremony marking the first production of Sakhalin-1 Project. Minister of State for Science and Technology, Kapil Sibal, visited Russia in September 2005.

The Commerce Secretary visited Russia during 20-24 January 2006 to conclude negotiations on the WTO Agreement with Russia, as per the commitment given at the time of Prime Minister's visit to Moscow. Mr. German Gref, Minister of Trade and Economic Development of Russia visited India during February 4-7, 2006. The WTO Agreement with Russia was signed during the visit. Mr. Gref also visited Bangalore to explore possibilities of strengthening cooperation between the two countries on the IT front.[7]

The Prime Minister of India, Dr. Manmohan Singh had a 20-minute conversation over the telephone with the President

Vladimir Putin of Russian Federation on March 4, 2006. The Indian side initiated the conversation.

The two leaders discussed implementation of areas of cooperation identified during their last summit meeting held in Moscow in December. President Putin also briefed Prime Minister Singh about the G-8 Summit being hosted by Russia in St. Petersburg in July 2006. Prime Minister conveyed his acceptance of President Putin's invitation to participate in a broader dialogue with the G-8 at St. Petersburg.

The discussion between President Putin and Prime Minister Singh also covered India-Russia bilateral economic and commercial relations. Prime Minister Singh expressed satisfaction that the bilateral agreement on Russia's accession to the World Trade Organization had been signed recently, in accordance with his commitment to President Putin during their last meeting. The two leaders also discussed ongoing cooperation in the field of civilian nuclear energy.

The leaders exchanged views in context of the forthcoming meeting of the Board of Governors of the IAEA on March 6. Prime Minister welcomed Russia's efforts to address the issue related to Iran's nuclear program through dialogue and consultations.[8]

Prime Minister Mr. Mikhail Fradkov Visits to India

Prime Minister of Russian Federation Mr. Mikhail Fradkov visited to India on March 17, 2006. During the visit of Prime Minister of Russia, Mr. Mikhail Fradkov, the discussions focused on giving a new depth to the strategic partnership. Prime Minister of Russia said, "As large modernizing economies, we have an interest in strengthening bilateral cooperation and in jointly making global interdependence beneficial. In this context, I am happy that we have concluded a bilateral agreement on Russia's accession to WTO last month. The formation of the India-Russia Trade and Investment Forum headed by our Commerce Minister and his Russian counterpart is a valuable step forward in revitalizing our trade and economic relations. We aim to expand bilateral trade to $ 10 billion in the next five years. A Joint Study Group has been formed to recommend ways to achieve this goal and to examine the feasibility of signing a

Comprehensive Economic Cooperation Agreement. We will continue discussions to conclude an Agreement allowing investment of funds from the Rupee Debt Account in India." "Our two growing economies also offer considerable scope for cooperation in energy, information technology and biotechnology and high technology commerce. Along with trade, these sectors must supplement the excellent cooperation we enjoy in the political, strategic and defence spheres," he added. The lists of Agreements signed during the visit of the Russian Prime Minister Mr. Mikhail are the following:

(i) Agreement between the Indian Space Research Organisation (ISRO) and the Federal Space Agency (ROSCOSMOS) for launching of Russian navigation satellites GLONASS-M by a variant of Indian Geo-Synchronous Satellite Launch Vehicle (GSLV): this is a follow-up agreement to the umbrella GLONASS agreement signed in December 2004. This agreement would facilitate launching of GLONASS-M types of satellite of Russia using Indian GSLV.

(ii) Agreement between the Indian Space Research Organisation (ISRO) and the Federal Space Agency (ROSCOSMOS) on joint development of GLONASS navigation satellites GLONASS-K: this is a follow-up agreement to the umbrella GLONASS agreement signed in December 2004. Indian and Russian space agencies would cooperate in developing GLONASS-K satellite with technological inputs from either side.

(iii) MoU between Indian Oil Corporation and Joint Stock Company Stroytransgaz of the Russian Federation: this MoU is declaration of intent for pursuing petro-infrastructure projects worldwide jointly through a consortium.

(iv) Agreement between Vneshtorg Bank of Russian Federation and EXIM Bank of India on new credit line. It is understood that EXIM Bank would open a credit line of $ 100 million with Vneshtorg Bank. This is the largest such credit line so far.

(v) Agreement on cooperation between ICICI Bank and Vnesheconom Bank of the Russian Federation.

(vi) Agreement on cooperation between Confederation of Indian Industries (CII) and the Russian Union of Industries & Enterprises (RUIE).

(vii) Agreement between the Federation of Indian Chambers of Commerce & Industry (FICCI) and the Indo-Russian Business Council set up by the Russian Federation Chamber of Commerce & Industry (RFCCI) and the Expert Magazine of Russia.[9]

ECONOMIC AND SCIENCE & TECHNOLOGY COOPERATION

Economic and Science & Technology Cooperation constitutes a core element in India-Russia relations. A strong commitment from both sides to mutually beneficial cooperation in these sectors, and to translate this into effective bilateral trade, investment and S&T exchanges has been a basic dimension of India-Russia relations throughout the decades. This has also been one of the major factors ensuring stability and continuity of the relationship in the Soviet period and beyond.

Economic

Bilateral trade grew steadily from the early fifties, encompassing a wide range and volume of goods and services and reached a volume of US $ 10 billion by the mid-1980. There was also substantial Russian investment, mainly in industrial infrastructure sector, which was a major input in the first generation industrial growth of India. S&T exchanges grew substantially in scope.

Specific mechanisms and structures were created to facilitate trade and investment; essentially, the rupee-trade system and annual trade plans and a series of state credits, for Russian investment in projects in India lost their relevance with the dissolution of the Soviet Union. What was required was not merely finding new structures and mechanisms to replace them, but coming to terms with a radically new milieu of bilateral economic cooperation. The major readjustments required could not be made immediately and not surprisingly, there was a considerable decline in bilateral trade and investment. The dislocations of the Russian economy, culminating in the 1998 financial crisis, compounded this trend.

Throughout the last decade, both countries have worked in the national framework and jointly, to reactivate our economic relations. It was realised early that this task involved not restoration as such, but re-establishing trade, investment and other related cooperation on a fundamentally new basis and radically new milieu especially the free market economy, entrepreneurship and democracy. India was ready for this challenge considering that this period also coincided with the beginning of serious reform and liberalisation of the Indian economy as well. This had generated new strengths in Indian side, which could be brought to bear on economic relations in the new situation. In this framework, both sides have sought over the last decade to work out a new practical approach to cooperation and to identify the parameters.

This effort has been particularly focused during the last three years, centered on the recognition of the larger framework for economic cooperation, as set by the fact that India and Russia have large and growing economies with abundant human and natural resources, well established, versatile and productive capacities in industry, agriculture, services as well as science and technology. In the last few decades, driven by comprehensive reform and liberalization, the economies of the two countries have acquired a new dynamism. Thus, at the time of economic slowdown around the globe, India and Russia are among the few economies that continue to grow at substantially high rates. In terms of average annual GDP growth during the last some years, the two countries rank among the top 10 in the world. Both India and Russia are active in developing high technology and are in the forefront of the knowledge revolution. This overall process gained strength for being broad-based—both on the domestic and external front—and, for being guided by a basic consensus and clear-sighted leadership.

Basic economic indices relating to both countries are relevant: In GDP, India ranks among the first twelve in the world and is fourth in purchasing power parity; within the first fifteen in industrial production and the first four in agricultural output. Global ranking is high in many indices of production—both in industry and agriculture. Industrial capability has grown substantially and is versatile. There are areas of excellence, notably IT, biotechnology, space, peaceful nuclear technology applied to energy, automobile components, pharmaceutical and precious stones. Among the other core strengths of the Indian economy are small and medium enterprises in industry, agriculture and services, a sound financial, banking and managerial infrastructure and, above all, rapidly growing entrepreneurship, which is a driving force in the economic growth. A 200 million strong middle class with increasing purchasing power is also a factor sustaining the growth. Current economic indicators are very positive. There is concerted effort to rectify the serious shortcomings of the economy, i.e. upgrading infrastructure in transport, communication and power, enhancing domestic and foreign investment, improving productivity and quality of life, reinforcing economic reforms with effective regulation and reducing inequalities.

In this context, we have also noted the dynamic growth of the Russian economy, particularly intensive and rapidly expanding entrepreneurial activity and increased investment, positive economic indicators on foreign investment, consumer purchasing power, external reserves, foreign trade, debt repayment capability, energy exports and revenues, inflation, tax collection, etc. and progress in implementation of a far reaching programme of reform and liberalisation, as well as in creating a facilitating environment for domestic and foreign investment. Underlying these trends is the basic fact that along with the other attributes of a great power of historical standing, Russia is also inherently a major economic power—and its current direction of economic growth is very positive.

The new capabilities and requirements that have developed in both countries as outlined above have created a qualitatively new and greatly improved environment for bilateral economic cooperation. There is recognition in both countries, that we should make the best use of the enhanced opportunities and synergies that have thus emerged, for mutually beneficial interaction which would strengthen the two national economies as well as the welfare and prosperity of the two countries. This would also be essential for reinforcing the overall relationship and providing more substance and long-term sustainability to the strategic partnership. The basic endeavor is to optimize the exchanges and realise the tremendous potential for economic cooperation, bringing it to a level commensurate with our excellent political relations. This would apply specifically to the last bilateral trade turnover as well as investment.

This approach is well reflected in the landmark Joint Declaration on Strengthening and Enhancing Economic, Scientific and Technological Cooperation signed by the Prime Minister of India, Atal Bihari Vajpayee and the President of Russia, Vladimir Putin, during the Presidential visit to India in December 2002. This document embodies the shared vision and resolve of countries to give a renewed impetus to trade, investment and S&T cooperation. It sets out a road map as well as facilitating measures for building a strong and mutually beneficial partnership.

It is recognised that bilateral trade, which declined to US $1.5 billion by the end of the last decade was well below potential and that special efforts were made to reactivate it. There has been steady progress in this regard. In 1992, an attempt was made to revive the mechanism of 'ordered' trade in a modified form under the Indo-Russian Trade and Economic Agreement. In January 1993, it was decided that instead of being governed by inter-governmental protocols, Indo-Russian trade should be conducted on normal international practice. Accordingly, an arrangement was made which provided for regulated annual repayment in US dollars billion equivalent in Rupees to Russia over a period of 12 years, and smaller amounts thereafter for a further period of 33 years. The rupee debt repayment funds were to be used by Russia for import of goods and trade related services from India. Approximately 80 per cent of Indian exports to Russia are now routed through the Rupee debt channel.

Experience has made it clear that while the Rupee trade mechanism provides some stability, it has also encouraged a non-competitive, sheltered approach with inadequate emphasis on quality. This is one of the reasons for many exporters in India shying away from Russia and moving to other markets over the last decade. There is a strong perception that reactivating of trade will require phasing out the traditional Rupee debt system. Already about 20 per cent of Indian exports are effectively dollarised and Russian exports to India have been against freely convertible currency. There are indications showing an increase in trade turnover (i.e. US $2 billion in the first nine months of 2003). Both sides are also devoting special attention to ensuring stability in trade during the current transition from the Rupee debt system to open trade. The main items of Indian export are tea, coffee, pharmaceutical, textile and garments and tobacco while major imports from Russia are fertilizers, non-ferrous metals, newsprint, iron and steel. While consolidating the traditional items of trade, there is also an effort to establish new areas, e.g. machinery and equipment, IT and telecom, automobile components, gems and jewels, processed food, agro items, rough diamonds, etc.

Investment is another large priority and a test case for the health of any economic relationship. There has been progress on this front as well—the outstanding example is large Indian investment of about US$ 1.7 billion in Russia in the Sakhalin-I oil and natural gas project. Under the agreement signed in February 2001 between ONGC (Videsh Limited) with Rosneft, the Indian side has acquired a combined 20 per cent interest in the project from Rosneft-S and SMNG-S, two subsidiaries of Rosneft. Besides, an upfront cash payment for its share, ONGC-VL (OVL) will also invest further in the development of the project, and finance Rosneft in its remaining participation until the project generates a positive cash flow. Russia has made a comparable investment in India through provision of a credit in the construction of a nuclear power plant in Kudankulam in South India. This involves setting up of two units of 1000 MW each based on the standard and widely used Russian VVER nuclear reactor design. Both projects are progressing satisfactorily, i.e. preparatory work for Sakhalin-I and actual construction in Kudankulam. These projects start in the year 2005-2006. Yet another important development is the production-sharing contract for joint exploration and development of natural gas reserves in one bloc on the east coast of India signed between Gas Authority of India Ltd. (GAIL) and GAZPROM in October, 2000. It was agreed earlier that the two companies would further explore the possibilities of energy cooperation, including transportation.

There is great interest on both sides to move further in mutual investment, even beyond the large projects mentioned above. While India is seeking new investments in energy, fertilizers, cement, electronics, other hi-tech sectors, Russian firms with expertise and surplus capacity are welcome to bid for investment in our infrastructure sector—where there are new opportunities—e.g. the 15,000 kms National Highway Project, in sea and airports, new metro systems and power generation, transmission and distribution. A Russian firm had won a contract for construction of a section of the National Highway. India looks forward to other Russian firms who have shown interest in investing in the oil sector, power and other infrastructure to follow up and work out mutually feasible projects and modalities.

Both sides are looking for ways to raise capital needed for new investments as above. Apart from surplus capital from national sources, another possible channel would be the money accumulated over the years in Russian Central Bank, through annual repayment by India of the Rupee debt. A reserve fund set up out of this money, could be used for selected, mutually agreed projects in either countries. The fund would function as venture capital for helping to kick-start investment.

There is also steadily growing business-to-business interaction and information flow—through direct personal contact as well as electronic means. Indian businessmen in various trade exhibitions in Russia—both general and specialised, reflect this in significantly larger number of Indian trade delegations visiting Russia and greater participation. The thirteen Indian business groups that have visited Russia in 2004 represented important sectors such as engineering goods, textile, pharmaceuticals, gems and jewelery, tea, tobacco, leather products, tourism, IT and telecom. Russian business delegations are now more active in visiting India and participating in business events here. This includes the premier international Indian Engineering Trade Fair held in New Delhi in March 2003. There is enhanced Russian participation in the annual India International Trade Fair in New Delhi. The exclusive Indian trade and industry exhibition organised in Moscow in February 2004 was attended by 200 Indian companies representing nearly 40 categories of products and services to Russia. This event was also well attended by

Russian business entities. Interactions of Indian entrepreneurs with various regions, republics and territories of Russia are expanding, and the Indian businessmen are building new linkages in areas outside Moscow. Many Indian states like Karnataka, Andhra Pradesh and Gujarat have established contact relation with Samara, Tatarstan and Astrakhan. It also helps to promote business contacts. Other such linkages with a business fall-out are being considered.

Also noteworthy is the renewed activity of the Joint Business Council in which the parties are the leading national chambers, i.e. Federation of Indian Chambers of Commerce and Industry (FICCI), and the Russian Federation of Chambers of Commerce and Industry. The Council met in Moscow in February 2004, and the visiting Indian business leaders further renewed their contact. The other major apex Indian trade and industry business federation, the Confederation of Indian Industry (CII), and its counterpart, the Russian Union of Industrialists and Entrepreneurs (RUIE) have also reactivated their exchanges. The Moscow Office of CII was opened during the visit of the Prime Minister of India Dr. Manmohan Singh.

The high point in direct business interaction was the visit to Russia of the nearly 100 strong business team accompanying the Prime Minister. Their interactions with their Russian counterparts have set the tone for greater mutual interest in the business sectors of the two countries in increased trade investment and S&T exchanges. Their visit has helped identify specific areas and there are promising indications of follow up.

A sector closely related to trade and investment, with great potential for mutually beneficial exchanges, but somewhat neglected, is Small and Medium Enterprises (SMEs). SMEs have developed in India as a crucially important component of our economy, contributing not only to employment, but also to the production of quality goods, supplied directly or as ancillaries feeding into big industry. They also contribute substantially to our exports. India continues to pay great attention to the healthy development of this sector. We know that Russia also attaches high priority to SMEs. Cooperation in this sector could cover areas such as training, exchange of experts, management, supply of machinery and equipment, and turnkey execution of projects.

During the Prime Minister's visit, a MoU between the Federation of Indian Chambers of Commerce and Industry and Russian Public Organisation of Small and Medium Enterprises was concluded and further contacts are being built in this sector.

A strong banking linkage is essential to sustain trade and investment and contacts between the banking sectors of two countries have grown substantially in recent years. Indian banking teams have visited Russia to establish the parameters for closer banking cooperation. The license for operation of the new Commercial Bank of India in Russia has been issued and the unit will start functioning shortly. A Russian bank is also working actively for establishing a presence in India. Leading Russian banks are interested in corresponding agreements with the Indian counterparts. A working sub-group on banking functioning in the inter-governmental Joint Commission framework meets regularly to work out arrangements for further improvement in this sector.

Improved transport and communication is obviously another very important dimension in bilateral trade and investment. The multi-mode North-South international transport corridor is of particular significance. This trilateral arrangement involving India, Iran and Russia, established in September 2000, through an inter-governmental agreement is meant to facilitate movement of goods from India to Iran through a sea route and onward by road or rail to the Caspian Sea, and then Russia and beyond. The route greatly reduces transit time and shipping costs and is already being used for moving cargo. Parties to the agreement have met regularly to review progress in operationalisation of the corridor. The essential requirement is upgrading of seaport, road and railway communications, and improvement in procedures such as documentation. A good part of the action in this regard lies inside Russia. All sides can contribute by increasing utilisation of this route, so that it becomes economically more viable.[10]

The 10th session of the Indo-Russian Inter-Governmental Commission on Trade, Economic, Scientific, Technological and Cultural Cooperation (IRIGC) was held in New Delhi from 18-19 November 2004. Deputy Prime Minister Mr. Alexander Zhukov led Russia and Minister of External Affairs

Shri K. Natwar Singh led India. Mr. Zhukov called on the President of India and met the Minister of Finance and the Minister of Commerce and Industry. Some of the important decisions taken during the Inter-Governmental Commission were:

1. A first Indo-Russian Round Table on Information Technology was held in Bangalore from 1-2 December 2004.
2. The first Indo-Russian Energy Meet was held in New Delhi on 15 January 2005.
3. Canara Bank and State Bank of India signed agreements with two Russian banks to facilitate trade and mutual bank guarantees.

Other areas of cooperation include projects for development of software products and also Indian assistance in the establishment of software parks in Russia, cooperation between Russian company Sudoimport and Magnum International Trading for construction of auxiliary fleet ships in India and the development of the Indo-Russian Joint Venture Company to produce Titanium Dioxide in Orissa.

India and Russia have identified Energy, IT, Banking, Communications, and Biotechnology as new areas of growth. Special emphasis has been given in expanding cooperation in thermal, hydro and nuclear energy for power production. Both the countries also supported development of cooperation between India and Russia with the purpose of participation of Indian and Russian companies in the exploration of new oil and gas fields in Russia and third countries.

Agreement was also reached to hold the "Days of Indian Culture" in Russia in September-October 2005 and develop cultural cooperation within the framework of Exchange Programme of "Days of the Cities: Moscow and Delhi" in 2005-06.

As part of efforts to enhance bilateral relations, the "Year of Russia in India" was inaugurated in early 2008. The year-long programme covers wide-ranging events in the field of culture, economy and commerce, science and technology, arts, etc. which is to be followed by the "Year of India in Russia in 2009."

India and Russia established a new milestone in bilateral trade and economic relations, with India giving its consent to

Russia's accession to the World Trade Organisation (WTO) and both sides setting up a Joint Study Group (JSG) to finalise a road map for increasing the bilateral trade turnover to US $10 billion by 2010. The Protocol on Completion of Bilateral Negotiations on the Accession of Russia to the WTO and the Memorandum of Understanding (MoU) on Cooperation between the Ministry of Commerce & Industry of India and the Ministry of Economic Development and Trade of the Russian Federation were signed on February 6, 2006 in New Delhi by Shri Kamal Nath, Minister of Commerce and Industry on behalf of the Government of India and by Mr. German Gref, Minister for Economic Development and Trade, on behalf of the Government of Russian Federation respectively.[11]

The highlights of the agreements are:

1. Signing a deal on the long-standing Russia's accession to the World Trade Organisation (WTO).
    - Russian side agreed to recognise Darjeeling tea, Basmati rice and Alphonso mango as some of India's geographical indicators. This means that any other country selling products under these names will now have to pay royalties to Indian producers.
    - Russia also agreed to consider providing market access to Indian meat and poultry items.
2. Signing a MoU on cooperation between the Ministry of Commerce and Industry of India and the Ministry of Economic Development and Trade of the Russian Federation.
    - The MoU provides for setting up of a Joint Study Group (JSG) with a view to assessing the feasibility of signing Comprehensive Economic Cooperation Agreement (CECA) between the two countries. CECA is much wider in scope than a Free Trade Agreement (FTA) as it not only includes goods, but also services and investment.
    - By the end of 2006, the JSG to be co-chaired by the Commerce Secretary from the Indian side and his counterpart from the Russian side will look for ways to increase bilateral trade turnover to $10 billion by

2010. It is also expected to suggest specific measures to stem the decline in India's exports to Russia.

Shri Kamal Nath said that India was looking forward to Russia's early accession to the WTO for further cooperation in the multilateral trade forum on the basis of mutual benefit. As per the WTO accession procedures, the country seeking accession is required to negotiate bilaterally with each member country of the WTO. It is in accordance with this principle that both the Ministers signed the protocol on completion of bilateral negotiations on the accession of Russia to the WTO.

The JSG is likely to prepare a road map for achieving a significant increase in bilateral trade turnover by diversifying and strengthening relations in a wide range of areas particularly trade in goods, services, investment and economic cooperation.

Even though bilateral trade is increasing—with growth of 11 per cent in two-way trade in 2004-05—India's exports to Russia have been declining over the last few years. But during 2006-07 and 2007-08 the trend reversed and it increased substantially.

During the visit many other issues of interest were discussed between the two sides:

- Both sides agreed to strengthen cooperation in oil and natural gas.
- An early finalisation and signing of the draft inter-governmental agreement concerning higher off-take of Indian tobacco by Russia through the purchase of cigarettes/tobacco or procuring of cigarettes from a Joint Venture proposed to be set up in Russia by any Indian company which would procure tobacco from India.
- Cooperation in diamond trade between Russia and India also figured in the discussions and Shri Kamal Nath urged the Russian Minister to expedite the decisions agreed by both sides for inclusion of MMTC in the list of regular participants for auction and tenders for selling of rough diamonds by Alrosa, the Russian diamond mining company as also to explore the action taken by the Russian side for setting up a joint venture by Alrosa with MMTC for manufacturing jewellery in India.

- Indian side sought facilitating measures for setting up joint ventures of Indian tea companies and Russian business houses in order to augment the export of quality tea from India. The Indian side also asked to quicken the release of payment due to Indian exporters and delink this issue from the overall settlement of state credit.
- The issue of early conclusion of simplified visa procedure agreement to enhance trade and economic cooperation also figured in the deliberations.

The Russian Minister also attended a meeting organized by Federation of Indian Chambers of Commerce and Industry (FICCI). He said, "It is about time that Indian business turned its attention to its counterparts in Russia and vice versa." He, however, expressed disappointment at the current level of bilateral trade, saying India's exports to Russia had declined from US$ 800 million in 2001 to US$ 657 million in 2005. But in the subsequent years it rose to US$ 733.5 million in 2005-06. It further increased to US$ 902.17 million during 2006-07. The rising trend in exports continued during 2007-08 when it reached US$ 939.7 million. Russia's exports to India during the period had risen marginally from US$ 1.3 billion to US$ 2.5 billion. Russia's export to India continued to rise during the period. It reached US$ 2,022.19 million, US$ 2,407.61 million, and US$ 2,468.49 million in 2005-06, 2006-07 and 2007-08 respectively.

Mr. German Gref said his visit to India was aimed at facilitating the launch of CECA in a year. He pointed to the opportunities for cooperation in energy, defence and hi-tech areas, apart from mentioning that Russia could help India in developing infrastructure and business-to-business deals in automobiles. "We will do all that is possible to remove procedural and other irritants like delays in issuance of visas," he said.

Russia's Ambassador Vyacheslav Trubnikov said his government was considering the issue of five-year, multiple-entry visas for genuine business travelers, but had to guard against illegal migrants masquerading as businessmen to seek entry to Europe from Russia.[12]

Earlier, Shri Kamal Nath had a bilateral meeting with Mr. Gref during which trade issues were discussed. Shri Kamal Nath requested for early finalisation and signing of the draft inter-governmental agreement regarding higher off-take of Indian tobacco by Russia through the purchase of cigarettes/tobacco or procuring of cigarettes from a joint venture proposed to be set up in Russia by any Indian company which would procure tobacco from India. He also requested Mr. Gref to accord protection to "Darjeeling tea" as a geographical indication and to recognise "Assam", "Nilgiri" and "Indian tea logo" as labels/ well known original brands and facilitating setting up of joint ventures of Indian tea companies and Russian business houses in order to augment the export of quality tea from India.[13]

The G8+4 Finance Ministers' meeting took place in Moscow on the 11th of February 2006. The Finance Ministers of the G-8 countries, along with their counterparts from India, Brazil, China and South Africa, took part in the breakfast meeting organized under the chairmanship of Russia in Moscow. Indian Finance Minister P. Chidambaram, in his intervention at the Meeting, made a forceful plea for a successful conclusion of the Doha Developmental Agenda (DDA) under the aegis of the ongoing WTO negotiations.

Mr. Chidambaram informed that while the Hong Kong Ministerial declaration signaled a marginal forward movement in the ongoing WTO negotiations, the main area of negotiation, i.e. agriculture, continued to pose a serious problem. He emphasized the sensitivity in India to the issue of agriculture, which employed 65 per cent of the Indian population while contributing about 22 per cent of the country's GDP. He made it clear that India would not accept any settlement, which adversely affected the rural sector and would look for effective safeguards for the farmers of India.

With respect to Non-Agricultural Market Access (NAMA), he felt substantial progress still had to be made. He conveyed that India had been autonomously pursuing the policy of tariff reduction and had sharply brought down import duties over the last few years. While signaling active participation in the NAMA negotiations, he conveyed, "the 'water' between our bound and applied tariffs is an asset which we would trade off only if comparable benefits in other areas, particularly services, were obtained".

He signaled India's concern over negotiations relating to services. He confirmed India's significant interest in Mode-1 (cross-border supplies), Mode-2 (consumption abroad), and Mode-4 (movement of natural persons) processes. "India expected meaningful offers in the services area from developed countries in the next phase of negotiations," he said.

In conclusion, he felt, as outlined in the Hong Kong Ministerial Declaration, "Aid for trade cannot be a substitute for the development benefits that will result from a successful conclusion to the DDA, particularly in areas of market access." He confirmed India's full participation in the ongoing negotiations and her determination to play a constructive role in enabling an early conclusion of the ongoing negotiations in the year 2006, as envisaged by the Trade Ministers in the Hong Kong Ministerial Declaration.

In his interaction with the press, he said that he was particularly happy to visit Moscow for the G-8+4 Finance Ministers' meeting since Russia had taken up the chairmanship of G-8 in 2006 and India's relations with Russia were close and friendly. He said that India was supportive of energy security being high on the G-8 agenda and felt that large and long-term producers of energy required large and long-term consumers in the interests of global energy stability.[14]

Science & Technology Cooperation

India and Russia are ideal partners in the field of Science & Technology (S&T), considering Russia's powerful S&T tradition and achievements and India's strong capabilities. Cooperation in this field has indeed developed well especially through the Integrated Long Term Programme (ILTP), initiated in 1987, and valid till 2010. This is one of the largest S&T international cooperation programs, and has been operating actively and has enabled several exchange visits and joint research projects.[15]

India and Russia have been successfully executing for the past seventeen years probably one of the largest mutual cooperation programs in science and technology between any two countries. The dimensions of research cover the widest possible spectrum. The interaction in the field of Science & Technology between India and Russia is conducted through the following two types of programs:

(i) Programs Based on Inter-Governmental Bilateral Agreements

These include the Integrated Long-Term Programme of Cooperation (ILTP), the Working Group on Science & Technology, and the Academy Exchange Program.

These programs are based on Protocols, MoUs, and Agreements between Russian and Indian agencies. Mr. Mikhail Gorbachev signed the agreement on ILTP on July 3, 1987 the then President of the erstwhile Soviet Union and Mr. Rajiv Gandhi, the then Prime Minister of India. It has been renewed for another 10 years on 3rd October 2000. It is the largest bilateral Science & Technology program that India has entered into with any country. The Department of Science & Technology coordinates the ILTP on the Indian side and the Russian Academy of Sciences on the Russian side. Continuous dialogue and interaction between Indian and Russian scientists result in identification and implementation of joint projects in the areas of mutual interest. In its 16 years of implementation, the ILTP is credited with about 3000 exchange visits from the countries, 300 completed joint research projects and establishment of 6 joint research centers in important areas of science. Currently, about 150 joint research projects are being implemented and one joint center in the areas of Biomedical Instrumentation is on the anvil. The ILTP comprises of cooperation in 11 thrust areas related to frontiers of S&T, namely: Biotechnology and Immunology; Materials Science & Technology; Laser Science & Technology; Catalysis; Space Science & Technology; Accelerators & their Applications; Hydrology; Computer & Electronics; Biomedical Science & Technology; Oceanology & Oceanic Resources and Engineering Sciences; and seven select areas of basis research in science, which include Mathematics; Applied Mechanics; Earth Sciences; Physics & Astrophysics; Ecology and Environmental Protection; Chemical Sciences and Life Sciences.

ILTP Centres of Exellence

Under this program six joint Indo-Russian centers have been established to pursue the concerted areas where large interactive research work progresses. Among the technology export capable countries, India is placed better in some areas such as technology licensing, number of scientists and engineers, and science and mathematical education levels. It is hoped that both the countries will resolve and take steps to benefit by industrial realization of high technologies and commercialization of products developed by joint research.

Setting up of Advanced Research Centre for Powder Metallurgy and New Materials at Hyderabad is a proud example of accomplishments of ILTP. Presently, the Centre is operational with thrust on three major areas, namely Powder Metallurgy; Surface Engineering and Ceramic Materials. This is a unique example where scientists and technologists work together for joint R&D and transfer of technologies to industry.

Another important accomplishment of the programme has emerged in the form of polio vaccine production facility, BIBCOL (Bharat Immunological and Biologicals Corporation Limited) at Bulandshahar. This plant with a capacity of 100 million doses of polio vaccine annually has been receiving continuous help and cooperation from Russia.

Setting up of Indo-Russian Centre for Advanced Computing Research in Moscow has been another important milestone of this programme. The parallel computing system PARAM 10000, designed and developed by Centre for Development of Advanced Computing (C-DAC) has been installed at the Indo-Russian Centre for Advanced Computing Research. Initially, the system is of 12.8 GFLOPS peak performance which would be subsequently upgraded after the multidisciplinary applications are optimized.

Indo-Russian Centre for Biotechnology at Allahabad is another addition to the list of Centres of Excellence created under ILTP. The agreement for establishment of this Centre was formally concluded on 5th November 2001 in Moscow during the visit of the Indian Prime Minister to Russia between the Department of Science & Technology on the Indian side and the Russian Academy of Sciences on the Russian side.

Indo-Russian Centre for Gas Hydrates is the latest addition to the list of Centres of Excellence created under ILTP. The agreement for establishment of this Centre was formally concluded during the visit of Indian Prime Minister to Russia in November 2003 between the Department of Science & Technology on the Indian side and the Russian Academy of Sciences on the Russian side. The Centre was inaugurated at National Institute of Ocean Technology, Chennai on 12th March 2003.

A MoU for the establishment of Indo-Russian Centre for Earthquake Research has been signed in November 2003 between Department of Science & Technology and Russian Academy of Sciences. The Centre is coordinating with seventeen joint R&D projects.

Working Group on Science & Technology

This Group has been in operation since 1993. It is coordinated from the Indian side by the Department of Science and Technology, Government of India and from the Russian side by the Ministry of Education and Science. Sub-Working Groups are functioning in the following areas:

1. Agriculture—Indian Council for Agricultural Research
2. Standardization, Meteorology and Certification—Bureau of Indian Standards
3. Building Materials—National Council for Cement and Building Materials
4. Meteorology—India Meteorology Department
5. Biotechnology—Department of Biotechnology
6. Medical Sciences—Indian Council for Medical Research
7. Ocean-technology—Department of Ocean Development
8. Industrial Realization of High Technology—Deptt. of Science & Technology
9. Seismology—Deptt. of Science & Technology

The progress in most of the 9 sub-working groups under the Working Group on Science and Technology of the Inter-Governmental Commission has also been satisfactory.

Inter-Academy Exchange Program

INSA-RAS Cooperation

This program was initiated in 1970 through an agreement signed between the erstwhile USSR Academy of Sciences and the Indian National Science Academy. The program has since continued by renewal of the agreement every five years. The thrust of this program is on pure sciences.

ICAR-RAAS Cooperation

An agreement for cooperation in the field of agriculture and related subjects between the Indian Council of Agricultural Research (ICAR) and the Russian Academy of Agricultural Sciences (RAAS) was signed in New Delhi on 5th October 1995. The agreement provides for scientific and technical cooperation, joint research projects, exchange of information and materials between both the countries and organization of bilateral workshops and seminars.

(ii) Programs Based on Agreements Between Governmental Agencies

There are many programs that are based on the direct agreements between various Govt. agencies of both the countries. These are pursued as per their contractual agreements.

Fourth Meeting of Indo-Russian Joint Working Committee for ILTP

The fourth meeting of the Indo-Russian Joint Working Committee (JWC) for Integrated Long-Term Programme of Cooperation in Science & Technology (ILTP) was held in Moscow during May 20-21, 2004. Academician G.I. Marchuk, Co-chairman ILTP Joint Council expressed his satisfaction on the implementation of the program as per decisions taken during 11th Session of Joint Council held in Bangalore on November 6-7, 2002. The JWC considered 54 new proposals and approved 50 for inclusion in the program.

The Committee also considered progress made under various ILTP Centres. It was noted that the Indo-Russian Centre for Gas Hydrates was inaugurated on 12th March 2004 at National Institute of Ocean Technology, Chennai. Nine projects have been identified for implementation. It was noted that Russian Indian Centre for Ayurvedic research has been registered in Russia as per Russian national law. First Joint Committee Meeting of the centre was held and the centre was inaugurated shortly.

The Joint Working Committee discussed various issues connected with ILTP and made the various recommendations to the Joint Council. The Committee also recommended that both sides should make efforts to increase number of exchange visits.

S&T–CII Summit

The Department of Science & Technology (DST) and the Confederation of Indian Industry (IIC) with the initiative of ITLP organized a "Technology Summit with Russia as a Partner Country" in New Delhi on October 19-20, 2004. Approximately fifty scientists/technologists/industry persons attended the event from Russia. About 150-200 Indian technologists/industrialist participated in it. Apart from these delegates a large number of interested scientists and senior government officials also took part in it. Hon'ble Minister of State for Science & Technology and Ocean Development Shri Kapil Sibal inaugurated the Summit.

Fifteen Letters of Intend (LOIs) agreements were singed at the end of the Summit in the areas of mutual interest from the two sides.[16]

The Integrated Long-Term Programme for cooperation in the field of science and technology (ILTP) completed 20 years of successful working during the year 2007. Joint Council of the ILTP co-chaired by Chairman of the Scientific Advisory Council to the Prime Minister, Prof. C.N.R Rao met in Moscow during 11-12 Oct. 2007. During the meeting several MoUs were signed for the cooperation in the field of science and technology. Besides, in August 2007, Department of Science and Technology of India and the Russian Foundation of Basic Research, Moscow signed a Memorandum of understanding on cooperation in basic science.

COOPERATION ON COUNTER-TERRORISM

India and Russia share a common resolve to fight terrorism. Both countries are faced with secessionist movements in their respective regions of Kashmir and Chechnya. The two countries project and equate these movements for self-determination with terrorism. Both also believe that these movements have strong support from neighboring countries, which are extending them their moral, political and financial support.

In the Joint Statement issued at the end of President Putin's visit to India in October 2000, the two sides underlined the importance of joint efforts in "combating international terrorism".[17] In his address to the Joint Session of the Indian

Parliament during the visit, Putin had said that the same extremist organisations that were creating problems in Jammu & Kashmir were behind the troubles in Chechnya and other northern territories of Russia. In order to further institutionalize and consolidate their cooperation on terrorism, both countries signed the "Moscow Declaration on International Terrorism" during Indian Prime Minister, A.B. Vajpayee's visit to Russia in November 2001.[18]

The two sides have reaffirmed that global terrorism in all its forms and manifestations constitutes one of the most serious threats to international peace and security, and condemned, in the strongest terms, all acts of terrorism irrespective of their motivation, whenever and by whomsoever committed. They underscore that there can be no justification for terrorism on any grounds, including ideological, religious, racial, ethnic or any other. They believe that the fight against terrorism has to be long-term, sustained and comprehensive. In this regard they emphasize the need for giving substance and credibility to the global fight against terrorism and avoid selective approaches and political expediency. With the recent targeting of open societies around the world, Russia and India as two large and influential democracies, have reasons to be concerned about the vulnerability of democracies to terrorist attacks, because terrorism exploits the strengths of democracies such as, human rights, freedom of expression and movement, etc. Both countries welcome the unanimous adoption of the UN Security Council resolution 1566 (piloted by the Russian Federation).[19]

Both countries have sought heightened cooperation in fighting the scourge of terrorism by working on a coordinated and synchronised approach to counter the policy of using terrorism to achieve political objectives. "What prevents us from coming forward in a coordinated and synchronised manner against the policy which employs terrorism as a means to achieve political objectives," asked Gen. A.I. Nikolaev, Chairman of Russian Duma's (Parliament) Committee on Defence at a seminar on Indo-Russian Strategic Partnership in 21st century. Gen. Nikolaev asserted Russian troops would "never" be withdrawn from Chechenya as "it is part of Russia". On 29 November 2002, inaugurating the seminar organised by Indian Defence Review,

Minister of State for External Affairs Digvijay Singh spoke about increased international cooperation in fighting terrorism saying Moscow and New Delhi were among countries, which were at the forefront of this fight. "Both our countries believe that combating this global scourge of terrorism should be on a comprehensive and long-term basis and directed also at those supporting, harboring or providing safe haven to terrorists," Singh said hinting at Pakistan.[20]

Russia and India re-emphasize the need for an early adoption by the General Assembly of the Comprehensive Convention on International Terrorism and the International Convention for the Suppression of Acts of Nuclear Terrorism. Bilateral cooperation in this field is conducted through discussions in the framework of bilateral Joint Working Groups on "Global Challenges" and "Combating International Terrorism".[21]

First Meeting of the Joint Working Group on Combating International Terrorism

The first meeting of the India-Russia Joint Working Group (JWG) on Combating International Terrorism was held in Moscow on 29-30 September 2003. The Joint Working Group on Combating International Terrorism was established as a result of the Memorandum of Understanding signed between the two countries during the visit of the President of the Russian Federation Mr. Putin to India in December 2002. The MoU seeks to further strengthen the cooperation between India and Russia in combating international terrorism in accordance with the determination of the two countries to fight this phenomenon, which is also reflected in the bilateral declaration signed during the visit of the Prime Minister of India Mr. A.B. Vajpayee to Russia in November 2001.

The two sides discussed a wide range of issues relating to combating international terrorism and the contribution they have already made and that they are prepared to make to global, regional and sub-regional efforts in combating terrorism including mutual assistance and assistance to third countries in developing their potential to combat terrorist threats. They also informed each other about the efforts undertaken at the national level in the fight against terrorism. The two sides agreed to develop cooperation against terrorist organizations with transnational links.

The two sides examined the matter relating to mutual interaction between India and Russia in this area in the United Nations and other international forum. During the exchange of views on the need to strengthen the international legal basis for combating terrorism, special attention was paid to the progress in the UN on India's Draft Comprehensive Convention on International Terrorism and Russia's Draft International Convention Against Acts of Nuclear Terrorism.

The Group also discussed in detail the measures that could be taken for the suppression of the financing of terrorism, including through funds raised from illicit drug trafficking.

The Joint Working Group was in agreement that terrorism must be eliminated wherever and in whatever form it exists. To this end, the meeting also served to reiterate the resolve of both India and Russia to continue cooperating in the fight against international terrorism.

Second Meeting of the Joint Working Group on Combating International Terrorism

The second meeting of the India-Russia Joint Working Group on Combating International Terrorism was held on 8th April 2004 in New Delhi. Mrs. Meera Shankar, Additional Secretary (International Security) in the Ministry of External Affairs led the Indian delegation, while Mr. Anatoly E. Safonov, Deputy Foreign Minister of the Russian Federation led the Russian side. Both delegations included an inter-agency group of counter-terrorism and law enforcement officials. The two sides recalled that the India-Russia Joint Working Group on combating international terrorism was established following the MoU signed during the visit of the President of the Russian Federation to India in December 2002 and constitutes an important element of the strategic partnership between the two countries. They unequivocally condemned all acts, methods and practices of terrorism as criminal and unjustifiable and reiterated their determination to further strengthen their cooperation in combating it.

The two sides shared their assessment of law enforcement, legislative, financial and other measures taken against terrorists and their networks since the last meeting in September 2003.

International and regional developments were reviewed. The Indian side provided an assessment of terrorism challenges in the South Asian region, including cross-border terrorism affecting India while the Russian side gave their perspective on terrorism challenges confronting Russia.

The two sides reviewed multilateral efforts to counter terrorism and agreed that the institutional mechanisms set up by the UN Security Council in this regard should be further strengthened and made more effective. They shared their assessment of progress on various multilateral initiatives under consideration with specific emphasis on India's initiative for a Comprehensive Convention on International Terrorism and the Russian Initiative for a Convention on Suppression of Nuclear Terrorism. The two sides exchanged views on new challenges including the threat of proliferation of WMDs to terrorist organisations. They also discussed linkages between trafficking in narcotics and the financing of terrorism. Both sides agreed that continued cultivation of opium poppy and trafficking in narcotics pose a serious threat to security, political stability and economic development in many regions.

The Joint Working Group attached special importance to strengthening bilateral mechanisms. The two delegations agreed to deepen their counter-terrorism cooperation, in particular through:

- Exchange of information and sharing of experience in their fight against international terrorism;
- Strengthening cooperation in curbing trafficking in narcotics;
- Continuing cooperation to address the threat of terrorist financing;
- Extending support for the full and effective implementation of UN Security Council Resolution 1373 and the work of the Security Council's Counter Terrorism Committee; and
- Continuing consultations on the Comprehensive Convention on Terrorism and the Convention against Acts of Nuclear Terrorism with a view to their finalization.

Third Meeting of the Joint Working Group on Combating International Terrorism

The third meeting of the India-Russia Joint Working Group on Combating International Terrorism was held in Moscow during January 19-20, 2005. Ms. Meera Shankar, Additional Secretary in the Ministry of External Affairs, Government of India, led the Indian delegation. The Russian delegation was led by Mr. Anatoly Safonov, Special Representative of the President of the Russian Federation for international cooperation in fight against terrorism and transnational organized crime. Both the delegations included representatives of relevant ministries and agencies.

The Indian and Russian delegations reiterated that cooperation in combating international terrorism constitutes an important part of the strategic partnership between the two countries. They unequivocally condemned all acts, methods and practices of terrorism and reiterated their commitment to further strengthen cooperation in the field of counter-terrorism. The two sides reviewed the situation surrounding their respective nations and the security challenges that they face. They shared concern on cross-border terrorism and emphasized the importance of action by all States to deny safe haven for terrorist groups and their members.

The two sides exchanged views on the measures taken by both countries domestically as well as in the international arena to strengthen the war against terrorism. They also discussed linkages between terrorism and illegal narcotics as well as new challenges, such as the threat of proliferation of WMD to terrorists. The two sides reviewed the findings of the report submitted by the high-level panel appointed by the UN Secretary General insofar as it relates to terrorism and decided to work closely with each other in advancing negotiations currently underway in the UN on India's initiative for a Comprehensive Convention on International Terrorism and the Russian initiative for an International Convention for the Suppression of Acts of Nuclear Terrorism.

The Joint Working Group attached special importance to strengthening bilateral mechanisms and agreed to continue to exchange information and share experience in the fight against international terrorism. To this aim, participants will hold a targeted discussion on suppression of financing of terrorism in the near future.

Fourth Meeting of the Joint Working Group on Combating International Terrorism

The fourth meeting of the India-Russia Joint Working Group on Combating International Terrorism was held in New Delhi on October 24, 2006. Mr. K.C. Singh, Additional Secretary (International Organisations) and Counter-Terrorism Coordinator in the Ministry of External Affairs, Government of India led the Indian delegation. The Russian delegation was led by Mr. Anatoly Safonov, Special Representative of the President of the Russian Federation for International Cooperation in the Fight against Terrorism and Transnational Crime. Both delegations included representatives of relative ministries and agencies.

The negotiations were held in an atmosphere of trust, frankness and mutual understanding. The two sides shared concern on cross-border terrorism and emphasized the importance of actions by all States to deny safe haven to terrorists. They stressed the necessity to take more efficient measures on preventing the propagation of terrorism, including in the Cyberspace. The importance of broader dialogue on cultures and civilizations to counter divisiveness, on which terrorists thrive, was underlined. In this context the two sides called for unconditional implementation of the UNSC Resolution 1624 on fighting incitement to terrorism.

The Russian and Indian delegations reiterated that cooperation in combating terrorism constitutes an important part of strategic partnership between the two countries. They unequivocally condemned terrorism in all its forms and manifestations and reiterated their commitment to further strengthen counter-terrorism cooperation.

The two sides expressed their concern regarding the increase in the spread of narcotics in the region and agreed that this directly threatens the security of both countries. They stressed the need to consolidate bilateral mechanisms for sharing information in curbing drug trafficking. They shared concern over the financing of terrorism noting that its prevention is the key component in the counter-terrorism strategy and agreed to strengthen bilateral interaction in this field.

The two sides agreed to enhance cooperation in the international forum, especially in suppressing WMD terrorism. In this regard they noted that early entry into force of the International Convention on Suppression of Acts of Nuclear Terrorism (ICSANT) would facilitate this objective. They stressed the need to further improve the legal framework for the fight against terrorism. The two sides also urged the early finalization of the Comprehensive Convention on International Terrorism (CCIT) at the UN.

Issues of regional anti-terrorist cooperation were reviewed. It was noted that India-Russia partnership within the SCO and ASEAN Regional Forum must be enhanced, including in eliminating new threats and challenges in Central, South and South-East Asia.

The two sides also discussed the emerging threat to oil and gas installations from terrorists and agreed to exchange experiences to counter it, underscoring energy security as a vital component of national and international counter-terrorism strategies. Both sides agreed to hold the next session of the India-Russia Joint Working Group on Counter-Terrorism in 2007.

The domestic executive and legislative measures taken by India, Russia and other countries to put an end to this menace cannot be effective without a sustained and collective international counter terrorist effort. This is so, because, in most cases, terrorism affecting sovereign nations is being actively sponsored and promoted from outside. This is confirmed by the experience of India and Russia and of other countries, e.g. as in the events of September 11, 2001, terrorists attack in Moscow on the night of August 31, 2004 and subsequent terrorist occurrences. These acts of terror are yet another reminder to the world that joint efforts at a global level are necessary to combat the menace of international terrorism. An additional crucial element is that these external forces of international terrorism have their roots in our common neighborhood, which for many years has been built up as a centre and base for this activity, through deliberate state action of nurturing terrorist groups with the intention of using them as an instrument of policy. This activity is directed against other sovereign states, to secure blatantly unacceptable objectives including territorial claims, and also as part of a policy of confrontation and hostility. In this regard, there is no room for double standards, or a distinction between terrorism from one source and terrorism from other source, or between "good" and "bad" terrorists, made usually basis of self-serving calculations and narrow strategic consideration. The leaders of the two countries have repeatedly emphasized these points. The international community should not also equivocate about countries that profess to support the global coalition against terrorism, but are themselves active promoters of terrorism across their own borders.

All these dimensions of the problem of international terrorism are duly reflected in the historic UN Resolution 1373. They are also emphasized in the Moscow Declaration on Terrorism of November 2001 issued by the two leaders. Both documents set effective benchmarks for the world community's effort to root out international terrorism.

Strengthening the international legal basis of the counter-terrorism effort is also a very important requirement. Apart from the bilateral consultation and action on this issue, India and Russia are actively cooperating in the UN and other multilateral forum for this purpose. The present focus is on adoption of two key treaties, i.e. the Comprehensive Convention on International Terrorism proposed by India and the Convention on Suppression of Acts of Nuclear Terrorism, proposed by Russia.

Another crucial and relevant dimension on which India and Russia share a close concern is the dangerous linkage between terrorism and weapons of mass destruction. Besides, "non-state actors" we must reckon with the fact that a state that uses terrorism as a policy instrument, also possesses weapons of mass destruction and these weapons may fall in the hands of terrorist groups, who have been cultivated and established as a matter of policy on the soil of that very state. This concern is enhanced by the fact that the states in question are also unstable and very undemocratic and unaccountable. The international community needs to work out foolproof regime of collective measures and legally binding instruments that will prevent terrorists gaining access to WMD. Some states where there is a clear and present danger of a terrorist-WMD nexus are also collaborating in transfer of weapons and nuclear technology to other States, thus seriously imperiling international security and stability of other countries.

Open democratic societies, and in particular those pluralistic composition are the most vulnerable terrorist targets. The perpetrators of terror and their sponsors exploit their very commitment to freedom including media, civil liberties, and human rights. India and Russia have paid special attention to this aspect.

Much progress has been made in the fight against international terrorism. There is now a collectively higher level of international cooperation than ever before, and new international standards for international cooperation have been worked out and adopted. There is also a more concerted effort in tracking and disrupting flows of financial support to terrorists and dismantling their bases. However, much more co-operations need to be done for the global counter-terrorism effort to produce results.[22]

COOPERATION IN THE ENERGY SECTOR

Cooperation in this field is yet another area of great potential and mutual interest. Russia is among the world's leading producers and suppliers of energy. India is one of the largest and fastest growing markets for energy. Successful cooperation in the Sakhalin-I and Kudankulam Project underlines the synergy in this sector. Our exchanges could cover upstream and downstream projects and other aspects. India is ready to invest in the Russian energy sector on this basis, taking into account India's experience in overseas investment. During the recent high-level visit, it was agreed to set up a bilateral energy dialogue between the business sectors of the two countries.[23]

India and Russia interact and cooperate regularly in multilateral trade, economic and financial bodies. Both countries support strengthening of these institutions for facilitating progress towards a rational and equitable international economic order which is responsive to the needs of the world. India supports

Russia's early accession to the World Trade Organisation, not only in the spirit of our strategic partnership, but also in the firm belief that Russia's membership will provide more balance and strength to the WTO. India's convergent views on globalisation, provide great opportunities for accelerated economic growth, these also highlight disproportions, which need to be rectified. We also have an ongoing discussion on global environmental issues.

The high level Inter-Governmental Commission for Economic, Scientific and Technology Cooperation headed by a Russian Deputy PM and the Indian Foreign Minister, has played an important role in our economic relations, through regularly reviewing cooperation and providing coordination, regulation and guidance. Its work is supported by Working Groups and Sub Groups devoted to specific aspects of our wide ranging economic and S&T engagement. The ninth session was held in Moscow.

The two governments and business sectors have also devoted particular attention to proper facilitation of trade, i.e. a friendly visa regime, and expeditious immigration, customs, documentation and other procedures. Other facilitating measures such as warehousing are also being considered.

TOURISM

India and Russia mutually offer very attractive and cost-effective tourist destinations. A good beginning has been made in exploiting these possibilities. The current focus is on Goa, which has tremendous potential for tourism. Other destinations of interest in India include wildlife sanctuaries, adventure tourism sites, the Himalayan areas, the deserts of Rajasthan, etc. which are now being considered by the Russian tourists as great tourist attractions in India. We also look forward to Indian tourists visiting Russia. Measures for facilitation of travel are also being taken. Among them is the authorising additional flight of Aeroflot on a reciprocal basis (this move would also help business).[24]

COOPERATION IN PEACEFUL USES OF ATOMIC ENERGY

An Inter-Governmental Agreement (IGA) on the construction of a 2×1000 MW Nuclear Power Station in India was signed between the then Prime Minister Mr. Rajiv Gandhi and the then Soviet President Mr. Mikhail Gorbachev in November 1988.

The Supplement to the 1988 IGA was signed in June 1998. A bilateral MoU in the Peaceful Uses of Nuclear Energy was signed during the visit of President Putin to India in October 2000. An Inter-Governmental Memorandum on the Implementation of Kudankulam Project was signed during Prime Minister Atal Bihari Vajpayee's visit to Russia in November 2001.

India has one of the world's oldest programs of peaceful use of atomic energy—mainly for production of electricity, as well as in other areas, going back almost to the dawn of the atomic age. Starting from the first research and industrial reactors in the mid-50's India today has 22 power reactors with nine more being under construction, of which all except one are indigenous. The existing network of reactors is also largely indigenous. India has the infrastructure for R&D, engineering, construction and manpower to build its own nuclear power generation industry. However, our requirements are large and hence the demand for additional through involvement of foreign investors. This is the rationale of cooperation with Russia in the construction of the Kudankulam nuclear power plant. Nuclear power is environmentally the cleanest source of energy and considering India's very large energy requirements, and our shared commitment to reduce carbon dioxide emissions from the burning of fossil fuels, make it vital for us to increase the share of nuclear power in our total energy production.[25]

To overcome the shortage of hydrocarbon, India has sought expansion of the civil nuclear co-operation with Russia, besides talking about the possibility of using its expertise in the Iran-India gas pipeline project. Thanking Russia for its decision to supply 60 tonnes of uranium to Tarapur Atomic Plant Station (TAPS), on 18 March 2006 the Prime Minister, Dr. Manmohan Singh said, "I would like to convey our warm appreciation to the Russian Government for responding positively to meet the requirements for nuclear fuel supplies to Tarapur I and II. I am confident that both countries will utilize opportunities to expand our partnership in civil nuclear energy cooperation."

NORTH-SOUTH TRANSPORT CORRIDOR

An Inter-Governmental Agreement on International North-South Corridor between India, Iran and the Russian Federation was signed in St. Petersburg on 12 September 2000. All the three signatory states have ratified this, which came into force on 16 May 2002. The Agreement will facilitate easier movement of goods along the corridor connecting India through the sea route to Iran and then via the Caspian Sea to the Russian Federation and beyond. This new initiative is expected to reduce transit time and cost of transportation of goods to the Russian Federation and European countries. The Coordination Council held its second meeting in Tehran in April 2003. The third meeting of the Coordination Council was held in January 2005. Both sides recognize the potential of the corridor to boost bilateral trade by substantially reducing the transit time for movement of goods between the two countries.[26]

DEFENCE COOPERATION

On the defence front, India and Russia cooperation goes back to 40 years and substantial acquisitions have been made over this period. A major part of the inventories of the armed forces of India is of Russian origin. The tempo of acquisition has progressively increased as indicated in the large items such as T-90 tanks, frigates, Sukhoi aircraft, and the envisaged purchase of the aircraft carrier Admiral Gorshkov on which negotiations are being held. Average annual acquisitions over the last 10 years are estimated at US$ 1 billion. Prospective purchases will enhance this figure. A vitally important dimension of defence cooperation is that it is no longer a mere buyer/seller relationship, but involves to an increasing extent, technology transfer as well as joint design, development, production and marketing. The outstanding example of the application of this principle is the Brahmos Missile developed by an Indo-Russian joint venture. The missile which completed its fifth successful test confirming its all round capability, have been inducted into the Indian Navy, and the Indian Army and look forward to its being made part of the Russian Navy's arsenal. The same principle also applies to T-90 tanks and in particular, to Su-30 MKI aircraft, i.e. after initial purchase of a few aircraft, the rest will be manufactured in India under license. Based on increasing capabilities, India can also set up facilities for maintenance and servicing of a wide range of military equipment. All this will involve sharing of work and technology, which would, in the context of the growing relationship, benefit both sides. With the objective of increasing efficiency and intensifying our military technical cooperation, a ministerial level Inter-Governmental Commission for Military Technical Cooperation was set up in 2000, and has provided guidance and coordination.

Yet another important aspect of the defence cooperation is the joint naval exercise conducted in the Indian Ocean region on April 2003. The first in many years, this demonstrated the capability of the armed forces of the two countries, as well as the commonality of our strategic interests.[27]

Mr. Sergei Lavrov, Defence Minister of Russian Federation visited India on 1-2 December, 2004 to co-chair, along with Defence Minister of India, the fourth session of the Indo-Russian International Governmental Commission on Military-Technical Cooperation (IRIGC-MTC).[28]

The strategic partnership between India and Russia was further consolidated during the year through exchange of high level visits and signing of documents in the field of defence and military cooperation. Minister of Defence, A.K. Antony visited Moscow during 17-19 October 2007 to co-chair the 7th session of the India-Russia Inter-Governmental Cooperation on military technical cooperation. During the visit an agreement on the joint development and production of prospective multi-role fighter aircraft was signed. India and Russia conducted joint naval exercise in the Sea of Japan on 24-27 April 2007 and counter-terrorism exercise with the joint participation of the Indian Army, the Indian Air Force and the Russian Airborne Forces during 11-20 September 2007.

It is widely recognised that India and Russia defence cooperation meets not only India's security needs, but has also contributed to stability. Further, it has helped the economies of the two countries, including several defence production enterprises all over Russia.

SPACE COOPERATION

Peaceful exploitation and use of outer space is a traditionally important area of cooperation. Our first generation space satellites in the 70's and 80's were launched from a Soviet Cosmodrome. Among the high points for cooperation was the joint space flight in 1984. Since then, India has built very substantial launch capabilities of its own—as demonstrated in the Polar Satellite Launch Vehicle (PSLV), and Geo-stationary Satellite Launch Vehicle and (GSLV). The Russian cryogenic engines were an important element in the third stage of the latest and largest launch vehicle (GSLV). India also has developed state-of-the-art excellence in satellite technology and satellite applications, e.g. in meteorology, remote sensing and communication, etc. This is reflected in the large number of Indian satellites, which are now in orbit contributing directly to our economy and society. Taking these factors into account, we are ready to develop new areas of cooperation. Some of these are highlighted in the Inter-Agency Memorandum of Understanding on Space Cooperation signed during the recent Prime Ministerial visit. This is in the framework of the 1994 Inter-Governmental Agreement. The overall record on both countries trade relations, investment, S&T and other important functional cooperation is one of livening exchanges and forward movement. Recent experience indicates that this will be sustained, adding further substance to the relationship.[29]

CULTURAL COOPERATION

Over the decades, culture has emerged as one of the strongest areas for cooperation, with a special place in the relationship. This is not surprising, considering the long history of close cultural interaction. It is significant that the cultural contacts of earlier years has been sustained and enlarged in recent decades in the new framework. Deep-rooted mutual understanding and interest in our respective cultures strengthen this activity. Thus, Russian classics are widely popular in India and have been translated into all the major Indian languages. Russian theatres also regularly performed in India in translation and adaptation, Russian music, dance and film attract great attention among the Indian public. There is deep interest all over Russia in Indian music and dance, literature, language, philosophy, in special areas such as Yoga and Ayurveda. For example, there are presently 19 centres of Hindi teaching in Russia; nearly 1400 Russian students have been studying this and other Indian languages. There are an estimated 500 students of Indian dance and music, and similar numbers in other branches of Indian culture. Cultural centres in Kazan, Tver, Ufa, Vladivostok, Yakutsk, Samara, Izhevsk, Voronezh and Ekaterinberg set up with the cooperation of regional and republican authorities supplement this effort.

Similarly, Russian Cultural Centres in India are active in promoting Russian art and culture in its different manifestations among the Indian public. The Inter-Governmental Cultural Exchange Programme provides a strong framework for enabling regular and growing cultural exchanges. Cooperation in culture and the arts has been supplemented with exchanges in the academic world—especially in the humanities and social sciences. The Russian Academy of Sciences and corresponding institutes in India have a comprehensive programme in this regard. Exchanges have also been taking place on a regular basis between academics and scholars of the two countries in the shape of seminars, round-tables, conferences, etc. A Mahatma Gandhi Chair of Indian Philosophy was formally inaugurated in February 1999, at the Institute of Philosophy, Russian Academy of Sciences.

The October 2000 Declaration on Strategic Partnership also strengthened on promoting cultural cooperation, and people-to-people contact. India's most extensive cultural, academic, scientific, educational, sports and other exchanges are carried under the Cultural Exchange Programmes (CEP). Both countries also organised the "Days of Russian Culture"; the "Days of Indian Culture"; "Days of Moscow"; and the "Days of New Delhi" in their respective countries on alternate basis in the years 1995, 1996, 1998 and 1999 respectively.

Indian Prime Minister Atal Bihari Vajpayee's visit to Russia in November 2001, also witnessed signing of four agreements on promotion of education and research at four leading Russian institutes: Jawaharlal Nehru Cultural Centre and the Institute of Oriental Studies at the Russian Academy of Science; the St. Petersburg State University; the Kazan State University; and the Far Eastern National University in Vladivostok.

This review indicates that the two countries' relationship is substantial, contemporary and forward-looking. Dialogues and summit level of meetings have been more frequent than ever before. "This record has", as our Prime Minister puts it, "helped us evolve a comprehensive vision of Indo-Russian ties for the 21st century; reinforcing our conviction that the strategic partnership between India and Russia is a reliable factor in promoting peace, security and stability both in Asia and the world."[30]

RUSSIA SUPPORTS INDIA'S CANDIDATURE FOR THE UNITED NATIONS SECURITY COUNCIL (UNSC) PERMANENT SEAT

India is a founding member of the UN and is strongly committed to the ideals and principles of the UN Charter. India has consistently followed and implemented these commitments, participating actively in strengthening the UN in the political, cultural, social, economic and humanitarian spheres—for example, in the work of leading UN agencies: UNESCO, UNICEF, UNDP, UNIDO, etc. A key illustration is India's active involvement over the decades in UN peacekeeping activities in several countries, especially in difficult missions such as Korea, Indo-China, the Middle East, Yemen, Iran-Iraq, Kuwait, Namibia, Mozambique, Somalia, Rwanda, Angola, Sierra Leone, Cambodia, Lebanon, Ethiopia, Eritrea, Kosovo, Congo, etc. India has committed over 67,000 personnel to these missions. There are several other instances of India's active engagement in the UN. All this has created a basis for cooperation with Russia—which has historically played a leading role in the UN, as a member of the United Nations Security Council (UNSC) and because of its high standing in world affairs. There is regular consultation and cooperation between our countries, in the UN and other international forum on important international issues. The Joint Political Document reaffirms our shared conviction of the centrality of the UN and the need to strengthen it.

An important issue in this context is the UN reform. It is widely accepted by the international community that such reform is essential if UN is to be effective. This applies particularly to the UN agency principally entrusted with maintenance of peace and security—the UN Security Council. The crucial rationale for the UNSC reform is that while its deliberations and decisions overwhelmingly concern countries in the developing and non-aligned world, its permanent membership is predominantly from the developed world. Besides, the present structure of the Security Council was set about 60 years ago. While the world has changed considerably since then, this structure has remained essentially unchanged except for some adjustments in the number of non-permanent members. Taking this into account, it is clear that the UN reform would not be meaningful without restructuring of the UNSC, bringing into its ranks of permanent membership countries such as India that can make a responsible contribution to strengthening the UN. Russia has been supportive of India's candidature for permanent membership of the UN Security Council. The Russian leadership at the highest political level has repeatedly voiced such expressions of support.[31]

India and Russia have also found common ground on the vital subject of security. Both countries agree on the importance of maintaining Global Strategic Stability. India also supports all nuclear disarmament measures, which rectified the irrationalities of the Cold War. Both countries are also committed to non-proliferation: discussions on this subject relate to establishing rational and realistic instrumentalities. In this regard, as a responsible country, India firmly believes that there is a need to seriously address true proliferation concerns. India commits to working with the international community including Russia for this purpose. The strategic stability talks provide a forum for consultations on this subject. There is also need to reckon with the emergence of non-conventional military threats as a dominant element in the overall security picture. This places a special burden on territorially large pluralistic states such as India and Russia. These are essential elements of a sensible, cooperative security order, which must also take into account the specific security needs of countries, especially large ones dictated by their specific security environment. There are a number of other issues bearing on the crucial interests of both countries, which are part of the dialogue. Among these are the highly topical questions of Iraq and Afghanistan (and the related serious concern with international narco-trafficking). The convergence of the views on these subjects is adequately reflected in the Joint Declaration and the Joint Statement issued during the recent high-level visit. Also relevant to both countries' common interests is the Shanghai Cooperation Organisation (SCO). On this matter, India regularly keeps in touch with Russia as an important member of this organisation, as well as with other member countries. As a country with a serious regional and global interaction, India can make an effective contribution to strengthening SCO in its activities relating to economic cooperation as well as security.

India-Russia-China Trilateral Cooperation is a subject that finds frequent public mention. There are obvious common perceptions between the three countries on leading international issues and it is beneficial for all of us to develop these further through informal discussions, e.g. Foreign Minister level talks on the sidelines of the UNGA sessions—and through seminars held by research institutions. Both processes have been useful. An important factor relevant to this exercise is that India has an excellent relation with Russia, and its relations with China are also steadily improving.

EVALUATION

The relationships between the two countries—India and Russia—maintain a basic continuity from their accumulated inheritance stretching back to about 40 years after India got independence. India and Russia are democracies with a commitment to freedom of speech, assembly, press and a strong Parliament and judiciary. Besides these, both countries have large and rapidly growing economies with very substantial human and natural resources, augmented by new strengths generated through reforms and liberalization, emergence of active entrepreneurship and strong science and technology traditions and capabilities.

Both countries enjoyed a close strategic relationship during the major portion of the Cold War era. The peak point of this relationship was the conclusion of the Indo-Soviet Treaty of Peace, Friendship and Cooperation signed in 1971.

The India-Russia bilateral relation was comprehensive one, encompassing political, military, cultural and economic cooperation and exchanges. The proximity between the two countries led at times to India being labeled as a Soviet satellite. In international politics, there are contextual imperatives that prompt forging of strategic relationships or undoing them. This applies to the India-Russia bilateral relationship also.

With the end of the Cold War and the disintegration of the Soviet Union, the overall orientation of the Russian Foreign Policy was to establish a "Look West" policy with the United States as its top priority. Russian Foreign Ministry published the *Concept of Russian Federation's Foreign Policy*, in which Asia in general and South Asia in particular was accorded a low priority in Moscow's restructuring process. In the post-Cold War era Russia's initial foreign policy initiative towards West did not result in the kind of fruitful political and economic relations that it hoped for.

In relation to what was the cornerstone of the India-Russia strategic relationship, the both countries renewed the Treaty of Friendship and Cooperation, which was an extension of the previous Treaty of Peace, Friendship and Cooperation of 1971, that was extended for another twenty years in 1991. The time of Yeltsin, President of Russian Federation, was a period of exploratory interaction given the context of the Russian Federation engaged in structuring new global equations in the post-Soviet era. In addition, the bilateral relations between India and Russia improved as a result of eight agreements signed in December 1994 during the visit of Russian Prime Minister Victor Chernomyrdin to India. The agreements included military and technical cooperation from 1995 to 2000.

The purpose of detailing specifics of bilateral cooperation is to underline the fact that Indo-Russian relations are substantive. These joint orientations towards significant international issues have found expression in the Declaration on Strategic Partnership signed between the two countries in the year 2000 during President Putin's visit to India. The new Foreign Policy Concept, released by Russian Federation on July 10, 2000, stated that to develop friendly relations with the leading Asian states including India, Russia intended to strengthen its traditional partnership with India in every spheres, including international affairs. Following Russian President, Vladimir Putin's visit to India in October 2000 it led to intensification of political and economic cooperation. Both countries signed a Declaration on Strategic Partnership that spelt out in detail the long term nature of

Indo-Russian relations in all aspects of mutual cooperation, like political, defense, economic and trade, science and technological, and cultural spheres. During the second visit of President Putin to India in December 2002, both Russia and India signed a "Declaration on Further Consolidation of Strategic Partnership" between them creating a Joint Indo-Russian Working Group on dealing with global challenges. Furthermore, the assurances extended by the Putin administration during Prime Minister Vajpayee's visit to Russia in November 2003, are apart from the institutionalized and regular consultations between officials of the security councils of the two countries. Russia and India have a common approach on drafting an international anti-terrorism convention and also a comprehensive convention against acts of nuclear terrorism. And this commonality of approach has resulted in close and effective cooperation between them at the United Nations and its relevant specialized agencies.

President Putin visited India in December 2004 for the fifth India-Russia Annual Summit. During the visit, a number of agreements were signed, which include the Joint Declaration signed by President Putin and Prime Minister Dr. Manmohan Singh and four Inter-Governmental Agreements covering the areas of space, consular and regional cooperation. The Joint Declaration emphasizes the strategic partnership between the two countries and also notes the transformation in the global environment in the recent past and stresses the need for a new international architecture based on a multi-polar world. Both the countries also underlined the importance of fighting terrorism by the international community jointly without adopting double standards. The three agreements signed after summit level meetings with President Putin were: (i) Agreement on Reciprocal Protection of Intellectual Property Rights in the field of Military-Technical Cooperation; (ii) Agreement on Safeguard Technologies while implementing long-term cooperation in the area of joint development, operation and use of the GLONASS System for peaceful purposes; and (iii) Agreement between the Indian Space Research Organisation and the Federal Space Agency of the Russian Federation on Cooperation in the field of solar physics and solar-terrestrial relationships within the framework of the Coronas-Photon Project.

The heads of the state visit, regular inter-ministers and inter-parliamentary interactions provide an additional dimension to India-Russia political relations.

Economic and Science & Technology cooperation constitute a core element in India-Russia relations. A strong commitment from both sides to mutually beneficial cooperation in these sectors, and to translate this into effective bilateral trade, investment and S&T exchanges has been a basic dimension of India-Russia relations throughout the decades. This has also been one of the major factors ensuring stability and continuity of the relationship in the Soviet period and beyond. Particularly, India-Russia Science & Technology (S&T) Cooperation has indeed developed well especially through the Integrated Long-Term Programme (ILTP) initiated in 1987 and valid till 2010. This is one of the largest S&T international cooperation programmes, and has been operating actively and has enabled several exchange visits and joint research projects. It has been successfully executing for the past several years probably one of the largest mutual cooperation programmes in science and technology between any two countries.

Both countries share a common resolve to fight against terrorism. Both countries are faced with secessionist movements in their respective regions of Chechnya and Kashmir. Both countries project and equate these movements for self-determination with terrorism. Both countries have sought heightened cooperation in fighting the scourge of terrorism by working on a coordinated and synchronized approach to counter the policy of using terrorism to achieve political objectives. Bilateral cooperation in this field is conducted through discussions in the framework of bilateral Joint Working Groups on "Global Challenges" and "Combating International Terrorism". So far there are four meetings held on the Joint Working Group on Combating International Terrorism. Much progress has been made in the fight against international terrorism. However, much more co-operations need to be done for the global counter-terrorism effort to produce results.

Cooperation on energy sector is yet another area of great potential and mutual interest. Russia is among the world's leading producers and suppliers of energy. India is one of the largest and fastest growing markets for energy. Successful cooperation in the Sakhalin-I and Kudankulam project underlines the synergy in this sector. During the recent high-level visit, it was agreed to set up a bilateral energy dialogue between the business sectors of the two countries. In 1988 the then Prime Minister Mr. Rajiv Gandhi and then Soviet President Mr. Mikhail Gorbachev signed an Inter-Governmental Agreement (IGA) on the construction of a 2×1000 MW Nuclear Power Station in India. In order to overcome the shortage of hydrocarbon, India has sought expansion of the civil nuclear cooperation with Russia, besides talking about the possibility of using its expertise in the Iran-India gas pipeline project.

There are also possibilities of structuring equations between India, Russia and Iran. In order to strengthen regional security arrangements and augment economic cooperation, by building up infrastructures for such cooperation in terms of roads and communications. Negotiations on specific projects are in the pipeline for the said cooperation.

On the defense relations, India-Russia cooperation goes back to 40 years and substantial acquisitions have been made over this period. There has been a qualitative change in the terms of Indo-Russian military and technical cooperation. During the period of the Soviet Union this cooperation was concretized by a cash and carry procedure catalyzed through concession credit arrangements. These days military and technological cooperation is rooted in joint long-term programs of research and development and joint production projects between the military and industrial organisations of the two countries. Transfer of technologies and licenses for the production of sophisticated military and technical equipment like T-90 (Main Battle Tank) and the SU 30 MK-I fighters are examples of this phenomenon of transition. It is widely recognized that India and Russia defense cooperation meets not only India's security needs, but has also contributed to stability. Further, it has helped the economies of the two countries, including several defense production enterprises all over Russia.

Peaceful exploitation and use of outer Space is a traditionally important area of cooperation. Both countries organised the

"Days of Russian Culture"; the "Days of Indian Culture"; "Days of Moscow"; and the "Days of New Delhi" in their respective countries on alternate basis in the years 1995, 1996, 1998, and 1999 respectively. The October 2000 Declaration on Strategic Partnership also strengthened on promoting cultural cooperation, and people-to-people contact. India's most extensive cultural, academic, scientific, educational, sports and other exchanges are carried under the Cultural Exchange Programmes (CEP). Culture has emerged as one of the strongest areas for cooperation, with a special place in India and Russia bilateral relations.

There are several instances of India's active engagement in the UN peacekeeping activities in many countries, especially in difficult missions such as Korea, Indo-China, the Middle East, Yemen, Iran-Iraq, Kuwait, Namibia, Mozambique, Somalia, Rwanda, Angola, Sierra Leone, Cambodia, Lebanon, Ethiopia, Eritrea, Kosovo, Congo, etc. All this has created a basis for cooperation with Russia—which has historically played a leading role in the UN, as a member of the United Nations Security Council (UNSC) and because of its high standing in world affairs. Russia has been supportive of the India's candidature for permanent membership of the UN Security Council.

The two countries have managed the transition from economic and technological interaction being conducted under governmental arrangements to the conduct of these relations by private sectors of both countries. A wide range of inter-state and inter-departmental agreements is being implemented and monitored by a Russia-India inter-governmental commission on trade, economics, and scientific and technological cooperation.

Regarding India-Russia relation in trade, Russian Ambassador to India, Vyacheslav I. Trubnikov has expressed disappointment with the current level of trade and investment with India and identified "infrastructure constraints" as the chief obstacle in realizing the full potential of economic relations between the two countries. "Our potential has not yet been fully realized," the Russian envoy said at a seminar on 7 October 2006 on the topic "Russian-Indian Economic Relations: Problems and Prospects". The Russian envoy identified "several natural and artificial obstacles" hampering the expansion of commercial opportunities. Trubnikov also elaborated on the importance of

Russia's fast accession to the WTO in facilitating better and broader access of Indian goods to the Russian markets. "India and Russia have successfully completed the bilateral negotiations with India regarding Russia's joining the WTO, but the pace of negotiations with other countries has been slow," he said.

The overall record on both countries trade relations, investment, S&T and other important functional cooperation is one of the lively exchanges and forward movement.

Though Russia may have lost its position as a super power in Cold War equations, it is still a big power in terms of the ingredients of such power. It is territorially large; it's strategically adjacent to Central Asia, China and Iran—an area of political, security and economic interests to India. It is also still one of the most important military powers in the world after the United States of America. Most importantly, Russia gives a higher priority to India in its foreign policy and strategic calculations than America or other countries of the world in spite of the latter acknowledging India's importance incrementally. Realism requires that Russia remains a country of top priority in India's external relations. The compatibility in the national interests of both nations and their commonly shared perceptions in respect of various issues give rise to the expectation and hope that Indo-Russia relations are destined to develop further, more and more matured, warm and friendly in the years to come.

NOTES

1. "India-Russia Relations", Address of Ambassador to the Students of the Faculty of Philosophy, Moscow State University, 15 May 2004, Moscow. www.indianembassy.rec/does htm/en 16 30 t001. htm
2. N. Jayapalan, *Foreign Policy of India*, Altantic Publishers and Distributors (P) Ltd., New Delhi (2001), p. 167.
3. Sayed Adnan Ali Shah, "Indo-Russia Relations: Prospects in the 21st Century". www.issi.org.pk/journal/2003-file/no 4/article/3a.htm-75k
4. "Bilateral Relations between India and the Russian Federation" www.indianembassy.ru/does htm/ru ru01 01 t001.htm
5. *Ibid.*, No. 1.
6. *Annual Report 2004-2005*, Ministry of External Affairs, p. 48.
7. *Annual Report 2005-2006*, Ministry of External Affairs, pp. 39-40.

8. Prime Minister Dr. Manmohan Singh's Telephone Conversation with President Putin (Press Release) on 5 March 2006. www.meaindia.nic.in/newswire/2006/01 06.htm 9k.
9. Visit of Prime Minister of Russian Federation Mr. Mikhail Fradkov to India, (Press Release) March 17, 2006, New Delhi. www.indiaembassy.ru/docs thm
10. *Ibid.*, No. 1, pp. 9-14.
11. Summary of decisions taken at the 10th session of the Indo-Russian Inter-Governmental Commission on Trade, Economic, Scientific, Technological and Cultural Cooperation (18-19 November, 2004) at New Delhi, PIB (Press Release).
12. Visit of Economic Development and Trade Minister of Russia Mr. German Grief to India, 4-6 February 2006 (Press Release). www.indianembassy.rus/doc htm
13. *Ibid.*, No. 12.
14. Finance Minister P. Chidambaram visits to Russia on February 1, 2006, Moscow (Press Release). www.Indianembassy.rus/docs.
15. *Ibid.*, no. 1, p. 14.
16. "India-Russia Relations: Indo-Russia S&T Cooperation." www.indianembassy.ru/docs htm/en/en 16 03 t001.htm
17. Joint Statement, President Putin's Visit to India in October 2000 www.indianembassy.ru/docs htm
18. Joint Statement, Prime Minister A.B. Vajpaypee's Visit to Russia in November 2001. www.indianembassy.ru/docs htm
19. *Ibid.*, no. 16, p. 7.
20. "India, Russia for Increased Cooperation to Fight Against Terrorism," 29 November, 2002. www.whartonglobal.com/india/press/mi.pdf
21. *Ibid.*, no. 16, p. 8.
22. Joint Working Group on Combating International Terrorism (Press Release 2003, 2004, 2005, 2006). www.indianembassy.ru/doc
23. *Ibid.*, no. 16, p. 8.
24. *Ibid.*, no. 1, p. 15.
25. *Ibid.*, no. 1, p. 16.
26. *Ibid.*, no. 16, p. 15.
27. *Ibid.*, no. 1, p. 17.
28. *Ibid.*, no. 6, p. 48.
29. *Ibid.*, no. 1, p. 16.
30. *Ibid.*, no. 1, p. 17.
31. *Ibid.*, no. 4, p. 9.

4

India-China Bilateral Relations

BACKGROUND

India has consistently viewed bilateral relations with China in a positive spirit. India seeks friendly, cooperative, good-neighbourly and mutually beneficial relations with China on the basis of the five principles of peaceful coexistence, mutual sensitivity to each other's concerns and equality. India remains committed to the process of dialogue to resolve outstanding differences and to build a strategic and cooperative partnership for peace and prosperity.

India and China are two of the world's oldest civilizations with a history of close contacts. Buddhism arrived in China from India. Two Indian Buddhist monks—Kasyapa Matanga and Dharmaratna arrived in China in 65 A.D. The golden period of Buddhist influence in China lasted 8 centuries from the 5th to 12th century A.D. Tang dynasty in China played an important role in promotion of Buddhism. Among the well-known Chinese scholars who visited India were Fa Hien (early part of 5th Century A.D.), Xuan Zang (633 to 643 A.D.) and Yi Qing (673- 695 A.D.). However, the first travellers from China to India were not Buddhist scholars. They were traders who came from south-western China to northern India. The Chinese travellers introduced silk, vermillion and items made of Chinese bamboo. General Zheng He from the Ming dynasty arrived in Cochin/ Calicut in the early 15th Century A.D. Chinese brought porcelain, silk, iron, copperware, gold and silver for trade.

Nationalist movements in the two countries against colonial oppressors led to renewed contacts in the late 18th/early 19th century. Rabindranath Tagore visited China in 1924. A 5-member Indian medical mission visited North China during the anti-Japanese war in late 1930s. Contribution of one of the doctors Dr. Dwarkanath Shantaram Kotnis, who died in China in December 1942, is still remembered by the Chinese.

POLITICAL RELATIONS

India extended official recognition to the People's Republic of China (PRC) on December 30, 1949. India was the second among the non-socialist countries (after Burma) to recognise PRC. India and China established diplomatic relations on April 1, 1950. In 1954 India and China evolved the Panchsheel (Five Principles of Peaceful Coexistence). In the same year Premier Zhou Enlai visited India in June and Prime Minister Nehru visited China in October. The circumstances leading to the war of 1962 led to a serious setback in bilateral relations. India and China restored ambassadorial relations in 1976.

In February 1979, the External Affairs Minister A.B. Vajpayee paid a visit to China, which marked the resumption of political level exchanges with China, thus defreezing the relationship. At his invitation, the Chinese Foreign Minister Huang Hua visited India in June 1981. Following this exchange of visits between the two Foreign Ministers, India and China agreed to Official Level Talks on the boundary question and all other aspects of India-China relations. Eight rounds of Official Level Talks were conducted between 1981 and 1987. The general trend since 1979 has been of steadily improving relations.

The visit of Prime Minister Rajiv Gandhi to China in December 1988 marked the resumption of political dialogue at the highest level. Both sides agreed to develop and expand bilateral relations in all fields, while continuing to address the outstanding differences. It was also agreed to establish a Joint Working Group (JWG) on the boundary question to seek a fair, reasonable and mutually acceptable solution. Besides the JWG (on the border issue) and the Joint Economic Group (JEG) (on economic and commercial issues), it was agreed to encourage bilateral exchanges in science and technology, outer space, mining, audit, defence, personnel and culture.

Premier Li Peng visited India in December 1991. Prime Minister Narasimha Rao visited China in September 1993 during which the Agreement on the Maintenance of Peace and Tranquillity along the Line of Actual Control (LAC) in the India-China Border Area was signed and the India-China Expert Group of Diplomatic and Military Officers to assist the JWG was set up. This Agreement provides for both sides to respect the status quo on the border, clarify the LAC where there are doubts and undertake Confidence Building Measures (CBMs).

President R. Venkataraman paid a state visit to China in May 1992 and Vice President K.R. Narayanan in October 1994. From the Chinese side, CPPCC Chairman Li Ruihuan visited India in December 1993 and NPC Chairman Qiao Shi in November 1995. President Jiang Zemin's state visit to India in November 1996 was the first by a Chinese Head of State. During his visit, the two countries agreed to work towards a constructive and cooperative relationship while continuing to address outstanding differences. Four agreements were signed, of which the most important was one on CBMs in the Military Field along the LAC in the India-China Border Areas. A prominent feature of the CBM Agreement is the adoption of concrete measures between the two militaries to enhance exchanges and promote cooperation and trust. The two countries agreed to exchange maps indicating their respective perceptions of the entire alignment of the LAC.

Bilateral relations suffered a setback after the India's nuclear tests in May 1998, but soon, in early 1999, both countries made efforts to resume official level dialogue, with both Foreign Ministries holding talks in February 1999. The then External Affairs Minister Jaswant Singh visited China in June 1999. Both sides reiterated that neither country is a threat to the other. High-level exchanges were renewed with the visit of President K.R. Narayanan in May-June 2000. This was the second visit to China by an Indian Head of State in the last 50 years and marked a return to normalcy in bilateral relations.

Senior Chinese leader and Chairman of the Standing Committee of the National People's Congress (NPC) Li Peng visited India in January 2001 at the joint invitation of Chairman,

Rajya Sabha and Speaker, Lok Sabha. This was the highest-level visit from China since the visit of President Jiang Zemin in 1996. During the visit, the formation of an India-China Parliamentary Friendship Group was announced.

By the time Premier Zhu Rongji visited India in January 2002, there was a new vigour in the bilateral relations, especially in the economic area. This was the first visit by a Chinese Premier in ten years, since Premier Li Peng came to India in December 1991. MoUs and agreements on cooperation in tourism, provision of hydrological data by China to India, peaceful uses of outer space, science & technology and phyto-sanitary measures were signed during the visit. The visit of then External Affairs Minister Jaswant Singh to China in March-April 2002 led to further enhancement of mutual understanding and trust. He met Premier Zhu Rongji and a dialogue architecture instituting regular meetings at various levels was agreed to during the visit. Mr. Jia Qinglin, Chairman of National Committee of Chinese People's Political Consultative Conference paid an official visit to India in November 2003.[1]

Prime Minister A.B. Vajpayee visited China in June 2003. A Joint Declaration on Principles for Relations and Comprehensive Cooperation and ten agreements were signed. The Joint Declaration provides a roa dmap, based on shared perspectives between India and China, in an extensive range of areas. The mechanism of Special Representatives was established to explore from the political perspective of the overall bilateral relationship the framework of a boundary settlement. India and China concluded a border trade protocol to add a border trade point between Sikkim and the Tibet Autonomous Region.[2]

Chinese Premier Wen Jiabao visited India in April 2005. During the visit, the two Prime Ministers signed a Joint Statement, which establishes a strategic cooperative partnership for peace and prosperity between the two countries. Eleven other agreements were signed. The agreement on political parameters and guiding principles for the India-China boundary question represents the successful conclusion of the first phase of the work of the Special Representatives and lays down the parameters and principles for their future discussions to explore the political settlement of the boundary question. A protocol on Confidence Building Measures was also concluded which further underpins the maintenance of peace and tranquility along the Line of Actual Control in the India-China border areas.[3]

Apart from the high-level exchanges, the bilateral dialogue mechanism provides greater depth to India-China bilateral relations and a systemic means of facilitating enhancement and implementation of existing initiatives and identifying newer ones. The various mechanisms evolved and instituted between India and China include Strategic Dialogue, Joint Working Group (JWG), Expert Group (EG) dealing with the boundary issues, meeting of Special Representatives (SR), Foreign Office Consultations, Security Dialogue, Policy Planning Dialogue, and the Dialogue on Counter-Terrorism.

TRADE RELATIONS

Sino-India trade initiated in 1951. In 1954, the governments of the two nations endorsed a trade agreement, which is renewed in August 1984. Seven yearly trading agreements have been signed in sequence since 1986. The bilateral trade between China and India has been developing in a rapid pace with trade volume increasing continuously and variety of exchanging commodity gradually expanding. Since 1990, interactions between the economic and trade circles of China and India have kept expanding, and the bilateral trade volume has grown even faster. In 1991, the total trade volume between China and India registered only US$ 265 million, whereas in 1999 it rose to US$ 1,988 million. In 2000, it shot up to US$ 2,910 million, an increase of 46.4 per cent of the previous year, of which China's exports amounted to US$ 1560 million and imports US$ 1350 million, an increase of 34.3 per cent and 63.9 per cent respectively. India has become China's largest trading partner in South Asia.

Bilateral Economic Cooperation

Meanwhile project-contracting and mutual investment have already started and the level of the bilateral cooperation is continuously upgrading. Now, there are Indian companies investing in pharmaceutical area in China and some software enterprises setting up liaisons too. Konka Electrics (India) Ltd., coming into existence in December 1998, has carried out its business of assembling of TV SKD (system knock down). What's more, a number of Chinese companies have enjoyed a reciprocal cooperation with Indian enterprises in the field of power.

Major Export and Import Commodities

The principal exports from China to India include raw silk, beans, sheet and paper pulp, rosin, coke, medical product, light industry product, textile product, chemical industry product, food, metal product, machinery facility, etc. The principal imports from India include iron ore sand, chrome ore, gem, steel, leather, plant oil, southern medicine, raw material for chemical industry, etc.

Sino-Indian Commercial Exchanges

In celebration of the 50th anniversary of the establishment of the diplomatic relations between China and India, China Engineering and Commodities Fair, sponsored by the Ministry of Foreign Trade and Economic Cooperation (MOFTEC) of China, was held from 6th to 9th December 2000 in New Delhi. The fair was a comprehensive exposition covering machinery, power, iron & steel, chemical engineering, telecom, and electronics, etc. It had an exhibition area of over 4,600 sq. m., with over 130 exhibitors. Industrialists and entrepreneurs from the two countries had extensive interactions through various presentations, negotiations and seminars.

Mr. Li Peng, Chairman of the Standing Committee of the National People's Congress of China, paid a formal friendly visit to India from 9th to 17th January 2001. During his visit in India he met a Confederation of Indian Industries (CII) team consisting of leading Indian entrepreneurs, and visited Huawei Technologies R&D center and Infosys, both located in the International Tech Park, Bangalore.

Associated Chambers of Commerce and Industry of India (ASSOCHAM) had sent a business delegation to China in April 2001. The Indian businessmen met the China Council for Promotion of International Trade (CCPIT) and have *vis-à-vis* interactions with their Chinese counterparts.

China's Economic Developments and Investment Policies

The last twenty years and more of China's reform and opening-up have witnessed a sustained and speedy economic development, growing national strength and remarkable improvement in people's living standards. In 1998-99 China ranked the seventh in terms of overall economic volume and the ninth in terms of foreign trade in the world. China is now the largest producer of agricultural and industrial products such as coal, steel, grain, cotton, rapeseeds, meat, cement, and TV sets, and the second largest producer in power generation. The Chinese government has taken series of measures to spur the economy, such as boosting the domestic demand, adopting positive financial policy and steady monetary policy. As a result, China's economy has withstood the adverse impacts of the Asian financial crisis, and enjoyed a sustained, rapid and healthy development. Its economic growth rate reached 7.1 per cent in 1999. In 2000, China's national economy and fiscal revenue mounted up to a new scale. Foreign trade witnessed a considerable rise; domestic market turned brisk; banking performance became smooth going, and international payments saw favorable balance. In 2000 China's GDP exceeded US$ 1,000 billion, an increase of 8.0 per cent over 1999. Its total volume of exports and imports in 2000 totaled US$ 474.3 billion, 31.5 per cent higher than 1999. China's foreign exchange reserves reached US$ 165.6 billion at the end of 2000, ranking the second in the world. In 2003 China carried out its "Tenth Five-Year Plan of Economic & Social Development". China will continue restructuring its economy, deepening economic system reforms, and widening its opening-up to the outside world.

As an important component of China's basic national policy of reform and opening-up, absorbing foreign investment plays an irreplaceable role in China's sustained, rapid and healthy economic development. In 2000, 22,532 new overseas-funded enterprises were approved, with contractual overseas investment of US$ 64.188 billion and actual inflow of US$ 42.09 billion. The end of 2000 had approved over 360,000 overseas-funded enterprises in total approved, with an overall overseas investment by contract registering US$ 678.25 billion and actual inflow of US$ 379.942 billion. Nearly 400 out of the top 500 multinational corporations in the world have started their business in China. Meanwhile, following the ever-growing tendency of economic globalization, China encourages big companies to invest abroad also. By the end of 2000, there have been over 6000 foreign-based Chinese companies with an overall investment volume of more than US$ 10 billion.

With the acceleration of China's paces of entering the WTO, China's opening-up to the outside world will come up to a new phase. This phase indicates a shift of opening-up from limited sphere and limited fields, to all dimensions; a shift from policy-driven opening-up based on experiments, to foreseeable opening-up within the legal framework, i.e. in accordance with the timetable undertaken to keep; and a shift from unilateral opening-up, to two-way opening-up between China and other WTO members.

The acceleration of China's reforms, opening-up and its modernization drive have provided foreign investors with good business opportunities. China's pursuance of its policy of boosting domestic demand and acceleration of strategic economic restructuring offers a wide scope for overseas investment in the fields of agriculture, water conservation, energy, transportation, communication, raw material, environmental protection and high-tech. China is now embarking on the strategy of developing its west. The industrial infrastructure, technical strength, rich natural and human resources existing in the central and western regions of China will provide attractive conditions for overseas investors to participate in the development of these regions.[4]

By the end of 2003, bilateral trade had increased to US$ 7.6 billion and it crossed the 10 billion mark for the first time in 2004 to record US$ 13.6 billion in two-way trade. The increase in trade volume has not been uniform over the years. Since 2000, bilateral trade has shown substantial increase in both in terms of total volume and rate of growth.

Chinese investment in India, for the year 2007, stands at US$ 16 million and cumulative investment till September 2007 is US$ 20.33 million. According to the Chinese Ministry of Commerce, the total amount of FDI from India to China in the form of project during 2007 is US$ 34 million. The cumulative FDI from India into China till November 2007 was US$ 200 million.

In 2007, bilateral trade between India and China totalled US$ 38.69 billion as per Chinese figures which is an increase of 54.42 per cent year-on-year.

Table 4.1: Growth Trends in India-China Bilateral Trade for the Period 1993-2007

(US$ million)

Year	Indian Imports	Indian Exports	Trade Balance	Trade Volume
1993	259.16	416.57	+157.41	675.73
Growth	63.5%	131.3%		99.6%
1994	573.00	322.00	-251.00	894.00
Growth	121%	-22.75%		32%
1995	765.00	398.00	-367.00	1,162.00
Growth	34%	24%		29,9%
1996	689.54	719.16	+29.62	1,406.00
Growth	-10.1%	80.9%		20.9%
1997	933.06	897.26	-35.8	1,830.32
Growth	36%	24.7%		30.2%
1998	1,016.59	905.70	-110.89	1,922.30
Growth	8.9%	0.9%		5%
1999	1.161.890	825.792	-336.098	1,987.68
Growth	14.3%	-8,8%		3.4%
2000	1.569.465	1350.414	-219.051	2,914.223
Growth	34.3%	63.9 %		46.6%
2001	1.896.268	1,699.966	-196.302	3,596,234
Growth	21.5%	25.6%		23.4%
2002	2.671.728	2274.180	-397.548	4,945.908
Growth	40.8%	33.7%		37.5%
2003	3.344.993	4252.802	+907.81	7,597.79
Growth	25.1%	86.9%		53.6%
2004	5.925.58	7672.51	+1746.94	13,598,09
Growth	77.15%	80.41%		78.99%
2005	8.936.91	9780.083	+843.17	18717
Growth	50.82%	27,47%		37.64%
2006	14.558.04	10469.18	-4118.86	25,057.22
Growth	+63.23%	+7.05%		+33.87%
2007	24.036.440	14658.791	-9377.649	38,695.231
Growth	+64.77%	+40.02%		+54.42%

Source: General Administration of Customs of the People's Republic of China.

In the year 2006, India-China bilateral trade grew by 33.87 per cent from corresponding period in 2005 to reach US$ 25.05 billion. As per statistics released by China's General Administration of Customs, India's exports to China during this period recorded a total value of US$ 10.46 billion increasing by 7.05 per cent while India's imports from China reached US$ 14.58 billion increasing by 63.23 per cent over the year 2005.

Following are the main trends in bilateral trade during the year 2006:

- Total bilateral trade rose by 38.69 per cent to US$ 25.05 billion. This is lower than the 79 per cent growth rate recorded in 2006.
- Exports from India reached US$ 14.65 billion, representing a year-on-year growth of 40.02 per cent which is almost 53 percentage points lower than that in 2006. This makes India the 15th largest exporter to China in this period with a 1.53 per cent share in the country's total imports increasing from 1.32 per cent in 2006.
- Imports from China grew by 64.77 per cent to reach US$ 24.03 billion. During this period, India maintained its position as China's 10th biggest export destination accounting for 1.97 per cent of China's export volume as compared to 1.51 per cent during the year 2006.
- India's trade surplus has contracted to US$ 800 million which turned into a trade deficit of US$ 4.11 billion in 2004.

Table 4.2: Bilateral Trade in 2007

(US$ million)

Month/Year	Indian Exports	Indian Imports	Total	Trade Balance for India
Jan-Dec 2007	14658.791	24036.440	38695.231	-9377.649
Jan-Dec 2006	10469.185	14588.047	25057.232	-4118.862
% Growth	+40.02%	+64.77%	+54.42%	

Source: General Administration of Customs, PRC.

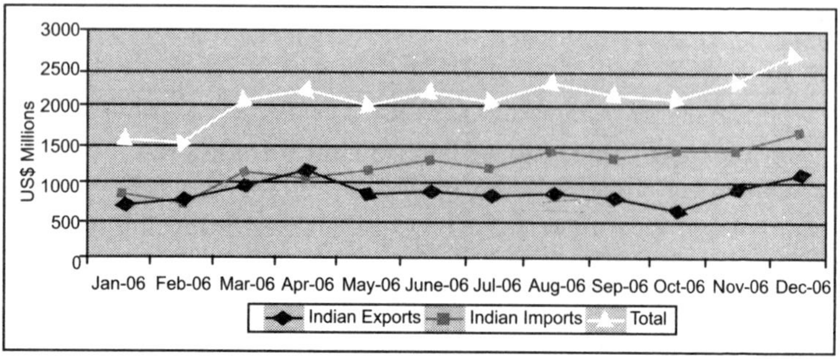

Figure 4.1: India-China Bilateral Monthly Trade

Monthly trade volume in December 2006 reached to an all-time monthly high of US$ 2.66 billion from US$ 1.63 billion in November largely riding on a month-to-month increase in imports from China. Imports from China recorded its highest value of the year in December at US$ 924.12 million as compared to US$ 815.12 million in preceding month. Indian exports to China in December dipped slightly to US$ 813.5 million from US$ 822.86 million in November. India therefore recorded a monthly trade deficit of US$ 110.6 million.

Indian Exports

Table 4.3: India's Top 15 Exports to China (2006 & 2007)

HS	Description	Value Million US$		% Share		% Change
		2006	2007	2006	2007	2007-2006
	India	10469.18529	14658.79094	1.32	1.53	40.02
26	Ores, Slag, Ash	5263.354967	8834.536477	50.28	60.3	67.85
52	Cotton+Yarn, Fabric	905.215689	1015.863418	8.65	6.93	12.22
29	Organic Chemicals	599.853265	759.921549	5.73	5.18	26.68
74	Copper+Articles Thereof	354.84663	678.233504	3.39	4.63	91.13
71	Precious Stones, Metals	287.102018	384.646249	2.74	2.62	33.98
72	Iron And Steel	341.171256	364.748071	3.26	2.49	6.91
39	Plastic	490.489853	328.965385	4.69	2.24	-32.93
84	Machinery	429.490621	303.642152	4.1	2.07	-29.3
25	Salt; Sulfur; Earth, Stone	239.214943	269.09036	2.29	1.84	12.49
28	Inorg Chem; Rare Earth	315.915188	249.487488	3.02	1.7	-21.03
85	Electrical Machinery	143.807	196.827102	1.37	1.34	36.87
41	Hides And Skins	151.851946	196.566031	1.45	1.34	29.45
67	Artif Flowers, Feathers	74.962224	119.726206	0.72	0.82	59.72
32	Tanning, Dye, Paint, Putty	63.150516	86.371128	0.6	0.59	36.77
03	Fish And Seafood	90.86974	86.102701	0.87	0.59	-5.25

Source: China Customs Statistics.

In January-December 2005, India exported 68.58 million tons of iron ore to China valued at US$ 5.2 billion. Year-on-year growth rate of iron ore in value and volume terms was 29 per cent and 37 per cent respectively. Share of iron ore in Indian exports was 53.5 per cent. In the month of December, iron ore exports amounted to 5.75 million tons valued at US$ 389.3 million. Australia remains China's top source for iron ore supplying 112 million tons worth US$ 6.1 billion in 2005. Overall, China imported 275 million tons of iron ore in 2005 as compared to 208 million tons in 2004.

Economic ties between India and China are rapidly emerging as one of the most important bilateral relationships in the world. Trade between the two countries has grown very robustly. Each country's aggregate international trade is expanding by 23-24 per cent annually. In comparison, India-China trade grew at a 50 per cent rate during 2002-2006. It further increased 54 per cent in 2007 and reached US$ 37 billion. It is expected to increase the bilateral trade target from US$ 40 billion by 2010 to US$ 60 billion.

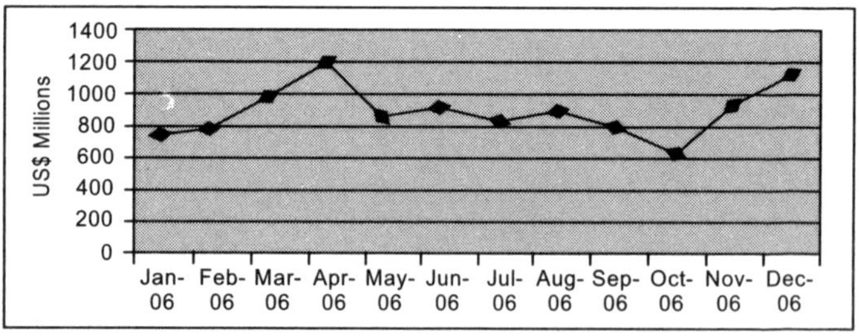

Figure 4.2: Indian Exports to China in 2006

Indian Imports

Table 4.4: India's Top 15 Imports from China in (2006 & 2007)

HS	Description	Value in US$ Millions 2006	2007	% Share 2006	2007	% Change 07/06
	India	**14588.0473**	**24036.44036**	**1.51**	**1.97**	**64.77**
85	Electrical Machinery	3640.8644	7009.997017	24.96	29.2	92.54
84	Machinery	2722.16069	4232.503634	18.66	17.6	55.48
29	Organic Chemicals	1711.31993	2409.835098	11.73	10	40.82
72	Iron And Steel	612.395389	1462.060601	4.2	6.08	138.74
73	Iron/Steel Products	715.68819	1198.747698	4.91	4.99	67.5
31	Fertilizers	85.351058	743.870239	0.59	3.1	771.54
39	Plastic	312.837589	609.708041	2.14	2.54	94.9
59	Impregnated Text Fabrics	338.738643	441.025128	2.32	1.84	30.2
50	Silk; Silk Yarn, Fabric	354.430356	414.282982	2.43	1.72	16.89
87	Vehicles, Not Railway	222.951936	374.908478	1.53	1.56	68.16
28	Inorg Chem; Rare Earth	227.851178	362.216377	1.56	1.51	58.97
54	Manmade Filament	239.615308	325.091031	1.64	1.35	35.67
90	Optic, Nt 8544; Medical Instruments	222.497988	320.875882	1.53	1.34	44.22
27	Mineral Fuel, Oil etc	525.040898	305.005278	3.6	1.27	-41.91
76	Aluminium	120.757846	279.481528	0.83	1.16	131.44

Source: China Customs Statistics.

Chinese exports to India have picked up in the year 2007 across all major segments. Composition of exports has remained more or less the same with only one new product segment breaking into the top 15, namely tanning and dye, paints, etc.

Fast-growing export segments from China include machinery, iron and steel, impregnated text fabrics, iron/steel products, plastic, and medical/surgical instruments. Chinese exports of silver and pearls to India have also shown rapid growth during the year to reach US$ 68.1 million and US$ 13.5 million respectively.

Indian Imports from China in 2005 (US$ Millions)

Feb-05	Mar-05	Apr-05	May-05	Jun-05	Jul-05	Aug-05	Sep-05	Oct-05	Nov-05	Dec-05
501.23	632.22	670.42	677.39	790.73	794.25	833.54	851.98	840.32	815.12	924.12

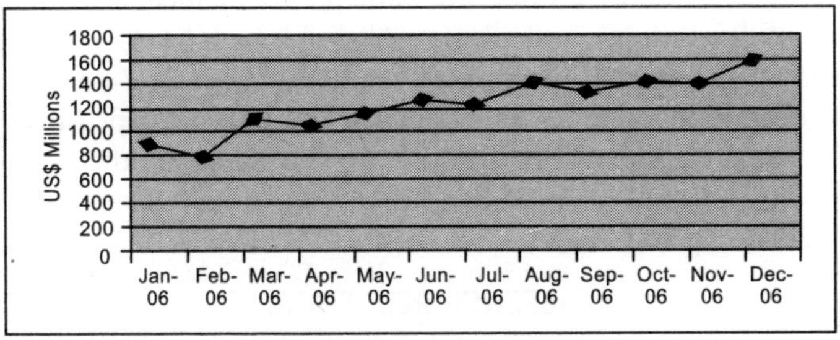

Figure 4.3: Indian Imports from China in 2006

China's Trade with The World

Table 4.5: China's Top Trading Partners for Jan-Dec 2006

(US$ million)

China's Exports					China's Imports				
Rank	Country	Value 2006	%Share 2006	% Change 06/05	Rank	Country	2006	%Share 2005	% Change 06/05
0	–World–	969323.62	100	27.15	0	-World-	791793.90	100	19.93
1	United States	203516.39	21	24.9	1	Japan	1 15810.93	14.63	15.27
2	Hong Kong	155434.52	16.04	24.84	2	Korea, South	89818.28	11.34	16.84
3	Japan	91771.96	9.47	9.13	3	Taiwan	87140.60	11.01	16.72
4	Korea, South	44557.92	4.6	26.88	4	China	73365.58	9.27	32.96
5	Germany	40302.12	4.16	23.87	5	United States	59222.47	7.48	21.52
6	Netherlands	30843.16	3.18	19.2	6	Germany	37887.52	4.79	23.54
7	United Kingdom	24158.46	2.49	27.26	7	Malaysia	23576.74	2.98	17.25
8	Singapore	23188.07	2.39	38.72	8	Australia	19195.72	2.42	18.88
9	Taiwan	20739.51	2.14	25.25	9	Thailand	17961.72	2.27	28.36
13	**India**	**14588.05**	**1.51**	**63.23**	**18**	**India**	**10469.19**	**1.32**	**7.05**

Source: General Administration of Customs of the People's Republic of China.

At the end of December 2005, China enjoyed a trade surplus of US$ 102.1 billion. Total trade for this period stood at US$ 1422.54 billion. While imports totaled US$ 660.22 billion in 2005, exports recorded a value of US$ 762.32 billion. Japan was the top exporter to China, while US remained the top importer of Chinese products.

Electrical Machinery (US$ 172.40 billion), machinery (US$ 149.83 billion), woven apparel (US$ 35 billion), knit apparel (US$ 30.87 billion) and optic photo/medical instruments (US$ 25.43 billion) constituted the top 5 exports from China in the year 2005. China's top 25 exports have all registered positive growth. In terms of imports top five categories include electrical machinery (US$ 174.91 billion), machinery (US$ 96.41 billion), mineral fuel (US$ 64.23 billion), optic photo/ medical instruments (US$ 49.95 billion) and plastic (US$ 33.33 billion). Amongst China's top imports, products that have registered a year-on-year decline in value include vehicles and parts except railways (–5.2%).[5] In 2006, China's trade growth makes it the world's third largest trading nation, and foreign direct investment in Russia, India and Brazil.

DEFENCE RELATIONS

The continuing progress in bilateral defence ties between India and China was manifested in increased defence exchanges, and mutual participation in training courses and joint activities. Chinese Defence Minister General Cao Guang Chuan visited India in March 2004, following the visit of then Indian Defence Minister George Fernandes visited to China in April 2003.

There were many contacts between India and China. The delegations led by Deputy Chief of Staff, People's Liberation Army (PLA) AF, President of Nanjiang Army Command College, General Wu Quanxu, Deputy Chief of General Staff, General Cao Ganchuan, Defence Minister and Lt. General Qian Haihao, Deputy President, Academy of Military Sciences. PLA CGS Liang Guanglie visited India in May 2005. From the Indian side, Chief of Army Staff (COAS) General N.C. Vij visited China in December 2004. The other delegations included Vice Adm. O.P. Bansal (this visit coincided with the port of call by INS Rajput, INS Kulish and INS Jyoti, which saw the first ever joint search and rescue exercise),

FoC-in-C eastern Naval Fleet, Lt. Gen. Mohinder Singh, GoC 4 Corps (which made the first visit by an Indian defence delegation to Tibet), and a Joint Training Committee visit by Air Marshall A.D. Joshi. A few Indian officers were undergoing courses at the National Defense University (NDU) while the Chinese officers were attending UN Peace-keeping Courses in India. As part of CBMs, activities have been organised along the Line of Actual Control (LAC), including a joint mountaineering expedition and sports matches between two forces and participation in each other's National Days and festivals.[6]

Besides that, important high-level visits that took place from India to China in 2005 were: Vice Chief of Naval Staff, Vice Admiral Yaswant Prasad in April; Director General of Military Intelligence; Lt. General D.H. Summanwar in May; Director General of Military Operations; Lt. General Madan Gopal in September; a delegation from National Defence College in May; and a delegation led by Vice Admiral Raman Puri to attend an academic seminar in China in June. An Indian delegation participated as observers in China-Russia joint military exercise "Peace Mission 2005" in August 2005 and later in China's military exercise "Northern Sword 2005" in September 2005.

Seven-member delegation led by the Deputy Chief of General Office of China's Central Military Commission visited India in July-August 2005. Three officers of Peoples Liberation Army (PLA) attended, as observers, the Indian military exercise "Desert Strike" in November 2005. A task force of two ships from PLA Navy visited India from 28 November to 1 December 2005 and held search and rescue exercises with the Indian Navy on the coast of Kochi.[7]

The defence ties between the two countries further strengthened during the year 2007 through different defence exchanges. The first meeting of India-China Annual Defence Dialogue which was held in Beijing in November 2007, successfully concluded in the year. The year also saw the organisation of the first ever joint training exercises held between the ground forces of the two countries. Army Chief General J.J. Singh and also Chairman, Chief of Staff Committee visited China during the year 2007.

COOPERATION ON COUNTER-TERRORISM

The first meeting of the India-China dialogue mechanism on counter-terrorism was held in New Delhi on April 23, 2002. Mr. Li Baodong, Director General (International Organizations) of the Chinese Ministry of Foreign Affairs led the Chinese delegation and the Indian delegation was led by Mr. Nalin Surie, Joint Secretary (East Asia) of the Ministry of External Affairs. Agreement to establish this dialogue mechanism was reached between the two Prime Ministers during the visit of Chinese Premier Zhu Rongji to India in January 2002. During the visit of the External Affairs Minister George Fernandes to China in March 2002, it was agreed that the dialogue will be held annually with the first meeting in New Delhi in April 2002.[8]

The two countries shared their national experiences on dealing with phenomenon of terrorism, and exchanged views on the international counter-terrorism, situation including developments in the region, cooperation at the United Nations and possibilities of bilateral cooperation. Both countries agreed that the first meeting of the dialogue mechanism was useful in enhancing mutual understanding. Both sides also agreed on the terms of reference for the dialogue.

The Second meeting of India-China dialogue mechanism on counter-terrorism was held in Beijing on June 13, 2003. The Indian delegation was led by Mr. Ashok K. Kantha, Joint Secretary (East Asia), Ministry of External Affairs. The Chinese delegation was led by Mr. Jhang Jun, Acting Director General of the Department of International Organizations Conferences, Ministry of Foreign Affairs. The delegates of the two sides included representatives from the concerned ministries. Both sides recalled that the regular counter-terrorism dialogue mechanism was established in January 2002.

Both countries exchanged views on the international and regional counter-terrorism situation, Sino-India cooperation on counter-terrorism, role of the United Nations in combating global terrorism, and enhancing counter-terrorism capabilities. Both sides stressed the important role of the United Nations in the international counter-terrorism cooperation and expressed their willingness and readiness to strengthen cooperation bilaterally and multilaterally.

Mr. Shen Guofang, Assistant Minister of the Ministry of Foreign Affairs, also received the Indian delegation. Mr. Shen underlined the importance of enhancing bilateral relations and made a positive appraisal of bilateral counter-terrorism dialogue, which would contribute to further development of cooperation between the two countries.[9]

Prime Minister Shri Atal Bihari Vajpayee's visit to China during 22-27 June 2003, which took place after a gap of ten years, was a major step forward in the ongoing process of building mutual trust and understanding between India and China. Both India and China recognized the threat posed by terrorism to them and to global peace and security and resolutely condemned terrorism in all forms.[10]

The momentum of bilateral defence exchanges was maintained with the visit of General N.C. Vij, Chief of Army Staff (COAS) to China during 22-29 December 2004. The COAS called on Chinese Vice-President Zeng Qinghong and Defence Minister General Cao Guangchun, and had extensive interaction with the Peoples' Liberation Army (PLA). There was also consensus on further enhancing military exchanges and cooperations at different levels. Cooperation in facing non-traditional threats, particularly against international terrorism was also discussed.[11]

India-China cooperation in the field of counter-terrorism and public security was also marked by the visit of Home Minister Shri Shivraj Patil to China during 7-11 September 2005. During the visit, a MoU was signed between India's Ministry of Home Affairs and China's Ministry of Public Security, which provided for cooperation in combating international terrorism, transnational crimes including money laundering, drug trafficking, illegal trading of arms, forgery of passports and visas, cyber crime, training and capacity-building of law enforcement agencies, and cooperation between national Interpol agencies in a mutually beneficial manner.[12]

As for the cooperation on transnational crimes, the MoU provides for specifics "exchanges of information and experiences, bilaterally as well as in the context of regional and international initiatives".

SCIENCE AND TECHNOLOGY COOPERATION

The Science and Technology relations between India and China function within the overall ambit of the Agreement on Cooperation in Science and Technology, signed between the Department of Science and Technology and the People's Republic of China (PRC) Ministry of Science and Technology in Beijing on December 22, 1988.[13] Since then, the two countries have signed a number of Memorandums of Understanding (MoUs) to cover a range of scientific and technological activities.

During the India visit of PRC State Councillor Chen Zhili in November 2004, Indian Minister for Science and Technology and Ocean Development Kapil Sibal suggested the setting up of a Joint Steering Committee on Science and Technology Cooperation, to be headed by Science and Technology Ministers on both sides.[14] A reference to the Joint Steering Committee was made in the joint statement issued during the India visit of PRC Premier Wen Jiabao in April 2005.

The Indian Minister of Science and Technology Kapil Sibal visited China during 10-16 September 2006. During the visit he signed a memorandum of understanding on science and technology cooperation with his Chinese counterpart Xu Guanhua. He said that India and China have a good time to strengthen cooperation in the field of science and technology sector. Sibal, also India's Minister of Ocean Development said in an interview with Xinhua that the 2006 India-China Friendship Year is the best time for the two countries to conduct cooperation. India and China have a lot to learn from each other. The Chinese have very strong capability in hardware production and the Indians have strength in software production.

Sibal said there is not so much competition between India and China because the two nations have adopted different strategies. One is more home consumption-driven and the other is more export-oriented. He said, "China and India in total have almost one-third of the world's population, If working and managing their resources together, the two can actually lead the world community in many areas, even in the science and technology."[15]

ENERGY COOPERATION

Five memoranda of understanding on energy between India and China were signed by Indian Petroleum and Natural Gas Minister Mani Shankar Aiyar and China's National Development and Reforms Commission (NDRC) Minister in charge Ma Kai, in Beijing on January 12, 2006.

Future exchanges will be on "a full spectrum", said the Indian Petroleum and Natural Gas Minister Mani Shankar Aiyar. Aiyar visited China as guest of Ma Kai. He was accompanied by a batch of major Indian petroleum firms. According to NDRC, the Indian delegation met with major Chinese players, including China National Petroleum Corporation (CNPC), China Petrochemical Corporation (SINOPEC), and China National Offshore Oil Corporation (CNOOC). Aiyar said China and India have agreed to strengthen the exchange of information when bidding for oil resources in a third country in order to realize mutual benefit.

In December 2005 China and India won a joint bid to buy Petro-Canada's 37 per cent stake in Syrian oilfields, marking the first cooperation in bidding for overseas oil resources. "Unbridled rivalry between Indian and Chinese companies is only to the advantage of the seller," said Aiyar.

Aiyar said that the memoranda, of which four are commercial, cover a full scope of areas, including upstream exploration and refining in the oil sector, the laying of national and trans-national oil and gas pipelines, frontier and cutting-edge research and development, as well as a joint energy efficiency program.

The two countries will also tap potential for working together on bio-fuels, such as vegetable oils blending with diesel and ethanol blending with gasoline. A working group will be established soon, said Aiyar. The group will meet at least once a year to keep track of the cooperation. This year 2006 dubbed as the "Year of Friendship between China and India."[16]

AGRICULTURAL COOPERATION

Senior officials from China and India agreed on 28 March 2005 to enhance cooperation to boost the agricultural industry. In a meeting with Sharad Pawar, Indian Minister of Agriculture,

Food and Civil Supplies, Consumer Affairs and Public Distribution, and his party, Chinese Vice Premier Hui Liangyu suggested the two countries share experience in agriculture and cooperate to research new agricultural technology. Hui said both China and India are agricultural countries and the cooperation between them will not only benefit their people but also help secure global food safety. Hui also suggested the two sides enhance exchanges between their administrative and technical staff. Pawar, who said India is ready to actively promote agricultural exchanges with the China, echoed Hui's suggestion.[17]

COOPERATION ON GLOBAL OIL QUEST

With rapidly growing oil demand and increasing dependence on imports – in 2004, over 40 per cent of China's crude and some 70 per cent of India's came from abroad—the two countries have more than just their rivalry in common. They are linked by similar business models, with cash-rich, State-controlled oil firms seen having more appetite for risk than companies beholden to earnings-conscious shareholders. "Although there is competition, both sides share a common aim," said Zhou Fengqi, a high-level adviser in the Energy Research Institute of China's National Development and Reform Commission. "There is a basis for cooperation between the two sides, because they are both developing countries with oil demand...but the specifics of any cooperation still needs to be researched." A deal could include agreements for each country to refrain from trying to buy certain assets to prevent bidding wars, or working on joint projects in areas of interest, analysts said. "We are pitted against each other almost always to the advantage of the third country," Indian Oil Minister Mani Shankar Aiyar said.

Although Chinese and Indian companies are partners in Sudan's Greater Nile Project, widespread cooperation could be a long way off with both countries on a global prowl for assets. "The Chinese in particular, I think, would be reluctant to start excluding themselves from ... areas of certain countries just so they could avoid having Indians bidding on one or two assets," said Gavin Thompson, a Beijing-based analyst with Wood Mackenzie. "It's just a little bit too competitive for that to happen," he added.

If China and India can't cooperate over oil and gas deposits, there may still be a future for lower-level cooperation. "Both countries have large populations without access to modern forms of energy and we need to work together developing technologies appropriate for rural areas," said R.K. Pachauri, Director General of the Energy and Resources Institute in New Delhi. Cleaner coal-burning techniques would offer another opportunity for cooperation, but neither side had promoted this kind of deal amid the jostling about overseas oil resources, he said.[18]

STRATEGIC AND COOPERATIVE PARTNERSHIP

China and India have agreed to establish a "strategic and cooperative partnership for peace and prosperity" between them, according to a joint statement signed by the premiers of the two countries in New Delhi on 11 April 2005. The statement, signed by visiting Chinese Premier Wen Jiabao and Indian Prime Minister Manmohan Singh, said that the two premiers agreed that China-India relations have now acquired a "global and strategic character". Wen paid an official visit to India from April 9 to 12 at Singh's invitation, the last leg of his four south Asian nation tour, which also took him to Pakistan, Bangladesh and Sri Lanka. "The leaders of the two countries have, therefore, agreed to establish a China-India Strategic and Cooperative Partnership for Peace and Prosperity, " the statement said. "Such a partnership is based on the principles of Panchsheel, mutual respect and sensitivity for each other's concerns and aspirations, and equality, provides a sound framework for an all around and comprehensive development of bilateral relations based on mutual and equal security, development and prosperity of the two peoples, and contributes to jointly addressing global challenges and threats, " the statement said.

According to the statement, the two sides agreed that China-India relations have entered a new stage of comprehensive development. The two sides also reiterated their intention to promote regular ministerial-level exchanges and make full use of the China-India strategic dialogue and other bilateral dialogue mechanisms, the statement added. The statement said the year of 2005 marks the 55th anniversary of the establishment of diplomatic relations between China and India, and to mark the occasion, the two countries would organize a series of commemorative activities.

China and India have agreed that an all-round expansion of economic cooperation between the two countries constitutes an important dimension of their stronger relationship and they should make joint efforts to increase bilateral trade volume to 20 billion US dollars or higher by 2008. The two sides welcomed the report of the Joint Study Group (JSG) that was set up to examine the potential complementarities between the two countries in expanded trade and economic cooperation. The JSG in its report has identified a series of measures related to trade in goods, trade in services, investments and other areas of economic cooperation, and recommended their expeditious implementation to remove impediments and facilitate enhanced economic engagement between China and India.

The Prime Ministers agreed to appoint a Joint Task Force to study in detail the feasibility of, and the benefits that may be derived from, the China-India Regional Trading Arrangement and give recommendations regarding its content, the statement said. The two sides also agreed to further promote cooperation in the spheres of education, science and technology, health care, information, tourism, youth exchange, agriculture, dairy development, sports and other fields on the basis of mutual benefit and reciprocity. The statement also said that the two sides noted useful exchanges and interactions in the military field and decided to further promote such exchanges and interactions.

China and India have reiterated their readiness to seek a fair, reasonable and mutually acceptable solution, through equal and friendly consultations and proceeding from the overall interests of bilateral relations in the settlement of the boundary question. The two sides expressed satisfaction over the progress made in the discussions between the Special Representatives of the two countries and welcomed the conclusion of the Agreement on the Political Parameters and Guiding Principles for the Settlement of the Boundary Question.

Pending a final resolution, the two sides would continue to make joint efforts to maintain peace and tranquility in the border areas in accordance with the Agreements of 1993 and 1996, the joint statement said. Both sides agreed that while continuing the discussions between the Special Representatives, it is also important that the Joint Working Group (JWG) continues its work to seek an early clarification and confirmation of the Line of Actual Control (LAC). Progress made so far on the clarification of the LAC in the China-India border areas was noted. It was agreed to complete the process of exchanging maps indicating their respective perceptions of the entire alignment of the LAC on the basis of already agreed parameters, with the objective of arriving at a common understanding of the alignment, as soon as possible, the statement said. The two sides expressed satisfaction at the progress achieved in the implementation of the agreements of 1993 and 1996 and agreed to fully implement them expeditiously.

Towards that end, they concluded a Protocol on Modalities for the Implementation of Confidence Building Measures in the Military Field along the Line of Actual Control in the China-India Border Areas. In the joint statement, the Indian side reiterated that it recognized the Tibet Autonomous Region as part of the territory of the People's Republic of China and that it did not allow Tibetans to engage in anti-China political activities in India.

The Indian side recalled that India was among the first countries to recognize that there is one China and its one China policy remains unaltered. The Indian side stated it would continue to abide by its one China policy. Both sides reviewed with satisfaction the implementation of the memorandum on the border trade through the Nathula Pass between the Tibet Autonomous Region of the People's Republic of China and the Sikkim, a state of the Republic of India.

The two large Asian neighbors have expressed in the joint statement their desire to develop "closer and more extensive" understanding and cooperation in regional and international affairs. "Aware of their linked destinies as neighbors and the two largest countries of Asia, both sides agreed that they would, together, contribute to the establishment of an atmosphere of mutual understanding, trust and cooperation in Asia and the world at large, and facilitate efforts to strengthen multilateral coordination mechanisms on security and cooperation," said the statement.

As two large developing countries, China and India were both aware of each other's important role in the process of promoting the establishment of a new international political and economic order, it said. The statement noted that the two sides are supportive of democratization of international relations and multilateralism, stand for the establishment of a new international political and economic order that is fair, rational, equal and mutually beneficial, and promote North-South Dialogue and South-South Cooperation.

They agreed in the statement that reform of the United Nations should be comprehensive and multi-faceted and should put emphasis on an increase in the representation of developing countries. According to the document, the Indian side reiterated its aspirations for permanent membership of the UN Security Council, and the Chinese side also reiterated that India is an important developing country and is having an increasingly important influence in the international arena. The two sides also resolutely condemn terrorism in any form, admit that the struggle between the international community and global terrorism is a comprehensive and sustained one.[19]

FINANCIAL DIALOGUE MECHANISM

The Chinese Ministry of Finance has set up a Financial Dialogue Mechanism with its Indian counterpart in a bid to boost their exchanges and cooperation in major international financial issues. The mechanism will help promote the global economy in a balanced and orderly manner. The move also indicates that China has made new progress in cementing financial exchanges and cooperation with other developing countries.

The Chinese and Indian government officials signed a MoU on Financial Dialogue during the visit of Chinese Premier Wen Jiabao. The Chinese Ministry said the dialogue between the two countries, their financial policies, financial reforms and exchanges on matters, related to international economic forums and institutions. China has also set up financial dialogue mechanism with the US, Britain, the European Union, and France on a regular basis at ministerial levels.[20]

CHINA SUPPORTS INDIA'S CANDIDATURE FOR UNSC SEAT

Chinese Premier Wen Jiabao who was paying an official visit to India said on April 11, 2005, China supports India's bid for a permanent seat in the United Nations Security Council (UNSC). "We fully understand and support the Indian aspiration to play an even bigger role in international affairs and in the United Nations (UN)," Premier Wen said while addressing a question at a press conference before winding up his four-day visit to India. He said he had conveyed the support to Indian Prime Minister Manmohan Singh during their talks in Delhi. "China attaches 'great importance' to India's role in both international and regional affairs, India is a very populous developing country and also a very important developing country," Wen added.[21]

COOPERATION ON CIVIL AVIATION

China and India first signed an aviation agreement in 1988. In March 2002, China Eastern Airlines made a maiden flight from Beijing to New Delhi and the following year Indian Airlines opened regular flights of Mumbai-New Delhi-Bangkok-Shanghai. China and India signed a memorandum of understanding on the expansion of aviation transportation between the two countries, the General Administration of Civil Aviation of China announced on April 13, 2005. The new agreement allows the two countries to open freight market to each other. Passenger planes can fly to six cities in each country up to 14 flights per week, which will keep increasing year by year. The agreement also includes details on code-sharing cooperation of airline companies, aircraft leasing and foreign pilots hiring.

China Eastern Airlines launched new flights from Beijing to Mumbai via Shanghai on April 18, 2005. Four weekly flights started operating: Air China and relevant Indian Airlines also prepare to join the route. In recent years, the relations between the two countries in trade and tourism have developed rapidly. Bilateral trade volume reached US$ 13.6 billion in 2004, up to 80 per cent over the previous year and will surpass US$ 20 billion by 2008.[22]

COOPERATION ON BORDER TRADE

The historic re-opening of Nathu La Pass between the Sikkim and Tibet on July 6, 2006 after 44 years for trans-border trade is a milestone in the growing India-China bilateral relations. An inaugural function was held on July 6, 2006 at Nathu La, Sikkim on the occasion of resumption of border trade between India and China through the pass. The function was presided over by Dr. Pawan Chamling, Chief Minister of Sikkim and H.E. Mr. Champa Phuntsok, Chairman of the Tibet Autonomous Region.

It may be recalled that India and China had signed the Memorandum on Expanding Border Trade on June 23, 2003. The said Memorandum provided the use of Nathu La for the purpose of border trade between India and China. This is the third border trade point between the two countries, the other two being Lipulekh pass in Uttarakhand and Shipki La in Himachal Pradesh.

Modalities for conducting border trade between India and China are laid out in the Memorandum on the Resumption of Border Trade signed between the two countries in December 1991 and the Protocol on Entry and Exit Procedures for Border Trade signed in July 1992. All provisions of these two documents would be applicable for border trade through Nathu La. Other details were worked out between the two countries when an Indian delegation visited the Tibet Autonomous Region during June 17-20, 2006.

The following aspects of border trade through Nathu La may be of interest:

(i) Border Trade through Nathu La resumed on July 6, 2006 at the Changgu border trade mart at Sherathang on the Indian side and Renqinggang trade mart on the Tibetan side.

(ii) The border trade mart shall be opened from June 1—September 30 every year. It will be opened to the designated authorities of the two sides to extend or reduce the period of trade when considered necessary on account of exigencies like weather conditions.

(iii) The border trade marts on both sides will be opened from Monday to Thursday every week. The daily opening time for the marts for border trade shall be from 07.30-15.30 hours Indian Standard Time.

(iv) The traders from both sides would use trade passes for the purpose of border trade. Trade passes would also be issued to drivers of vehicles, which are utilized for the purpose of border trade. To start with, 60 four-wheeled vehicles including passenger buses, if any, would be issued border trade pass. This number could be increased or decreased based on mutual agreement.

(v) Border trade would be transacted for items contained in the agreed list of commodities for border trade between the two countries, which presently includes 29 items for exports from India to China and 15 items of import into India from China.[23]

Border trade linkages continued to expand during 2007. The period of border trade through Nathula was extended from the earlier June to September in 2006 to the period from May to November in 2007. Both sides are discussing the possibility of expanding the basket of tradeable goods across Nathula.

CULTURAL AND EDUCATIONAL COOPERATION

The early 1950s and the Hindi-Chini Bhai Bhai phase of 1950s witnessed a further strengthening of these ties. Various Indian films like *Awaara, Caravan, Do Bigha Zameen*, etc. as well as actors like Raj Kapoor and Nargis left a lasting impression on Chinese audiences. The resumption of political relations in 1980s has provided an impetus to cultural exchanges.

India and China signed an Agreement on Cultural Cooperation in May 1998, which provides for an executive Cultural Exchange Programme (CEP) for implementation.[24] The CEP signed in June 2003 provides for cooperation in a gamut of cultural fields including exchanges of visits of artists, officials, writers, archivists and archaeologists, organising cultural festivals, exchanges in the field of mass media, youth affairs and sports. During the visit of Prime Minister A.B. Vajpayee to China in June 2003, a MoU was signed on reciprocal setting up of Cultural Centres in the two capitals. An Indian Studies Centre was also inaugurated in Peking University in June 2003.

In June 2003, the bilateral Education Exchange Program (EEP) was signed which provides for exchange of scholars, mutual recognition of academic degrees, cooperation in the field of teachers training, exchanges between higher education institutions, and exchanges of Hindi and Chinese language teachers. Under EEP, each side offers scholarships for postgraduate and higher level studies for a maximum of 25 persons per year. The trend of self-financed students of India and China going to each other's country for higher studies is also on the rise. Exchange of students between India and China continued under the bilateral Education Exchange Program (EEP).

The India-China Cultural Exchange Program (2003-05) continued to provide framework for various exchanges and activities, which included dance, theatre, painting, photographic exhibitions, films, and literary exchange and cultural restoration. As part of the commemorative activities for the "50th Anniversary of Panchsheel", cultural programs were organised and a joint exhibition of Indian and Chinese postage stamps was held.

In response to the interest shown by the Chinese side, Government of India indicated its willingness to build an Indian-style Buddhist Temple in the International Garden on the west side of the White Horse Temple in Luoyang, which is the oldest icon of India-China exchanges in the field of Buddhism. During Premier Wen Jiabao's visit to India in April 2005, a memorandum was concluded to this effect. An Advisory Committee constituted by the Prime Minister has selected the design and the architect for the project. It is expected that the Temple, once completed, will become an enduring symbol of the centuries-old Indian influence in China and epitomize how Buddhism from India became an integral part of Chinese culture and life.[25]

55TH ANNIVERSARY OF CHINA-INDIA DIPLOMATIC TIES

The Chinese People's Association for Friendship with Foreign Countries (CPAFFC) and the China-India Friendship Association hosted a reception on 31 March 2005, to mark the 55th anniversary of the establishment of diplomatic relations between China and India. Addressing the reception, Chen Haosu, President of CPAFFC, said that the relationship between China and India has experienced its ups and downs, but the friendship between the two peoples has never changed.

As developing countries, China and India have many similarities. Pushing the friendly and mutual-beneficial ties not only benefits the interests of the two countries, but also benefits regional peace and stability, said Chen. Nalin Surie, Indian Ambassador to China, said the reception this year (2006) has a special meaning because it was held just before Chinese Premier Wen Jiabao's visit to India. He said, "Wen's visit will be a milestone that will push forward bilateral ties and promote mutual understanding and trust."[26]

Chinese and Indian leaders exchanged congratulatory messages on 31 March 2005 on the 55th anniversary of the establishment of diplomatic ties between the two countries. In his message to Indian President Avul Pakir Jainulabdeen Abdul Kalam, Chinese President Hu Jintao noted that recent years witnessed a remarkable progress in the two countries' exchanges and cooperation, especially their coordination in international and regional affairs. "Further strengthening of the long-term partnership of constructive cooperation between the two countries serves the fundamental interests of the people of both countries," Hu said, adding that "it also contributes to mutual prosperity." He said China is ready to work with India to promote good-neighborly friendship and mutually beneficial cooperation on the basis of the five principles of peaceful co-existence, which were jointly initiated by India and China. Kalam, for his part, said the five principles of peaceful co-existence not only serve as the foundation of India-China relations, but as a guide to peace, stability and development in the world at large. He said bilateral ties developed fairly well in recent years and he is confident of better cooperation in the future.

In his message to Indian Prime Minister Manmohan Singh, Chinese Premier Wen Jiabao said the Chinese and Indian peoples have a long history of friendly contacts.

Since the establishment of diplomatic ties 55 years ago, and especially since the beginning of this century, the good-neighborly friendship and mutually beneficial cooperation between the two countries has entered a new era of comprehensive development, he said.

Indian Prime Minister Manmohan Singh said the frequent exchanges of visits by Indian and Chinese leaders in recent years have greatly promoted mutual understanding and trust. India hopes the two countries take a global and strategic perspective and continue to enrich and enhance their partnership of constructive cooperation, he said. Chinese Foreign Minister Li Zhaoxing and Indian Foreign Minister Natwar Singh also exchanged congratulatory messages on the same day.[27]

PRESIDENT HU JINTAO VISITS TO INDIA

Mr. Hu Jintao, President of the People's Republic of China visited to the Republic of India from 20 to 23 November 2006 at the invitation of Dr. A.P.J. Abdul Kalam, President of the Republic of India. President Hu Jintao held talks with Prime Minister Dr. Manmohan Singh, and President Dr. A.P.J. Abdul Kalam. Vice President Shri Bhairon Singh Shekhawat, Speaker, Lok Sabha Shri Somnath Chatterjee, and leader of the opposition in Lok Sabha Shri L.K. Advani paid courtesy calls on President Hu Jintao. Smt. Sonia Gandhi, Chairperson, United Progressive Alliance, met him. Minister of External Affairs Shri Pranab Mukherjee called on the visiting Chinese President. President Hu Jintao delivered a policy address at the Vigyan Bhawan, New Delhi and attended the India-China Friendship Year commemorative function. He also visited Agra and addressed a business summit in Mumbai, among other engagements.

The leaders of the two countries noted with satisfaction the all-round progress made over recent years in India-China relations and their regional and multilateral cooperation. They reiterated the shared vision and fundamental principles for the future development of India-China relations, as embodied in the Declaration on Principles for Relations and Comprehensive Cooperation of 23 June 2003 and the Joint Statement of 11 April 2005 signed between the Prime Ministers of the two countries.

Both sides agreed that the relationship between India and China, the two biggest developing countries in the world, is of global and strategic significance. Both countries are seeking to avail themselves of historic opportunities for development. Each side welcomes and takes a positive view of the development of the other, and considers the development of either side as a positive contribution to peace, stability and prosperity of Asia and the world. Both sides hold the view that there exist bright prospects for their common development, that they are not rivals or competitors but are partners for mutual benefit. They agree that there is enough space for them to grow together, achieve a higher scale of development, and play their respective roles in the region and beyond, while remaining sensitive to each other's concerns and aspirations. Strategic partnership between the two countries with a similar worldview is consistent with their roles as two major developing countries. With the growing participation and role of the two countries in all key issues in today's localizing world, their partnership is vital for international efforts to deal with global challenges and threats. As two major countries in the emerging multi-polar global order, the simultaneous development of India and China will have a positive influence on the future international system.

In order to promote the sustainable socio-economic development of India and China, to fully realise the substantial potential for their cooperation in a wide range of areas, to upgrade India-China relations to a qualitatively new level, and to further substantiate and reinforce their Strategic and Cooperative Partnership, the leaders of the two countries have committed themselves to pursuing the following ten-pronged strategy:

I. Ensuring Comprehensive Development of Bilateral Relations

Both sides are committed to making the positive development and diversification of India-China relations in recent years an irreversible trend.

The two sides agree to hold regular summit-level meetings, in each other's country and in multilateral forums. They agree that high-level exchanges between Governments, Parliaments and political parties play an important role in expanding overall bilateral cooperation.

In order to sustain, facilitate and promote greater engagement between the two countries, an additional Consulate General shall be opened in each other's country. The Indian side shall open a new Consulate General in Guangzhou, while the Chinese side shall open a new Consulate General in Kolkata. In this context, the mutually satisfactory resolution of the long-pending issue of the property of the Consulate General of India in Shanghai is a positive development.

II. Strengthening Institutional Linkages and Dialogue Mechanisms

The two sides shall strengthen institutional linkages between their Governments in different areas and levels with a view to foster synergy and cooperation and promote greater understanding of each other's policies and positions on important national, regional and international issues. The concerned ministries and organisations of the two countries shall intensify exchanges under the existing dialogue mechanisms and revitalise those that have not been regularly used. The signing of the Protocol of Cooperation between the Ministry of External Affairs of India and the Ministry of Foreign Affairs of China during the visit is an important step in this direction.

III. Consolidating Commercial and Economic Exchanges

Both sides believe that comprehensive economic and commercial engagement between India and China is a core component of their Strategic and Cooperative Partnership. They will endeavour to raise the volume of their bilateral trade to US$ 40 billion by 2010. They shall make joint efforts to diversify their trade basket, remove existing impediments, and optimally utilise the present and potential complementarities in their economies, in order to sustain and further strengthen bilateral commercial and economic cooperation. Towards this end, both sides will attach utmost priority to an early implementation of the decisions taken in March 2006 by the Ministerial-level Joint Economic Group, including the recommendations of the Joint Study Group, through mechanisms already created for this purpose. The Joint Task Force set up to study the feasibility and benefits of an India-China Regional Trading Arrangement shall complete its work by October 2007.

The conclusion of the Bilateral Investment Promotion and Protection Agreement during the visit is a welcome development that will provide the institutional and legal basis to encourage and promote greater investment flows between the two countries.

The Chinese side has invited India to participate in the World Exposition Shanghai 2010. The Indian side expressed its appreciation and stated that it will actively support and participate in the event.

IV. Expanding All-Round Mutually Beneficial Cooperation

The two sides agree to further strengthen positive trends in the all-round development of relations and fully realize the substantial potential of cooperation, including in trade, industry, finance, agriculture, water resources, energy, environment, transportation, infrastructure, information technology, health, education, media, culture, tourism, youth affairs and other fields.

Both sides agree to fully implement the provisions of the Memorandum on Cooperation in the field of Oil and Natural Gas signed in January 2006 and encourages collaboration between their enterprises, including through joint exploration and development of hydrocarbon resources in third countries.

Given the complementarities that India and China enjoy in the area of information and communication technology, the two sides agreed to strengthen mutually beneficial cooperation in this sector, through closer policy dialogue and enhanced collaboration among their enterprises, including in third countries.

The two sides shall fully implement the Memorandum of Understanding on Agricultural Cooperation, step up the exchange of experience in the field of agriculture and rural development, including food security, and hold discussions and consultations on the standards for agricultural goods at an early date in order to facilitate trade in such goods.

The two sides will set up an expert-level mechanism to discuss interaction and cooperation on the provision of flood season hydrological data, emergency management and other issues regarding trans-border rivers as agreed between them. The ongoing provision of hydrological data for the Brahmaputra/Yarlung Zangbo and the Sutlej/Langqen Zangbo Rivers by the Chinese side to the Indian side has proved valuable in flood forecasting and mitigation. The two sides agree to continue bilateral discussions to finalise at an early date similar arrangements for the Parlung Zangbo and Lohit/Zayu Qu rivers.

Both sides shall intensify their consultations, bilaterally and in multilateral forum, on sustainable development, biodiversity, climate change and other related environmental issues of common concern. The cooperation in wildlife conservation, particularly in tiger conservation, shall be stepped up.

V. Instilling Mutual Trust and Confidence through Defence Cooperation

The exchange of visits in the field of defence has resulted in building of mutual trust and enhancement of mutual understanding between the defence establishments of the two countries. Both sides shall fully implement the provisions of the Memorandum of Understanding for Exchanges and Cooperation in the field of Defence signed on 29 May 2006, which provides a sound foundation and institutional framework for further development of defence cooperation.

VI. Seeking Early Settlement of Outstanding Issues

Both sides are committed to resolving outstanding differences, including on the boundary question, through peaceful means and in a fair, reasonable, mutually acceptable and proactive manner, while ensuring that such differences are not allowed to affect the positive development of bilateral relations.

The Special Representatives of India and China on the boundary question have taken steps and shall continue to strive to arrive at a boundary settlement on the basis of the Agreement on Political Parameters and Guiding Principles for the Settlement of India-China Boundary Question signed on 11 April 2005. An early settlement of the boundary question will advance the basic interests of the two countries and shall, therefore, be pursued as a strategic objective. The Special Representatives shall complete at an early date the task of finalising an appropriate framework for a final package settlement covering all sectors of the India-China boundary. Pending the resolution of the boundary question, both sides shall maintain peace and tranquillity in the border areas in accordance with the agreements of 1993, 1996 and 2005.

Along with the talks between the Special Representatives, the Joint Working Group on the India-China Boundary Question shall expedite their work, including on the clarification and confirmation of the Line of Actual Control and the implementation of confidence-building measures. It was agreed to complete the process of exchanging maps indicating their respective perceptions of the entire alignment of the LAC on the basis of already agreed parameters as soon as possible.

VII. Promoting Trans-border Connectivity and Cooperation

Both sides shall promote greater trans-border cooperation at mutually agreed sites in India-China border areas with the objective of transforming their border from being a dividing line into a bridge that unites them in cooperative pursuits. In this context, border trade between India and China, including the recent resumption of border trade through the Nathula La Pass, is of significant importance. The two sides shall strengthen border trade through the existing locations, while continuing to explore the possibility of opening additional trading routes in India-China border areas.

The two sides welcome the organisation of a car rally, recommended by the BCIM Forum, between Kolkata and Kunming via Bangladesh and Myanmar. The Chinese side shall provide greater facilitation to Indian pilgrims for the Kailash Mansarovar Yatra. Both sides shall explore the possibility of opening an additional route for the Yatra.

VIII. Boosting Cooperation in Science and Technology

Bearing in mind the priority attached by India and China to scientific and technological development and innovation as a cornerstone of their efforts towards sustainable socio-economic development, the two sides shall establish an India-China Partnership in Science and Technology. The two sides welcome the establishment of the Ministerial-level Committee on Science and Technology Cooperation as a positive step in guiding, coordinating and facilitating cooperative activities. They agree to launch joint projects in the areas of: (i) Earthquake engineering; (ii) Climate change and weather forecasting; (iii) Nano-technology with focus on advanced materials; and (iv) Biotechnology and medicines with focus on bio-nano. The cooperation framework shall include entrepreneurs on both sides, besides the two Governments and their respective institutions.

Considering that for both India and China, expansion of civilian nuclear energy programme is an essential and important component of their national energy plans to ensure energy security, the two sides agree to promote cooperation in the field of nuclear energy, consistent with their respective international commitments. As two countries with advanced scientific capabilities, they stress the importance of further deepening of cooperation bilaterally as well as through multilateral projects such as ITER, and enhance exchanges in the related academic fields.

As countries, which have made advances in space technologies, both sides reiterate their commitment to the use of outer space for peaceful purposes. They agree to strengthen their cooperation in the use of space-based technologies for peaceful and developmental applications, including through satellite remote sensing, satellite communications, satellite meteorology and satellite launch services. Cooperation in practical applications of space technology, such as those related to disaster management and distance education shall also be actively explored. Towards this end, both sides shall fully implement the provisions of the Memorandum of Understanding on the peaceful use of outer space signed between India and China in December 1991 and January 2002.

IX. Revitalising Cultural Ties and Nurturing People-to-People Exchanges

The centuries-old cultural contacts between the two peoples provide a strong foundation for enduring friendship between India and China. The initiatives to rediscover these historical linkages and revitalise them in the present day context, including through an early completion of the Xuanzang Memorial in Nalanda and the Indian-style Buddhist Shrine in Luoyang, will further strengthen these bonds. The two sides agree to strengthen cooperation in the area of spiritual and cultural heritage, discuss collaboration in the digitisation of Buddhist manuscripts available in China as well as the re-development of Nalanda as a major centre of learning with the establishment of an international university on the basis of regional cooperation. In order to promote greater awareness of each other's culture, the two sides shall organise a Festival of India in China and a Festival of China in India, with a joint logo. The concerned authorities through mutual consultations in this regard will decide detailed modalities.

In order to promote greater academic exchanges between India and China, the two sides agree to work towards the establishment of an India-China Exchange Foundation. Detailed modalities of the Foundation will be worked out through mutual consultations. India-China relations in the field of education will be further strengthened through a new Educational Exchange Programme concluded during the visit.

The two sides also agree to launch a five-year programme for mutual exchange of youth delegations. In this context, the Chinese side invites five hundred youth from India over the next five years. With a view to vigorously promoting tourism between India and China, the two sides decided to organise the India-China Year of Friendship Through Tourism in 2007 with a joint logo and take other initiatives, such as opening of the office of the China National Tourism Administration in India and an Indian Tourism Office in China, improved air connectivity, and continued liberalisation of the visa regime.

The two sides welcome cooperation linkages between the Indian states and the Chinese provinces in order to promote greater people-to-people exchanges.

X. Expanding Cooperation on Regional and International Stage

The two sides shall hold regular exchange of views on the emerging security environment in the Asia-Pacific and in the world, and undertake proactive consultations on issues of immediate and emerging concern, so as to coordinate their positions and to make positive contribution towards peaceful resolution of such issues. They shall also have regular consultations on issues pertaining to regional peace, security and stability, such as regional maritime security, proliferation of weapons of mass destruction and related materials and their means of delivery, pandemics, natural disasters, illegal trafficking in arms, narcotics and people, and environmental degradation.

The two sides positively assess the trilateral dialogue mechanism among India, China and Russia and agree that exchanges and cooperation under it should be further substantiated. Recognising that terrorism constitutes a crime against humanity that cannot be justified on any ground and condemning it in all forms and manifestations, the two sides agree to revitalise and broaden the India-China Dialogue Mechanism on Counter-Terrorism. They shall strengthen their efforts, bilaterally as also in the international fora, to fight against terrorism, separatism and extremism, and the linkages between terrorism and organized crime and elicit arms and drugs trafficking.

Recognising the central role of the United Nations in promoting international peace, security and development, both sides reiterate their determination to strengthen the UN system. The reform of the UN should be comprehensive, ensure balanced representation of developing and developed countries in the UN Security Council, and add to the efficiency and efficacy of the UN and its Security Council. The two sides shall conduct consultations on the question of UN reform, including the reform of the UN Security Council. The Indian side reiterates its aspirations for permanent membership of the UN Security Council. China attaches great importance to the status of India in international affairs. It understands and supports India's aspirations to play a greater role in the United Nations.

Energy security constitutes a vital and strategic issue for producing and consuming countries alike. It is consistent with the common interest of the two sides to establish an international energy order, which is fair, equitable, secure and stable, and to the benefit of the entire international community. Both sides shall also make joint efforts, bilaterally as well as in multilateral forum, to diversify the global energy mix and to increase the share in it of renewable energy sources. Global energy systems should take into account and meet the energy needs of both countries, as part and parcel of a stable, predictable, secure and clean energy future. In this context, international civilian nuclear cooperation should be advanced through innovative and forward-looking approaches, while safeguarding the effectiveness of international non-proliferation principles.

Both countries are committed to non-proliferation objectives and agree to expand their dialogue on the related issues, in bilateral and international forum. As two large developing countries with relatively successful developmental experiences, India and China share unique responsibilities to protect and promote the interests of the developing world in the emerging international order and to help them benefit from the positive forces of globalisation. In this context, the two sides shall hold a two-part international seminar in Beijing and New Delhi, co-hosted by their Ministries of Finance, to share their developmental experience with other developing countries and the international community at large.

The two sides agree to strengthen their cooperation in the World Trade Organisation. They support the establishment of an open, fair, equitable, transparent and rule-based multilateral trading system, early resumption of Doha negotiations, and are determined to safeguard the legitimate rights and interests of the developing countries. As founding Members of the G-20 and the G-33, they are determined to strengthen their cooperation and to coordinate with other members of the WTO, especially the developing countries, in order to secure an early resumption of the negotiations on the Doha Work Programme, placing the development dimension at its heart.

Recognising that regional integration is an important feature of the emerging international economic order, the two sides agree to expand their coordination within regional organisations and explore a new architecture for closer regional cooperation in Asia. They positively view each other's participation in Asian inter-regional, regional and sub-regional cooperation process, including in the progress towards the East Asian Community. In this context, the two sides agree to cooperate closely in the East Asia Summit. The Indian side welcomes China's attainment of observer status in the South Asian Association for Regional Cooperation. The Chinese side welcomes India's membership of the Asia-Europe Meeting. The two sides agree to expand their cooperation on issues on common interest under the Shanghai Cooperation Organisation.

The Indian side recalls that India was among the first countries to recognize that there is one China and that its one China policy has remained unaltered. The Indian side states that it would continue to abide by its one China policy. The Chinese side expresses its appreciation for the Indian position. The Indian side reiterates that it has recognized the Tibet Autonomous Region as part of the territory of the People's Republic of China, and that it does not allow Tibetans to engage in anti-China political activities in India. The Chinese side expresses its appreciation for the Indian position.

The following agreements were signed during the visit:

(i) Protocol on the Establishment of Consulates-General at Guangzhou and Kolkata;

(ii) Protocol on Cooperation between the Ministry of External Affairs of India and the Ministry of Foreign Affairs of China;

(iii) Agreement on the Issue of Property of the Consulate General of India in Shanghai;

(iv) Agreement on Bilateral Investment Protection and Promotion;

(v) Memorandum of Understanding on Inspection of Export Cargo (Iron Ore);

(vi) Protocol on Phytosanitary Requirements for Exporting Rice from India to China;

(vii) Memorandum of Understanding between Forward Markets Commission of India and China Securities Regulatory Commission regarding Commodity Futures Regulatory Cooperation;

(viii) Memorandum of Understanding on Cooperation between the Indian Institute of Public Administration and the Central Party School of the Communist Party of China;

(ix) Agreement on Forestry Cooperation;

(x) Memorandum of Understanding between the Indian Council of Agricultural Research and the Chinese Academy of Agricultural Sciences;

(xi) Exchange Program on Cooperation in the Field of Education;

(xii) Memorandum of Understanding on Cooperation in the Conservation of Cultural Heritage; and

(xiii) Agreement on Preventing Theft, Clandestine Excavation and Illicit Import and Export of Cultural Property.

The two sides believe that the highly successful visit of President Hu Jintao to India marks the high point of the

India-China Friendship Year in 2006, promotes mutual understanding and trust, helps in substantiating the Strategic and Cooperative Partnership between the two countries and leads to a qualitative and quantum improvement in bilateral relations. Both sides also agree that the 'Joint Statement' issued during the president's visit provides a valuable blueprint for enduring development and diversification of the relations between India and China and sustained enrichment of their strategic partnership.[28]

HU JINTAO'S FIVE POINTS ON SINO-INDIAN TIES

Chinese President Hu Jintao on 22 November 2006, made five-points proposal for further developing Sino-India relations, which focuses on increasing political trust, business cooperation, cultural and social exchanges, boundary issues and multilateral cooperation.

Hu made the proposal in a keynote address dubbed "Working Together to Expand Cooperation and Create a Bright Future" at Vigyan Bhavan in New Delhi during his state visit to India. "China is ready to work with India to ensure that the China-India strategic and cooperative partnership grows in both depth and width," Hu said.

I. Mutual Political Trust

Hu proposed first to increase mutual political trust and consolidate the basis of bilateral relations. He said, "We should continue regular leadership meetings and expand high-level exchanges between the governments, legislatures and political parties to enhance mutual understanding." Furthermore, the two should make full use of the bilateral consultation mechanisms to maintain regular dialogue and enhance communication on issues of respective concern, he said.

II. Business Cooperation

The two-way trade volume between China and India registered an averaged annual growth rate of 32 per cent between 1995 and 2005, Hu said, adding that China had become India's second biggest trading partner and India was China's largest trading partner in South Asia. "We should work vigorously to increase the varieties of goods traded and add more value to them", the president said, noting their goal is for the two-way trade to reach US$ 40 billion in 2010.

He proposed to encourage and support cooperation between the business communities of the two countries in information technology, energy, resources, infrastructure, science, technology and agriculture.

III. Cultural and Social Exchanges

Hu said the two countries should continue to carry out cultural exchanges in various forms, strengthen cooperation in education and tourism, expand air links, increase media and youth exchanges and forge closer ties between sister cities. The two countries agreed to jointly host the China-India Year of Friendship through Tourism in 2007, the president said.

IV. Early Settlement of the Boundary Issue

The early settlement of the boundary issue would contribute to peace and stability in the region, Hu said, noting it should be pursued as a strategic goal of the two countries. China is ready to work with India, guided by the Five Principles of Peaceful Co-existence and the overall interests of the two countries, to actively seek a fair, just and mutually acceptable solution through friendly consultation on an equal footing, the president said. "We hope to turn the China-India boundary into a bond of good-neighborliness and mutually beneficial cooperation," Hu added.

V. Multilateral Cooperation

Hu suggested that the two countries should develop multilateral cooperation and jointly uphold the legitimate rights and interests of developing countries. "We should increase communication and coordination on major international issues to jointly uphold the overall interests of developing countries," he said. Furthermore, the two countries should promote multi-polarity in the world and democracy in international relations and work to make the international political and economic order fairer and more equitable, Hu proposed.

HU JINTAO'S FIVE POINTS ON ECONOMIC COOPERATION

Chinese President made a five-points proposal on 23 November 2006, for promoting Sino-Indian economic and trade cooperation at the India-China Economic, Trade and Investment Cooperation Summit and CEO Forum.

I. To Expand and Upgrade Bilateral Trade

The two countries have set a new goal for bilateral trade to reach US$ 40 billion in the year 2010. To achieve this goal, Hu said, both sides should work to improve the trade structure, increase the technology content in commodities and add value to them, increase the share of new and high-tech products and electron mechanical products in bilateral trade, expand the scale of trade and upgrade the level of cooperation.

II. To Strengthen Cooperation in Key Areas

Hu said the respective strength of China and India in information technology, energy resources, infrastructure, science and technology and agriculture is mutually complementary and offers great potential for cooperation. The two sides should explore business opportunities in these fields and nurture new growth stimulus to boost business ties. The Chinese Government will continue to encourage competent Chinese companies to invest and do business in India, and Indian companies are welcome to explore business opportunities in China.

III. To Improve Environment of Trade and Investment

He said the Chinese and Indian governments should act in the overall interests of the two countries, strengthen consultation and dialogue and properly resolve problems in business and trade. He said both sides should take measures to remove obstacles to trade and investment, promote trade and investment facilitation and create an enabling business environment. The two governments should create better conditions for bilateral economic and technological cooperation and ensure a fair and favorable trading environment for business communities of the two sides.

IV. To Strengthen Cooperation in Multilateral Fields and with Third Countries

He said China and India should strengthen coordination in the World Trade Organization and other multilateral economic organizations to jointly uphold the legitimate rights and interests of developing countries. The two countries should encourage

Chinese and Indian companies to enter into energy cooperation in third countries, and they may conduct joint project contracting in third countries by drawing on mutual strength, noted Hu.

V. To Actively Explore Trade Liberalization

He said a China-India free trade area would lift the bilateral business relations to a higher level and promote regional economic integration in Asia.

China and India have started joint feasibility study on regional trade arrangement and agreed to conclude the study by October 2007, said Hu, hoping this will lay a good foundation for launching negotiation on regional trade arrangement. China-India two-way trade, growing at an average annual rate of 32 per cent, rose to 18.7 billion dollars in 2005 from 1.16 billion dollars in 1995, a jump of 15 times in ten years. The bilateral trade touched US$ 38.6 billion in 2007, according to Chinese statistics.

China is now India's second largest trading partner and India is China's largest trading partner in South Asia. Besides, India is also one of China's most important project contracting markets. Bilateral mutual investment is growing, and it covers new industries such as telecommunications, software and pharmacy, which serve as an example for investment in other sectors.

Hu said, "China-India business cooperation, which is mutually beneficial in nature, has brought much benefit to both countries, and solidified the foundation of the relations. China takes India as a friend and partner and sincerely wishes India greater progress in development. The development of the two countries cherishes good opportunities to deepen bilateral all-round cooperation and achieve win-win progress, both sides should also seize the opportunity to advance bilateral economic cooperation and trade in depth and width." "Business communities of the two countries would be future-oriented and work together to boost the bilateral business ties and contribute to both national development of the two countries and the rejuvenation of Asia. More than 400 government officials and business people from both sides attended this summit meeting," he added.[29]

EVALUATION

India and China are two of the world's oldest civilizations with a history of close contacts. Freedom struggle in the two countries against colonial rule led to renewed contacts in the late 18th/early 19th century. In 1954, India and China evolved the Five Principles of Peaceful Co-existence. In the same year Chinese Premier Zhou Enlai visited India in June and the first Indian Prime Minister Jawaharlal Nehru visited China in October. The war of 1962 led to a serious setback in bilateral relations. India and China restored ambassadorial relations in 1976. India seeks friendly, cooperative, good-neighborly and mutually beneficial relations with China on the basis of the Five Principles of Peaceful Co-existence.

Indian Prime Minister Narasimha Rao visited China in September 1993 during which the Agreement on the Maintenance of Peace and Tranquillity along the Line of Actual Control (LAC) in the India-China Border Area was signed and the India-China Expert Group of Diplomatic and Military Officers was set up to assist the JWG. This Agreement provides for both sides to respect the status quo on the border, clarify the LAC where there are doubts and undertakes Confidence Building Measures (CBMs).

President Jiang Zemin visited to India in November 1996. During his visit the two countries signed four agreements of which the most important was one on Confidence Building Measures (CBMs) in the Military Field along the LAC in the India-China Border Areas. A prominent feature of the CBM Agreement is the adoption of concrete measures between the two militaries to enhance exchanges and promote cooperation and trust. The two countries agreed to exchange maps indicating their respective perceptions of the entire alignment of the LAC. Both countries also agreed to work towards a constructive and cooperative relationship while continuing to address outstanding differences.

India-China relations suffered a setback after the India's nuclear tests in May 1998, but in June 1999, both countries' Foreign Ministers resumed official level dialogues. Both sides reiterated that neither country is a threat to the other. High-level exchanges were renewed with the second visit of President K.R. Narayanan in May-June 2000 which marked a return to normalcy in bilateral relations.

Senior Chinese leader and Chairman of the Standing Committee of the National People's Congress (NPC) Li Peng visited India in January 2001. During the visit formation of an India-China Parliamentary Friendship Group was announced. Premier Zhu Rongji visited India in January 2002. During the visit there were many agreements on cooperation in tourism, provision of hydrological data by China to India, peaceful uses of outer space, science & technology and phytosanitary measures were signed.

During Prime Minister A.B. Vajpayee's visit to China in June 2003 both countries issued the Joint Declaration, which provides a roadmap, based on shared perspectives between India and China, in an extensive range of areas. The mechanism of Special Representatives was established to explore from the political perspective of the overall bilateral relationship the framework of a boundary settlement. India and China concluded a border trade protocol to add a border trade point between Sikkim and the Tibet Autonomous Region.

During the visit of the Chinese Premier Wen Jiabao to India in April 2005, the two Prime Ministers signed a Joint Statement, which establishes a strategic cooperative partnership for peace and prosperity between the two countries.

India-China relations have gone through a tortuous process—from friendship to confrontation, from confrontation to détente and then to normalization. The relations have been growing in a substantive manner in recent years. When discussing relations between the two countries, one has to recognize the differential priorities in each country. China remains a country of top priority in India's foreign policy, probably next only to her relations with Pakistan and Russia and more recently, the USA.

The bilateral trade between China and India was initiated in 1951, and in 1954 the governments of the two countries endorsed a trade agreement, which was renewed in August 1984. Seven trading agreements have been signed in sequence since 1986 every year. The trade between China and India has been developing at a rapid pace with trade volume increasing continuously and variety of exchanging commodity gradually expanding. Since 1990, interactions between the economic and trade circles of China and India have kept expanding, and the bilateral trade volume has grown even faster. By the end of 2003, bilateral trade had increased to US$ 7.6 billion; the increase in trade volume has not been uniform over the years. Since 2000, bilateral trade has shown substantial increase in both total volume and rate of growth.

In 2004, bilateral trade between India and China stood at US$ 13.6 billion as per Chinese figures. At the end of December 2005, China enjoyed an overall trade surplus of US$ 102.1 billion. Total trade for this period stood at US$ 1422.54 billion. While imports totaled US$ 660.22 billion in 2005, exports recorded a value of US$ 762.32 billion. Japan was the top exporter to China, while US remained the top importer of Chinese products.

Trade and economic relation has emerged as one of the most visible indicators of recent positive developments in India-China relations. According to Chinese statistics bilateral trade touched US$ 38.6 billion in 2007. According to the Department of Commerce statistics, bilateral trade was Rs. 43661.72 crores during April-October 2007. China has emerged as our second largest trade partner. For China India became an important export market with China's export to India registering the fastest growth. Both countries realised the importance of placing bilateral trade on a strong diversified and mutually beneficial foundation.

China and India have agreed that all-round expansion of economic cooperation between the two countries constitutes an important dimension of their stronger relationship and they should make joint efforts to increase bilateral trade volume to US$ 20 billion or higher by 2008.

India and China are two growing economies and emerging powers. Both countries are great powers with legitimate aspirations and a fair amount of competition and rivalry is natural. The two nations have struggled hard to find a place in the international community. Being neighbors, each of the two is also unlikely to accept an inferior position *vis-à-vis* the other.

There are many similarities in the challenges both countries face in modernizing their economies and in their participation in the process of globalisation. Given the prevailing flux in the international economic situation and evolving international trade regimes, there is ample room for exchanges of experience between Indian and Chinese socio-economic experts. Both countries are pursuing their foreign policy goals more assertively as each country tries to position itself as the major political and economic force in Asia.

Bilateral defense ties between India and China is manifested in increased defense exchanges, and mutual participation in training courses and joint activities. Chinese Defense Minister General Cao Guang Chuan visited India in March 2004, following the visit of then Defence Minister George Fernandes, to China in April 2003.

India and China share their national experiences in dealing with phenomenon of terrorism, and exchange views on the international counter-terrorism situation including developments in the region, cooperation at the United Nations and possibilities of bilateral cooperation. The two sides resolutely condemn terrorism in any form, admit that the struggle between the international community and global terrorism is a comprehensive and sustained one. Both countries agreed that the first meeting of the dialogue mechanism was useful in enhancing mutual understanding. Both sides also agreed on the terms of reference for the dialogue. India-China cooperation in the field of counter-terrorism and public security was also marked by the visit of Home Minister Shri Shivraj Patil to China during 7-11 September 2005.

The Science & Technology relations between India and China function within the overall ambit of the Agreement on Cooperation in Science & Technology, signed between the Department of Science and Technology and the People's Republic of China (PRC) Ministry of Science and Technology in Beijing on December 22, 1988. Since then, the two countries have signed a number of Memorandums of Understanding (MoUs), agreements on energy cooperation, agricultural cooperation, cooperation on global oil quest, etc.

China and India have agreed to establish a "strategic and cooperative partnership for peace and prosperity" between them, according to a joint statement signed by the premiers of the two countries in New Delhi on 11 April 2005. The two sides also reiterated their intention to promote regular ministerial-level exchanges and make full use of the China-India strategic dialogue and other bilateral dialogue mechanisms, the statement added. The statement said the year of 2005 marks the 55th anniversary of the establishment of diplomatic relations between China and India, and to mark the occasion, the two countries organized a series of commemorative activities.

Both sides reiterated their readiness to take the India-Chinese Strategic and Cooperative Partnership for Peace and Prosperity to a new level. The Prime Minister of India Dr. Manmohan Singh during his visit to China in January 2008 said that the relation with China is a high priority for India. Both sides agreed that India-China relations are of regional and global significance. During the time both sides issued "A Shared Vision for the 21st Century". This document reflects not only the common perceptions of India and China but also their desire to purposefully cooperate in the future and to promote global peace and common prosperity following the principles of *Panchsheel.*

Chinese side reiterated that India is an important developing country and is having an increasingly important influence in the international arena. Chinese Premier Wen Jiabao who was paying an official visit to India said on April 11, 2005, China supports India's bid for a permanent seat in the United Nations Security Council (UNSC).

China and India signed a Memorandum of Understanding on the expansion of aviation transportation between the two countries, the General Administration of Civil Aviation of China announced on April 13, 2005. The new agreement allows the two countries to open freight market to each other.

The India-China Cultural Exchange Programme (2003-05) continued to provide for cooperation framework for various exchanges and activities, which included dance, theatre, painting, photographic exhibitions, films, and literary exchanges and cultural restoration. As part of the commemorative activities for the "50th Anniversary of Panchsheel", cultural programs were organised and a joint exhibition of Indian and Chinese postage stamps held.

Since the establishment of diplomatic ties 55 years ago, and especially since the beginning of this century, the good-neighborly friendship and mutually beneficial cooperation between the two countries has entered a new era of comprehensive development. Further strengthening of the long-term partnership of constructive cooperation between the two countries serves the fundamental interests of the people of both countries. The frequent exchanges of visits by Indian and Chinese leaders in recent years have greatly promoted mutual understanding and trust. India hopes the two countries take a global and strategic perspective and continue to enrich and enhance their partnership of constructive cooperation.

Mr. Hu Jintao, President of the People's Republic of China's visit to the Republic of India from 20 to 23 November 2006, signifies an important milestone in bilateral relations. It was only the second visit to India by any Chinese president. The President's visit showed that there is a mutual willingness to keep the irritants aside and move forward. The timing was appropriate since it also marked the high tide of "Sino-Indian Year of Friendship". A number of commitments have been made in 2005 when Wen Jiabao, the Chinese Premier was in India and Hu was here mainly to consolidate those gains.

The various agreements signed in New Delhi, to upgrade India-China relations, to further substantiate and reinforce their Strategic and Cooperative Partnership, committed them to pursuing the "Ten-Pronged Strategy" which embodied in the Joint Declaration. Indeed, it is a "road map" for comprehensive development of bilateral relations. Now people hope that in the days to come both the countries would adjust their relationship in such a way that the nations in South-East Asia and South Asia do not have to fear Beijing or New Delhi. Both India and China can jointly formulate programs to help the countries in the region develop a common market, like the arrangement in Europe.

During President Hu's visit "Five-point proposals" seek to increase political trust, business cooperation, cultural and social exchanges, and multilateral cooperation on the one hand and address the boundary issues on the other.

The visit also reminds that India's foreign policy has yet to make the full transition to realism. Let us have a look at the following two paragraphs in the joint statement: "The Indian side recalls that India was among the first countries to recognize that there is One China and its One China policy has remained unaltered. The Indian side states that it would continue to abide by its One China policy." "The Indian side reiterates that it has recognized the Tibet Autonomous Region as part of the territory of the People's Republic of China, and that it does not allow Tibetans to engage in anti-China political activities in India." The People's Republic of China (PRC) expresses its appreciation for the Indian position. From Chinese side, without any reciprocal commitment to a "One India Policy", India again pledged to abide by a "One China Policy" despite recently, just before Hu's visit, Chinese officials released a barrage of statements claiming Arunachal Pradesh as part of China. How can India's diplomacy become so one-sided that India propitiates and China merely records its "appreciation"?

The boundary issues remain the sore point. The two countries have a long-standing territorial dispute in the Himalayas that led to a border war in 1962. The Prime Minister of India, Dr. Manmohan Singh did not shy away from giving vent to India's disquiet over the slow progress of the 25-year-old border negotiations even after eight rounds of talks by calling for efforts to settle the "outstanding issues in a focused, sincere and problem-solving manner". For the first time, China suggested acceleration of border talks and seeking an early settlement of outstanding issues realizing that unresolved border issue is a hurdle to normalization of bilateral relations.

At the same time India should seriously think about the proposal to exchange Aksai Chin with particular reference to Tawang tract of Arunachal Pradesh if China's old proposal still stands. China should, in the meanwhile, make certain gestures by accepting the 1962 Colombo Proposals which suggested—(i) from nowhere would Indian troops be required to withdraw further; (ii) the McMahon Line would be more or less the ceasefire line (India gave an assurance that it would not take its troops right up to the McMahon Line even though the Colombo Conference had allowed it to do so).

China still seems anxious to maintain good relations with India. During President Hu's visit to India, he speaks of Panchsheel, that China and India are "true friends", not rivals but partners; even on the nuclear issue, it doesn't have too many reservations. However, India-China partnership cannot be achieved unless China walks a step ahead.

It is quite significant that in spite of many drawbacks in the bilateral relations, the two nations have upgraded their diplomatic relations to the current level of "strategic comprehensive partnership for peace and prosperity". Looking at the emerging world order in terms of the developments especially since World Trade Center bomb blast, combating terrorism, the nuclear crisis in North Korea and President Hu Jintao's South Asia tour, one can have more optimistic view of the future India-China bilateral relations.

In Pakistan, General Pervez Musharraf himself received Hu Jintao at the airport. China and China's 'evergreen' friend Pakistan are anxious to show the world that those ties have not been diminished by Hu's visit to India. In order to counter-balance India in South Asia and prevent India's rise as a regional power, China has long been supporting Pakistan morally, financially and militarily. China's close alliance with Pakistan is also one of the most dangerous strategic ties of the South Asian region as Pakistan is viewed by China as having considerable potential to offer it foothold in the region. Thus, it is a very special relationship that it would never think of losing. Both China and Pakistan are intransigent neighbors of India having nuclear warheads. Both are common in interests and close to each other. Both nations fought wars against India.

India's problems with both China and Pakistan are territorial, strategic, and above all, emotional. These problems are not going to be resolved in a few sittings or a few years. There is no easy solution. Therefore, India has to rise above its personal gains and past hurt, it would have realized that accommodating a bit of China and Pakistan's concerns may not be a bad investment. The approach should be based on consensus, buttressed by the spirit of give and take.

CHRONOLOGY OF EVENTS

Agreements/MoUs Signed between India and China

1954: Agreement between the Republic of India and the People's Republic of China on Trade and Intercourse between the Tibet region of China and India. (Note: The Agreement was valid for eight years and it lapsed in 1962).

1954: Trade Agreement between the Republic of India and the People's Republic of China. (Note: The Agreement was valid for two years, with the provision that it could be extended. It lapsed in 1962).

1984: Trade Agreement between the Government of the Republic of India and the Government of the People's Republic of China.

1988: Protocol between the Republic of India and the People's Republic of China on Resumption of Border Trade between the Tibet region of China and India.

1991: Memorandum of Understanding between the Ministry of Aero-Space Industry of the People's Republic of China and the Department of Space of the Republic of India on Cooperation in the Peaceful Application of Outer Space Sciences and Technology.

1991: Memorandum between the Government of the Republic of India and the Government of the People's Republic of China on Resumption of Border Trade.

1991: Trade Protocol between the Government of the Republic of India and the Government of the People's Republic of China for the Calendar Year 1992.

1991: Consular Convention between the Republic of India and the People's Republic of China.

1992: Protocol between the Government of the Republic of India and the Government of the People's Republic of China on Custom Regulation, Banking Arrangements and Related matters for Border Trade.

1992: Memorandum of Understanding on cooperation in the field of Civil Services, Personnel Management and Public Administration between the Ministry of Personnel, Public

Grievances and Pensions of the Government of the Republic of India and the Ministry of Personnel of the People's Republic of China.

1992: Protocol between the Government of the Republic of India and the Government of the People's Republic of China on Entry and Exit Procedures for Border Trade.

1992: Memorandum of Understanding between The Office of the Comptroller and Auditor General, Republic of India and The Audit Administration, People's Republic of China.

1992: Memorandum of Understanding on cooperation in Agriculture between the Ministry of Agriculture of the Republic of India and the Ministry of Agriculture of the People's Republic of China.

1993: Protocol between the Government of the Republic of India and the Government of the People's Republic of China for Extension of Border Trade across Shipki La Pass.

1993: Agreement between the Ministry of Information and Broadcasting of the Republic of India and the Ministry of Radio, Film, Television of the People's Republic of China on Radio and Television Cooperation.

1993: Memorandum of Understanding between the Government of Republic of India and the Government of the People's Republic of China on cooperation in the Field of Geology and Mineral Resources.

1993: Agreement on the Maintenance of Peace and Tranquility along the Line of Actual Control in the India-China Border areas signed in Beijing on September 7, 1993.

1994: Memorandum of Understanding on Simplifying the Visa Procedures between the Government of the Republic of India and the Government of the People's Republic of China.

1995: Memorandum of Understanding between Ministry of Metallurgical Industry of the Government of the People's Republic of China and the Ministry of Steel of the Government of the Republic of India.

1996: Agreement between the Government of the Republic of India and the Government of the People's Republic of China on Confidence-Building measures in the Military Field along the Line of Actual Control in the India-China Border Areas.

1996: Agreement between the Government of the Republic of India and the Government of the People's Republic of China concerning the maintenance of the Consulate General of the Republic of India in the Hong Kong Special Administrative Region of the People's Republic of China.

1996: Agreement on Maritime Transport between the Government of the Republic of India and the Government of the People's Republic of China.

1997: Protocol on cooperation between the Ministry of External Affairs of the Republic of India and the Ministry of Foreign Affairs of the People's Republic of China.

2000: Memorandum of Understanding signed during the 6th Joint Economic Group Meeting in Beijing during February 21-22, 2000 on cooperation in the field of steel between India and China.

2000: Memorandum of Understanding on cooperation in the field of Information Technology.

2000: Memorandum of Understanding on cooperation in the field of Labour (Employment services, vocational training and social security).

2002: MoU on the Application of Phytosanitary Measures between the Ministry of Agriculture of the Republic of India and the State General Administration of the People's Republic of China for Quality Supervision, Inspection and Quarantine (AQSIQ).

2002: MoU between ISRO and the China National Space Administration on Cooperation in the Peaceful Use of Outer Space.

2002: MoU between Department of Science and Technology of the Republic of India and the State Administration of Foreign Experts Affairs of People's Republic of China on Exchange of Personnel between India and China.

2002: MoU between Department of Science and Technology of the Republic of India and the Chinese Academy of Sciences of the People's Republic of China on Cooperation in Science and Technology.

2002: Agreement between India and China on Cooperation in the field of Tourism.

2002: MoU between the Ministry of Water Resources of India and Ministry of Water Resources of China upon provision of hydrological information of the Yaluzangbu/Brahmaputra river in flood season by China to India.

2002: MoU between Department of Tourism and China National Tourism Administration (CNTA) on the Implementation Plan for organised group travel by Chinese citizens to India.

2003: Declaration on Principles for Relations and Comprehensive Cooperation between the People's Republic of China and the Republic of India.

2003: MoU between the Government of the Republic of India and the Government of the People's Republic of China on Expanding Border Trade.

2003: Memorandum of Understanding on Cooperation between the Ministry of Law and Justice of the Government of the Republic of India and the Supreme People's Prosecution Service of the People's Republic of China.

2003: Executive Program on Educational Cooperation and Exchange between the Ministry of Human Resource Development, Government of the Republic of India and Ministry of Education, the People's Republic of China.

2003: Protocol of Phytosanitary Requirements for Exporting Mangoes from India to China between the Ministry of Agriculture of the Republic of India and General Administration of Quality Supervision, Inspection and Quarantine of the People's Republic of China.

2003: Memorandum of Understanding on Simplifying Visa Procedures between the Government of the Republic of India and the Government of the People's Republic of China.

2003: Memorandum of Understanding for Enhanced Cooperation in the field of Renewable Energy between the Ministry of Non-Conventional Energy Sources, Government of the Republic of India and the Ministry of Water Resources, Government of People's Republic of China.

2003: Memorandum of Understanding for Cooperation in the field of Ocean Science and Technology between Department of Ocean Development, Government of the Republic of India and State Oceanic Administration, People's Republic of China.

2003: Memorandum of Understanding between the Department of Science and Technology of the Republic of India and the National Science Foundation of China.

2003: Memorandum of Understanding between the Government of the Republic of India and the Government of the People's Republic of China on the Reciprocal Establishment of Cultural Centres in their capitals.

2003: Executive Programme of Cultural Exchanges between the Government of the Republic of India and the Government of the People's Republic of China for the years 2003-2005.

2005: Agreement on the Political Parameters and Guiding Principles for the Settlement of the India-China Boundary Question.

2005: Protocol on Modalities for the Implementation of CBMs in the Military Field along the Line of Actual Control in the India-China Border Areas.

2005: Report of the India-China Joint Study Group on Comprehensive Trade and Economic Cooperation.

2005: Agreement on Mutual Administrative Assistance and Cooperation in Customs Matters between India and China.

2005: Memorandum of Understanding on Civil Aviation between India and China.

2005: Protocol of Phytosanitary Requirements for the Export of Grape from India to China between the Ministry of Agriculture of India and the General Administration of Quality Supervision, Inspection and Quarantine of China.

2005: Protocol of Phytosanitary Requirements for Exporting Bitter Gourds from India to China between the Ministry of Agriculture of India and the General Administration of Quality Supervision, Inspection and Quarantine of China.

2005: Memorandum of Understanding on Cooperation between the Indian Council of World Affairs, India and the Chinese People's Institute of Foreign Affairs, China.

2005: Memorandum of Understanding on the Launch of the India-China Financial Dialogue.

2005: Memorandum of Understanding between the Ministries of Water Resources of India and China upon Provision of Hydrological Information of the Sutlej/Langqen Zangbo River in Flood Season by China to India.

2005: Protocol on India China Film Cooperation Commission.

2005: Memorandum on the Construction of an Indian Style Buddhist Temple on the Western Side of the White Horse Temple in Luoyang, China.

2006: Agreements/Protocols/MoUs signed during the visit of Chinese President Hu Jintao to India (Nov. 20-23, 2006).

Following is the synopses of Agreements/Protocols/MoUs signed during visit of Chinese President Hu Jintao to India (November 20-23, 2006):

1. **Protocol between the Government of the Republic of India and the Government of the People's Republic of China on the Establishment of Consulates-General at Guangzhou and Kolkata**

   (Signatories: Shri Pranab Mukherjee, Minister of External Affairs and Mr. Li Zhaoxing, Minister of Foreign Affairs of the People's Republic of China)

   This Protocol provides for an Indian Consulate-General in Guangzhou, with its consular district covering the seven Chinese Provinces of Guangdong, Fujian, Hunan, Hainan, Yunnan, Sichuan and Guangxi Zhuang Autonomous Region. The Chinese Consulate-General in Kolkata will have its consular district covering the five States of West Bengal, Orissa, Chhattisgarh, Jharkhand and Bihar. This Protocol will help sustain, facilitate and promote greater engagement between India and China.

2. **Protocol on Cooperation between the Ministry of External Affairs of the Republic of India and the Ministry of Foreign Affairs of the People's Republic of China**

   (Signatories: Shri Pranab Mukherjee, Minister of External Affairs and Mr. Li Zhaoxing, Minister of Foreign Affairs of the People's Republic of China)

   This Protocol institutionalizes the bilateral dialogue and consultation mechanisms between the two Foreign Offices and provides for the establishment of a hotline between the two Foreign Ministers. The Protocol is expected to intensify dialogues, interaction and cooperation on issues of mutual interest between the two Foreign Offices.

3. **Agreement between the Government of the Republic of India and the Government of the People's Republic of China on the Issue of Property of the Consulate-General of the Republic of India in Shanghai**

   (Signatories: Shri Pranab Mukherjee, Minister of External Affairs and Mr. Li Zhaoxing, Minister of Foreign Affairs of the People's Republic of China)

   Under this Agreement, the Chinese side shall provide the Indian side with a plot of land measuring an area of 5,000 square meters, free of charge for the construction of the premises of the Consulate-General of India, Shanghai. The plot of land is provided to Indian side in lieu of the old Indian Consulate property in Shanghai. The signing of the agreement will bring to a close an issue, which has remained outstanding for over 40 years now.

4. **Agreement between the Government of the Republic of India and the Government of the People's Republic of China for the Promotion and Protection of Investments**

   (Signatories: Shri Kamal Nath, Minister of Commerce and Industry and Mr. Bo Xilai, Chinese Minister of Commerce)

   The Agreement provides for a framework for bilateral investment flows between the two countries, thereby creating favorable conditions for investors of one country to make investments in the other. This will send a positive signal to prospective Indian and Chinese investors and contribute to strengthening of the economic engagement between the two countries.

5. **Agreement of Cooperation on Inspection of Iron Ore between Export Inspection Council of the Republic of India (EIC) and the General Administration of Quality Supervision, Inspection and Quarantine of the People's Republic of China (AQSIQ)**

   (Signatories: Shri Kamal Nath, Minister of Commerce and Industry and Mr. Li Changjiang, Administrator, AQSIQ)

   The Agreement establishes a mechanism to inspect trade in iron ore between China and India. The Export Inspection Council of India and the General Administration of Quality Supervision, Inspection and Quarantine of China shall respectively recognize and designate inspection agencies in India and China. This Agreement is expected to give a further boost to bilateral trade in iron ore—the single largest export item from India to China.

6. **The Protocol between the Ministry of Agriculture of the Republic of India and the General Administration of Quality Supervision, Inspection and Quarantine of the People's Republic of China on Phytosanitary Requirements for Exporting Rice from India to China**

   (Signatories: Shri Sharad Pawar, Minister for Agriculture and Mr. Li Changjiang, Administrator of AQSIQ)

   This Protocol, which provides, the phytosanitary requirements regarding the entry into China of Basmati rice produced in India, will facilitate the export of Indian rice to China. Accordingly, Basmati rice that is exported to China shall comply with the Chinese plant quarantine laws and regulations and also adhere to the relevant measures under the WTO.

7. **MoU between the Indian Council of Agricultural Research (ICAR) and the Chinese Academy of Agricultural Sciences (CAAS) for Cooperation in Agricultural Research**

   (Signatories: Dr. Mangala Rai, Secretary, Department of Agricultural Research and Education and Director General, ICAR and Mr. Sun Yuxi, Ambassador of the People's Republic of China to India)

   Under this MoU, the ICAR and CAAS agree to promote cooperation in the exchange of scientific personnel; germplasm and breeding material; scientific literature, information and methodology; equipment, etc. The signing of this MoU will facilitate cooperation in areas that are crucial to the well-being of a large part of their respective populations.

8. **Exchange Program between the Ministry of Human Resource Development of the Government of the Republic of India and the Ministry of Education of the Government of the People's Republic of China on Cooperation in the Field of Education**

   (Signatories: Shri R.P. Agarwal, Secretary, Ministry of Human Resource Development and Mr. Cui Tiankai, Assistant Minister of Foreign Affairs of the People's Republic of China)

   Through this Agreement the Ministry of Human Resource Development of India and the Ministry of Education of the Government of China seek to encourage the development of contacts and cooperation between the educational institutions of the two countries. As two developing countries with large human resources potential, cooperation in the area of education will contribute to the further broad basing of the bilateral relationship.

9. **MoU between Forward Markets Commission, India and China Security Regulatory Commission Regarding Commodity Futures Regulatory Cooperation**

   (Signatories: Shri S. Sundareshan, Chairman, Forward Markets Commission and Mr. Sun Yuxi, Ambassador of the People's Republic of China to India)

The purpose of this MoU is to promote investor protection and integrity of the commodity futures markets by providing a framework for cooperation, including channels of communication, increasing mutual understanding and exchange of regulatory and technical information.

10. **MoU on Cooperation between the Indian Institute of Public Administration, India and the Party School of the Central Committee of the Communist Party of China, the People's Republic of China**

    (Signatories: Shri P.L. Sanjeeva Reddy, Director General, IIPA and Mr. Cui Tiankai, Assistant Minister of Foreign Affairs of the People's Republic of China)

    The MoU provides for cooperation between the IIPA and the CPS on issues of common interest such as rural development, agriculture, poverty alleviation, public administration, public policy, role of government in a market economy and role of Planning Commission. The signing of the MoU reflects the desire of the public administration institutions of the two sides to better understand each other's systems of governance and promote cooperation and exchange of experience.

11. **The Agreement on Forestry Cooperation between Ministry of Environment and Forests of the Republic of India and State Forestry Administration of the People's Republic of China**

    (Signatories: Shri Gopal Krishna Prasad, Director General of Forests & Special Secretary, Ministry of Environment and Forests and Mr. Cui Tiankai, Assistant Minister of Foreign Affairs of the People's Republic of China)

    Under this Agreement the two sides shall support cooperation and development in forestry related fields of economy, manufacturing, processing, and science & technology. This would provide an opportunity for the two sides to gain better insight into an important part of the other's natural ecosystem and the activities that influence them.

12. **MoU between the Archaeological Survey of India of the Republic of India (ASI) and the State Administration of Cultural Heritage (SACH) of the People's Republic of China on Cooperation in the Conservation of Cultural Heritage**

    (Signatories: Shri C. Babu Rajeev, Director General, Archaeological Survey of India and Mr. Shan Jixiang, Director General of State Administration of Cultural Heritage of China)

    The MoU provides for cooperation between ASI and SACH in the field of cultural heritage. Cooperation shall include exchange of professional experience; training of personnel; and joint scientific and academic research in related spheres of activity. Such cooperation assumes significance for the two countries, which are inheritors of the oldest civilizations in the world.

13. **Agreement between the Government of the Republic of India and the Government of the People's Republic of China on Preventing Theft, Clandestine Excavation and Illicit Import and Export of Cultural Property**

    (Signatories: Shri C. Babu Rajeev, Director General, Archaeological Survey of India and Mr. Shan Jixiang, Director General of State Administration of Cultural Heritage of China)

    Under this Agreement, the Ministry of Culture of India and the State Administration of Cultural Heritage of China shall collaborate in adopting preventive, mandatory and remedial measures to combat unlawful and criminal practices concerning the theft, clandestine excavation and illicit import and export of cultural property.[30]

NOTES

1. India-China Bilateral Relations: Political Relations. www.indianembassy.org.cn/Bilateral relations.htm
2. *Annual Report 2003-2004*, Ministry of External Affairs, p.15.
3. *Annual Report 2005-2006*, Ministry of External Affairs, p.6.
4. Bilateral Trade between China and India: Basic Information, A Survey before 2003.

http://www.chinaembassy.org.in/eng/jjmy/

5. India-China Bilateral Trade from Jan-June, 2006. http://www.indianembassy.org.cn/
6. *Ibid.*, no. 2, p. 18.
7. *Ibid.*, no. 3, p. 7.
8. The First Meeting of Sino-Indian Dialogue Mechanism on Counter-terrorism (Press Release). www.chinaembassy.org.in/eng/ssygd/zygx/xy/t807o2.htm
9. The Second Meeting of Sino-Indian Dialogue Mechanism on Counter-terrorism (Press Release). www.chinaembassy.org.in/eng/ssygd/zygx/xy/t807o2.htm
10. *Ibid.*, no. 2, pp. 15-16.
11. *Annual Report 2004-2005*, Ministry of External Affairs, p. 7.
12. *Ibid.*, no. 3, p. 7.
13. Agreement on Cooperation in Science and Technology between India-China in 1988 (Press Release). www.chinaembassy.org.in/eng
14. *Ibid.*, no. 11, p. 6.
15. Indian Minister Calls Better Cooperation with China, 11 September, 2006. www.chinaembassy.org.in/eng/ssygd/zygx/xy/t807o2.htm
16. China, India signs Five Memoranda On Energy Cooperation, 12 January, 2006. www.chinaembassy.org.in/eng/ssygd/zygx/xy
17. China, India Agricultural Cooperation (2005/03/30). www.chinaembassy.org.in/eng/ssygd/zygx/xy/t189435.htm
18. China, India Seek Cooperation In Global Oil Quest (2005/04/05). www.chinaembassy.org.in/eng/ssygd/zygx/xy/t190213.htm
19. China, India Agree on "Strategic Partnership"(2005/04/13). www.chinaembassy.org.in/eng/ssygd/zygx/xy/t191496.htm
20. China Supports India's Bid for UNSC Seat. www.chinaembassy.org.in/eng
21. China, India Renew Aviation Agreement (2005/04/15). www.chinaembassy.org.in/eng/ssygd/zygx/xy/t191746.htm
23. On the Inaugural Function for the Resumption of Border Trade at Nathula (2006/07/06), MEA, *News Wire*, July 6, 2006, New Delhi.
24. Cultural Agreement between the Government of the China and India. www.chinaembassy.org.in/eng/ssygd/zygx/xy/t191746.htm
25. *Ibid.*, no. 3, p. 8.
26. 55th Anniversary of China-India Diplomatic Ties Marked (2005/04/01). www.chinaembassy.org.in/eng

27. China, India Hail 55 years of Diplomatic Ties (2005/04/03). www.chinaembassy.org.in/eng

28. Chinese President Hu Jintao Visits India November 2006: Joint Declaration. http://www.indianembassy.org.cn/

29. President Hu Jintao Five Points on Sino-India Ties and Five Points on Economic Cooperation Proposal November 2006. http://www.indianembassy.org.cn/

30. Agreements/MoUs Signed Between India and China (1954-2006). http://www.indianembassy.org.cn/

5

India's Relations with the United Kingdom

BACKGROUND

The relationship between Britain and India is based on the solid bedrock of a democratic and pluralist society and commitment to mass prosperity. There are many constants in the relationship between Britain and India: the centuries of shared history, the commitment to democracy and to the values of a pluralist society.[1] The relationship between Britain and India is warm and based on deep cultural, historical and, above all, personal roots. Both countries celebrate the diversity of the multi-ethnic and multi-cultural societies.

India has very cordial relations with United Kingdom and this is so in spite of the fact that there was a lot of resentment against the British during their rule in India. The exemplary manner in which the British government granted independence to India won over the hearts of the people of India and a lot of goodwill was created in favour of Great Britain (United Kingdom). Even today, India buys the largest number of things from United Kingdom. Very often, the British Government consults the Government of India on many points. India received great help under the Colombo Plan. It got most of the military help from United Kingdom. It is the British officers who have helped in the development of the Indian Air Force and Indian Navy.

Although India became a Republic in January 1950, it has continued the Commonwealth link. That is a standing testimony to the close relations between the two countries. Pandit Nehru supported the Commonwealth tie in these words : "At the same time, it's made perfectly clear that each country is completely free to go its own ways; it may be that sometimes they may go so far as to break away from the Commonwealth. In the world today where there are so many disruptive forces at work, where we are often on the verge of war, I think it is not a safe thing to encourage the breaking up of any association that one has. Break up the evil part of it; break up anything which comes in the way of your growth because nobody dare to agree to anything which comes in the way of a nation's growth. Otherwise, apart from breaking the evil parts of the association, it is better to keep a cooptive association going which may do good in this world rather than break it."[2]

India's multi-faceted bilateral relationship with the UK has developed substantially over the past few years. There have been regular and close consultations at the highest levels. Strong ties with the UK are a priority for India given the political and cultural ties, substantial economic linkages and the large community of Indian origin in the UK.[3] The 1.5 million strong community of Indian origin is acquiring a growing profile in British society, economy and politics. It remains a valuable catalyst in promoting the bilateral cooperation. This friendship between the two countries is now stronger and more important than ever before.

On foreign policy and defense, too, India and UK are cooperating more than ever before. Both nations are working hard to find a fair and lasting solution to the world trade negotiations. Both countries also extend cooperation on the issues such as security and terrorism which have an impact on both our global and domestic agendas. India, of course, is one of the world's most successful countries. It is the world's largest democracy—a rich, diverse and tolerant society—and is rapidly becoming an economic powerhouse.

In March 2006 UK published a White Paper outlining the forward plan for British diplomacy. It identified ten strategic policy priorities, which focus on such issues as: counter-terrorism, sustainable development, climate change, weapons of mass destruction, energy supply, a liberal, global trading regime, etc.

The White Paper positions India as a global player with significant influence along with China, Japan and Russia. It states: "India is an important partner on global economic and political issues including energy and climate change, serious regional crises, and global non-proliferation. As the world's largest democracy, India will have a growing influence in international affairs and on the global economy. It will have particular strengths in the service and knowledge sectors, while broadening the base of its growth. We are strong advocates of India gaining a permanent seat on the UN Security Council. Our two countries share a modern relationship."

UK strongly supports India's candidature for a permanent seat in the UN Security Council and will continue to work with India to achieve this. India is a strategic partner for the EU. The UK is looking to develop this relationship, including in the area of counter-terrorism, on which the EU and India will work closely together. Promoting an effective EU in India complements the activity in promoting the UK. The UK wants India to take part in the work of the G-8, therefore invited Prime Minister Dr. Manmohan Singh to the G-8 Summit at Gleneagles in July 2006. This was the first time India had been invited to a G-8 heads of government meeting.[4]

Indo-UK Summits

Dr. Manmohan Singh visited the UK during 19-20 September 2004, his first visit to a western capital after he assumed office of the Prime Minister of India. The two Prime Ministers adopted a Joint Declaration titled "India-UK: Towards a New and Dynamic Partnership" which envisaged annual summits, meetings between Foreign Ministers and outlined areas for future cooperation in civil nuclear energy, space, defence, combating terrorism, economic ties, science and technology, education and culture.

British Prime Minister Tony Blair was the first G-8 leader to moot the idea of India joining G-8 discussions. At his invitation Indian Prime Minister visited the UK during 7-8 July 2005 for the "G-8 Plus 5" Gleneagles Summit (India, China, South Africa, Brazil and Mexico). British Prime Minister Tony Blair visited India during 6-8 September 2005 in his capacity as EU-President for the EU/India Summit and also in a bilateral capacity. This was the third meeting between the two Prime Ministers since the elections in May 2004. The bilateral summit was held on September 8 in Udaipur, a day after the 6th India-UK Summit. The delegation included Rt. Hon. Alan Johnson, Secretary of State for Trade and Industry and Dr. Ian Pearson, Minister of State for Trade responsible for trade policy and foreign affairs.[5]

The bilateral summit was follow-up to the Prime Minister's visit to the UK in September 2004 when the two Prime Ministers had adopted a joint declaration titled "India-UK: Towards a New and Dynamic Partnership", setting out plans for a comprehensive strategic partnership. The joint declaration envisaged annual summits as well as meetings between Foreign Ministers and outlined areas for future cooperation.

The two leaders exchanged views on a range of bilateral, regional and multilateral issues including UN reform, cooperation against terrorism, the Millennium Development Goals, climate change including technology transfers for sustainable development and education exchanges. The two sides agreed to move forward cooperation in the civilian nuclear energy sector. UK had reviewed its policy with regard to civilian nuclear technology cooperation and scientific contacts with India a few weeks prior to the visit. At the summit it recognized the need for a supportive international environment for meeting India's pressing energy requirements.

The two sides were in complete agreement on the need to strengthen cooperation against terrorism. Prime Minister reaffirmed his commitment to India's candidature for permanent membership of the expanded UN Security Council. Prime Minister urged a regular dialogue on regional issues. The two sides finalized agreements on air services (substantially increasing the direct flights between the two countries) and cooperation in the field of hydrocarbons. An agreement on films co-production was initiated.

Prime Minister announced that India would found a Chair at Cambridge in honour of Pt. Jawaharlal Nehru. Prime Minister announced a £10 million UK-India education initiative, which will fund scholarships and short-term academic exchanges; provide research awards to young Indians to go to Britain and young British researchers to spend time in Indian institutions.

At the India-EU Summit on September 7, progress was achieved on cooperation in high technology areas, with the EU under the UK Presidency reiterating support for India's participation in ITER and initiation of a framework agreement on India's participation in the Galileo Satellite Navigation Project. At the press conference following the Summit, Prime Minister announced the decision of Indian Airlines to purchase 43 aircraft worth US $2.2 billion from Airbus.

Visits to India

Ministerial visits to India in 2005 included Ms. Patricia Hewitt's visit to Delhi to launch Joint Economic and Trade Committe (JETCO) with Commerce and Industry Minister on January 13. EU Trade Commissioner Peter Mandelson visited India as the EU's Trade Commissioner from January 12-14 during which he participated at the "Partnership Summit" of the Confederation of Indian Industry (CII) in Kolkata and a seminar on "India-EU Strategic Partnership: Steps Ahead" organised by the Federation of Indian Chamber of Commerce and Industry (FCCI) in New Delhi.

Elliot Morley, Minister for Environment and Agri-Environment, visited India during 3-6 February 2005 to attend the opening ceremony of the Delhi Sustainable Development Summit (DSDS), organised by Tata Energy Research Institute (TERI) and also addressed the Summit's Ministerial Session on 3 February.

Lord Bach of Lutterworth, Undersecretary of State and Minister for Defence Procurement, led the British delegation to the Fifth Aero India aerospace exposition at Bangalore on 9-13 February 2005.

Ms. Tessa Jowell, MP, Secretary of State for Culture, Media and Sport visited India during March 27-31, 2005. Sir David King, Chief Scientific Adviser (CSA) to HM Government, visited India during 4-8 February 2005 to participate in the Delhi Sustainable Development Summit (DSDS) organised by TERI.

Sir Nigel Sheinwald, Foreign Policy Adviser (FPA) to PM visited India during 26-27 April, 2005, and Bill Rammell, Minister of State for Lifelong Learning, Further and Higher Education, visited India during 31 July-5 August 2005 to enhance bilateral ties and to explore possibilities for bilateral cooperation in the field of higher education.

Prime Minister Tony Blair led the EU and UK delegations to the Indo-EU and bilateral Summits (6-8 Sept. 2005). British Defence Secretary John Reid visited India during October 5-7, 2005. Mr. Jack Straw, Foreign Secretary, had paid his fifth official visit to India during 17-18 February 2005 (Mr. Straw has visited India nine times since he spent his honeymoon there). During his visit to Amritsar he issued an apology for the Jallianwala Bagh massacre.[6]

UK Minister of State for Trade, Trade Policy and Foreign Affair, Ian Pearson visited India from 15-18 January 2006. He spent a day each in New Delhi, Chennai and Kolkata, met Mr. Kamal Nath, Minister of Commerce and Industry, in New Delhi on 16 January, and addressed the Confederation of Indian Industry (CII) Partnership Summit in Kolkata on 18 January. He was accompanied by a 25-strong business delegation.

The delegation, led by Indo-British Partnership Network (IBPN) Chairman Karan Bilimoria CBE, DL, included senior officials from Standard Chartered Bank, GlaxoSmithKline, Virgin Atlantic and the London Stock Exchange. Minister for Defence Procurement, Lord Drayson was in New Delhi from 1-2 February 2006 to support the attendance of UK companies at DEFEXPO 2006. During his visit Lord Drayson met the Indian Defence Minister, Shri Pranab Mukherjee, to discuss a wide range of bilateral defence issues.

UK Minister for Biodiversity, Jim Knight visited India from 2-6 February 2006. During his visit he delivered a keynote speech at the Delhi Sustainable Development Summit, in New Delhi. Mr. Knight, also met Mr. A. Raja, Minister of Environment and Forests, and Mr. Mani Shankar Aiyar, Minister Panchayati Raj. Mr. Knight also visited the Vultures Breeding Centre at Pinjore (Haryana) and Ranthambore National Park to see the developments relating to tiger conservation. Minister for Science and Innovation, Lord Sainsbury of Turville visited India during 16-23 February 2006. During his visit he presented the 2006 Global Leadership Awards instituted by National Association of Software and Service Companies (NASSCOM) in Mumbai. He also visited Bangalore and Delhi. In Delhi Lord Sainsbury met Mr. Kapil Sibal, Minister for Science, Professor V.S. Ramamurthy, Secretary, Department of Science & Technology and Prof. Samir K. Brahmachari, Director, Institute of Genomics and Integrative Biology (IGIB).

Minister of State Climate Change and Environment, Elliot Morley visited India, during the time he attended the CII Conference on Energy Derivatives and Emission Trading in Mumbai on 20 February. Mr. Morley also visited New Delhi, Bhopal and Corbett National Park and discussed issues on wildlife conservation and management. In New Delhi, the Minister attended a seminar on Mainstreaming Clean Development Mechanism (CDM) opportunities in the Indian Finance sector organised by IT Power India.

The Chancellor of the University of Oxford, Lord Chris Patten's visit aimed at strengthening the UK-India education relationship and to promote Oxford as a centre of academic and creative excellence for Indian students aspiring to study in Britain. The Chancellor of the University of Oxford attended alumni receptions in New Delhi, Bangalore and Mumbai and met prominent business leaders to explore possible industry-academia linkages. He also attended the UK-India Round Table in Goa.

Lord Mayor of City of London, Lord Mayor David Brewer visited India during 19-28 March 2006, who represents the global financial services industry based in the City of London, at the head of a business delegation to strengthen links with India in business, financial, legal and education sectors. The Lord Mayor visited Delhi, Mumbai, Chennai and Hyderabad encompassing more than 60 meetings and seminars. In Delhi, he inaugurated and addressed a seminar on "The City of London—Your Gateway to Global Business". He also took forward a project for a City of London office in Mumbai. Minister for Culture, Media and Sports, Tessa Jowell, who was in Mumbai as a guest speaker at Frames 2006 announced a "UK-India University Partnership Scheme" with a grant of £2 million. The grant is for measures that will allow international students to take their place in the global search for talent. The package will include £1 million in both 2006-07 and 2007-08 for UK-India scholarships, academic exchanges and university collaboration to help higher education sector benefit from global skills.

His Royal Highness the Prince of Wales and the Duchess of Cornwall visited India from 26 March to 31 March 2006. TRH the Prince of Wales last visited India from 28 October to 5 November 2003. This was "Their Royal Highnesses" second joint overseas tour, following a visit to the United States of America in November last year. Their Royal Highnesses visited New Delhi, Punjab and Rajasthan. In New Delhi, TRH attended the British High Commissioner's annual reception for diplomats, politicians and businessmen. In Punjab and Rajasthan, where the Prince of Wales and the British Indian community have been taking forward a range of charitable initiatives, the Chief Minister invited TRH to support plans to help promote sustainable farming, water conservation and employment generation.

UK's Secretary of State for Northern Ireland, Rt. Hon. Peter Hain MP visited India to promote investment, trade, tourism and academic cooperation between India and Northern Ireland. Representatives from some of Northern Ireland's most innovative companies and universities accompanied Mr. Hain on his tour of Delhi, Mumbai and Chennai. He met a range of political and economic representatives and also delivered a lecture on Northern Ireland's political process. The delegation also met tourism trade operators and Bollywood producers, in a bid to attract more Indian tourists to Northern Ireland.

A delegation of prominent British Muslims led by Lord Adam Hafejee Patel, Member of the House of Lords, visited Delhi, Lucknow and Hyderabad during 15-19 May 2006. Other members of the delegation were Waqar Azmi, Museji Takolia, Waqqas Khan, Rabia Malik, Unaiza Karim. The delegation met with key representatives from the social, educational and political fields, in a bid to understand key concerns of the Muslims. The visit was to help project a constructive image of Islam in Britain and enable cross-fertilisation of ideas between British and Indian Muslims.

The leader of the Conservative Party in the United Kingdom, David Cameron, visited India during 4-7 September. He was accompanied by the Shadow Chancellor, George Osborne. They visited Pune, Mumbai and New Delhi. In Pune, Mr. Cameron opened the JCB Plant. In Mumbai, they toured the campus of India's largest IT company TCS. Mr. Cameron also made a speech on the global economy and the Indo-British relationship in the 21st century to the city's business leaders. He met political and business leaders in New Delhi. UK's Special Representative for International Trade and Investment, His Royal Highness Prince Andrew, the Duke of York, visited India from 29 October to 4 November 2006. The Duke of York visited New Delhi, Mumbai and Chennai as the UK's Special Representative for International Trade and Investment, supporting UK companies trading internationally and encouraging foreign investment. His Royal Highness also presented the first-ever UK Trade & Investment India Business Awards in Mumbai on 1 November, 2006.[7]

Visits to UK

Among high level visits from India's side to the UK have been those by Dr. Manmohan Singh, Prime Minister of India to attend the G-8 Summit at Gleneagles. The bilateral leg of the visit had to be abandoned because of the London bombings in UK. Vice-President of India, Shri Bhairon Singh Shekhawat visited London during November 5-6, 2006. During his short transit, he visited Bhartiya Vidya Bhavan, where he inaugurated an exhibition on paintings by Indian artist entitled "Eastern Echos". He also watched a brief dance performance by artists from the Bhavan and unveiled a plaque commemorating his visit to the Bhavan. External Affairs Minister Shri K. Natwar Singh visited the UK during June 15-17 and in September 2004 and on March 9 and June 27-28 in 2005.

Other visits included those by Shri Arjun Singh, Minister for Human Resource Development during 12-15 October, 2005; Shri Kamal Nath, Minister for Commerce & Industry during June 16-19 and October 8-14 in 2004, and on January 29, July 6-8 and October 13-14 in 2005; Shri Kapil Sibal, Minister of State for Science & Technology and Ocean Development

(June 23-25); Shri Praful Patel, Minister of State for Civil Aviation (July 2004 and May 2005); Shri Dayanidhi Maran, Minister for Communication & IT (September 25-28, 2004 and 17-19 February, 2005); Smt. Renuka Chowdhury, Minister of State for Tourism (October 2-4 and November 2-5, 2004) and Shri P. Chidambaram, Minister of Finance (October 8-9). Finance Minister visited London again during February 3-5, 2005 at the invitation of Chancellor Gordon Brown to launch the Economic and Financial Dialogue. Shri Mani Shankar Aiyar, Minister for Petroleum, Natural Gas and Panchayati Raj visited the UK during 19-23 January, 2005. Shri Mufti Mohammad Syeed, CM of J&K visited the UK to promote tourism & investment during 7-10 February, 2005.[8]

Third Annual India-UK Summit

Prime Minister Dr. Manmohan Singh visited UK during 09-11, October 2006 and held the third annual India-UK Summit since the comprehensive strategic partnership was launched in September 2004. The Summit underlined the continued need for India and the UK as democracies to work together to counter terrorism and promote global economic growth. Following discussions on a host of bilateral, regional and multilateral issues, the two leaders told in a press conference that their nations enjoyed strong cooperation on business and education and on tackling terrorism and climate change. During their talks at 10, Downing Street, they also discussed the situation in North Korea and its nuclear test. Prime Minister Tony Blair stated that the difference between countries like Britain or India, and a country like North Korea, was that the former were democracies, abiding by the rule of law and their international obligations. He emphasized India's strong and impeccable record on counter-proliferation. Stating that the North Korea's test highlighted the dangers of clandestine proliferation, Dr. Singh reiterated that a further erosion of the non-proliferation regime was not in India's interest. India's own security had suffered due to clandestine proliferation linkages relating to our neighbours. The Prime Ministers addressed the concluding session of the India-UK Investment Summit. Chancellor of the Exchequer Gordon Brown and British Foreign Secretary Margaret Beckett called on the Indian Prime Minister.

India and the UK share a strategic relationship. Fourth India-UK annual summit was held in Delhi on January 21, 2008. The British Prime Minister Gordon Brown visited India to attend the summit. He was accompanied by high-powered business delegation. A joint statement was issued at the end of the visit and an agreement in the field of education was signed. Major areas of intense cooperation identified during the visit include education, science and technology, environment, etc. The British Prime Minister Gordon Brown was conferred on Honorary Doctorate by the Delhi University.

UK Foreign Secretary Visits India

UK Foreign Secretary Margaret Beckett visited to India during 2-8 November 2006. This was her first visit since becoming Foreign Minister. She visited New Delhi, Hyderabad and Mumbai. In Delhi she met with the Indian Prime Minister Dr. Manmohan Singh, Foreign Minister Mr. Pranab Mukherjee, Finance Minister P. Chidambaram, Home Minister Mr. Shivraj Patil and other senior members of the Parliament. In Hyderabad she visited a Department of International Development (DFID) funded project while in Mumbai she spoke on the growing business links between India and the UK. Mrs. Beckett met with Maharashtra Chief Minister Mr. Vilasrao Deshmukh and to share UK's view on terrorism.

Parliamentary Groups

Institutional linkages with all the major British political parties have been established to ensure that goodwill towards India cuts across party lines. In Parliament, the Friends of India Groups have been useful in promoting understanding of India's pluralist society and democracy. The Labour Friends of India (LFIN) was launched in 1999 and has sent six parliamentary delegations to India in April 2006. The Liberal Democrat Friends of India (LIB-DEM FIN) was launched in September 2000 and sent delegations to India in 2002, 2004 and 2005. The Conservative Parliamentary Friends of India (CPFIN) was launched in March 2001 and visited India in 2003, 2004 and 2006. Dr. Liam Fox, then Shadow Foreign Secretary of the Conservative Party led a delegation of four parliamentarians (three MPs and one MEP) to India during August 30-September 1, 2005. Members of important Parliamentary Select

Committees—the Trade & Industry Select Committee, the Home Affairs Committee and the Treasury Select Committee visited India in 2006. An All Party Parliamentary Group on India holds regular meetings.

The Indo-British Parliamentary Forum (IBPF) was launched in New Delhi in April 2003. The India-United Kingdom Parliamentary Friendship Group was launched by Hon'ble Speaker, Lok Sabha on 27 September 2005. Its President is Shri Gurudas Kamat. At the invitation of Hon'ble Speaker, Lok Sabha, a five member UK parliamentary delegation of CPA led by Lord Paul of Marylebone visited India in October 2005. The Lords and Commoners Cricket Team toured India in December-January 2005, led by Crispin Blunt, MP, Captain of the British Parliamentarian team. "Cricket diplomacy" reinforced the links between the two Parliaments, with an Indian Parliamentary Team paying a return visit to the UK on September 7-12, 2005.[9]

ECONOMIC RELATIONS

India was a British colony for more than 200 years till it got independence from the United Kingdom on August 15, 1947. Bilateral trade relations between India and UK have undergone a massive change from the colonial period. Once perceived as a less developed country, India had transformed itself into one of the fastest growing economies of the world. It is well known that India is world's fourth largest economy in purchasing power parity terms and UK is the 4th in GDP dollar terms.

"India and Britain can have a shaping influence for both progress and justice in the emerging global economy. And we will do that if we think boldly about opportunities that are ahead," said British Prime Minister Gordon Brown on the first day of his visit to India on January 21, 2008. During the visit he announced that the UK will invest another £ 825 million for development in India over the next three years, a major portion of which is expected to be spent on health and education.

The Indo-British Economic and Financial Dialogue was launched during the visit of Chancellor Gordon Brown to India in 2007.

Economic relations play a key role in the bilateral relationship, and the Indo-British Partnership is an important catalyst. All these economic links are, of course, based to a great deal on the multitude of personal connections — of family and friendship — between the two countries. Britain would be poorer in every way without the immense contribution of the 2 per cent of the population with roots in India. And these connections also continue to strengthen.[10]

A Partnership for World Trade and Investment Promotion

In 1993, in response to opportunities created by the bold and imaginative liberalization program introduced in India, the then British and Indian Prime Ministers publicly endorsed the creation of the Indo-British Partnership Initiative (IBPI). Its mandate is to increase bilateral trade and investment with particular emphasis on small and medium enterprises and to promote technology and science links between the two countries.

Backed by the two governments and led by industry, the initiative has become an ongoing partnership and is now called the Indo-British Partnership (IBP). In India the Confederation of Indian Industry (CII) in collaboration manages the IBP secretariat with the Trade & Investment department of the British High Commission, and in the UK by the Department of Trade and Industry (DTI). Co-chairmen N.R. Narayana Murthy, Chairman & CEO of Infosys Technologies Ltd. and Karan Billimoria, CEO of Cobra Beer led it.

Trade between the two countries is growing at 20 per cent a year. Britain has long been a leading investor in India—it is currently the third most important.[11]

The two countries' business links today are as much in cutting-edge sectors such as biotechnology, IT and pharmaceuticals as they are in more traditional industries. There are already 500 Indian companies operating in Britain, with investment of over £1 billion last year alone. With planned infrastructure projects in India which is expected to need investments of $150 billion over the next decade, this is in the interest of both countries. That is true as well of finding ways to use India's growing know-how and innovation to strengthen Britain's science base.

There has been an intensified exchange of visits by ministers and senior officials from both sides. British ministers have been regular participants at the CII Partnership Summits, the NASSCOM Annual Conferences, ITcom, Frames and other business events and exhibitions. Indian ministers and senior officials also regularly visit the UK, as do delegations from business chambers. The CII leads an annual Mission of CEOs every summer of the year, FICCI brought a CEOs Mission in October 2004, ASSOCHAM and PHDCCI brought delegations in 2006, and the Indian Merchants Chamber organized an "India Calling" conference in London during 2-3 October 2006. Besides, sectoral-industry delegations interact with their British counterparts, and India participates annually at the World Travel Mart in London and at other important trade events. In addition, NASSCOM and Financial Times organize a Conference on Outsourcing to India every year in London.

Various bilateral mechanisms have been established in recent years to facilitate economic cooperation between India and the UK including a Joint Economic and Trade Committee, Economic and Financial Dialogue (launched in February 2005), a Joint Working Group on Power and an Indo-British Coal Forum. Moreover, under the Indo-British Partnership established in 1993, the UK side has launched an Indo-British Partnership Network in the UK in December 2005. Lord Karan Bilimoria of Chelsea, Chief Executive, Cobra Beer chairs the IBPN while Shri Sunil Mittal, Chairman and Group Managing Director, Bharati Enterprises co-chairs the IBP Board from the Indian side.

The most important bilateral mechanism in the economic arena is the India-UK Joint Trade and Economic Committee (JETCO), which was launched in New Delhi on 13 January 2005 by Commerce & Industry Minister Shri Kamal Nath and Secretary of State for Trade & Industry Ms. Patricia Hewitt. The second plenary meeting of JETCO took place in London on 31 January 2006 under the co-chairmanship of the Rt. Hon. Alan Johnson, the then Secretary of State for Trade and Industry and Shri Kamal Nath, Minister for Commerce and Industry. Deliberations at the JETCO included reviewing the performance of the respective economies, trends and developments in bilateral trade and investment as well as the international economic context. The leaders noted the successful visit of the high-level UK business delegation to India led by Prime Minister Tony Blair in September 2005. Both sides agreed to establish a structured dialogue to address Intellectual Property Rights and a bilateral dialogue on venture capital for SMEs. It was further agreed that the first Investment Summit would be held in London in 2006. Both sides also welcomed the establishment of Indo-British Partnership Boards in both countries, and the establishment of the IBP Network (IBPN) in the United Kingdom, and were of the view that the two boards should play a leading role in driving private sector interaction between the two countries, together with other private sector bodies including the Confederation of British Industry (CBI), Commonwealth Business Council (CBC), Confederation of Indian Industry (CII) and Federation of Indian Chambers of Commerce and Industry (FICCI). The Ministers welcomed the progress made in the JETCO working groups on Agribusiness, Healthcare, High Technology and Infrastructure, which had held discussions on 30 January 2006, and invited the Chairmen to submit further reports to the mid-year JETCO review meeting of senior officials. It was also formally agreed to establish a bilateral experts group within the private sector to identify issues and opportunities in accountancy services in India and the UK. A British proposal to establish a working group to enhance links in creative industries was also received favorably.

Thereafter, an India-UK Business Summit was held in London during 26-28 June 2006. The Minister of Commerce and Industry, Mr. Kamal Nath and Minister of Science and Technology, Mr. Kapil Sibal attended the event, which included holding of the second India-UK Business Leaders Forum on Investment, Infrastructure and Innovation at Lancaster House on 27th June 2006. The CII CEOs Mission represented Indian business at the Forum. The Forum provided a platform to the highest levels of Government and business from both countries to discuss issues and seek mechanisms to increase investment flows as well as become partners of choice in science, innovation and progress. The event was a huge success. Prominent speakers included Lord Sainsbury, Secretary of State for Science and Innovation, Mr. Kamal Nath, Minister of Commerce and

Industry, Mr. Kapil Sibal, Minister of Science and Technology, Mr. Kamalesh Sharma, Indian High Commissioner to UK, Sir Michael Arthur, British High Commissioner to India and Dr. Ajay Dua, Secretary, Department of Industrial Policy & Promotion. Lord Sainsbury and Mr. Kamal Nath also signed a letter of intent to cooperate in the field of Intellectual Property Rights (IPRs). The Commerce and Industry Minister met his counterpart, the Rt. Hon. Alistair Darling, Secretary of State for Trade & Industry. The Indo-British Partnership Network also held its meeting in the margins of the Forum under the co-chairmanship of Lord Karan Bilimoria of Chelsea and Mr. Sunil Mittal, Vice President of CII.

A mid-term review of the JETCO was also held to coincide with the Summit. The meeting reviewed the progress made by working groups set up under JETCO. It was reiterated that the Investment Summit would be organised in London on 10 October 2006 during the visit of Prime Minister Manmohan Singh to London.

Bilateral Trade

India and the UK have had a long trading relationship. India is the UK's 15th largest export market and its largest export market in the developing world (ahead of China). In 2005, bilateral trade grew at the rate of 23.6 per cent. Trade in goods was £ 5.6 billion and trade in services £ 1.8 billion. Total bilateral trade turnover in 2006 was £8.74 billion of which trade in goods accounts for £5.8 billion and trade in services £2.9 billion. The total bilateral trade in goods has grown from £3.58 billion in 2001 to £5.83 billion in 2006 with UK being the second largest importer of Indian goods after the US. The total trade in goods and services in last five years from 2002-06 grew over 75 per cent. The balance of trade is currently in India's favor. India's main exports to the UK are engineering goods, ready-made garments, textiles, gold jewelery, footwear, marine products, rice and agricultural products, etc. The main imports from the UK are uncut diamonds, metal scrap, chemicals, machinery, transport equipment, scientific equipment, etc. The UK is the largest market in Europe for Indian IT services. It accounts for 6.4 per cent market share of India. The India-UK bilateral trade in the first 8 months of 2007 was up 13.2 per cent over the corresponding period in 2006. Many British blue chip companies (about 30) and some smaller companies have offshored work to India creating over 60,000 jobs. Conservative industry estimates are that British businesses now save upwards of £ 1 billion every year due to offshoring, the bulk of which is accounted for by India.

Table 5.1: Bilateral Merchandise Trade

(£ million)

Year	UK Exports to India	% Change	UK Imports from India	% Change	Total	% Change	India's Balance of Trade
1999	1450	+16.7%	1426	+3.2%	2876	+9.6%	-24
2000	2058	+41.9%	1651	+15.8%	3709	+30%	-407
2001	1797	-12.7%	1825	+10.5%	3622	-2.3%	+28
2002	1754	-2.4%	1793	-1.7%	3547	-2.1%	+39
2003	2293	+30.1%	2147	+16.1%	4375	+23%	-146
2004	2243	-2.18%	2340	+9.0%	4583	+3.0%	+97
2005	2813	+27.4%	2829	+20%	5632	+23.6%	+34
2006	2695	-3.6%	3136	+12.68%	5813	+4.48%	+441
2007 (Jan-Sept)	2062	-26.2%	2719	-13.29%	4781	-18%	+657

Table 5.2: Bilateral Trade in Services

(£ million)

Year	UK Exports	UK Imports	Total	% Change	India's Balance of Trade
2001	664	816	1780	+21.81%	+152
2002	623	808	1431	–3.31%	+185
2003	605	810	1515	+5.87%	+105
2004	981	1095	2076	+37.02%	+114
2005	1146	1311	2457	+18.06%	+165
2006	1424	1485	2909	+18.68	+61

Source: Office of National Statistics and Overseas Trade Statistics, HM Customs & Excise.

The bilateral trade has increased to 100 per cent in the last five years and it is increasing at a rate of 20 per cent per year. UK is the 4th largest trading partner of India with bilateral trade of US$ 9.8 billion in 2006-07 which is about three per cent of India's total trade.

Bilateral Investment Flows

FDI from the UK

UK is the 3rd largest investor in India, after Mauritius and the US during the fiscal year 2007-08. The actual inflow of investment from the UK in 2006 was 15.5 per cent of total foreign investment in India during the year. FDI inflows during the first quarter of fiscal 2007-08 were $4.9 billion, a growth of more than 185 per cent as against $1.7 billion received during the corresponding quarter of fiscal 2006-07. With a figure of £3.4 billion, the UK continues to be the largest cumulative investor in India and the 3rd largest in post-1991 era, which accounts for 8.5 per cent of total FDI inflows during 1991-2007.

The UK's total FDI outflow during 2002, 2003 and 2004 was US $50.3 billion, US $66.4 billion and US $65.4 billion respectively. However, very little of this investment found its way into India. While the UK was traditionally the largest cumulative investor in India, post-liberalization FDI inflow from the UK into India has been only US $2.026 billion (i.e. from August 1991 to May 2006), making it the 5th largest investor in terms of actual inflow accounting for approximately 6 per cent of the total investment of US $38.9 billion.

Top sectors attracting FDI inflows from UK are electrical equipment including computer software & electronics (22.29%), fuels i.e. power & oil refining (20.87%), services—both financial & non-financial (11.79%), timber products (8.28%) and telecommunications (5.59%). Some major UK insurance companies commenced their operations in India in 2002. Leading British oil and gas companies, including British Gas, Shell and Cairns Energy, have expanded their operations and increased their investments in India. Bilateral investment has also been in negotiations for investing in refinery and exploration and production. An increasing number of British companies are also moving to India for setting up BPO operations.

(million US$)

Year	Aug 1991- Mar 2003	2003-04	2004-05	2005-06	2006-07	Cumulative
Amount	1,106	167	101	266	47	2,026

Source: DIPP, GOI.

FDI from India

Meanwhile, the UK is one of the world's most attractive destinations for foreign investment and the top investment destination in Europe. In 2005-06, it received total foreign direct investment of US $165 billion (£91 billion), tripling the previous year's figure and making it the largest recipient of FDI in the world, beating both the US and China. The flow of Indian investments into the UK that began as a trickle in the late 1990s has now turned into a flood. In 2004-05, India became the eighth largest investor in the UK and in 2005-06 Indian companies doubled their investments in the UK to emerge as the third largest foreign investor in the country and the largest developing country investor (in terms of number of projects). According to the UK Inward Investment Report prepared by UK Trade & Investment, Indian companies invested £1.02 billion in 76 projects in 2005-06, creating a total of 1,449 jobs and safeguarding another 2,523 (Total number of jobs created and safeguarded—3,972). The number of investment projects increased by a whopping 111 per cent. This is all the more surprising as India was nowhere on the investment scene a decade ago.

While Information and Communications Technology remains the dominant sector for Indian investment accounting for 54 per cent of all investment (26 projects), there has been strong growth in investments in pharmaceuticals and healthcare (12 projects) and automotive and engineering sectors (6 projects). Financial services also received substantial investment with 8 projects. Nearly half of the 76 projects in 2005-06 are located in London, while the remaining is spread across various regions. India has now emerged as the second largest overseas investor in London, after the US. At the same time, more Indian companies are looking to do business outside London, reflecting the deepening of the bilateral investment relationship. A recent survey conducted by FICCI on outbound investment by Indian companies from January 2000 to July 2006 also confirms that the UK is the second most favored investment destination for Indian companies after the US.

The rise in Indian investment in the UK has been due to Indian investors taking advantage of Britain's expertise in high-value activities such as research & development, science and technology and innovative design, as well as the City of London's status as an international financial capital. Indian companies also find it convenient to locate their European headquarters in the UK to access Europe's 500 million consumers. A growing number of Indian companies are also listing on the London Stock Exchange to raise their international profile, tap some of the world's largest pools of capital and gain entry into European and global markets. Recent listings include IT services firm Rolta India ($100 million), Nagarjuna Construction ($115 million), Bajaj Hindustan ($135 million) and Federal Bank ($80 million).

It is encouraging to note that as the volume, scope and breadth of Indian projects expand in the UK, Indian investment is getting the recognition it deserves. In view of the growing investment ties, the City, the Mayor of London (who heads the Greater London Authority) and the London Stock Exchange are all in the process of opening offices in India. The local chambers of commerce are also waking up to the "India opportunity". The British Chambers of Commerce released India's Fact File in October 2006 containing detailed information of trade and investment with India. The Fact File was made available to the chambers' 135,000 members. The London Chambers of Commerce have meanwhile entered into a MoU with ASSOCHAM in May 2006 and partnering IMC's India Calling event in October 2006.

In this environment of all-round economic interest in India, the House of Commons' Select Committee on Trade & Industry in June 2006 published its report on "Trade and investment opportunities with India". The Committee focused on the difficulties and opportunities faced by UK businesses wishing to trade or forge investment links with India, with particular reference to opportunities in the IT, life sciences, aerospace and financial services sectors; the role of British institutions of higher and further education in developing such links; and the role of the UK Government in assisting businesses, including the relative responsibilities of UK Trade and Investment and the Regional Development Agencies. Their major findings were that the UK was not as engaged with India's markets as it should be; the Indian market was liberalizing at a pace not fully appreciated in the UK, and the UK's institutional arrangements to support trade and investment with India were characterized by enthusiasm but also by confusion. They encouraged the UK Government to focus on forging more economic links with India; else the UK may miss the last train to India! The Treasury Committee of Parliament also paid a visit to India in June 2006 as part of their study on globalization.[12]

The success of the partnership is reflected as follows:

- About 69 per cent increase in bilateral trade since the Indo-British Partnership was formed in 1993. The UK-India bilateral trade of goods and services was nearly £5 billion in 2002.
- Over 2000 joint ventures were signed between Indian and UK companies since 1993.
- UK is the third largest overseas investor after Mauritius and the US in terms of new investments approved.
- Excluding investment from Mauritius, UK is the second largest foreign direct investor in India after the US.
- UK is the largest market for Indian IT services (12% of IT services exports — nearly $1 billion).[13]

Other Economic Linkages

In addition to trade and investment, UK's Department for International Development (DFID) supports the Government of India in its efforts to achieve the poverty reduction objectives of the Tenth Plan and the internationally agreed Millennium Development Goals (MDGs). DFIDs is providing in India for the financial year 2005-06 £280 million. It aims to develop strategic program at the national level as well as supporting programs in its four partner states: Andhra Pradesh, Madhya Pradesh, Orissa and West Bengal. Out of 100 per cent DFID's total assistance 45 per cent to India was disbursed through national programs. These national programs are—the District Primary Education Program (DPEP), health interventions (AIDS, TB, Polio, etc.) and direct financial support to the activities of several partner agencies, including the ADB, World Bank and a number of UN organisations.

Trade and investment relations have been continuously strengthened by several bilateral interactions between the two nations. Among other things, one such linkage is the India-UK Round Table, a non-governmental body, set up in 2000 to make recommendations on development of bilateral relations in all spheres.

In August 2005, an agreement named "The Prime Ministers' Initiative", which was signed between India and UK sets out a new strategic partnership between the UK and India, which among other areas include education, culture, foreign and defence policy, and aims to strengthen bilateral economic and trade issues between the two countries.[14]

Besides, the third meeting of Joint Economic and Trade Committee (JETCO), constituted in 2005, was held in January 2007. The Committee has set up eight working groups in specific areas for special attention which include Hi-tech, IPR, Accountaincy, Legal Services, Infrastructure, Agribusiness, and Healthcare. Its next meeting was held in London in December 2007.

Information Technology

The UK and India are partners in the IT sector. The UK is the largest market in Europe for Indian IT services (12% of IT services exports—nearly $1 billion). The UK companies realise the benefits of outsourcing to India. There are about ten thousand Indian IT professionals working in the UK. Indian IT companies in UK are employing over 4000 UK citizens. The United Kingdom and India have emerged as major partner countries in the Information Technology sector. A large number of Indian IT companies have substantial operations in the UK. Indian professionals have also filled in skill shortages in the UK's IT sector. There are some fears of job losses on account of outsourcing to India, but the reality is that the UK economy is growing strongly and the employment situation, including in call centres, has never been better. Moreover, in a reversal of trends, the Indian IT firm HCL Technologies has set up a call centre in Belfast employing several hundred people. NASSCOM opened its UK Chapter in September 2003, its first such overseas office. It has a Memorandum of Understanding with its British counterpart, trade association, intellect, and also with the Welsh Development Agency, which has now been a Platinum Sponsor of NASSCOM's Annual Conference for many years. In association with the *Financial Times*, NASSCOM also held a prestigious annual conference in London on Outsourcing to India. In November 2005, FT-NASSCOM held the annual conference on "India Outsourcing Event" in London.

Air Services between India and the UK

Over 400,000 British tourists and a rapidly growing number of business people visit India every year. The UK-India air services market was grossly underserved and this was proving to be a hindrance in promoting tourist and business travel from the UK to India. India and the UK signed a MoU (Sept 2004) increasing the number of services per week from 19 to 40 for each side, to operate in three stages from 2004 to end 2005. A further expansion was agreed upon (April 2005), with 77 flights per week for British carriers (56 to Delhi and Mumbai, 14 to Chennai and Bangalore, and 7 to other international airports) and 56 flights per week by Indian carriers to London Heathrow and unlimited numbers to other British destinations. This additional capacity is expected to ease the situation through greater direct connectivity and lower fares.

In May 2005, Air India launched its first flight linking Amritsar via Birmingham to Toronto in Canada, with the service expected to boost religious tourism around the Golden Temple. Also in May, the British Airline British Midland International (BMI) began flying between London and Bombay making it the third British Airline after British Airways and Virgin. Airlines operating to the UK from India are Jet Airways, Air India and Sahara. During the visit of British Prime Minister Tony Blair to India in September 2005, both sides signed a new bilateral Air Services agreement in order to further enhance cooperation in the civil aviation sector.

Biotechnology and Healthcare

Biotechnology has been identified as one of the main areas for enhanced cooperation. Leading Indian biotechnology companies are collaborating with clients across the UK and Europe. AstraZeneca has established an R&D Centre in Bangalore (Bangaluru). GlaxoSmithKline and Ranbaxy have signed an agreement for joint research and development. Industry delegations from both countries visit each other regularly.

Healthcare is another potential area for cooperation. India has supplied doctors and nurses in substantial numbers for the UK's National Health Service (NHS), with about 26 per cent of doctors employed in the NHS being of Indian origin. However, the new immigration rules announced earlier this year (2006) have had a negative impact on the employment of Indian doctors, many of who are unable to find jobs. Meanwhile, Indian pharmaceutical companies are marketing their products in the UK and many such as Nicholas Piramal have invested in production facilities in the UK. The UK is also a major source of medical equipment. The Indian Healthcare Federation comprising top Indian private sector healthcare organisations and super-speciality hospitals visited the UK in September 2003 to explore potential partnerships and opportunities. UK Trade and Investment also regularly sends teams of experts from the healthcare sector to India to explore possibilities of cooperation. The second India Medical Tourism Expo was held in London in June 2006. UK consumers are also showing interest in complementary and alternative medicine in which India has considerable strengths.

New Regulations Affecting Indian Doctors

Approximately 30 per cent of the doctors in the UK's National Health Services (NHS) are Indian. At the India-UK Round Table, it was estimated that Indian doctors contribute £4.5 billion to the UK economy, taking into account the cost of training for approximately 20,600 Indian doctors on the UK register. Every year a number of junior doctors from India used to write the PLAB examinations and were subsequently allowed to seek employment in junior posts in NHS trusts/hospitals/ local councils under the "Permit Free Training" (PFT) scheme. However, the new immigration law announced in March 2006 by the UK abolished PFT. Now every NHS trust/hospital first has to ensure that there is no UK or EU national available. The new rules have added to their distress and several have been forced to leave for India. In June 2006, the GMC of the UK cancelled all overseas PLAB examinations till January 2007.

These issues have been taken up with the UK Department of Health and Members of Parliament in the UK. The need for suitable transitional arrangements for doctors already in the UK under previous regulations has been emphasized.

Education

The British Council Fellowship Programme, Commonwealth Scholarship and British Chevening Scholarships provide financial support to Indian students studying in the UK. Various other scholarships like the Inlaks Foundation, the Rhodes Scholarship, etc. are offered for study in various UK educational institutions.

The UK estimates the benefits to its economy brought in by the presence of overseas students at £9 billion. The number of Indian students in UK universities has increased dramatically from 4000 in 1999-2000 to more than 15000 in the year 2004-05, despite the extremely high tuition fees for overseas students.

The 2004 Joint Declaration identified educational linkages as a priority. India has (Nov. 2004) become a strategic partner in the Global Gateway Initiative of the UK Department for Education and Skills for linkages between schools. The British Academy is exploring university-level linkages with the UGC. The Eighth Indo-UK Round Table welcomed a comprehensive study funded by the British Council entitled "The India-UK Strategic Partnership: A Review of Academic and Educational Links". Its main recommendations were to institute financial support for an academic exchange program at Ph.D and postdoctoral levels, setting up an India-UK Academic and Educational Network, and expansion of school links between India and the UK. Mr. Bill Rammell, Minister of State for Lifelong Learning, Further and Higher Education, visited India from 31 July-5 August 05 to explore possibilities for bilateral cooperation in the field of higher education and met Shri Arjun Singh, HRD Minister of India.

A UK-India Education Investment Initiative of £10 million spread over a period of 5 years was announced by Prime Minister Tony Blair during his visit to New Delhi in September 2005. The UK-India Education Investment Initiative will fund scholarships and short-term academic exchanges and promote student exchanges between universities and schools. The main aim of the initiative is to build on existing academic linkages and to address imbalances in the bilateral relationship. Presently, only 100 British students go to India to pursue their studies.

A Chair had been established on Indian history and culture in the Oxford University by Government of India (GOI) with an endowment of £1.8 million in July 2002. It is intended to bridge the worlds of Indology and Modern History, as well as open up Indian studies to wider currents.

The issue of student visa fees and related issues has been taken up with the UK Government. From 1st April 2005, student visa fees have been increased from £36 to £85. For extension of visa in the UK, the fee for application through the post has been increased from £155 to £250 and for the same day service in person, the fee has been increased from £250 to £500. The removal in the Immigration and Asylum Bill of the right of Appeal for the refusal of student visas and its implications for Indian students needs to be addressed. The grounds for refusal to Indian students, who are a sought after resource by universities around the world, should be transparent and genuine cases should have some right of appeal. Even UK universities are critical of Government plans to abolish the right of appeal of students refused visas for the UK.

The market for international students in the UK is estimated to contribute £9 billion to the British economy as non-EU students pay up to five times that of UK and EU students. The number of student visas issued to almost entirely self-financed Indian students increased dramatically from under 4000 in 1999 to 15000 in 2005, contributing £300 million to the UK economy. After China, India is the second largest country to send students to UK. The UK aims to attract 100,000 more international students by 2011. UK universities are approaching students from small towns in India besides the four metropolitan cities. Over 14 UK Universities have opened full-time offices in India. In addition, several UK colleges have approached GOI for funding for Chairs/scholarships on India. In September 2005, India announced it would fund a Chair named after Pt. Jawaharlal Nehru at Cambridge University to project the Indian economy, business and management. Further, efforts are underway to create

Chairs dedicated to India supplemented by India Business Centres in leading Business Schools with the support of UK's corporates.

To increase Indian students enrolment, Prime Minister Tony Blair announced the UK-India Education and Research Initiative (UKIERI) in September 2005, and launched in London on April 18, 2006. The Initiative solicited contributions from industry and Shell, BP, BAE Systems and GlaxoSmithKline have pledged funds. 50 research fellowships have recently been announced. The first meeting of the India-UK Science and Innovation Council in London on June 2006 endorsed UKIERI and agreed to match the UK's contribution for bilateral research projects. The initiative would focus primarily on higher education and has accepted bids for projects from academic institutions during the current UK Financial Year. Mr. Blair said from May any overseas student who completed a postgraduate degree or undergraduates in sectors needing extra skills could work in Britain for up to 12 months after graduating. MPs from the Conservative Party have demanded that this period be extended to two years, as per the Scottish model.

Culture

An agreement on Film Co-production was initiated during Prime Minister Tony Blair's visit. The two sides recognized that there is a huge potential for the film industries of the two countries to work together. The Nehru Centre is based in London. Department of Culture has conveyed its support to the exhibition of Chola Bronzes at the Royal Academy of Art (December 2006-February 2007).

The Nehru Centre is among the most active of India's cultural centres abroad and organises a wide range of performances, exhibitions, lectures and film shows as a platform for Indian culture in the broadest sense, focusing on the role played both by British and Indian artistes in promoting greater cultural understanding. It has also launched several books, by both Indian and British authors and promoted the participation of British authors in Indian literary festivals. Department of Culture has conveyed its support to the exhibition of Chola Bronzes at the Royal Academy of Art (December 2006-February 2007). The Ministry of Culture has proposed an exhibition of Gupta Art in

France in early 2007. Discussions are continuing with Victoria & Albert Museum to host this exhibition in London from August to October 2007.

The year 2007 represents the 60th Anniversary of India's Independence. A series of events were planned to highlight the emergence of new cultural forms, such as the *British Natyam* and gradual mainstreaming of Indian culture in United Kingdom, thus abandoning the notion of a culture "historically frozen in time".

Film Co-Production Agreement

India and the UK, signed a film co-production agreement during the UK Secretary of State for Culture, Media and Sport, Ms. Tessa Jowell's visit to New Delhi on December 5, 2005. This will allow film producers from the two countries to pool creative, artistic, technical, financial and marketing resources to produce films and television programs. Indian film producers will also benefit from various tax benefits offered recently by the British Government for films producing under such Agreements. Minister Tessa Jowell again visited India in March 2006 for the FICCI Frames event.

Tourism

In 2004, out of 3.36 million international arrivals in India, about half a million were from the UK (15%), a 17 per cent growth over 2003. The High Commission in London alone issued 22 per cent more tourist visas and 29 per cent more business visas in 2004. During the first half of 2005, this upward trend has continued with a 21 per cent increase over the same period in 2004. Complaints persist concerning the quality of airports and immigration bottlenecks.

The India Tourism Office undertakes major efforts to publicize the potential of tourism in the UK market. Complaints persist concerning the quality of airports and immigration bottlenecks in India. Tourism Minister Renuka Chowdhury led a large Indian delegation to the World Tourism Mart that was held in London in November 2005. Tourism in Jammu & Kashmir will also get a boost if the UK withdraws the adverse travel advisory for the state.

UK Development Assistance to India

India has remained the single largest recipient of bilateral development assistance from the UK, with £198 million disbursed in 2003-04. The outlay for 2004-05 was £250 million. For India, the UK is the third largest source of ODA, and the largest in terms of grant aid. The UK was the only developed country which did not suspend ODA to India after the nuclear tests of 1998. The Parliamentary Committee on Development Assistance has however suggested in 2004 consideration of the possibility of gradually phasing out aid to India.

Energy

The Director General of Hydrocarbons, GOI and the Department of Trade & Industry, signed an MoU during the Indo-UK Summit in September 2005. On April 7, DGH also signed MoUs with two leading UK universities—Imperial College in London and the University of Aberdeen—to promote cooperation in the hydrocarbon sector. The road show for the sixth round of the New Exploration Licensing Policy (NELP-VI) offering 55 blocks was held in London on March 27, 2006. 38 prominent companies were present including BP, Shell, Total, Statoil, Chevron, BG, Repsol, Cairn Energy, Woodside, Petrobras, Maersk, Devon, ENI, Burren, BHP, Ensearch, Goepetrol and Premier oil. Shri Vilash Muttemwar, Minister for Non-Conventional Energy Sources (MNES) met Mr. Ian Pearson, Minister of State in the Department of Environment, Forest and Rural Affairs (DEFRA) in London on June 14, 2006. Issues discussed included R&D cooperation in the renewable energy sector, investment by the UK in an SEZ set up for renewable energy and sustainable development.

Environment

India and the United Kingdom signed a declaration on cooperation to meet global environmental, economic and social challenges during a visit by Shri A. Raja, Minister for Environment and Forests during 9-13 October 2005. The two sides agreed on a high-level Sustainable Development Dialogue as part of an initiative by their Prime Ministers to strengthen ties in research, environmental impact assessment, public-private partnerships, sustainable forestry, illegal trade in animals, and science and technology. Britain has already set up an India Task Force to aid cooperation in sustainable development. An immediate fallout of the agreement could be British help in cleaning the Yamuna river in Delhi. This is the first time the UK has signed a sustainable development pact with any country. The UK has conveyed the high priority it attaches to cooperation in this sector with India.

A delegation led by Shri Namo Narain Meena, the Minister of State for Environment and Forests attended the Dialogue on Climate Change, Clean Energy and Sustainable Development in London on November 1, 2005—organized in follow up to the Gleneagles G-8 Summit on climate change. UK's Biodiversity Minister Jim Knight visited India during 2-6 February, 2006 to attend the Delhi Sustainable Development Summit to take forward the UK-India Sustainable Development Dialogue. Shri Vilas Muttemwar, Minister for NES, visited London on June 14, 2006 and met Mr. Ian Pearson, Minister DEFRA (Deptt. for Environment, Forests and Rural Affairs).

Customs Cooperation

A MoU on Customs Cooperation was signed on 16 March 2001, which enables both countries to cooperate in combating economic and drug offences and contacts established with the newly established Serious Organised Crime Agency (SOCA).

Indian Community in the UK

Bilateral trade and economic relations are facilitated by the presence of about 1.2 million strong Indian community in the UK, which represents the single largest ethnic segment of the country's population. The contribution of NRIs in the UK has been notable from the economic point of view, especially in the fields of industry, medicine, accountancy, law, management, financial services and food. 40 per cent of the pharmaceutical trade of the UK is run by Indians who are also the mainstay of several other retail trades in the country. The Indian community has also made progress in the media, and has left other South Asian communities far behind in economic terms and educational achievement. It also has a significantly lower crime rate. There are 6 MPs and 17-18 members of the House of Lords of Indian origin.[15]

COOPERATION ON SCIENCE & TECHNOLOGY

India and the UK have a long tradition of scientific links, and there are several ongoing joint projects between scientists and institutes. There is an India-UK Joint Working Group on S&T, headed by Secretary (S&T) on the Indian side and the Chief Scientific Adviser to the British Government (Prof. Sir David King). The third meeting in London in July 2002 had led to an agreement to set up a joint Networking Fund, with an equal contribution from both sides. The operation of this Fund follows a 'bottom up' and 'blue skies' approach to collaborative proposals in order to eliminate constraints.

Several top British scientists have visited India regularly. The Royal Society, UK's premier scientific academy, celebrated an 'India Day' in London on 11 December 2002. This first-ever India Day was a showcase event celebrating the scientific links between the UK and India. There are long-standing links between the Royal Society and India. The first Indian Fellow of the Royal Society was elected in 1841, and the total number so far, which includes almost all the greatest Indian scientific luminaries and Nobel Prize winners, is 30. In 1972, an agreement was signed between the Royal Society and the Indian National Science Academy. Since then, over 400 British scientists have visited India and 500 Indian scientists have visited the UK.

S&T cooperation between India and UK is undertaken under an Inter-Governmental S&T Agreement signed in New Delhi in January, 1996. Sir David King, Chief Scientific Adviser to the British PM and Prof. V.S. Ramamurthy, Secretary, DST are the Co-Chairmen of the Joint Committee which held several meetings.

Bilateral arrangements also exist between the Indian National Science Academy (INSA) and the Royal Society (RS) and Department of Biotechnology and British Biotechnology Research Council (BBRC). The Council for Scientific & Industrial Research (CSIR) is also a party to a few of the programs being run in India by the Department for International Development (DFID) of UK. The Director of Ri, Professor Susan Greenfield, visited India in Jan. 2006.

Thematic Workshops on tuberculosis, e-sciences, industrial mathematics and biomarkers, which have generated Joint R&D proposals (on which a view has to be taken), have been held so far. The Joint Committee has also agreed to organize Joint Workshops in the following areas—stem cell research, climate change, alternative fuels, coastal defence and bio-nano technology. British and Indian scientists on climate change research held a workshop at Ahmedabad in September 2005.

An MoU was signed between ISRO and the British National Space Centre (BNSC) in March 1997 for cooperation in the different areas of space science, technology and applications. The UK also provides components and sub systems for the Indian space program. The European Space Agency (ESA) and ISRO have had discussions on cooperation in the area of lunar exploration. ESA has recently launched a mission called SMART-1 to the moon and has expressed willingness to share the data with India.[16]

The UK ranks fourth after the US, Germany and Japan in terms of technology collaboration. During the period 1991-2007, the number of technical collaborations approved from the UK stands at 855 which is 10.90 per cent of the total technology transfer approvals.

In order to enhance S&T cooperation between India and UK, it was decided in June 2005 to upgrade the Joint Committee on S&T to the Indo-UK Science and Innovation Council (SIC). Shri Kapil Sibal, Minister for Science and Technology, led a delegation to the UK during June 26-28, 2006 for its first meeting. The delegation included Prof. CNR Rao, Chairman, Scientific Advisory Council (SAC) of the Prime Minister, Dr. R.A. Mashelkar, Secretary, DSIR and DG, CSIR and Dr. T. Ramasamy, Secretary, Department of Science and Technology. The UK side was led by Lord Sainsbury, the UK Secretary of State for Science and Innovation and included Sir David King, Principal Scientific Advisor to Prime Minister Tony Blair. Both side discussed possibilities of cooperation in science and technology and agreed to be equal partners in future initiatives.

The meeting endorsed the UK-India Education and Research Initiative (UKIERI) announced by Prime Minister Tony Blair and agreed to develop a strategic relationship in meeting the challenges of the future—climate change, energy security, health and infectious diseases, etc. and on innovation and engagement with industry. The Council agreed that the UK and India could usefully collaborate on entrepreneurship, technology transfer and intellectual property.[17]

COOPERATION ON DEFENCE

The India-UK defence relationship has never been stronger. The modern relationship has been developed through the India-UK Defence Consultative Group (DCG) established in 1995; the DCG meets annually (the venue alternates between Delhi and London) and is co-chaired by the UK Permanent Undersecretary of State for Defence and his Indian counterpart. It has three sub-groups, covering military to military contacts, defence equipment and research and technology.

The bilateral program of exercises, exchanges, training courses and high-level visits continue to accelerate. Activity levels have tripled since 2002-03. Highlights include an average of 5 ships' visits per year, Exercise Emerald Mercury, a Joint Force Headquarters deployment planning exercise, conducted in field conditions, in Hyderabad in March 2005 and Konkan 2006, a large scale joint maritime exercise between the Royal and Indian Navies. Royal Navy participation comprised an Aircraft Carrier Group, a nuclear submarine and support vessels with the Exercise itself being held off the Indian west coast between Goa and Mumbai in May 2006. Furthermore, the heads of all three services and the British Chief of Defence Staff have visited each other's countries over the last 3 years.

This trend continued and major Royal/Indian Airforce joint exercises were held in Gwalior and Agra in October 2006. In line with Joint Declaration aspirations, the DCG meeting was held in New Delhi in November 2006 to identify further ways of deepening and broadening defence cooperation.

There has been a long-standing bilateral defence relationship between the two countries, which includes sales to India of Canberra, Jaguar and Sea Harrier combat aircraft, ex-RN aircraft carriers, VIP-transport aircraft and Sea King helicopters. In March 2004 a contract (initially worth £795 million to UK) for 66 Hawk Advanced

Jet Trainers from BAE Systems was agreed. Defence equipment cooperation continues, especially in terms of radars, army communications networks, VVIP helicopters, naval support vessels and upgrades to existing equipment.

Defence cooperation took place under the India-UK Defence Consultative Group (DCG) formed in 1995, which meets at the level of the Indian Defence Secretary and UK Permanent Undersecretary for Defence respectively. The Military Sub-Group, the Defence Equipment Sub-Group and the Defence Research and Technology Sub-Group and other Sub-groups hold their meetings simultaneously with the DCG and report to it.

Shri Shekhar Dutt, Defence Secretary, led a delegation to the 9th India-UK Defence Consultative Group meeting held during 26-28 September 2005 in London and the 10th meeting held in London on November 27-29, 2006.[18]

A MoU on the purchase of 66 Hawk Advanced Jet Trainers (AJT) from British Aerospace Systems of the UK for the Indian Air Force, 24 to be procured in fly away condition and the remaining 42 to be manufactured under license in India by M/s. Hindustan Aeronautics Limited, was signed in March 2004. The delivery of 24 aircraft in fly away condition was to be started from September 2007 and completed by February 2008.

The Joint Indo-UK exercises for ten-day—Emerald Mercury—held in India in March 2005 was the first of its kind between the two countries, marking the biggest land deployment of British military personnel in India. The Indian Air Force and the Royal Air Force have their first joint air exercise Inder Dhanush at Gwalior during 2-13 October 2006, which was to be regularised on an annual basis. Naval cooperation includes the Konkan series of bilateral exercises, product support for Sea King and Sea Harriers, training facilities offered by the Royal Navy and continuation of bilateral ship visits including participation in the 200th year Celebration of the Battle of Trafalgar in 2005 and RN ships visiting Indian ports. The first Navy to Navy staff talks were held in September 2004 in New Delhi. The Indian Navy and the British Royal Navy held one of their biggest joint exercises in Konkan in 2006 and on May 17-29, 2006 off India's west coast between Goa and Mumbai.[19]

COOPERATION ON COUNTER-TERRORISM

Terrorism which has spread all over the globe, cannot be fought successfully by any country alone. India and Britain have decided to set up a Joint Working Group (JWG) to counter terrorism, during the London visit of the Home Minister, Mr. L.K. Advani in September 2000, and firmed up on the arrival of the British Home Secretary, Mr. Jack Straw in New Delhi. The JWG provides an institutional mechanism to step up coordination in tackling the problems of drug trafficking and related crimes. Both countries already have an extradition treaty in place and the JWG should provide an ideal vehicle to maintain close contact and exchange information on terrorism and other major concerns. The Terrorism Act 2000 of the UK came into force from October 2000, the JWG could help plug the loopholes in the domestic legislation as well as the rules and regulations to be framed by the two countries in the future.

The relationship between India and Britain have returned to the fast track after the slowdown in 1998 over the Pokhran nuclear tests. The Foreign Minister, Mr. Jaswant Singh, the Defence Minister, Mr. George Fernandes, and Mr. Advani have had fruitful visits to London.[20]

There should be no discrimination. Trade and investment interests apart, terrorism is bound to top the Indian agenda in its dealings with the West. UK has unfortunately earned the dubious distinction of being the global headquarters for various terrorist groups—terrorist organizations of Punjab, Kashmiri groups, LTTE, etc. One of the hijackers of the Indian Airlines flight to Kandahar was reported to be a British national.

The joint declaration issued by India and Britain on 21 September 2004, to launch a drive against the menace together is significant in the sense that both have been its victims for a long time. India, first faced the problem in Punjab, and has been facing in Jammu and Kashmir since 1989 because of Pakistan who is using terrorism as an instrument of state policy. The UK, which had been earlier targeted by Northern Ireland terrorist group is now on the hit list of those associated with Al-Qaida.[21]

In the wake of 9/11, the UK Government has begun to adopt a robust approach to terrorism including terrorism affecting India. In foreign policy, the F-C-O Strategy Paper released on December 2, 2003, had identified international terrorism and the spread of weapons of mass destruction as the most "catastrophic" threats to the UK's national security in the early decades of twenty-first century, relegating conventional military threats to the background. The paper also identified religion as a force in international relations, with religious tensions abroad, for example, in the sub-continent, having the potential to affect the UK's domestic security.

Both UK Prime Minister Tony Blair and Foreign Secretary Jack Straw have earlier called for an end to Pakistan's support for terrorism in Kashmir. Mr. Straw had acknowledged to Parliament that there was a clear link between the ISI and terrorist groups operating in J&K. At the Joint Press Conference held in London between President Bush and Prime Minister Blair on the same day of the Istanbul bombings on November 2003, Prime Minister Tony Blair described the outrages as a struggle between fanaticism and extremism on the one hand, and freedom and tolerance on the other, and included Kashmir as one of the areas seriously affected by terrorism. In December 2003 Prime Minister Tony Blair stated in Parliament that the key to the problem was for Pakistan to end all support to terrorism in any form. Following the Beslan atrocities, Jack Straw underlined the total culpability of terrorists.[22] During the joint press conference with Indian Prime Minister in September 2004, Prime Minister Tony Blair totally condemned any terrorism in Kashmir, including the killing of innocents and the murder of elected politicians.

The UK had proposed (10th October 2003) adding several terrorist organisations of concern to India to its proscribed list (which contains Lashkar-e-Tayyaba, Babbar Khalsa, International Sikh Youth Federation, The Liberation Tigers of Tamil Eelam, and the old Hizbul Mujahideen and Jaish-e-Mohammad). If approved, the following would be added to the UK list of proscribed terrorist organisations:

- Harkat-ul-Jehad-e-Islami
- Hizbul Mujahideen—in its new incarnation Harakat-ul-Mujahideen/Alami (HuM/A) and Jundallah—the old HM was already on the banned list.

- Jaish-e-Mohammed (JeM) in its new incarnation Khuddam ul-Islam and splinter group Jamaat ul-Furquan—the old JeM was already on the banned list.[23]

In his remarks to the press following the September 8, 2005 Summit, Prime Minister Tony Blair acknowledged that the world had been reluctant to recognize the insurgency in Jammu and Kashmir as terrorism. He added that whether it was in Palestine, Iraq, Afghanistan, Kashmir, or Chechnya—terrorism should never be compromised and justified. The July 7 bombings in London and the recent foiled attempt to bomb aircraft flying between the UK and US have contributed to the Government taking tough measures domestically on counter-terrorism. The Indian Prime Minister who was in the UK for the Gleneagles Summit, strongly condemned the 7/7 bombings of London's subway and bus system. Following the Mumbai train blasts, Prime Minister Tony Blair condemned the attacks and said there could never be any justification for terrorism. He expressed his country's shared determination to defeat terrorism in all its forms and solidarity with India.

Following India's request, the terrorist organisation Harkat-ul-Jehad-e-Islami was one of the 15 newly banned terrorist groups by the UK government on October 10. The LTTE had been banned earlier. The Hizbul Mujahideen has been added to the EU list of terrorist organisations.

The last round of the JWG on Counter-Terrorism with UK was held on 27-28 June 2005 in London and there have been consultations in follow up.

The UK has a close relationship with India—a strategic partner on counter-terrorism. The British Prime Minister, and Prime Minister Manmohan Singh, reaffirmed their commitment to this relationship, and to developing it further, during the UK-India Summit on 8 September. "We are developing this relationship through, for example, the UK-India Joint Working Group on terrorism. Operational links between our two countries are good. We are happy to share our experiences of dealing with terrorist incidents and appreciate the opportunity to learn about Indian experiences," said the British Prime Minister. Both India and the UK have suffered serious terrorist threats over the years, and both are among the strongest proponents of international cooperation against terrorism in the UN and elsewhere. Both Prime Ministers reiterated their belief in the international community working with unity and resolve to counter terrorism and extremism.

India and the UK are working together to promote in the UN the Comprehensive Convention for the Suppression of International Terrorism. Both countries continue to promote closer international cooperation in the fight against terrorism, within the rule of law and with respect for human rights. Recently, India and Britain on November 2, 2006 decided to step up cooperation to tackle threats posed by terrorism and climate change besides boosting the already buoyant bilateral economic relations. At a joint press conference British Foreign Minister Beckett said that they had constructive discussions to take forward the promise of cooperation on counter-terrorism that the Indian Prime Minister Manmohan Singh and the British Prime Minister Tony Blair had made earlier in London.

MoU on Return of Illegal Immigrants

Indian nationals used to account for the highest (40%) number of asylum applications in the UK, with around 2000 Indian nationals applying in 2002. To address this problem, a MoU on the return of illegal immigrants, agreed upon as a pilot project for a period of one year, was signed during the UK Home Secretary's visit on 30 January 2004. Following India's inclusion in the White List on 15 February 2005, intake fell by 46 per cent from March 2005 to September 2005. The MoU has been renewed till January 29, 2007. All efforts have been made to streamline the implementation of the MoU, resulting in an appreciable improvement in the number of verifications. According to UK official sources so far it confirmed the credentials of about 450 Indians who have been repatriated. The records of a further 1,000 have been verified and removal orders are awaited from the UK Home Office.

The New Points Based System of Managed Migration

The UK had indicated that tackling illegal immigration was a priority during its EU Presidency. A new point based system was introduced by the Home Office on March 7, 2006. This seeks to ensure that only those who benefit Britain can come to work or study in the UK, and also to crack down on abuse and illegal immigration and increase removals. There would be quantitative limits set according to immigration risk. With the large number of workers available from new EU countries, entry routes for low skilled migrants from non-EU countries would be quota based, time limited and only from countries with which the UK has effective returns arrangements (for repatriating immigration offenders). The new system should not adversely impact the movement of peoples. More than 470 Indian companies are already represented in the UK in the IT sector alone and several Indian companies source their key personnel from their Indian branches. India is the largest developing country investing in the UK and is in the first 10 overall. In a few years the number of students coming to the UK, primarily self-financed, has gone up from 4,000 to over 16,000 per year and the trend is increasing. Indian tourists form a substantial proportion of overseas high-spending visitors in the UK.[24]

In the India-UK annual summit, which was held on January 21, 2008, both sides agreed that terrorism is a global threat requiring a global response. They underlined the importance of joint international efforts in countering terrorism. They emphasised the need to intensify mutual exchange of veiws, experiences and practical cooperation in the fight against terrorism—both through bilateral channels and through multilateral forum. Multilaterally, the two countries remain committed to pursuing as soon as possible agreement in the UN on the Comprehensive Convention against International Terrorism.

MEETINGS OF ROUND TABLE

UK Foreign Secretary Robin Cook and Indian Foreign Minister Jaswant Singh established the UK-India Round Table, a non-governmental body in April 2000. They were looking for ways to regenerate and strengthen the bilateral relationship. The Co-Chairmen were Lord Swraj Paul and Mr. K.C. Pant, Chairman of the Indian National Economic Commission. The Round Table consists of about 30 people drawn equally from India and the UK. They come from many different backgrounds and include academics, officials, businessmen and journalists.

The Foreign Secretary invites all the UK members personally. The two High Commissioners take part ex-officio as ordinary members of the group. The Round Table meets approximately every nine months, alternately in India and the UK.

The primary purpose of the Round Table is to discuss issues that may affect the bilateral relationship and to reflect on ways in which it can be strengthened. After each meeting the Co-Chairmen submit to their respective Governments at the highest-level recommendations to that end. The aim of the Round Table is not to duplicate inter-governmental discussions but rather to put forward ideas from different perspectives. Outside experts are sometimes brought in to introduce the discussions on specific subjects. The discussions of the Round Table have covered very widely, reflecting the fact that the ties between the two countries are exceptionally broad; to work together for mutual advantage on both bilateral and multilateral issues, e.g. from international security or the WTO to visa policy and educational exchanges. Many ideas have been submitted to respective governments on how close cooperation might be achieved in the field of trade and investment, notably in the field of high technology. The Round Table has debated the importance of IT and biotechnology and put forward proposals for collaboration in research in these areas. Culture, tourism, air services, biodiversity, cultural and educational exchanges and legal services are among the many other issues that have been discussed. The efforts of the Round Table were acknowledged in the New Delhi Declaration of 6 January 2002, signed by the two Prime Ministers.[25]

The Sixth Meeting of the Round Table was held during 7-9 May 2003, at the Lygon Arms Hotel in Broadway, in the heart of the Cotswolds. Before going to Broadway Mr. Pant, the Indian Co-Chairman of the Round Table, and the Indian members, accompanied by Lord Paul, the UK Co-Chairman and some members of the UK delegation, called on the Foreign Secretary, Rt. Hon. Jack Straw MP, at the Foreign & Commonwealth Office. The Foreign Secretary said that the relationship between India and the UK was of profound importance to the UK. The UK was a friend of India and he himself had a very constructive relationship with his Indian colleague Mr. Yashwant Sinha. Mr. Pant reciprocated these comments and noted that mutual understanding between the two countries was much improved.

During the discussions Mr. Straw welcomed the initiative taken by the Indian Prime Minister, Mr. Atal Behari Vajpayee to re-establish contacts with Pakistan and the encouraging Pakistani response – he wished it every success. Mr. Straw also expressed appreciation for the position adopted by the Government of India during the war in Iraq. He fully supported the involvement of the UN in the post-war reconstruction of Iraq. Regarding the UN, he said that the UK strongly supported reform of the Security Council and hoped that India, Japan and Germany would become permanent members. He also stressed the importance of the Cancun ministerial meeting in September for a successful outcome to the Doha Round of trade negotiations. The theme chosen for this meeting of the Round Table was "multilaterallism and multilateral institutions". Previous meetings have dwelt on the many issues that might be termed purely bilateral. The UK and India worked together to promote their mutual interest in this multilateral forum. Recommendations of the meeting are as follow:

Bilateral Trade and Investment

While the Round Table welcomed the changes and reforms taking place in India and noted the upsurge of business confidence and pride in India, it urged further robust action to address the problem of negative perceptions among potential British investors and the British media, by trade bodies and government officials on both sides.

Multilateral Trade Negotiations

Recognising the fundamental importance of the Doha Round for the sustainable development of the economies of developing countries, that the two Governments should:

(a) Explore areas in which their interests converged and cooperate to apply pressure for a successful outcome, and

(b) Encourage the CII/CBI Working Group established in July 2002 at the UK-India Economic Summit to redouble its efforts to identify scope for bilateral cooperation in this context.

Climate Change

That the two governments at the highest level should reaffirm their concern for the adverse effects of global warming, and that they should take the following steps:

(a) Further develop exchanges, perhaps through the establishment of a bilateral mechanism, to share experiences of measures taken to arrest global warming. These included high profile publicity campaigns in support of new initiatives and policies to induce more environmentally friendly lifestyles and business practices, and to assist in the rapid penetration of new technologies that have beneficial environmental consequences;

(b) Aim for agreement on a long-term stabilisation target;

(c) Share experience in experimentation with the development of non-conventional fuels, e.g. biofuels, and means of production at competitive cost, in particular, solar energy especially in India where the development/production of solar panels at competitive cost would have dramatically beneficial consequence;

(d) Explore the potential for innovative financing for hedging against 'weather risk' (including insurance), in order to reduce the negative impact of climate change;

(e) Exchange experience on the beneficial effects of forest management in tackling climate change; and

(f) Sensitise industry in both countries to the need to respect investor sensitivity to environmentally unfriendly practices, taking into account current UK practice on Social, Ethical and Environmental (SEE) policies and activities as a basis for inclusion of SEE guidelines for the contents of public company annual accounts.

Visas

That the two governments give early and serious consideration to a review of existing visa issuing arrangements with the aim of increasing efficiency and transparency, and of facilitating legitimate visits and exchanges in all categories on a reciprocal basis, including academic, commercial and economic, scientific and technological, cultural and sporting.[26]

The Seventh Meeting of the UK-India Round Table took place from 9-11 January 2004 at the historic Oberoi Grand Hotel in Kolkata. The Chief Minister of West Bengal, Shri Buddhadeb Bhattacharya, attended lunch on the first day and gave a presentation on the attractions of West Bengal for overseas investors. The British delegates called on the Governor of West Bengal, Shri Viren Shah, before the meeting and had the opportunity to see the excellent restoration of the Raj Bhavan. The main themes of the meeting were the fight against international terrorism, the movement of peoples, bilateral economic relations and the multilateral trading system. Recommendations from the Seventh Meeting are the following:

Bilateral Trade and Investment

The Round Table welcomed the continuing process of economic reforms in India, which had led to dramatic and broad-based GDP growth. The fact that FDI in India enjoyed rapid returns needed to be highlighted in investment promotion efforts. Removal of barriers to doing business and improvements in infrastructure had made India more attractive for foreign investment, especially from UK SMEs; there is a need to continue to encourage foreign investment and it is recommended that foreign institutional investment (FII) should not be included within FDI limits.

The Round Table appreciated the process of Business Process Outsourcing to India of a range of services, which it felt was mutually beneficial. The Indian side expressed appreciation of the supportive position taken by the UK government and business on this issue. Greater publicity needed to be given to the job creation by Indian investments in the UK, which have grown rapidly in the past few years.

That the Confederation of Indian Industry (CII) and Confederation of British Industry (CBI) conduct a factual analysis of investment by SMEs in both countries, with regard to their profitability and also to determine government hurdles/obstacles to increased bilateral trade, including export guarantees, lack of information about opportunities, trade fairs and expositions and to implement a plan of action with a specific timeframe.

Terrorism

India and the UK should intensify their bilateral cooperation in the fight against international terrorism in all its forms and manifestations.

Multilateral Trade Negotiations

India and the UK should work together to build bridges between the developed and developing world in order to achieve meaningful progress in the current trade Round Table towards a fair and equitable global trading system; to promote the advantages of such a system, in particular the need for further movement by the developed world on agriculture.

Academic, Cultural and Scientific Exchanges

Both Prime Ministers should commission an independent study to report by the end of 2004 to assess the state of academic, cultural and scientific exchanges and visits between India and the UK and make recommendations to further develop such exchanges.

Airline Services

The Round Table was most discouraged that the two governments have been unable to find ways to expand direct flight availability between the UK and India. This constitutes a serious obstacle to efforts to expand tourism, trade and bilateral cooperation in general.[27]

The Eighth Meeting of the UK-India Round Table was held at the Devonshire Arms Hotel, Bolton Abbey, and Yorkshire on 6 and 7 February 2005. In the chair there were Lord Swaraj Paul, the UK Co-Chairman and Mr. Hamid Ansari, the Indian Co-Chairman.

Lord Paul warmly welcomed Mr. Ansari as the new Indian Co-Chairman. He also requested that his expression of gratitude to the former Indian Co-Chairman, Mr. K.C. Pant for his skilful and patient chairmanship, be placed on the record. Lord Paul announced that this would be his own last meeting as UK Co-Chairman of the Round Table. He said that it had been an honour and privilege for him to have co-chaired the Round Table for the last five years and thanked Round Table members for their valuable contributions and support.

The main themes of the meeting were drawn from the Joint Declaration of 20 September 2004 and the exercise known as the Prime Ministers' Initiative, namely the Movement of Peoples, Education, Trade & Investment and Public Diplomacy.

Public Diplomacy and the Bilateral Relationship

In their introductory remarks the two Co-Chairmen pointed to the excellent state of the bilateral relationship, spearheaded by the two Prime Ministers. A strategic partnership has been established, as reflected in the commitments contained in the Joint Declaration of September 2004. Further progress was already being made in various areas, notably the Joint Economic and Trade Committee (JETCO), which had held a constructive first meeting. Another vital area of progress was air services; the Round Table had pressed hard for an increase on many occasions. The recent breakthrough would have a positive effect in all the areas under discussion. One field of particular concern was education, an area of fundamental importance to future ties.

A recurring theme was the fact that India was now beginning to realise its true potential. There was no turning back. Progress had hitherto been incremental but India was on the verge of a quantum leap in many fields. Recent long-term forecasts of economic growth suggest that India would be a major economic power before the middle of the century. India was not merely a source of inexpensive labour. It would also be wrong to categorise her, as a provider of services while China remained the manufacturing powerhouse of the world. India's manufacturing was reaching a high standard in several sectors. The establishment of R&D centres in India by leading multinationals reflected the high calibre of its graduates. India was enthusiastic about cooperation in trade and investment and science and technology.

Both governments recognised their mutual interest in working together on global governance. Contacts were taking place across a wide field. Nevertheless, despite all this and while all the architecture was in place for stronger bilateral ties, mutual perceptions in the two countries were not keeping pace with the efforts of governments. One description of India's relationship with Britain was that it was 'a fully laden ship waiting for the wind to blow'. Far more needed to be done, in particular, to get across the message of change in both countries.

The UK decision to mount a major public diplomacy campaign was very welcome, but efforts on both sides to open up communication and the means to greater mutual awareness must be unstinting. Younger Indians were not looking to the UK for inspiration; they had their eyes on the United States. Respect for age for its own sake was eroding in India; the future lay with its vast well-educated youth. Younger people would have a greater say in the future of India than hitherto. In this discussion, as in those on the other themes, great emphasis was placed on the vital need for Britain to connect with the younger generation of India. They must be made aware of the fact that the UK had transformed itself in recent years. Its economy was already considerably larger than those of France and Italy. People in the UK, too, must be made aware of these changes. The Government of India, as well as the corporate sector in both countries, also had an important role to play in facilitating mutual awareness of advances and changes.

Improvement in all forms of communication between the two countries must be a priority for Governments. They could start by giving strong encouragement to the promotion of middle level tourism given the recent agreement on increased flights. The low capacity in air travel hitherto had been a serious drag. The planned increase was a start but there was scope for many more flights between the two countries.

If the UK really felt that its interest lay in a close partnership with India, then it should take radical steps to achieve this. A study should be made of where the relationship might stand in 20 years. The Round Table should use such a study to identify the means to accelerate progress towards closer cooperation. Perhaps, the greatest opportunity lay in the field of education given the view that the real basis for a strong future relationship lay with the younger generation.

Recommendations

1. That the Round Table should commission a study of what the relationship might be in 20 years time, taking into account such factors as forecast economic growth, globalisation, evolving attitudes to the movement of peoples and technological progress. The study should be presented to the next meeting of the Round Table. The Round Table should then regularly look back from the study, and make recommendations on areas where progress towards certain goals might be accelerated.

2. That the report and recommendations of the meetings of the Round Table be circulated to opinion formers in each country and posted on High Commission websites.

The Movement of Peoples

Members noted that globalisation had created a situation in which the lowering of barriers to the supply of goods and services had outstripped progress of the freer movement of peoples. Many countries continued to restrict movement by means of immigration laws and visa and other forms of immigration control, sometimes for wholly justifiable reasons, for example, security. But some others did so for political reasons. It was hoped that policy on immigration in the UK would continue to be based on analysis of broader requirements and not political pressures. The free movement of peoples was crucial to a closer relationship.

National policies on immigration must take into account security and employment but they must also make clear distinctions between different categories of immigrants. The movement of workers and professionals was a phenomenon of modern economic growth. Demographic changes in advanced countries, for example, in the EU, made the cross-border flow of labour an absolute necessity. It would remain so increasingly in the future. But governments must be relentless in stamping out the ill-treatment of guest workers and illegal immigrants, in particular, the nasty crime of people trafficking. It was noted that the UK Government had publicly recognized that the benefits of the freedom of movement of workers and outsourcing, which were factors of globalisation, perhaps, inevitably, abuses of the system had led to a tightening of certain regulations. The Indian side expressed concern over the Voluntary Vetting Scheme which was detrimental to academic exchanges in high technology areas, identified as one of the important areas of cooperation in the Prime Ministers' Initiative. Controls were necessary but not barriers. It was accepted that there had been improvements but there was still a lack of transparency, notably in the operation of quotas in the UK.

The Round Table was deeply concerned for the growth in illegal immigration since this often involved grave abuses of human rights and outright criminal behaviour. Everything should be done to stamp out trafficking in people with especial efforts made to catch and punish the intermediaries responsible.

Serious attempts should be made to assess the labour market requirements in both countries and regulations should permit the free flow of workers in strong demand, especially professionals. Educational institutions in India were concentrating on qualifications, which met international standards, a further argument in favour of lowering barriers to cross-border movement of skilled workers and graduates. The UK had loosened its regulations on foreign students working both during and after their studies but a perceived lack of transparency still caused problems for them.

Recommendations

1. That the Governments should work together to eradicate illegal immigration into the UK, in particular, targeting those responsible for trafficking people.

2. That an analysis should be made of the future labour market requirements of the UK with a view to the establishment of India as a preferred source of skilled labour, taking account of India's own employment and skills needs.

3. That every effort should be made to facilitate travel between the two countries, in particular for students, businessmen, research scholars and professionals, for example, through further improvements in the processing of visas and the issue of work permits.

Trade and Investment

Indian members emphasized the huge benefit of the incremental economic reforms since 1991. Economic reform would continue; witness the recent lifting of caps on Foreign Direct Investment (FDI) in civil aviation and telecommunications. Political factors might, occasionally, slow the pace of reform but they would not prevent it. The focus of the economic reform program had now shifted:

(a) to the rural, agriculture and food sectors. The aim was to bring 300-500 million more people into the mainstream of the Indian economy.

(b) to the development of improved infrastructure. There was, of course, close interface between (a) and (b).

(c) to the SME sector.

In addition to the above, the huge efforts were being made in the fields of air services (investment by airlines, in airports) and urban infrastructure (using corporate townships as models). The banking sector was in good shape, with NPLs at a low level by international standards.

There was exponential growth in the service sector. One trend was that well-educated young people were not following traditional career patterns and increasingly working on their own account or setting up small companies. British SMEs should be encouraged to network with them. There would be explosive growth in healthcare, education and training. A scheme, based on the UK City & Guilds system, to provide one million Indians with skills, was being put in place.

India was 'going global' in a big way. The mindset of Indian was changing radically. Growth of trade with China had been exponential. A free trade agreement between the two countries was under discussion. The relationship with the USA was being transformed across a broad front.

There were black spots, for example, transport infrastructure and power generation. Much of the latter was the responsibility of the States where it was a political rather than economic problem. But they were being addressed. The high fiscal deficit of the states was another matter of serious concern. Another major task for the Government was to balance the pace of economic growth with the distribution of economic prosperity. The eradication of poverty was of vital concern.

A strong pitch was made for the UK to look at cooperation in the healthcare sector. The modern Indian healthcare sector was mainly in private sectors. Large firms were now investing heavily. Serious efforts were being made to increase the supply of well-trained medical personnel. Attitudes towards healthcare provision were changing in both countries. It was noted that the UK NHS had already been looking at the Indian market. Reliance on remote diagnostics could reduce costs substantially. The economics of patient movement might make treatment in India a real attraction. There was substantial potential benefit for Britain from the growth of this sector in India: investment by UK healthcare providers, technical and regulatory support and the supply of hospitals, equipment and even insurance.

Recommendations

1. Noting the importance of much closer contact between younger people for the future growth of business links between the two countries, that the Indo-British Partnership and other relevant UK bodies pursue efforts to increase contacts between SMEs in both countries and also to connect the platform of Young Indians in India with their counterparts in the UK.

2. That leaders of Indian companies investing in the UK and British companies investing in India should be enlisted widely to publicize the overall attractions of investment in each other's country, notably, at the annual investment conference proposed by JETCO, in order to change negative perceptions in the UK about investment in India.

3. Noting the extensive benefits of increased travel in both directions for closer links between people in many walks of life, that the two governments strive to achieve further increases in air services, in particular, with the aim of boosting middle level tourism.

4. That British and Indian firms pay especial attention to the opportunities thrown up by reforms in India in services, manufacturing and infrastructure, most particularly in the food and agriculture sectors, which offer considerable scope for partnership.

5. That an early study be commissioned on the scope for greater cooperation in healthcare.

6. Noting a new trend for networking and cooperation between professional associations in the two countries that a survey should be made of existing contacts and strong encouragement given to the promotion of further contacts.

Education

Both British and Indian members expressed deep concern over the erosion of educational exchanges between the two countries. India's exchanges with other countries had been on the increase supported by much more generous government funding. Whereas many current leading Indian academics and leaders in other sectors had benefited from a British university education, after fifteen to twenty years from today there would be very few. If this really happens then there would be grave implications for the bilateral relationship. It was also noted that while numbers of Indian students in the UK had risen substantially, mainly in vocational courses, it was feared that they were not of the highest caliber. Indian students were discouraged by the discontinuation of scholarships.

The Round Table strongly endorsed the findings of the British Council review, which recommended funding for faculty exchanges and graduate and post-doctoral fellowships in both directions, in addition to action to attract more students of the highest quality to the UK. However, notwithstanding the value of this study, the meeting was strongly of the view that a more radical approach was needed with much bolder funding proposals. Recalling that a really radical initiative had earlier been suggested as necessary to achieve a step change in the bilateral relationship, members were convinced that education was the area in which this could be undertaken. Such an initiative would meet the finding of members that far greater interchange between younger people was essential to change the erroneous mutual perceptions that persisted. Its benefits would transform the relationship over many years and would impact on every sector of the relationship, not least trade in goods and services and investment.

Bearing in mind that the imbalances in the relationship are at present very much in the UK's favor and that the Government of India has endowed at a cost of nearly £2 million a chair (an independent department) in Indian Studies at Oxford, that the UK government should make a strong commitment to addressing this weakness in the relationship, with bold initiatives and funding of at least £5 million per year rising over a period of 5 years to £10 million per year, to implement the recommendations of the British Council review and to attract more students of the highest quality to the UK.[28]

The Ninth Meeting was held in Goa from March 10-11, 2006. Lord Chris Patten is the Co-Chair from the UK side, while Dr. Nitin Desai is the Indian Co-Chair. It was decided to commission further studies on India-UK relations up to 2020 and on possibilities for cooperation in the health sector. The Indo-UK Round Table also called for two science and innovation studies. In follow up the UK has drawn up two draft documents (i) the "Mapping Study", which will "map" the extent and depth of existing S&T collaboration links between India and the UK; and (ii) the "Wealth Creation & Innovation Study" which will examine models of R&D collaboration and other examples of successful commercialization to suggest how the increasingly close connections between the UK and Indian science bases can better be exploited commercially.[29]

The Tenth Meeting of the India-UK Round Table was held in Ditchely, UK during 11-13 April 2007. It was co-chaired by Nitin Desai and Chris Patten. The Round Table made recommendations in areas such as education, healthcare, research, financial services, bilateral business and investment besides a re-think on global issues as well as studies on the wider horizons of the relationships. The MoU on Return of Illegal Immigrants, signed in January 2004, was renewed for another period of one year in 2007.

EVALUATION

The relationship between Britain and India has been very cordial, in spite of the fact that there was a lot of resentment against the British during their rule in India. There is something special that binds both nations together, that is based on people to people links, language, culture and values.

Both countries celebrate the diversity of the multi-ethnic and multi-cultural societies. The exemplary manner in which the British government granted independence to India won over the hearts of the people of India and a lot of good will was created in favor of UK. Even today, India buys the largest number of things from United Kingdom very often; the British government consults the Government of India on many points. Although India became a Republic in January 1950, she has continued the Commonwealth link. That is a standing testimony to the close relations between the two countries.

At the start of the 21st century both UK and India are trying to adapt fast to the challenges of a new world order, new security threats, the globalized economy, and revolution in communications. The globalisation has brought the spread of new threats and problems—terrorism, weapons of mass destruction, cross border crime, health, new shared challenges like climate change, the rapid spread of new diseases like HIV/AIDS, etc.

India's multi-faceted bilateral relationship with the UK has developed substantially over the past few years. Strong ties with the UK are a priority for India given the political and cultural ties, substantial economic linkages and the large community of Indian origin in the UK. It remains a valuable catalyst in promoting the bilateral cooperation. This friendship and partnership between the two countries is now stronger and more important than ever before.

In March 2006, UK published a "White Paper" that identified ten strategic policy priorities, which focus on such issues as counter-terrorism, sustainable development, climate change, weapons of mass destruction, energy supply, and a liberal and global trading regime. The "White Paper" positions India as a global player with significant influence along with China, Japan and Russia. UK supports India's candidature for a permanent seat in the UN Security Council and will continue to work with India to achieve this.

The bilateral Summit was in follow up to the Prime Minister Dr. Manmohan Singh's visit to the UK in September 2004 when the two prime ministers had adopted a joint declaration titled "India-UK: Towards a New and Dynamic Partnership", setting out plans for a comprehensive strategic partnership. The joint declaration envisaged annual summits as well as meetings between foreign ministers and outlined areas for future cooperation in civil nuclear, energy, space, defense, combating terrorism, economic ties, science and technology, and culture.

The two leaders also exchanged views on a range of bilateral, regional and multilateral issues including UN reform, the Millennium Development Goals, climate change including technology transfers for sustainable development and education exchanges. The UK had reviewed its policy with regard to civilian nuclear technology cooperation and scientific contacts with India a few weeks prior to the visit. At the Summit it recognized the need for a supportive international environment for meeting India's pressing energy requirements.

Prime Minister Tony Blair was the first G-8 leader to moot the idea of India joining G-8 discussions. He visited India during 6-8 September 2005 in his capacity as EU President for the EU/ India Summit and also in a bilateral capacity. The bilateral Summit was held on September 8 in Udaipur, a day after the 6th India-UK Summit.

Prime Minister reaffirmed his commitment to India's candidature for permanent membership of the expanded UN Security Council. Prime Minister urged a regular dialogue on regional issues. The two sides finalized agreements on air services (substantially increasing the direct flights between the two countries) and cooperation in the field of hydrocarbons. An agreement on films co-production was initiated. Prime Minister announced that India would found a Chair at Cambridge in honour of Pt. Jawaharlal Nehru. Prime Minister announced a £10 million UK/India education initiative, which will fund scholarships and short-term academic exchanges; provide research awards to young Indians to go to Britain and young British researchers to spend time in Indian institutions. At the India-EU Summit on September 7, progress was achieved on cooperation in high technology areas, with the EU under the UK

Presidency reiterating support for India's participation in ITER and initiation of a framework agreement on India's participation in the Galileo Satellite Navigation Project.

The heads of the state exchange of visits, the interaction between ministers, the parliamentary members, etc. strengthened the bilateral relationship between the two countries. Institutional linkages with all the major British political parties have been established to ensure that goodwill towards India cuts across party lines. In Parliament, the Friends of India Groups have been useful in promoting understanding of India's pluralist society and democracy.

Both nations' economies are increasingly linked. Trade between the two countries is growing at 20 per cent a year. This is no surprise given that Britain provides an easier base, linguistically, legally, and culturally, and given open business environment. But it is important that Indian businessmen continue to think in these terms too—Britain as the easy gateway into Europe.

Trade relations between India and UK have undergone a massive change from the colonial period. Once perceived as a less developed country, India had transformed itself into a the fastest growing economies of the world currently. It is not a secret that India is world's fourth largest economy in purchasing power parity terms and UK is the 4th in GDP dollar terms. Economic relations play a key role in the bilateral relationship, and the Indo-British Partnership is an important catalyst. All these economic links are, of course, based to a great deal on the multitude of personal connections—of family and friendship—between the two countries. Britain would be poorer in every way without the immense contribution of the 2 per cent of the population with roots in India.

Several bilateral mechanisms have been established in recent years to facilitate economic cooperation between India and the UK including a Joint Economic and Trade Committee, Economic and Financial Dialogue (launched in February 2005), a Joint Working Group on Power and an Indo-British Coal Forum. The most important bilateral mechanism in the economic arena is the India-UK Joint Trade and Economic Committee (JETCO), which were launched in New Delhi on 13 January 2005 by Commerce & Industry Minister Shri Kamal Nath and Secretary of State for Trade & Industry Ms. Patricia Hewitt.

A British proposal to establish a working group to enhance links in creative industries was also received favorably. India and the UK have had a long trading relationship. India is the UK's 15th largest export market and its largest export market in the developing world (ahead of China). The UK is the largest market in Europe for Indian IT services. Conservative industry estimates are that British businesses now save upwards of £1 billion every year due to offshoring, the bulk of which is accounted for by India.

The flow of Indian investments into the UK that began as a trickle in the late 1990s has also now turned into a flood. In 2004-05, India became the eighth largest investor in the UK and in 2005-06, Indian companies doubled their investments in the UK to emerge as the third largest foreign investor in the country and the largest developing country investor (in terms of number of projects). The number of investment projects increased by a whopping 111 per cent. This is all the more surprising as India was nowhere on the investment scene a decade ago.

While Information and Communications Technology remains the dominant sector for Indian investment accounting for 54 per cent of all investment (26 projects), there has been strong growth in investments in pharmaceuticals and healthcare (12 projects) and automotive and engineering sectors (6 projects). Financial services also received substantial investment with 8 projects. Nearly half of the 76 projects in 2005-06 are located in London, while the remaining is spread across various regions. India has now emerged as the second largest overseas investor in London, after the US. A recent survey conducted by FICCI on outbound investment by Indian companies from January 2000 to July 2006 also confirms that the UK is the second most favored investment destination for Indian companies after the US.

The rise in Indian investment in the UK has been due to Indian investors taking advantage of Britain's expertise in high-value activities such as research and development, science and technology and innovative design, as well as the City of London's status as an international financial capital. It is encouraging to note that as the volume, scope and breadth of Indian projects expand in the UK, Indian investment is getting the recognition it deserves. In view of the growing investment ties, the City, the Mayor of London (who heads the Greater London Authority) and the London Stock Exchange are all in the process of opening offices in India.

In this environment of all-round economic interest in India, the House of Commons Select Committee on Trade & Industry in June 2006 published its report on "Trade and Investment Opportunities with India," that focused on the difficulties and opportunities faced by UK businesses wishing to trade or forge investment links with India, with particular reference to opportunities in the IT, life sciences, aerospace and financial services sectors; the role of British institutions of higher and further education in developing such links; and the role of the UK Government in assisting businesses, including the relative responsibilities of UK Trade and Investment and the Regional Development Agencies.

Trade and investment relations have been continuously strengthened by several bilateral interactions between the two nations. Among other things, one such linkage is the India-UK Round Table, a non-governmental body set up in 2000 to make recommendations on development of bilateral relations in all spheres.

In 2005, an agreement was signed between India and UK named as "The Prime Ministers' Initiative," which sets out a new strategic partnership between the UK and India, which among other areas like education, culture, foreign and defense policy, aims to strengthen bilateral economic and trade issues between the two countries.

Both countries have a long tradition of scientific links, and there are several ongoing joint projects between scientists and institutes. In order to enhance S&T cooperation between the two it was decided in June 2005 to upgrade the Joint Committee on S&T to the Indo-UK Science and Innovation Council (SIC). Shri Kapil Sibal, Minister for Science and Technology, led a delegation to the UK from June 26-28, 2006 for its first meeting.

Both side discussed possibilities of cooperation in science and technology and agreed to be equal partners in future initiatives.

On foreign policy and defense cooperation too, India and UK are cooperating more than ever before. The India-UK defense relationship has never been stronger. In 1995, India-UK Defense Consultative Group (DCG) was established. The DCG meets annually (the venue alternates between Delhi and London) and is co-chaired by the UK Permanent Under Secretary of State for Defense and his Indian counterpart. The modern relationship has been developed through the India-UK DCG. The bilateral program of exercises, exchanges, training courses and high-level visits continues to accelerate. Activity levels have tripled since 2002-03. This trend set continued and major Royal/Indian Airforce joint exercises held in Gwalior and Agra in October 2006. In line with Joint Declaration aspirations, the DCG meeting held in New Delhi on November 2006 to identify further ways of deepening and broadening defense cooperation.

Both countries also extend cooperation on the issues such as security and terrorism which have an impact on both our global and domestic agendas. Terrorism itself is indeed age-old. Both Britain and India have each had their own difficult and painful, experience of terrorism.

The Joint Working Group (JWG) to counter-terrorism provides an institutional mechanism to step up coordination in tackling the problems of drug trafficking and related crimes. Both countries already have an extradition treaty in place and the JWG should provide an ideal vehicle to maintain close contact and exchange information on terrorism and other major concerns.

The Terrorism Act 2000 of the UK takes effect from October 2000; the JWG could help plug the loopholes in the domestic legislation as well as the rules and regulations to be framed by the two countries in the future. The UK has unfortunately earned the dubious distinction of being the global headquarters for various terrorist groups—terrorist organizations of Punjab, Kashmiri groups, LTTE, etc.

The joint declaration issued by India and Britain on 21 September 2004, to launch a drive against the menace together is significant in the sense that both have been its victims for a long time. The UK, which had been earlier targeted by Northern Ireland terrorists, is now on the hit list of those associated with Al-Qaida. In India, which first faced the problem in Punjab, has been grappling with the monster in Jammu and Kashmir since 1989, it is due to Pakistan which is using terrorism as an instrument of state policy.

Strike on World Trade Center and Pentagon on 9/11 showed the degree of internationalization of terrorist networks, and the high degree of expertise some of these groups were able to bring to their deadly operations. It also showed that there existed networks with the willingness to cause unlimited destruction, not to achieve a political objective but in pursuit of an apocalyptic goal. Ultimately, the fear is that these terrorists will be able to get hold of weapons of mass destruction.

In the wake of 9/11, the UK Government has begun to adopt a robust approach to terrorism including terrorism affecting India. In foreign policy, the FCO Strategy Paper released on December 2, 2003 had identified international terrorism and the spread of weapons of mass destruction as the most "catastrophic" threats to the UK's national security in the early twenty-first century, relegating conventional military threats to the background. The paper also identified religion as a force in international relations, with religious tensions abroad, for example, in the subcontinent, having the potential to affect the UK's domestic security.

Terrorist activities can sabotage any good work being done anywhere. Terrorist activities in any form cannot be justified, whatever the pretext. Those who are involved in this heinous activity deserve no sympathy, as their victims are mostly non-combatants, innocent people, including women and children. Both UK Prime Minister Tony Blair and Foreign Secretary Jack Straw have earlier called for an end to Pakistan's support for terrorism in Kashmir. During the joint press conference with Indian Prime Minister Dr. Manmohan Singh in September 2004, Prime Minister Blair totally condemned any terrorism in Kashmir, including the killing of innocents and the murder of elected politicians. The British Prime Minister, and the Indian Prime Minister, reaffirmed their commitment to this relationship, and to developing it further. Both India and the UK have reiterated their belief in the international community working with unity and resolve to counter terrorism and extremism. Both countries continue to promote closer international cooperation in the fight against terrorism, within the rule of law and with respect for human rights.

The UK-India Round Table was established in April 2000; the primary purpose of the Round Table is to discuss issues that may affect the bilateral relationship and to reflect on ways in which it can be strengthened. The Round Table meets approximately every nine months, alternately in India and the UK. After each meeting the Co-Chairmen submit to their respective Governments at the highest-level recommendations to that end. The aim of the Round Table is not to duplicate inter-governmental discussions but rather to put forward ideas from different perspectives. Outside experts are sometimes brought in to introduce the discussions on specific subjects. The discussions of the Round Table have covered very widely, reflecting the fact that the ties between the two countries are exceptionally broad; to work together for mutual advantage on both bilateral and multilateral issues, e.g. from international security or the WTO to visa policy and educational exchanges.

Many ideas have been submitted to respective governments on how close cooperation might be achieved in the field of trade and investment, notably in the field of high technology. The Round Table has debated the importance of IT and biotechnology and put forward proposals for collaboration in research in these areas. Culture, tourism, air services, biodiversity, cultural and educational exchanges and legal services are among the many other issues that have been discussed. There was many meetings of the Round Table held, it has now met ninth times: The Ninth Meeting was held in Goa during March 10-11, 2006. The Ninth Meeting was decided to commission further studies on India-UK relations up to 2020 and on possibilities for cooperation in the health sector. It also called for two science and innovation studies. In follow up the UK has drawn up two draft documents, (i) the "mapping study", which will "map" the extent and depth of existing S&T collaboration links between India and the UK; and (ii) the "wealth creation & innovation study" which will examine models of R&D collaboration and other examples of successful commercialization to suggest how the increasingly close connections between the UK and Indian science bases can better be exploited commercially.

There are growing links between universities, colleges and schools, helped by the UK-India Education and Research Initiative, which are funded by both countries. Both countries also adopted various policies to improve bilateral relationship through cooperation in Information Technology, Air Services, Biotechnology and Healthcare, Culture, Film Co-Production, Tourism, Energy, Environment, and Customs Cooperation. Besides, both countries work together on tackling issues which confront us all, such as the fight against terrorism, global warming, and poverty or sustainable development. Today both India and UK increasingly have shared goals too, and a common will to achieve them by active engagement in various activities. Britain and India can do more together than which have already been done bilaterally on education, fight against terrorism, trade, combating climate change, etc.

NOTES

1. *The Indian Express*, New Delhi, 6 February, 2004.
2. N. Jayapalan, *Foreign Policy of India*, Atlantic Publishers and Distributors (P) Ltd., New Delhi(2001), pp. 197-198.
3. India-UK Bilateral Relations. www.indianhighcommission.org
4. UK and India: Global Partners (2006). www. Britishhighcommission.gov.uk/servlet/
5. *Ibid.*, p. 2.
6. India-UK Relations. www. Hcilondon.net/India-uk-relations2005.html
7. UK Ministers Visit to India in 2005-2006. www.indianhighcommission.org
8. *Ibid.*, p. 6.
9. *Ibid.*, p. 3.
10. Tony Blair, *The Hindu*, New Delhi, 6 March 2006.
11. India-UK Bilateral Relation. www. Britishhighcommission.gov.uk/servlet/
12. *Ibid.*, p. 3.

13. India-UK Relations: Economic Relations.
www. Britishhighcommission.gov.uk/servlet/
14. Other Economic Linkages.
http://www.economywatch.com/world economy/united-kingdom/indo-uk-trade-relation.html
15. *Ibid.*, p. 3.
16. *Ibid.*, p. 6.
17. *Ibid.*, p. 3.
18. *Ibid.*, p. 6.
19. *Ibid.*, p. 3.
20. *The Hindu*, New Delhi, 6 September 2000.
21. *The Tribune,* Chandigarh, 22 September 2004.
22. *Ibid.*, p. 3.
23. *Ibid.*, p. 6.
24. *Ibid.*, p. 3.
25. UK-India Round Table: India-UK Relations.
www. Britishhighcommission.gov.uk/servlet/
26. Report on the Sixth Meeting of the UK-India Round Table, 7-9 May, 2003.
http://www.ukinindia.com/htdocs/aboutus.asp
27. Report on the Seventh Meeting of the UK-India Round Table, Kolkata, 9-11 January 2004.
www.britishhighcommission.gov.uk/.../Xcelerate
28. Report of the Eighth Meeting of the India-UK Round Table, Yorkshire, 6 and 7 February 2005.
www.britishhighcommission.gov.uk/.../Xcelerate
29. Indo-UK Round Table: India-UK Bilateral Relations.
http://www.hcilondon.net/bilateral-relations.html

6

India and the European Union

BACKGROUND

India and the EU States as the largest democracies in the world, share common values and beliefs that make them natural partners in the modern inter-connected world. Both share a common commitment to democracy, pluralism, human rights and the rule of law and seek to pursue economic progress and prosperity for the peoples in a peaceful, stable and secure global environment. EU-India relations go back to the early 1960s. India was among the first countries to establish diplomatic relations with the (then) EEC. Then bilateral agreements were signed in 1973 and 1981.[1]

Based on the 1993 Joint Political Statement, Ministerial and Senior Official's Meeting have successfully carried forward the political dialogue. The intensity of dialogue improved as in 1997 the Commission suggested five "mechanisms" for reinforcing political relations. They were agreed with India at the 1997 Luxembourg Ministerial meeting:

1. Senior Officials Meetings (nine held);
2. Meetings between Commission and Indian planners (three held);
3. Bilateral meetings in margins of multilateral forum (two meetings on Biological and Toxicological Weapons);
4. Working groups of specialists (one meeting on Export Controls; five on Terrorism Experts, eight on Consular Affairs).

5. Think tank network: A Think Tank Seminar took place in Brussels, October 2001.[2]

The 1994 Co-operation Agreement signed between EU and India provides for an EC-India Joint Commission as the central guardian mechanism to oversee and inspire the entire range of co-operation activities between India and the EC. Three separate sub-commissions on Trade, Economic Co-operation and Development Co-operation, cover a more detailed agenda and report directly to the Joint Commission.[3] The 1994 cooperation agreement took bilateral relations beyond merely trade and economic cooperation. Together with the Joint Political Statement signed in 1993 it opened the way for annual ministerial meetings and a broad political dialogue. The Commission Communication for an "EU-India Enhanced Partnership" of June 1996 was also a leap forward and contributed to put the Commission in the driver's seat of EU-India relations. Council and EP endorsed the Commission's approach. Since then, dialogues have been held at different levels and at regular intervals.

POLITICAL DIALOGUE

India has traditionally had a multi-dimensional relationship with the EU, which is the largest trading partner, with an annual bilateral trade close to Euros 25 billion, biggest source of foreign direct investment, major contributor of developmental aid, important source of technological assistance and home to a large and influential Indian diaspora. India was one of the first Asian nations to accord recognition to the European Community in 1962. Since then EU has grown from a common market to a common currency and from a Community to a Union with increasing political and economic influence in the world. It was natural, therefore, that the growth of bilateral relations between India and the Members of the EU also evolved into an institutionalized dialogue with the EU itself. Accordingly, in 1983, the two sides agreed to formally institute the India-EC political dialogue.

Partners in Progress

India and the European Union are committed to an equal and dynamic dialogue on all subjects of interest and concern to them as major entities in their own regions, and as emerging global actors on the world stage. The European Union is already India's first partner in terms of trade and actual investment inflows and is in the front rank of its partners in the fields of economic and development cooperation.

As exemplified by the great impact of the terrorist attacks of 11 September 2001 on both India and Europe, in today's "global village" political, social and economic developments in one part of the world have a rapid outreach across the globe. In the rapidly evolving international order of new groupings and new challenges, India and the EU are called upon to play a major role, both within their respective regions and beyond.

As mentioned by Mr. Michel Caillouet, Ambassador—Head of Delegation of the EC Delegation in India, in of the 2nd EU-India Summit that took place in New Delhi in November 2001, "The challenge is to give effect to our intentions stressed in Lisbon and reaffirmed in New Delhi to build a strong partnership and to create at all appropriate levels of our institutions and or our civil societies the framework and the mechanisms which will sustain the necessary political will and give joint endeavors their fullest realization."

Indeed, deepening of the political partnership is embedded in a strong institutional architecture. Annual ministerial meetings and summits are the most visible feature of the ongoing political dialogue between the EU and India. Senior officials and experts also regularly meet on issues of common concern such as terrorism. Political relations are also strengthened by the regular exchange of visits between EU and Indian parliamentarians. One should also mention the increasing number of visits of European Commissioners to India. For instance, in 2001: External Affairs Commissioner Chris Patten; Agriculture Commissioner Franz Fischler; Trade Commissioner Pascal Lamy and, of course, President Prodi on the occasion of the Delhi Summit visited India. In 2002, Commissioner for Enterprise and Information Society Erkki Liikanen visited India, as well as the Commissioner for Development and Humanitarian Aid Poul Nielson, and Commissioner for External Relations Chris Patten, who returned to India.

India's bilateral interactions with the countries of Europe have gathered considerable momentum during 2007. Sumit-level interaction has taken place with Italy, Netherlands, Germany, Portugal, the U.K. and France. There has also been extensive interaction at ministerial and official levels, besides growing exchanges of parliamentarians and civil society dialogues.

Civil Society Links

The wider relationship of the EU and India can be seen from their strengths of the two civil societies. Their vibrancy and diversity reflect the strengths of both the respective democracies, and the multi-lingual, multi-cultural societies in Europe and India. The launching of a "EU-India Round Table" of eminent personalities and the creation of a EU-India network of "Think Tanks" are significant steps in this direction. In the same spirit, the development of academic and cultural exchanges should play an increasing role in order to broaden the spectrum of EU-India relations. For instance, if EU Film Festivals are already a familiar event in Delhi and a few Indian metros, the momentum generated by various projects going on under the EU-India Economic Cross-Cultural Programme should set an important example to boost a much-needed co-operation in the fields of media, academia and business enterprises.

Growth of EU-India Relations

The relations between India and the Member States of European Union have a long history. But EU-India relations really took root in their present form in 1963, when India was amongst the first developing countries to establish diplomatic relations with the then six-nation European Economic Community. Over the years, the EU and India have developed a close relationship that covers key areas such as political relations, trade and investment, economic and development co-operation as well as cultural exchanges. A strong impetus came from the Cooperation Agreement on Partnership and Development, which was signed between the EU and India in December 1993 and came into force in August 1994. In July 1996, the European Commission presented a "Communication", "EU-India Enhanced Partnership" which suggested a number of steps to reinforce this relationship. The Council as well as the European Parliament subsequently endorsed the recommendations of the Commission.

A quantum leap occurred in the EU-India relations in June 2000 in Lisbon with the first-ever EU-India Summit. On this occasion, the Prime Minister of India, Mr. Atal Bihari Vajpayee, the Prime Minister of Portugal, Mr. Antonio Guterres in his capacity as the President of the European Council, the Secretary General of the European Council, Mr. Xavier Solana, the President of the European Commission, Mr. Romano Prodi, along with several Ministers and European Commissioners, launched a new strategic partnership based on shared values and aspirations. The Republic of India and the European Union, each in its own way, bring together in a vast geographical area a great diversity of peoples and cultures. Both derive strength from their traditions of diversity, plurality and tolerance. The Second EU-India Summit was held in New Delhi in November 2001 and the third EU-India Summit was held in Copenhagen on 10th October 2002. The European Commission has also presented "Country Strategy Paper 2002-2006" for India, which aims to chart out the course for development and economic co-operation between India and the European Commission for the period 2002 to 2006.[4] India is the world's largest democracy, ethnically and linguistically the most diverse nation state next to China, the only other population billionaire. India has made enormous strides since it achieved independence more than 50 years ago: literacy, health and life expectancy have substantially improved, and poverty that once afflicted a majority of its citizens has been reduced dramatically.

India has developed the world's fourth largest economy with a growth rate that since 1980 ranks amongst the highest in the world, and a rapidly expanding global imprint in information technology. At the same time the challenges India faces are becoming more complex and urgent as the global village raises expectations and as people are demanding their fair share in improving their economic and social fortunes.

India's overriding challenge for the first decade of the new millennium is to lift between two to three hundred million of its citizens out of poverty. All of India's co-operation partners, including the EC, subscribe to this objective and are seeking to mobilise their particular strengths towards helping the Indian government to achieve this goal.

The EC's co-operation strategy will build on the experience of two decades of successful co-operation and adapt its interventions to the changing political and economic landscape in India. It will assist India to build its "human capital" by dedicating its resources to:

- making elementary education universal;
- improving health services in favour of the hitherto deprived population groups;
- restoring and safeguarding a healthy environment.

The EC will work with the Indian authorities to create an enabling economic environment. It will share its expertise, including in science and technology, to help India unlock the full potential of its economy, induce better returns on its vast economic assets through regulatory reform, privatisation and fiscal reform. It will also seek to facilitate the exchange of talented students and scholars and the collaboration of scientists from both sides.

The central cross-cutting themes for the EC's co-operation strategy will comprise improved governance, the devolution of decision-making and management and the participation of stakeholders, in particular women and segments of the population traditionally disadvantaged in articulating their interests. The EC will assist communities at risk to be better prepared for natural disasters.

As political decentralization in India is increasingly shifting the dynamics for change from the centre to individual state governments, the EC will in the years to come invest resources in a "Partnership for Progress" with initially one Indian State that is committed to reducing poverty by pursuing a social and economic reform agenda. The first "Partnership" could be followed by second "Partnership" in due course.

In the pursuit of these objectives the EC will continue to work closely with India and through non-governmental organisations, the Indian civil society and private sector. It is expected that the Budget Authority will make available some €225 million for the forthcoming five-year period for EC development and economic co-operation.[5]

SUMMITS

First EU-India Summit

The First Summit between the EU and India was held in Lisbon, Portugal on 28th June 2000. The Prime Minister of Portugal Antonio Guterres represented the EU in his capacity as President of the European Council assisted by the Secretary General/High Representative for Common Foreign and Security Policy Xavier Solona, and the President of the European Commission Romano Prodi. The Indian Prime Minister Atal Bihari Vajpayee represented India. It was one of the most important milestones in enhancing EU-India relations since the European Commission took the initiative in the mid-1990 to communicate to Council and Parliament its blueprint for a substantially enhanced partnership in India. For the EU the Summit represented the long overdue acknowledgement that India is an increasingly significant political and economic player on the global stage, ever since India had been left in the Cold War after its key ally, the Soviet Union crumbled at the end of the Cold War.

For India the Summit was a welcome opportunity to be recognised as a truly global player, receiving the same attention as other major partners of the EU. This Summit provides additional impetus to its policy of engaging India on all major issues of interest and concern.[6] It was also a manifestation of the EU's will to engage India as a major player in an emerging multi-polar world and a milestone in EU-India relations. The topics discussed covered the entire range of political, economic and global developmental and environmental issues between two democratic, responsible and influential partners on the world stage.

Concrete results are defined in a wide-ranging Joint Summit Declaration. It foresees that bilateral dialogue be enhanced by holding further regular Summits, Foreign Ministers' meetings every year and Senior Officials and experts' meetings each semester which will address foreign policy and security issues of common concern.

From an economic point of view India and the EU agreed to examine all impediments to trade and investment in India. The most important result certainly was the agreement to improve co-operation in WTO matters. This first Summit was a success. Contacts at the highest political level have given additional impetus to EU-India partnership, which is reflected in the Summit Declaration. On this historic occasion, both EU and India resolved to build a new strategic partnership founded on shared values and aspirations characterized by enhanced and multi-faceted co-operation.

Both EU and India, based on the shared universal values of democracy and the respect for human rights, rule of law and fundamental freedoms, stress the commitment to promote socio-economic development and prosperity, as well as international peace, stability and security. The EU, which has strategic partnerships with only five other countries (USA, Canada, Russia, Japan and China), now sees India as a "regional and global leader engaging increasingly on equal terms with other world powers".

Agenda for Action

Towards the achievement of these objectives both EU and India agreed on the following actions:

- Enhancing bilateral dialogue by holding further regular Summits, Foreign Ministers' meetings every year and Senior Officials and experts' meetings each semester, which will address foreign policy and security issues of common concern.
- Co-ordinate efforts to promote and protect all human rights and fundamental freedoms referred to in the Joint Declaration.
- Initiate dialogue on preventing and combating terrorism and to strive for a Comprehensive Convention on International Terrorism.
- Strengthen co-operation to combat international drug trafficking and drug abuse.
- Co-operate closely in identifying and furthering common interests in international organisations.
- Continue to work together to eradicate chemical and biological weapons.

- Work together for the complete elimination of nuclear weapons, proliferation and their means of delivery.
- Launching of the India-EU Round Table.
- Launching of the EU-India Think Tank Network.
- Continue to strengthen the High-Level Economic and Commercial Dialogue on bilateral and multilateral trade, economic and financial issues.
- Commence joint initiatives in the fields of information technology and telecommunications.
- Work towards an Agreement on Co-operation in Science & Technology.
- Draw up plans on co-operation in culture and education and for exchange of expertise in the field of management.
- Endeavour to complete the elaboration of a new sector programme in elementary education within the year.
- Join efforts towards setting up an Institute of Environment Technology in India.
- Promote bilateral initiatives in the field of environment and facilitate co-ordination on multilateral environmental issues.
- Further enhance economic co-operation for rapid development of infrastructure, including telecommunications, energy and transport in India.
- Work jointly to promote and increase flows of goods and services between the EU and India.
- Address all obstacles with a view to stimulating EU investment in India.
- Facilitate industry and business links.
- Consult each other within the existing fora on anticipated regulatory and other measures affecting the flow of trade, investment and services with a view to resolving problems at an early stage.
- Establish a regular high-level dialogue on WTO issues.[7]

Civil Society Relationship

The Lisbon Summit endorsed the EU-India Think Tank Network and the India-EU Round Table, already decided upon at the December 1999 Helsinki Ministerial Summit.

EU-India Think Tank Seminar

There were 40 leading European and Indian Think Tanks met in Brussels on 15-16 October 2001. The EU-India Think Tank Seminar, a European Commission initiative under the umbrella of the EU-India partnership, is opening the stage to a broad think tank network, a project triggered by Chris Patten, European Commissioner for External Relations.

The plan to foster interaction between European and Indian Think Tank is one of the two elements of the EU-India Lisbon Summit's action plan for closer involvement of the civil society in the partnership, the other decision being the setting up of a Round Table.

Commissioner Patten and Omar Farooq Abdullah, Indian Minister of State for External Affairs, the key speakers at the Seminar, expressed their views that this gathering of Think Tank contributes to feeding the EU-India relationship with challenging and new ideas and to enhancing contacts and understanding between the two societies. The participating Think Tank came from a wide cross-section of areas of activity: security, economy, law, international relations, environment, energy, science & technology, etc. The Think Tank met in four closed working groups on issues of common concern to the world's two largest democratic entities: security, energy, federalism/decentralization, and democratic traditions & governance. Two plenary sessions produced frank and forthright exchanges on EU-India relations and on prospects for co-operation between EU and Indian Think Tank.

The Commission has launched an EU-India Small Projects Facility Programme (SPF) to foster links, promote dialogue, facilitate interaction and encourage networking between EU and Indian civil society organisations, including also Think Tank.[8]

India-EU Round Table

As a direct implementation of the Lisbon Summit Agenda for Action, the India-EU Round Table held its first meeting in New Delhi on 29-30 January 2001.[9] Rt. Hon. Christopher Patten, External Relations Commissioner and Mr. Jaswant Singh External Affairs Minister of India inaugurated the first session of the India-EU Round Table. Mr. Patten's visit to India provided the opportunity to underline the importance that the European Union attributes to the development of its partnership with India, in accordance with the spirit of the first Summit which held in Lisbon in June 2000. The Commissioner met with various personalities, among which the Indian Finance Minister Mr. Yashwant Sinha, leaders of the Congress party, representatives of the Indian and European business communities, and also NGO representatives. Thus Mr. Patten could approach the complete spectrum of co-operation between the EU and India. He particularly emphasized the importance of a further deepening of the political dialogue as much as enhancing trade and investment relations; on this topic he announced that the Commission would submit a concrete initiative to the EC-India Joint Commission at the beginning of February. This initiative, decided upon at Lisbon is a very significant step towards the establishment of greater links between European and Indian civil societies. This visit was equally marked by its coincidence with the dramatic earthquake, which hit Gujarat, and hence Mr. Patten could discuss in detail with his Indian interlocutors the need for EU and international assistance.[10]

The 15 members of the European Economic and Social Committee (EESC) represent the European Civil Society. The Indian side has nominated an equal number of representatives from its civil society. The Round Table was launched by the Indian Minister for External Affairs, Mr. Jaswant Singh and the European Commissioner for External Relations Mr. Chris Patten.

It has held ten excellent meetings so far:

- Vienna, 7-8 June 2006.
- Hyderabad, 18-20 September 2005.
- London, 6-7 December 2004.
- Srinagar, 17-20 June 2004.

- Bangalore, 8-10 February 2003.
- Rome, 16-17 December 2003.[11]
- Jaipur, 4-5 February 2002.
- Cascais, 12-13 September 2002.
- Brussels, 16-17 July 2001.

The summit between India and the European Union will pay the way for much closer cooperation between the two in the future. A broad understanding with the EU on international issues is essential if New Delhi has to establish itself as a global actor of consequence.

Second EU-India Summit

The Second Summit between India and the EU was held in New Delhi, India on 23rd November 2001 in which India was represented by Prime Minister Atal Bihari Vajpayee. The Prime Minister of Belgium, Guy Verhofstadt, represented the EU in his capacity as President of the European Council and the President of the European Commission Romano Prodi. Indian Ministers Jaswant Singh (External Affairs), Murali Manohar Joshi (Human Resource Development, Ocean Development and Science & Technology), Murasoli Maran (Commerce & Industry), as well as the Belgian Minister of State Ms. Anne-Mie Neyts-Uytterbroeck (Foreign Affairs) and the European Commissioner Pascal Lamy (Trade) participated in the Summit.

Building on the success of the 1st Summit held at Lisbon in June 2000, the 2nd Summit (New Delhi, 23 November 2001) consolidated the strategic EU-India partnership further.

Encouraged by the solid achievements against the targets agreed in Lisbon, the New Delhi Summit, adopted a fresh "Agenda for Action", with concrete objectives to be implemented in time for the 3rd Summit due in Copenhagen in the second half of 2002. A joint statement on international terrorism stresses the congruence of EU and Indian views.

During the Summit meeting, both sides discussed the international situation, focusing on Afghanistan and Pakistan. The exchange of views offered insights into each side's approach and priorities for the way forward.

Perhaps the most striking results were achieved on the economic front. The EU-India Business Summit that preceded the political event sparked a lively debate amongst the Indian and visiting business participants, as well as government representatives. Recommendations generated under the "Joint Initiative for Enhancing Trade and Investment" were endorsed by business and presented to the highest political leadership of both sides. Furthermore, ministers signed a landmark Agreement on Scientific & Technological Co-operation and adopted a Joint Vision Statement on Information Society. A € 200 million EC contribution to the Indian universal elementary education programme was signed.

Both European Commission President Prodi and Trade Commissioner Lamy used the occasion of the Summit for meeting NGOs, academics and the media, and short trips to other Indian states. Mr. Prodi visited Mumbai where he met with the Council of EU Chambers of Commerce, the Governor of the Central Bank and inspected an EC funded port management project. Mr. Lamy took up an invitation by the Chief Minister and business community of Andhra Pradesh, and inaugurated an EC funded community development project. President Prodi highlighted India's importance, as cornerstone of the EU's South Asia policy. Trade Commissioner Lamy had intensive discussions on the outcome and follow-up to the WTO ministerial meeting of Doha. The extensive press coverage showed that EU arguments were very well taken.[12]

Third EU-India Summit

The Third EU-India Summit held in Copenhagen on 10 October 2002, brought together Indian and EU leaders. The two sides took stock of achievements across a wide range of issues; reviewed the challenges and possible responses in the area of peace and stability and, exchanged views on, amongst other things, sustainable development, the integration of developing countries into the global economy, the fight against poverty and for improved health and education.

The Summit also endorsed the objectives of a new five-year co-operation strategy for bilateral development and economic co-operation, and agreed activity to enhance investment and trade.

A Joint Press Statement and an "Agenda for Action" set out the objectives to achieve in time for the 4th Summit planned for the 2003. The 3rd Business Summit was a huge success. It preceded the political summit by one day, following a tradition set at the Lisbon Summit in June 2000, and continued in New Delhi in November 2001. In the context of the the "EU-India Joint Initiative for Enhancing Trade and Investment" it discussed and adopted specific recommendations in four sectors consisting of specific pro-investment investor-friendly measures aimed mostly at Indian, but also at EC policy makers.[13]

The Business Summit preceding the Political Summit was the main venue for enhancing EU-India business dialogue. The 4th Meet in New Delhi during 28-29 November 2003 showed huge interest in India as investment destination and in Europe as growing market. A gathering of leading CEOs, business federations and political leaders from both sides, has already preceded the EU-India Political Summits in Lisbon, New Delhi, and Copenhagen. This edition produced recommendations for endorsement by the Political Summit on improving EU-India business partnerships, trade and investment, including those related to the Joint Initiative for Enhancing Trade and Investment. The EU was seen as a source of expertise, investment funds and markets. India was presented as the "happening" place for business: growth had been good, prospects were even better.[14]

Fourth EU-India Summit

The Fourth Summit between India and the EU was held in New Delhi, India on 29th November 2003. The Prime Minister Mr. Atal Bihari Vajpayee represented India while External Affairs Minister Mr. Yashwant Sinha assisted him. The EU was represented by the Presidency of the European Council, Italian Minister of State for External Affairs, Mrs. Margherita Boniver, President of the European Commission, Mr. Romano Prodi, Secretary General High Representative for Common Foreign and Security Policy Mr. Xavier Solana and the Commissioner (External Relations), Mr. Chris Patten. The fourth Summit and Commissioner Patten's visit to India were instrumental in further enhancing EU-India relations. The Summit was a successful event. It took place in a positive atmosphere, and was marked by a determination on both sides to strengthen further EU-India relations, shared views across a range of regional issues, and progress on the business/economic front. Intense press coverage was noted. Among the main "deliverables", a Customs Co-operation Agreement was initiated. This should help cut red tape, help both sides to fight fraud, and generally improve cooperation between administrations.

A Trade and Investment Development Programme was signed and it was ready to be launched in early 2004. It was agreed to launch negotiation on Indian participation in Galileo. It should allow our high-technology industries to co-operate on this major industrial project. It was also agreed to start negotiations on a Maritime Agreement. On the Doha Development Agenda, both sides felt that it was necessary to make progress towards resumption of negotiation.[15]

Fifth EU-India Summit

The Fifth EU-India Summit was held on 8th November 2004 in The Hague. At the summit the EU and India showed a strong determination to build a solid and broad strategic partnership. The meeting was held in a very friendly atmosphere and the dialogue was open and intense, with many areas of mutual agreement. Leaders officially endorsed the launching of a EU-India "Strategic Partnership" and decided to prepare an Action Plan for its implementation as well as a new Joint EU-India Political Declaration, to be presented at the 6th Summit in Delhi in 2005.[16] This "Partnership" as more than just the sum of its parts, it sees as a qualitative transformation in the way, which engages as equal partners and work together in partnership with the world at large.

Strategic Partnership Joint Action Plan

India-EU relations have developed substantially since the adoption of the 1993 Declaration. An extensive bilateral political dialogue has evolved, which includes regular annual summits, Troika Ministerial and Senior Official level meetings covering a wide range of issues. In the economic sphere, ties have expanded and it has worked closely together to strengthen the multilateral trading system and to pursue a constructive dialogue on trade and investment and economic cooperation.

India and the EU also have much to contribute towards fostering a rule-based international order—be it through the United Nations (UN) or through the World Trade Organization (WTO). Both hold a common belief in the fundamental importance of multilateralism in accordance with the UN Charter and in the essential role of the UN for maintaining international peace and security, promoting the economic and social advancement of all peoples and meeting global threats and challenges.

As the EU evolves and enlarges, and as it faces diverse and complex global challenges, it is critically important to expand the multifaceted relationship and build upon these foundations. Both India and the EU commit themselves accordingly to:

- Strengthening dialogue and consultation mechanisms;
- Deepening political dialogue and cooperation;
- Bringing together people and cultures;
- Enhancing Economic Policy Dialogue and Cooperation;
- Developing trade and investment.

I. Strengthening Dialogue and Consultation Mechanisms

India and the EU have effective mechanisms for dialogue at all levels. With the launching of the India-EU Strategic Partnership, it is necessary to further intensify the dialogue, both by actively strengthening existing mechanisms and making them more efficient as well as initiating dialogues in new areas being considered for cooperation. It would also be necessary to put follow-up mechanisms in place in order to effectively implement the decisions taken, with a view to ensuring a more sustained and cohesive approach to issues affecting India and the EU over an increasingly wide range of sectors.

Towards this end, India and the EU will:

- Maintain the high level dialogue at Summit and Ministerial level on all issues of mutual interest. Make full use of opportunities for contacts between Indian Ministers and their EU counterparts on issues of mutual relevance;

- Continue to exchange views on regional issues and the international situation at the official and ministerial level; and
- Review at the Senior Officials Meeting and EU-India Joint Commission the effective implementation of decisions taken at the political level.

The progress in the implementation of the Joint Action Plan will be placed before each annual Summit, and an overall assessment will be made for the 2008 India-EU Summit.

II. Political Dialogue and Cooperation

Pluralism and Diversity: Both India and the EU are multi-cultural, multi-religious and multi-lingual societies. India is a microcosm of the globe because of its sub-continental size and a population that accounts for nearly one-sixth of humanity. The EU, with its expanding geographical boundaries and diversifying demography, is one of the most demographically diverse entities in the world and yet able to synthesize the diversity of its member states into a coherent whole. These are areas where both India and the EU could benefit from an exchange of experiences. Both sides share the objective of contributing to the promotion of cultural and linguistic diversity, which consider an inalienable value, and the promotion of dialogue among cultures at the international level.

Towards this end:

- India and the EU will initiate a dialogue on Pluralism and Diversity with a view to sharing experiences and enhancing mutual knowledge of the cultural and linguistic diversity existing within India and EU; and
- India and the EU will continue to encourage academic exchanges on the dynamics of pluralistic societies in Europe and Asia.

Dialogue on Regional Cooperation in the EU and SAARC: The SAARC and the EU are large entities with complex structures and diverse demography. India and the EU would benefit from a deepened exchange of views on developments in Europe and South Asia. The European Commission already has a Memorandum of Understanding with SAARC, the main focus of which is technical assistance. The European Commission and the SAARC Secretariat are currently exploring the possibilities of strengthening cooperation for technical assistance in various projects.

Towards this end, India and the EU will seek to have a regular exchange of views on regional cooperation in the EU and in SAARC.

Democracy & Human Rights: Both India and the EU are committed to upholding human rights and fundamental freedoms and have ratified the major international human rights instruments. These shared values, based on democracy, pluralism and respect for the rule of law give strength to the relationship.

They propose to:

- Continue in a spirit of equality and mutual respect, the dialogue on Human Rights—both in a multilateral and bilateral context, with the objective of building greater mutual understanding and expanding common ground in order to strengthen the foundations of the strategic partnership;
- Consult and discuss positions on human rights and democracy issues and look at opportunities for co-sponsoring resolutions on thematic issues in relevant forum such as UN Commission on Human Rights or UNGA Third Committee; and
- Look together for possible synergies and initiatives to promote human rights and democracy.

Effective Multilateralism: India and the EU believe that a multilateral approach, in which the UN plays a central role, is the best way to address global challenges such as development, effective management of globalization, terrorism, drug trafficking, organized crimes, natural disasters, pandemics, and energy security.

It will accordingly:

- Work closely to promote effective multilaterality;
- Continue to hold regular consultations on thematic issues prior to the UN General Assembly (UNGA), and work together on negotiation and implementation of the

outcome of major international conferences and summits including on security, trade, environment, development and human rights;

- Exchange views on the issues raised by the Secretary General of the United Nations in his comprehensive report entitled "In Larger Freedom: Towards Development, Security, and Human Rights for All"; and
- Endeavor to invite each other reciprocally for conferences sponsored by either side where the other is, or can be, a participant.

Peacekeeping, Peace-Building and Post-Conflict Assistance: India and the EU have a common interest in UN peacekeeping and in post-conflict political and economic rehabilitation and reconstruction.

They propose to work together in the first instance in the following areas:

- Consultation before major UN debates on peacekeeping and peace-building and in the preparation of major peace conferences;
- Establishing a dialogue at official level on UN peacekeeping and peace-building to exchange perspectives on conceptual and operational aspects of peacekeeping operations, including post-conflict reconstruction and rehabilitation, in order to identify and develop specific areas of cooperation in the following sectors:
  1. Training for military and civilian components of peacekeeping missions, including police and other security forces;
  2. Exchange of trainees and instructors between Peacekeeping Training Centres of India and EU Member States;
  3. Joint support of UN peacekeeping and peace-building efforts, including as regards improved analytical capacities and greater cooperation between EU and Indian components of UN peacekeeping missions;
  4. Trade and development in peace-building;

5. Post-conflict and confidence-building projects in other regions of the world; and
6. Seminars and other activities designed to facilitate post-conflict management.

Disarmament and Non-Proliferation of WMD and Security Dialogue: India and the EU have a shared interest in working towards achieving the goals and objectives of universal disarmament and non-proliferation of weapons of mass destruction and their means of delivery. The proliferation of weapons of mass destruction and its linkages with terrorism poses a threat to international peace and security.

In this context, both resolve to enhance collective action to fight the proliferation of WMD as well as their means of delivery. Both believe that the response to proliferation challenges requires strengthened multilateral consultations and the pooling of all efforts and resources. Both agree that effective export control measures for duel use goods can play an important role in preventing proliferation, and at the same time, such measures should not hamper international co-operation in materials, equipment and technology for peaceful purposes.

It has been decided to initiate a bilateral India-EU Security Dialogue at senior official level which will include regular consultations on global and regional security issues, disarmament and non-proliferation to increase mutual understanding and identify possible areas of cooperation.

Fight against Terrorism and Organized Crimes: India and the EU recognize the fact that terrorism constitutes one of the most serious threats to international peace and security, and reaffirm their condemnation of all acts of terrorism as criminal and unjustifiable, irrespective of their motivations, forms and manifestations.

Both propose to work together to strengthen the cooperation in counter-terrorism efforts in accordance with the UN Charter and applicable principles of international law.

India and the EU both agree to:

- Support the work of the UN to ensure universal respect for and full implementation of all relevant UN Security

Council Resolutions (UNSCRs), UN conventions on terrorism and related protocols;

- Cooperate in the fight against terrorism and establish contacts between the Indian and EU Counter-Terrorism Coordinators;
- Cooperate in the fight against trafficking in drugs and psychotropic substances, and the diversion of chemical precursors related to their production;
- Work closely to promote the early entry into force of the International Convention for Suppression of Acts of Nuclear Terrorism and for the early conclusion of the Comprehensive Convention on International Terrorism;
- Work together to reduce terrorist access to financing and to fight money-laundering, and monitor suspicious transactions, taking into account international standards adopted by the Financial Action Task Force (FATF);
- Exchange views on how to develop the comprehensive United Nations counter-terrorism strategy based upon the recommendations in the Secretary General's report "In Larger Freedom";
- Expand the EU-India dialogue to include the link between drug trafficking and terrorism, document security, illicit arms trafficking and cyber-terrorism;
- Promote cooperation between Europol on the EU side and the Central Bureau of Investigation (CBI) on the Indian side; and
- Establish an Indian contact point in India for Eurojust.

III. Bringing Together People and Cultures

Migration and Consular Issues: The subjects of Migration and Consular Issues are increasingly important in the context of globalization, given the large-scale movement of people from region to region for economic or other reasons and the large migrant communities in both India and the EU. It is important to note that India is a source, transit point and a destination for migrants. Both recognize that it needs to maintain a constant dialogue on all aspects relating to migration and consular issues.

Both also recognize that facilitation of movement of people is an important aspect of improving people-to-people contacts.

Given the inter-connections between migration and other issues such as public security, both are convinced of the need for an exchange of views in this area. It is, therefore, felt useful to hold a comprehensive dialogue on migration issues.

The India-EU Joint Working Group on Consular Issues was set up following the first India-EU Summit in Lisbon in 2000, in order to enhance cooperation in facilitating the movement of people between India and the EU, including the speedy delivery of consular and visa services and enhancing business relations and tourism. The Working Group meets twice a year to discuss issues of concern on either side. It encourages continuing its work, with a view to further facilitating progress. It, therefore:

- Holds dialogues on all aspects of migration and consular issues of interest to us; and
- Encourages institutions on either side to undertake joint studies on problems relating to skill-set shortages and the changing demographic profiles in our regions.

Parliamentary Exchanges: As the two largest democracies in the world, the importance of regular parliamentary interactions between India and the EU can hardly be overemphasized. They are essential to enhance understanding of eachother's points of view on matters of interest to both sides. They also encourage greater understanding of eachother's democratic systems and areas of responsibility.

They propose to:

- Work towards the further development of EU-India friendship groups in the Indian Parliament and the European Parliament;
- Organize regular exchanges of visits by Parliamentary delegations, including by the Speaker of the Lok Sabha to the European Parliament and the President of the European Parliament to the Indian Parliament; and
- Encourage greater interaction between subject-specific Parliamentary Committees on both sides.

Education & Academic Exchanges: Both EU and India are convinced that cooperation between institutions of higher education and the exchange of scholars and students play a significant role in enhancing mutual knowledge. Therefore, it proposes to build on existing programmes between India and EU Member States and develop new initiatives to accord greater opportunities to students from both sides to study in each other's universities.

It seeks to:

- Promote the implementation of the India Window of the Erasmus Mundus Scholarship Programme, and encourages continuation of the programme;
- Link up websites of Indian and EU Universities and academic institutions in order to better inform students of academic opportunities in each other's areas;
- Encourage the development of EU studies in India and Indian studies in the EU, by encouraging installation of Chairs/or Centres of Modern Indian Studies in EU Universities and of EU Studies in Indian Universities including EU languages; and
- Facilitate access to academic institutions and residence in each other's territory of students admitted into bona fide programmes of such institutions.

Civil Society Exchanges: The First India-EU Summit held in Lisbon in June 2000 recognised that the involvement of organized civil society in the dialogue between the two sides would add a new dimension to India-EU relations. Given the vibrant and free civil societies that flourish in India and in the EU, it was felt that the creation of a forum to institutionalize such interaction would enhance each other's understanding of regional and global problems through open and frank discussions. In pursuit of this approach, the India-EU Round Table was inaugurated in January 2001 so as to complement the existing political, economic and social links. EU and India will seek to expand cooperation through:

- Promoting cooperation between political parties, trade unions, business associations, universities and civil society (including Think Tanks and NGOs);

- Developing the India-EU Civil Society Internet Forum enabling enhanced exchange of ideas between civil society actors; and
- Continuing to support the work of the India-EU Round Table, and its integration into the institutional architecture of the India-EU relationship.

Cultural Cooperation: The EU and India, which enjoy rich and diversified cultural traditions, recognize culture as an important instrument to foster close cooperation among States. Both sides express satisfaction at the ongoing programmes and cultural exchanges between India and EU Member States and will endeavor to increase these exchanges both at the institutional level as well as at the level of public and private organisations. Both sides also believe that more areas of cooperation can be further considered and exploited, especially in the fields where long-standing cultural traditions, as well as contemporary creations, can enrich such cooperation and make it fruitful.

Both will identify such areas and explore ways of collaboration:

- Work towards full implementation of the Cultural Declaration;
- Hold India-EU Cultural weeks on a reciprocal basis as part of the India-EU Summit activities, with both sides facilitating participation, funds and logistics;
- Facilitate participation by both sides in Film Festivals and other relevant cultural events to be organized in each other's territories;
- Develop cooperation programmes in preservation and restoration techniques;
- Promote dialogue between respective audio-visual industry with a view to stimulating cooperation and exchange programmes; co-production, circulation of cultural works between Europe and India and training professionals;
- Exchange views on cultural diversity including on developments such as the adoption of the UNESCO Convention on the Protection and the Promotion of the Diversity of Cultural Expressions;

- Undertake possible joint action to increase awareness of European culture in India and Indian culture in Europe, including meetings, seminars and thematic conferences which gather professionals, in particular from the audio-visual sector; and
- Undertake twinning between European and Indian cities, in accordance with each other's guidelines.

Increasing Mutual Visibility: India and the EU are large geographical entities, with complex and diverse demography and rich histories and cultural traditions. This necessitates a conscious effort on both sides to aware and educate each other's public about this. Both societies are evolving rapidly and there is a constant need to update the media image on both sides. The strategy to enhance mutual visibility should include enhancing the effectiveness of available instruments at our disposal, in addition to exploring new ones.

To this end, it proposes to:

- Promote more intensive media coverage of India in the EU and vice versa;
- Enhance journalistic exchanges between the two sides;
- Organize short-term information courses and thematic conferences for journalists on a reciprocal basis;
- Promote tourism in both directions and especially promote interaction between youth groups including cooperation in the field of sports; and
- Organise periodically EU-India thematic cultural years (e.g. cinema, music, dance and literature).

IV. Economic Policy Dialogue and Cooperation

A strengthened exchange of views and information between India and the EU on matters of mutual interest in the areas of economic cooperation will improve the business environment, leading to strengthened economic relations. Moreover, in the long-term, it will help to reduce obstacles to bilateral trade and investment.

For this purpose, both sides agree to the setting up of discussion platforms including several new Working Groups.

Interlinkages between the Working Groups will be through the existing Sub-Commissions and the Joint Commission.

Industrial Policy: Cooperation between India and the EU on industrial issues and understanding of the regulatory framework has been growing in recent years. Under the "Joint Initiative to Enhance Trade and Investment", the two sides jointly carried out general as well as eight sector-specific studies on trade and investment matters. On the basis of the results of the studies, Indian and European business associations brought out a set of recommendations, which were placed before the 2001 and 2002 Summits.

Considering the potential for a further enhanced dialogue, both sides agree to:

- Establish a platform for the exchange of information and views on industrial policy and to enhance mutual understanding of regulatory frameworks;
- Continue and reinforce dialogues in existing and strengthened Working Groups and encourage discussion in various sectors;
- Exchange information on competition policy in areas of mutual interest, with a view to increasing cooperation;
- Develop a dialogue on best practices in the field of corporate governance; and
- Establish a Working Group on Food Processing Industries.

Following the useful joint initiative studies, both sides also agree that a new initiative on enhancing bilateral Trade and Investment would be taken up.

Science and Technology: Both in India and the EU, the development of Science and Technology (S&T) capabilities, to help boost innovation and competitiveness, has taken center stage in policy-making. India and the EU began cooperation in the S&T sectors in the mid-1980s, which has now led to more than a hundred joint research projects. Research collaboration has mainly focused on sustainable development. Key themes have been health, agriculture, natural resources management, etc. The India-EC Science and Technology Cooperation Agreement came into force on 14 October 2002. It has been a major milestone in bringing together our S&T expertise for our mutual interest.

Yet the potential for more India-EU collaboration in many new and emerging high-tech areas is huge. India is a priority country for collaboration under the international dimension of the EU's Sixth Framework Research Programme (FP6) and for participating in the preparation of FP7 so as to synergise it with India-EC S&T Cooperation Agreement. Both share a firm commitment to foster European and Indian joint research, for mutual benefit and as a contribution to solving global issues.

In order to build upon well-established policy dialogue and partnership in S&T, India and the EU propose to:

- Organize joint workshops on research in the fields of mutual interest among EU's thematic research priorities;
- Promote participation of Indian researchers in the Research and Technological Development (RTD) Framework Programme;
- Explore with India other scientific and technical collaboration possibilities, such as joint research in the areas of frontier technology/cutting edge technology;
- Seek to increase mobility, exchanges and promote access of researchers between India and Europe;
- As agreed at the 2nd India-EC Science and Technology Steering Committee meeting held at New Delhi on 29th April 2005, make further pro-active use of the India-EC S&T Agreement to co-sponsor collaborative activities and research projects in areas, such as:
  - Information Science and Technology;
  - Genomics and Biotechnology for Health;
  - Nanotechnology and Functional Materials;
  - Road Transport Research and Development; and
  - High Energy Physics (Accelerator Science and Technology).

Finance and Monetary Affairs: India and the EU have a strong and growing presence in international financial discussions. The introduction of the Euro has strengthened the

EU's role and responsibilities in the international monetary arena. In an increasingly interdependent and global economy, where the financial and monetary policies of one major economic actor affect others, India and the EU share a common interest in developing an in-depth policy dialogue on global financial and monetary issues.

For this reason, India and the EU should promote exchange of views and information between relevant institutions and policy makers in the economic and financial domain. This would allow an exchange of views on macroeconomic and financial matters of common interest. Dialogue already taking place in various forums should be further strengthened.

To this end, it is agreed to:

- Hold regular consultations at an appropriate senior level on matters of common interest as and when necessary for issues considered appropriate by mutual consent;
- Establish a regular macroeconomic dialogue on matters of common interest;
- Identify academic institutions on both sides for increasing academic cooperation and exchange in these areas;
- Exchange information on financial services regulatory policies, banking systems and accounting standards; and
- Encourage the European Investment Bank to continue its involvement in investment in India, and to explore strengthening it in the future.

Environment: India and the EU are committed to creating the conditions necessary for sustainable economic development. Each recognizes the interdependencies in the field of environment and the trans-boundary character of many environmental problems. As major global actors, both partners are fully conscious of their capacity to play a central role in international efforts towards better environmental global governance.

India and the EU are signatories and active contributors to the main multilateral instruments, including the Kyoto Protocol, and the UN Convention on Biodiversity.

To realize the vision of making sustainable development a reality, India and the EU will seek to:

- Strengthen the dialogue on global environmental issues with a view to building mutual understanding in particular on the UN Framework Convention on Climate Change (UNFCCC) and the Kyoto Protocol, the Montreal Protocol on substances that deplete the ozone layer, the UN Convention to Combat Desertification and the Convention on Biological Diversity;
- Hold meetings of the Joint Working Group (JWG) on Environment on a yearly basis and develop high-level visits;
- Organize an India-EU environment forum in 2005 with stakeholders involving business, academia and civil society to exchange views and information;
- Hold an experts' meeting to exchange views on voluntary eco-labeling schemes; and
- Identify key environmental issues and approaches to sustainable development where exchange of experiences and cooperation could be mutually beneficial.

Clean Development and Climate Change: India and the EU agree that urgent action is required by all countries to address the issue of climate change on the basis of equity and in accordance with their common but differentiated responsibilities and respective capabilities. Both sides are of the view that in the years to come the UNFCCC and the Kyoto process must gain further momentum. India and the EU also urge parties to the Kyoto Protocol to achieve their targets, where obligated for the first commitment period. India and the EU further commit themselves to work together closely on future global negotiations for tackling climate change, consistent with the principles of UNFCCC beyond 2012.

Accordingly, India and the EU agree to launch an India-EU Initiative on Clean Development and Climate Change. This Initiative will focus on voluntary practical measures, and be taken forward at successive India-EU Summits. In view of the particular importance of cleaner technologies for tackling climate change, both sides further agree to:

- Identify and develop ways of widening access and overcoming the barriers to dissemination of such technologies in India and the EU and more widely;
- Increase funding and promote public-private partnerships for research and development of cleaner technologies;
- Promote adaptive research and development to suit the resource endowment of both parties;
- Reduce the price gap between "cleaner" and "less efficient" technologies by seeking economies of scale; and
- Hold experts' meetings on climate change, including on the Clean Development Mechanism (CDM) in 2005.

It was further decided that India and the EU would take steps to encourage and promote sustainable patterns of consumption and production to lessen the causes and adverse impacts of climate change.

India and the EU agree to strengthen the implementation of the CDM to promote cooperation on CDM between India and the EU and to encourage our companies to engage in CDM projects. The proposed India–EU Seminar on CDM would also explore the possibilities of making CDM processes more efficient, and with reduced transaction costs.

India and the EU will cooperate on improving adaptation to climate change and integrate adaptation concerns into the respective sustainable development strategies. Both sides agree to cooperate to enhance the scientific, technical and institutional capacity to predict climate change and its socio-economic impacts. India and the EU will further pursue research and development on technologies and measures to adapt to climate change.

Energy: Energy is of major significance for both India and the EU. Both sides recognize the need to work towards achieving safe, secure, affordable and sustainable energy supplies. Joint efforts in the development of more efficient, cleaner and alternative energy chains will be paramount.

In this context, an India-EU Energy Panel has been set up to coordinate joint efforts and discuss energy related matters of mutual interest. The Energy Panel has decided to set up Working Groups in the areas of:

- Energy efficiency and renewable energies;
- Coal and clean coal conversion technologies; and
- Fusion energy including India's membership in ITER.

Both sides agree to cooperate closely in the areas of:

- Promoting energy efficiency and energy conservation;
- Development of affordable clean energy technologies;
- Identification of new technologies in the field of new, renewable, conventional and non-conventional energy sources;
- Oil and gas, with a view to promoting security of supplies and stability in prices;
- Nuclear energy;
- Technology and expertise in exchange of energy between different grid systems and development of energy markets;
- Development of hydrogen and fuel cells; and
- Methane recovery and use.

Information and Communication Technologies: Information and Communication Technologies (ICT) influence all areas of society, business and government. The development and widespread adoption of new ICT services and networks have powerful effects on economic and social development.

India has developed strong capacity in ICT, capturing a large and growing share of the world market for IT and software services. With its large pool of talented IT specialists and world-class facilities for IT research and development, India is considered an important partner for Europe and vice versa.

Many ICT researchers and businesses on both sides are keen to strengthen links with their counterparts.

In 2001, India and the EU took further concrete steps to promote mutual cooperation in the development of ICT and a modern information society, as expressed in the Joint EU-India Vision Statement on IT adopted at the Second Summit in New Delhi.

By building upon already extensive Information Society dialogue, the EU and India have agreed to:

- Enhance India-EU cooperation in the Seventh Framework Programme;
- Exchange views on a regular basis on e-commerce, Internet-governance, and universal service under the umbrella of the India-EU Information Society Dialogue.
- Exchange views between relevant authorities of India and EC on these areas of common interest in appropriate forum;
- Encourage India-EU joint research proposals and collaboration activities in particular for the following fields: 4G, e-governance, e-education and e-health;
- Exchange best practices and information on regulatory frameworks (internet governance, privacy and security, spamming) and for electronic communications (e.g. mobile aspects, universal service);
- Exchange views on Telecommunication spectrum management and on roaming and inter-operability of telecommunication services;
- Work towards GEANT-ERNET connectivity with the objective of connecting EU and Indian Information Networks to facilitate research and technology linkages; and
- Continue Information Society Technologies (IST) awareness through workshops and seminars.

Transport: India and the EU have a common interest to explore synergies in developing reliable, safe and secure transport networks and linkages, which respond to the needs of individuals and business. Efficient transport systems will increase competitiveness on both sides and enhance our attractiveness as investment locations.

The EC's economic cooperation with India in the field of transport is well established. The India- EC Civil Aviation Project is the largest bilateral economic cooperation project in India. The project aims to strengthen civil air safety and stimulates cooperation between Indian and the EU civil aviation authorities and European aerospace industries.

The India-EC Maritime Transport Project, which ended in late 2003 inter alia, contributed to electronic data interchange programme in the port sector in India.

To advance the mutual interests in this important sector, India and the EU have agreed to:

- Work towards the conclusion of a Maritime Agreement;
- Launch a broad-based dialogue in the sector of civil aviation including closer cooperation in air transport technology, regulation and infrastructure and assess the scope for mutual benefits that could derive from such dialogue;
- Explore the possibility of continuing and expanding the scope of the existing Civil Aviation Project; and
- Continue discussions, as a matter of priority, on a horizontal agreement between India and the EU resolving legal issues in bilateral air services agreements.

Space Technology: Both India and Europe are at the cutting-edge of research in the field of Space Technology, and there is a wide scope for cooperation. With a view to promote collaboration and provide an appropriate environment for fruitful cooperation in the space sector, both parties will:

- Support further collaboration and dialogue between Indian Space Research Organisation (ISRO), Department of Space (DOS) and the European Space Agency (ESA) and the European Commission, in areas such as earth observation and remote sensing for monitoring of natural resources and environment, communications, meteorology, navigation, life and material sciences under micro-gravity conditions, space exploration, space sciences and any other area relevant to our respective Space programmes;
- Jointly identify specific new areas/projects of cooperation between the respective space agencies for further discussion/implementation through the existing mechanism for technical cooperation; and

- Conclude a framework agreement on India's participation in Galileo Satellite Navigation Systems.

Pharmaceuticals and Biotechnology: The EU is the second largest center of biotechnology research activity in the world and Indian biotechnology sector is advancing rapidly. Opportunities for partnership in areas such as new discoveries, pre-clinical/clinical trials and bio-informatics already exist and the potential for collaboration in agro-biotechnology, food safety and pharmaceuticals are growing.

Greater interaction and enhanced cooperation between respective EU states and Indian administrations, industry and research institutions would lead to faster progress and greater benefits for all. For this reason the EU and India agree to:

- Set up a Working Group on Pharmaceuticals and Biotech and in this framework they agree to hold experts' meetings, as a matter of priority, with the participation of European Agency for Evaluation of Medicinal Products (EMEA) on the EU regulatory approach in the field of Ayurveda products;
- Exchange information on the regulatory framework, on best practice in funding, research, environmental issues, technical exchange programmes, and infrastructure support institutions; and
- Cooperate on confronting global challenges posed by diseases such as HIV/AIDS, tuberculosis and malaria, and as part of this seek to organize a conference on development of vaccines for HIV/AIDS, malaria and tuberculosis.

Agriculture: India and the EU appreciate the social and economic importance for both sides to develop and preserve a dynamic agricultural sector. To create the conditions necessary for an efficient, modern and diversified agricultural sector, the EU and India have agreed to:

- Exchange views in relation to our respective agriculture policies including modernisation and other issues;
- Explore issues of reciprocal interest in agriculture trade; and

- Reinforce the dialogue in the restructured Working Group on Agriculture and Marine products. Both sides will identify new areas of cooperation in this Working Group and meet in parallel with the newly created Joint Working Group on Sanitary and Phytosanitary (SPS) and Technical Barriers to Trade (TBTs).

Customs: The EU is India's largest trading partner and India-EU bilateral trade has been showing great dynamism. Both sides agreed that trade volumes can be further boosted. The EU and India are committed to understanding the problems faced by EU and Indian companies in relation to customs controls.

To help overcome various obstacles to trade and improve supply chain security, India and the EU propose to:

- Ensure full exploitation of the agreement between the EC and India on cooperation and mutual assistance on matters related to customs through development of a cooperation programme by the Joint Customs Cooperation Committee;
- Strengthen the dialogue on customs issues including issues such as valuation and classification, rules of origin etc.; and
- Discuss the role of customs in the implementation of relevant trade and commercial policy issues.

Both sides also agreed to:

- Deliberate on harmonization, implementation and enforcement of customs laws, procedures and working methods;
- Cooperate on security and facilitation in the international trade supply chain and in tackling commercial fraud;
- Discuss and cooperate in modernisation and capacity building; and
- Explore exchange of information within the framework of the customs agreement and to discuss the establishment of formal channels of communication.

Employment and Social Policy: Employment and social policies are core issues within the EU and the Government of India has put them at the heart of its policy approach. India and the EU are committed to promote full, freely chosen and productive employment with full respect for fundamental principles, fair wages and rights at work. India and the EU share a common interest to develop a policy dialogue on employment and social security to share experience, periodic exchange of views and information on:

- Labour and employment issues, including employment policies, restructuring, the global employment opportunities and requirements for trained manpower;
- Human resource management in particular through training and skills development; and
- Social security.

Business Cooperation: The close association of industry and business in India-EU cooperation as well as dialogue between businesses from both sides are crucial to achieving the common goal of enhanced trade and investment. Industry and business of India and the EU are not only competitors but also partners.

Regular business summits have been held since 2001. These summits have helped to create better understanding of the opportunities and obstacles in a broad variety of sectors. The recent phenomenon of Indian investments in EU especially in knowledge-based sectors of IT, Pharma, etc. has added a new dimension to overall India-EU economic relations.

Both sides should build on those experiences to promote a strategic discussion on improving business links. Therefore decided to:

- Hold a Business Round Table on a regular basis together with the Business Summits. Industry Associations concerned on both sides will take appropriate action to continue the Business Summit and Business Round Table initiatives. The Round Table will come up with innovative ideas to further trade and investment;
- Promote the development of networks for sectoral industrial cooperation and investment promotion;
- Further discuss strengthening of the existing information dissemination mechanism and explore the need for new instruments for facilitating EU-India trade and investment;

- Reinforce business-to-government dialogue based on the work undertaken under the Joint Initiative for Enhancing Trade and Investment, which should feed into the sectoral policy dialogues; and
- Operationalise the Trade and Investment Development Programme (TIDP) Web portal to provide both sides with comprehensive information on trade and investment issues.

Development Cooperation: Against the backdrop of thirty years of engagement between India and EU both sides are committed to achieve progress with regard to the Millennium Development Goals and related international agendas.

Since 1976, the EC has committed around €2 billion of development cooperation to India. The allocation for the 2002-2006 programming period is €225 million. An emphasis has been placed on health, education, water and environment.

This commitment should be further enhanced. With a view to provide impetus to India-EU cooperation it is proposed to deepen development cooperation in health and education sectors, under which the EU—working together with the Government of India—will aim to significantly enhance development cooperation to supplement Indian programmes, namely Sarva Shiksha Abhiyan (SSA) and the National Rural Health Mission (NRHM)—two important social sector programmes, for the periods of the 10th Five-Year Plan and the 11th Five-Year Plan of the Government of India.

India is itself becoming an increasingly active player in evolving development policy: it is a recipient and donor, a user of developmental innovations and an exporter of new concepts. India's position as an emerging bilateral donor under the "Indian Development & Economic Assistance Scheme (IDEAS)" could pave the way for a fruitful EU-India dialogue on optimal implementation of development cooperation in third countries.

Committed to implement the following actions:

- Operationalise States Partnership programme (€160 million) during 2005;
- Exchange views on global development issues;

- Evaluate the past fifteen years of India-EC bilateral cooperation and its impact, with the involvement of relevant authorities on both sides;
- Further explore EC-India cooperation in development projects in third countries; and
- Aim to enhance significantly EU development cooperation for the universalisation of elementary education (Sarva Shiksha Abhiyan) and the National Rural Health Mission of the Government of India.

V. Developing Trade and Investment

India and the EU agree to take positive steps to further increase bilateral trade and economic cooperation and to tackling barriers to trade and investment. Private sector contacts would also be further developed. While trade and investment flows between India and the EU have been increasing, they remain below potential. Therefore, to enhance economic cooperation the following steps are proposed:

High-Level Trade Group: India and the EU agree to establish a High Level Trade Group to study and explore ways and means to deepen and widen their bilateral trade and investment relationship. The Group was to report to the summit in 2006, including the possible launch of bilateral negotiations on a broad-based trade and investment agreement. Within this framework, and in order to increase investment in India and the EU, the scope of a possible investment agreement will be explored.

World Trade Organization (WTO)/Doha Development Agenda (DDA): India and EU are committed to a successful outcome of the Hong Kong Ministerial in December 2005 and agree to move forward the Doha Development Agenda (DDA) negotiations to a successful conclusion as a matter of priority. In this respect both parties agree to continue their dialogue with a view to greater convergence in areas of mutual interest.

To this end India and EU agree to strengthen their dialogue on the DDA negotiations which *inter alia* include Agriculture, Non-Agricultural Market Access (NAMA), Services, Trade Facilitation, Anti-dumping, Geographical Indications, Special and Differential Treatment, and Implementation, including as regards the relationship between Trade-related Intellectual Property Rights (TRIPs) and the Biodiversity Convention.

Public-Private Partnership (PPP): Both parties agree to initiate a discussion on Public-Private Partnership (PPP) and as a first step to exchange information and experiences with a view to, *inter alia*, enhancing investment in infrastructure. The two sides agree to set up an Expert Group to identify policy level changes required to promote PPP.

Intellectual Property Rights (IPR): India and the EU attach importance to achieving effective and comprehensive protection of Geographical Indications (GIs). As a first step, India and the EU exchanged information on their respective GI protection regimes and held an expert meeting on GIs in 2005 to strengthening their technical cooperation on GIs.

Both parties agree to establish an appropriate dialogue to discuss IPR policy, regulatory issues, implementation and enforcement, as well as the general objectives and/or framework. To this end, both parties agree to establish a forum for a regular exchange of views and information on domestic regulatory policies and practices and enforcement issues. This forum shall also cover related technical assistance and capacity-building initiatives.

Technical Barriers to Trade (TBT)/Sanitary and Phytosanitary (SPS) Issues: The two sides agreed to establish a TBT/SPS Working Group and held the first meeting in 2005. This deepened the dialogue on TBT and SPS issues respectively with a view to facilitating bilateral trade and increasing market access.

Trade Defence Instruments: India and the EU have agreed to activate the expert meetings according to the already agreed terms of reference.

Services: India and EU agreed to exchange information and initiate a dialogue on regulatory policy including Mutual Recognition Agreements (MRAs) and domestic regulations and market access issues related to services.

Public Procurement: Both parties agreed to exchange information on public procurement policies.[17]

Sixth EU-India Summit: The Sixth EU-India Summit, held in Delhi on 7 September 2005, was an excellent and fruitful meeting, which took place in a very amicable atmosphere. All objectives were reached: agreement was reached on a wide-ranging and ambitious Action Plan whose main features are highlighted in a Joint Political Statement covering all areas of the relationship to implement the Strategic Partnership. It is an important milestone in EU-India relations and provides a clear roadmap for the coming years.

The high-level gathering, including President Barroso, Commissioners Ferrero-Waldner and Mandelson, Prime Minister Tony Blair and HR/SG Solana, as well as Prime Minister Manmohan Singh and several Indian Ministers, attracted large media attention, an additional sign of the growing importance and awareness of EU-India relations. Press coverage focused largely on one of the most important breakthrough reached in the Action Plan, i.e. the decision to create a High Level Trade Group to report to the next summit in 2006, including the possible launch of negotiations on a broad-based trade and investment agreement.

The initiatives in the margins of the Summit of the Galileo framework agreement, the EU's firm support of India's wish to join ITER as well as Erasmus Mundus have also made it into headlines. The announcement by Prime Minister Manmohan Singh of Indian Airlines' purchase of 43 Airbus further enhanced Summit results. The parallel yearly Business Summit, which strongly endorsed the Action Plan, showed strong interest among the business communities for strengthening trade and investment opportunities. The creation of a CEO Business Forum is expected to inject innovative ideas into the process. Bilateral meetings with the President of India Abdul Kalam and Congress Party leader Sonia Gandhi also took place.[18]

Seventh EU-India Summit

The Seventh EU-India Summit was held in Helsinki during October 12-13, 2006 under the Finnish Presidency of the EU. Prime Minister Dr. Manmohan Singh led the Indian delegation while the Finnish President Tarja Halonen, President of the European Commission, Mr. Jose Manuel Barraso, led the EU delegation. The Helsinki Summit aimed at strengthening strategic partnership agreements in line with the joint action plan adopted in September 2005 in New Delhi. The areas of focus at the Summit were the economic aspects in the India-EU relations, energy, cooperation in counter-terrorism and the closer security and political dialogue. The two sides agreed to begin negotiations on a broad-based trade and investment agreement. A joint statement covering the multi-dimensional engagement between India and the EU, was issued at the end of the Summit.[19]

The Joint Statement highlights that the EU and India stand committed to the rule-based multilateral trading system and the successful outcome of the Doha Development Agenda and that multilateral trade negotiations remain their foremost trade policy priority. Furthermore, the Joint Statement stresses the importance of promoting international peace and security. It also raises questions regarding the situation in the Middle East, Nepal, Sri Lanka and Sudan and cooperation in the fight against terrorism.

An important outcome of the Summit was the EU-India High Level Trade Group report setting out a compelling argument for a new bilateral trade and investment agreement aimed at boosting trade and building on WTO rules. Other Summit "deliverables" include the establishment of new consultation mechanisms, which broaden the scope of the Partnership, such as the launch of a regular macro-economic policy dialogue and the establishment of a new bilateral Working Group on Hydrocarbons and Natural Gas.

The EU also pressed for further progress on the negotiation of an EU-India maritime transport agreement (a natural flanking measure to our ambition to expand two-way trade), push for progress on the conclusion of a bilateral horizontal civil aviation agreement and push for the conclusion of a Memorandum of Understanding on Cooperation in Employment and Social Affairs.

The EU-India relations have developed at a remarkable speed over the past few years. The EU-India Summit, held in September 2005 in Delhi, was the culmination of a gradual upgrading of EU-India relations which started at The Hague Summit, in 2004, with the upgrading of EU-India relations to a "Strategic Partnership", as recommended by a 2004 Commission Communication on

EU-India Relations. The 2005 Summit endorsed a wide-ranging Joint Action Plan giving substance to the Strategic Partnership. The Joint Action Plan covers all aspects of EU-India relations, for which it proposes practical steps to be achieved before 2008, when both parties are expected to review and update the document.

ECONOMIC COOPERATION

The EU-India relations can be traced back to the early 1960s, as India was among the first countries to set up diplomatic relations with the then EEC. Since then, India, as the world's largest democracy and the most diverse nation state—ethnically and linguistically—has become the world's 4th largest economy and by 2030 it is likely to be the 3rd biggest. The EU has been gradually establishing a strong economic relationship with India. Today India is one of the main trading partners and biggest foreign inward investors. The relationship between EU and India has gone beyond pure economic (trade and investment) interests. The EU is also seen as a critical actor in helping India achieve its development objectives.

India-EU economic cooperation takes place through several horizontal programs of the EU for Asia as well as India-specific programs. The total budget earmarked by EU for economic cooperation projects in India so far is around Euros 60 million of which only Euros 37 million has been actually committed. The EU implements its economic cooperation programs mainly through autonomous agencies guided and supervised by the EU. Since the year 2002, management of the India-specific programs has been de-concentrated and transferred from Brussels to the EU delegation in Delhi.

Some of the important horizontal programs are Asia Invest, Asia IT & C, Asia Eco-best and Asia Link. Although India is not a major beneficiary, these programs have helped a number of specific projects in India. Two programs that are specifically designed for India are Cross Cultural Program (Euros 30 mn) and Small Projects Facility (€7 m for 2002-06). The Cross Cultural Program, covering 3 sectors, viz. media, university and industry, has been revived after a lapse of almost 2 years. The EU has signed a MoU with GOI for implementing a National Indicative Programme (NIP) with a budget of €28 million for the year 2002-2006. The NIP provided outlays for the new programmes/activities, namely Trade & Investment programme (€15 m), and Disaster Management (€ 10 m). These programmes are being implemented by the EU delegation in New Delhi.

For the years 2005-2006, the EU had proposed a new NIP. This includes the Scholarship programme (€ 22 m), and the Small Projects Facility Phase II (€ 7 m).

With a view to promote business/industry collaboration, India-EU Partenariat has been organised in the past with the help of eonomic cooperation instruments of EU, e.g. Asia-Invest. The Partenariat took place in New Delhi in March 1999 bringing together 725 Indian and European companies. This event resulted in 110 agreements concluded between Indian and European SMEs.

India's Trade and Economic Policy

After independence in 1947 and until the beginning of the 1990s, India's trade policy was heavily influenced by the "Swadeshi" (self-sufficiency) mentality and the "licence raj" system of restrictions on production and imports. The first generation of reforms (1991-1996)—aimed at, *inter alia* liberalising trade—led to a reduction of import tariffs, elimination of quantitative restrictions, exchange rate reforms and deregulation of industry resulting in yearly growth rates of around 7 per cent (compared with 3 per cent before the reforms).

The second generation of reforms was initiated in 1999 to address issues related to lack of competitiveness, poor infrastructure and overregulation. India has set the ambitious target of an annual 8 per cent sustainable growth besides doubling the per capita income over 10 years.

India is a member of all major multilateral economic fora, including the International Monetary Fund (IMF), the World Bank and the Asian Development Bank (ADB). India was a founding member of both GATT and the World Trade Organisation (WTO).

At regional level, India is a member of SAARC, (South Asia Association of Regional Co-operation) BIMSTEC (Bangladesh, India, Myanmar, Sri Lanka, Thailand Economic Co-operation) and the Bangkok Agreement. India has a free trade agreement with Singapore and with the other SAARC countries (SAFTA) and is in the process of negotiating one with Japan, South Korea, GCC and ASEAN.[20]

EU-India Joint Action Plan

The EU-India Joint Action Plan, adopted during the Sixth EU-India Summit in New Delhi, on September 7, 2005, seeks to enhance economic co-operation between the EU and India in a number of areas where both parties have mutual interests. A broad range of sectors are envisaged under which EU-India co-operation broadened and enhanced. They include: Trade, Transport, Environment, Energy, Science and Technology, Space Technology, Information and Communication Technologies, Pharmaceuticals and Biotechnology, Industrial Policy, Customs Co-operation, Dialogue on Economic and Financial Matters, Employment and Social Policy, Agriculture and Business Dialogue & Co-operation. Below given are some of the areas where cooperation has been in progress. They are described in more detail:

Civil Aviation Project

The EU-India Civil Aviation Project was formally launched in February 2001 with a total investment of €32 million, contributed by the EU, the Government of India and the European aerospace industries. The EU-India Civil Aviation project is the EU's biggest economic cooperation project in India. The project aims firstly, to improve regulatory links and safety and, secondly, to facilitate business links. The project's main method is investment in human capital. Seven areas in particular have been targeted over the past five years:

1. Increasing local awareness of EU industry practice and safety standards.
2. Supporting the development of local air transport companies.
3. Providing technical assistance to Indian Air Traffic Management.
4. Providing training on the development of airports infrastructure.
5. Assisting in pilot training.

6. Stimulating collaboration between Indian and European aerospace manufacturers.
7. Developing local knowledge and practice of modern product support, maintenance and overhaul techniques.

Partnership has been the key to the project's success with co-financing provided by the EC, Indian partners and the European aerospace industry and technical assistance delivered by the Aerospace and Defence Industries Association of Europe.

Across the seven areas mentioned above and over a period of five years, more than two hundred and fifty training courses, workshops and seminars have been completed both in India and in Europe and over four thousand people have been trained. Achievements of note so far are:

- India has now adopted maintenance and aircraft parts manufacture regulations based on European standards. This means that Indian companies can now export to Europe and so have a vast new market while European companies have a vibrant and competitive new supplier and a host of potential new partners for design and manufacturing projects, truly a win-win outcome. In addition, the new regulations mean that the aircraft of European operators can be maintained in India and vice versa.
- Flight inspectors and airworthiness inspectors across India have been fully trained in accordance with European standards and practices.
- Several joint ventures have been founded, including one between SAFRAN of France and HAL of India for the manufacture of engine parts. This partnership has also led to the establishment of SAFRAN Aerospace India, which now has a technology centre employing some 200 engineers.
- Support has been delivered for the development and flight-testing of the Indian-built SARA aircraft.
- An official operations manual has been established for Indian helicopters and local pilots trained accordingly.

- EU aeronautical universities and the Indian authorities are currently designing an aviation-training institute based on a European model. This has followed the example of the French Aeronautical Universities and will provide the Indian civil aviation authorities with a centre of excellence. In addition, the curriculum for a Post Graduate Diploma in Aviation Management has been developed and the course was to be up and running by the end of 2007. This is the first step towards the creation of a Masters Degree course in Aviation Management at IIT Mumbai.[21]

Economic Cross Cultural Programme (ECCP)

The Government of India and the European Union are committed to the importance of raising public awareness on India-EU links and to the need of increasing mutual understanding between the two regions. Mobilizing civil society channels is recognized as being vital in achieving this objective. The EU-India Economic Cross Cultural Programme (ECCP) contributes to this commitment, as the key objective of the ECCP is to promote and support links and joint ventures between civil society organizations in India and the European Union in the fields of media, enterprise and university. The programme was first launched in 1997 and has since then funded 60 grant projects within three Calls for Proposals. Projects funded within the ECCP include networking, joint productions and studies, training activities and workshops, information exchange, research collaborations and organization of cultural events.[22]

Small Projects Facility Programme (SPF)

The EU-India Small Projects Facility Programme (SPF) reflects priorities set in the EU-India Co-operation Agreement (1993) and builds on joint strategies for enhancing mutual understanding, co-operation and dialogue between civil society representatives and local communities from India and the EU.

The main objective of the SPF is to support the ongoing reform process of India's economy and systems of governance through an enhanced involvement of civil society partners. The programme seeks to improve the mutual understanding and joint visibility of partners by promoting dialogue, the networking of policy makers and opinion formers, and by facilitating partnerships between Indian and EU operators in specific areas of intervention.

The SPF programme provides grants through the implementation of Calls for Proposals for small and innovative projects of high visibility in areas of strategic importance and mutual interest to India and the EU.[23]

Maritime Transport Project

Formal negotiations were launched at the Fourth EU-India Summit in November 2003. Such an agreement would improve the conditions and legal framework under which maritime transport operations to and from India are carried out for the benefit of both economies. It would be based on the principles of freedom to provide maritime services, free access to cargoes, unrestricted access to and national treatment in the use of ancillary services, and commercial presence of shipping companies. It would cover all aspects of door-to-door services, i.e. multimodal services.

The concluded EU-India Maritime Transport Project improved the efficiency of major Indian ports and helped the Government of India to introduce Electronic Data Interchange (EDI) in Indian ports, for the benefit of India and the EU alike.

Science & Technology Cooperation

The landmark agreement on Science & Technology Cooperation signed between India and the EU in November 2001 allows Indian scientists to participate in EU research activities and gives European scientists access to similar programmes in India.

Space Industries

The EU and Indian space industries have already collaborated in a number of areas and maintained close contact for some time. There is great potential for fruitful engagement for both sides in this sector, mainly through collaboration under the EU's Galileo Programme. Cooperation between India and the EU in the space sector took a major step forward at the Sixth EU-India Summit in Delhi, in September 2005, when the two partners initiated an agreement on India's participation in Galileo.

Environmental Issues

The past couple of years, have also experienced a closer cooperation on environmental issues, notably through the establishment of the Joint Working Group. The organisation of the so-called Environment Forum on a select key topic, provides for an active forum where EU and Indian policy-makers, business and civil society can exchange experiences and ideas. Tackling climate change, is another key global challenge, and in order to initiate an active dialogue, the Action Plan launched an EU-India Initiative on Clean Development and Climate Change, focusing on voluntary practical measures. This includes such essential elements as promoting clean technologies including in the context of the Clean Development Mechanism.

Energy Issues

Energy issues are central to both Europe and India, and in this context an EU-India Energy Panel, consisting of high-level officials, has been established in order to co-ordinate efforts and discuss matters of mutual interest. Three working groups have been established: energy efficiency and renewables, coal and clean coal conversion technologies, and fusion energy including India's membership in ITER. The EU has provided strong support for India's bid to join ITER, the high-tech civilian thermonuclear project, to be located in the south of France.

Customs Cooperation

The customs operation agreement was signed on 28 April 2004. The scope of the agreement is cooperation between the parties with a view to simplifying customs procedures and developing trade facilitation actions in matters related to customs in accordance with international standards. It also sets up mechanisms of mutual administrative assistance for exchanging information and carrying out inquiries, with a view to combating fraud against our respective customs legislation. It will, therefore, improve the effectiveness of the fight against fraud and counterfeiting. It also seeks to simplify and harmonise customs procedures.

Trade and Investment

In the area of Trade and Investment, following two key programmes stand out:

Joint Initiative to Enhance Trade and Investment: EU and India jointly carried out general as well as 8 sector-specific studies on trade and investment matters. On the basis of the results of the studies, Indian and European business associations put forward a set of "Joint Recommendations" to the political leadership.

Trade and Investment Development Programme: With an EU contribution of € 13.4 million the Programme has six components which aim to smoothen impediments to mutual trade and investment flows in various fields through training, technical assistance and provision of equipment. The programme was launched in 2006.

Asia-wide Horizontal Programmes

India also participates in a number of horizontal cooperation programmes, which are region-wide programmes. The Asia-wide programmes aim to support mutually beneficial partnerships. Projects are implemented in partnership between intermediaries from at least two different EU Member States and at least one of the eligible Asian countries.

India participates in Asia-Invest—a demand-driven EU-Asia horizontal cooperation programme, which seeks to build up business partnerships between Asia and Europe. A total of 43 projects have been approved to date involving Indian organizations. This included among other initiatives matchmaking events between European and Indian SMEs in various sectors in the EU and India (e.g. automotive industry, electronics, environmental technology, agri-foods, food processing, software, automation control, medical and biotechnologies).

India was also active under the Asia IT&C Programme, which is now a part of Asia-Invest: India is the most successful participating country in Asia IT&C, with 32 projects involving 40 partners and 3 applicants. The total EC contribution on Asia IT&C projects in India is of €8.5 million, i.e. 23.5 per cent of the total amount of the program.

Asia Pro Eco II (Asia Urbs has been merged with Asia Pro Eco) aims at strengthening the environmental dialogue between Asia and Europe through the exchange of policies, technologies and practices that promote cleaner, more resource-efficient, market-driven, sustainable solutions to environmental problems in Asia. The program aims at supporting a series of preventive and corrective actions which offer technical environmental solutions to contribute to both quality of life and economic prosperity in Asia. A total of 12 projects (out of 74) involving India have been recommended for funding by Asia Pro Eco I in 2003/2004.

Finally, India is also benefiting from funding under the Asia-Link, which commenced in 2002, and provided €53.2 million in funding for partnership projects involving EU and Asian higher education institutions.

EU-India Joint Action Plan

Sectoral Co-operation at the Fifth EU-India Summit of 8 November 2004 was formally decided to upgrade the EU-India relationship to the level of a Strategic Partnership, and to support this partnership through the implementation of an Action Plan that was endorsed by the 2005 Summit. A broad range of sectors are envisaged under which EU-India cooperation will be broadened and enhanced: Trade, Transport, Environment, Energy, Science and Technology, Space Technology, Information and Communication Technologies, Pharmaceuticals and Biotechnology, Industrial Policy, Customs Cooperation, Dialogue on Economic and Financial Matters, Employment and Social Policy, Agriculture and Business Dialogue & Cooperation.[24]

Economic Dialogue Between India and EU

India-EU economic relations are structured on the Agreement on Partnership and Development between India and the EU, which became effective from the beginning of 1994. There is an array of bilateral institutions, which derive their mandate from this Agreement and are used by both sides to engage in formal exchange of views and consultations on matters of bilateral interest. A Joint Commission headed by the Commerce Secretary on the Indian side and DG, External Relations (Relex) on the EU side functions to facilitate bilateral exchange on important policy issues relating to trade and economic relations.

Three Sub-commissions on: (i) Trade and commercial cooperation, (ii) Economic cooperation, and (iii) Development cooperation, function under the Joint Commission for closer and technical discussions on relevant issues. Six Working Groups in areas of bilateral interest, e.g. Agriculture & Marine Products, IT, Environment, Textiles, and Consular issues have also been set up which work to resolve the area-specific issues and report to the Joint Commission on their work. The 14th meeting of the India-EU Joint Commission was held in Brussels on 10th September 2004.[25]

Both India and EU have also adopted, in November 2004, a "Comprehensive Communication" prepared by the EU (in June 2004) on future cooperation with India with a view to raise the level of relations to that of a Strategic Partnership. India has also issued a response to the EU Communication. The Communication outlines the current state of India-EU relations in the political, social, cultural, economic, and strategic areas, etc. and proposes a programme of specific actions in areas of bilateral and multilateral interest. India has given its response to the Communication issues by the EC in which it has outlined its vision of similar cooperation with EU. India, EU on the one hand and the EU Member States on another have several specific bilateral agreements to foster cooperation in the area of trade, investment and economic relations.

The European Commission is currently drafting a Country Strategy Paper 2007-13 for India, which outlines the priorities and provides the financial framework for the funding of cooperation activities in India. In this context, an Action Plan Support Facility is being established to kick-start activities in select areas of priority.

EU and Indian experts exchanged information on company, company law and accounting standards, financial services policies and the supervision of financial institutions in a high level meeting of the EU-India Dialogue on Financial Services Regulation which took place on 9 June 2006 in Brussels.

Bilateral Investment Protection

India has signed Bilateral Investment Protection Agreements (BIPA) with 16 of the 27 EU Member States. However, with accession of 10 new countries from Central and East Europe into EU, new BIPAs need to be put in place in order to facilitate flow of investments and joint ventures between India and the new accession countries. India and EU are now likely to start negotiations on a bilateral agreement on investment protection.

Double Taxation Avoidance

India has Double Taxation Avoidance Agreements (DTAAs) with 18 out of 27 EU Member States. India is in advanced stages of signing of DTAAs with Lithuania, Estonia, Latvia, Slovakia and Slovenia. A proposal from Luxembourg for such DTAA is under consideration of the Ministry of Finance. India will also take up DTAA with the rest of Member States of EU.

S&T Agreement

India and EU have signed an agreement for cooperation in the field of Science & Technology in the year 2001. The agreement also assures a predictable and secure IPR regime for the EU companies and research institutions interested in cooperation with India. A steering committee was formed under the agreement to facilitate mutual discussions.

The Steering Committee held its first meeting in Brussels during 4-5th March 2004 where it drew up a Programme of Cooperation (PoC). As per the Programme, the two sides agreed to jointly organise 4 workshops during 2004-2005 in the areas of nanotechnology, genomics, health & food, surface transport (automotive sector) and sustainable development (natural disasters mitigation). The joint activities and projects were to be assisted within the Sixth Framework of Research and Technological Development (RTD) for 2002-2006 of the EU. The EU asked India to participate in its forthcoming Seventh Framework Programme. In its Communication on developing a "EU-India Strategic Partnership", issued in June 2004, the European Commission suggested various avenues of cooperation between the two sides in the field of S & T, including joint research in fusion energy. An Agreement for Scientific and Technological Cooperation was renewed during the Eight India-EU annual summit that took place on 30 November 2007 in New Delhi.

Information Technology

India and EU signed a Joint Vision Statement for promoting cooperation in the field of information and communications technology. The Vision Statement was issued at the India-EU Summit held in Delhi in November 2001. This provides a framework for exchange of views on regulatory practices, mutual cooperation in regulatory and industry initiatives and specific issues/projects of bilateral interest. For facilitating cooperation between India and EU in the area of development of Information Society Technologies (IST), which is supported by the EC under their Sixth Framework of RTD for 2002-06, a specific event Euro-India 2004 Cooperation Forum was organised in Delhi during 24-26th March 2004 where over 300 European and Indian agencies participated to launch partnerships and joint research/ technological development activities under EU's IST programme. A Joint Working Group on ICT sector also held its meeting in March 2004 in Delhi where certain areas of cooperation were identified. These include cooperation on information security, digital content in languages, broadband network, next generation mobile communications, open source software and development of Internet protocol version 6 (IPv6). Both sides also discussed the possibility of setting up an exclusive information network to facilitate direct communication and data sharing between the research and technology institutions of India and Europe.[26]

The first EU-India Ministerial Science Conference took place in New Delhi in February 2007. The meeting had a strong representation from EU Member States, from Science and Technology (S&T) Departments, and from leading scientists from both India and the EU. It allowed for an active discussion on key cooperation priorities, and on the potential benefits of a Coordinated Joint Call for proposals with co-investment of resources, including funds for sponsoring India-EU research projects and means to deepen EU-India Cooperation Agreement and the Seventh Framework Programme. It led to the release of "New Delhi Communique" which outlined the future of India-EU cooperation in the field of research and development.

Space

India has excellent credentials in space research. India's ongoing programme of exchange of scientists between the ESA (European Space Agency) and the ISRO (Indian Space Research Organisation) needs to be intensified. Eight Indian satellites have already been launched on board the Ariane series of launch vehicles. India has also assisted in the development of the German Bird satellite, which was launched aboard an Indian Polar Satellite Launch Vehicle (PSLV). The same launch carried a Belgian satellite called PROBA. India and France are cooperating in the joint satellite mission "Megha-Tropiques" to study the tropical monsoon system. India has developed considerable capabilities in the field of satellite navigation and is already embarking on technology demonstration for a satellite-based augmentation system called GAGAN. Specific new areas/projects for cooperation could be identified by the respective space agencies for further discussion/implementation. India participated in the Space Conference organized by the EU in February 2005.

In the Joint Press Statement issued at the conclusion of the Fifth India-EU Summit in November 2004, the two sides welcomed the progress in the ongoing discussion on the Draft Cooperation Agreement on the Galileo Satellite Navigation Project. Considering that India has well-proven capabilities in space, satellite and navigation-related activities, the agreement provides an important positive impulse for India.[27]

Business Summits

The Political Summits between India and EU have been supplemented by holding India-EU Business Summits organized by apex body Chambers of Commerce and Industry on our side and Union of Industrial Employers in Europe and the local national Chamber of Commerce from the Member States representing the Presidency on the EU side. Business Summits have been held between the industrialists/businessmen of India and EU in 2000 (Lisbon), 2001 (New Delhi), 2002 (Copenhagen) and 2003 (New Delhi) with a view to foster greater interaction between the industries of the two sides. This has generated greater interest and level of cooperation at the industry level. These Business Summits have also focussed on the recommendations emerging from the joint studies of specific sectors carried out by the industry. A total of eight (8) sectors, namely food processing, telecommunications, engineering, IT, financial sector, textiles, biotechnology, and energy/power have so far been studied jointly by the industry on both sides (CII and FICCI on Indian side) to suggest specific steps for promotion of trade and investment between India and EU.[28] The last summit was held in Helsinki on 12 October 2006.

EU-INDIA TRADE

The cornerstone of European Union's link with India lies in its trade and investment relationship. The EU is India's largest trading (1/5 of India's total external trade) and investment partner: the bilateral trade constitutes a quarter of India's total trade while total FDI inflows from the EU to India is US$ 10.86 that is 24 per cent of total FDI inflows during August 1991 to February 2007. At the Business Summit of the third EU-India Summit held in Copenhagen in October 2002, it was decided to set a bilateral trade target between EU and India of Euro 35 billion by 2005 and Euro 50 billion by 2008.[29] India's bilateral trade crossed € 46 billion in 2006. Bilateral trade has steadily grown between 2001-06 at over 10 per cent on average. EU and India are also key WTO partners and they have worked together in a number of areas to bring about greater liberalization within the ambit of WTO.

The EU remains India's largest trading partner, accounting for 21.77 per cent of India's exports and 18.33 per cent of total Indian imports during the year 2003-04. As per the figures available for the year 2004, total trade between EU and India increased from €28.4 billion in 2003 to €33.2 billion in 2004, registering a growth of 16.9 per cent.

EU exports to India show an impressive growth of 17.2 per cent in 2004 against a growth rate of 1.7 per cent in 2003. Exports increased to €22.3 billion in 2006 from €14.5 billion in 2003.

EU imports on the other hand increased from €13.9 billion in 2003 to €26.26 billion in 2007, recording a growth of 16.1 per cent.

Table 6.1: EU-India Trade

(million €)

Year	Imports	% change	Share of total EU imports	Exports	% change	Share of total EU exports	Balance	Imports + Exports
2000	12802		1.29	13626		1.59	824	26427
2001	13405	4.7	1.36	12894	-5.4	1.44	-512	26299
2002	13594	1.4	1.44	14271	10.7	1.58	676	27865
2003	13976	2.8	1.49	14516	1.7	1.65	540	28492
2004	16223	16.1	1.58	17013	17.2	1.77	790	33236
2005	19086	16.6	1.62	21322	24.3	2.03	2236	40409
2006	22613	18.5	1.67	24385	14.4	2.10	1772	46998
2007	26262	16.1	1.84	29481	20.9	2.38	3218	55793

Source: EUROSTAT.

During the year 2007, EU's major items of exports to India consisted of machinery (29.5%), chemicals (9.7%), transport equipment (5.7%) and primary products (6.1%). Also EU imported from India textiles and clothing (29.2%), chemicals (9.4%), agriculture and allied products (9%), machinery (7.7%) and transport equipment (5.5%) in 2004.

Evolution of EU-India Sectoral Trade during 2007

Table 6.2: European Union Imports from India (2007)

Products (Sitc Sections) by order of importance	Mio euro	%	Share of total EU imports
TOTAL	26.262	100,0	1,8
Manuf goods classif. chiefly by material	8.324	31,7	4,6
Miscell. manuf. Articles	6.875	26,2	3,9
Machinery and transport equipment	3.033	11,5	1,1
Chemicals and related prod., n.e.s.	2.781	10,6	2,5
Food and live animals	1.527	5,8	2,4
Mineral fuels, lubricants and rel. Materials	1.220	4,6	0,4
Crude materials inedible, except fuels	695	2,6	1,1
Animal and vegetable oils, fats and waxes	140	0,5	2,3
Commodit. and transactions n.e.c.	109	0,4	0,3
Beverages and tobacco	82	0,3	1,2

Source: EUROSTAT.

Table 6.3: European Union Imports from India (2007)

Products (Sitc Sections) by order of importance	Mio euro	%	Share of total EU imports
TOTAL	29.481	100,0	2,4
Machinery and transport equipment	10.873	36,9	2,5
Manuf goods classif. chiefly by material	9.399	31,9	5,7
Chemicals and related prod., n.e.s.	2.325	7,9	1,2
Miscell. manuf. Articles	1.585	5,4	1,3
Crude materials inedible, except fuels	1.208	4,1	4,5
Commodit. and transactions n.e.c.	499	1,7	1,5
Mineral fuels, lubricants and rel. Materials	126	0,4	0,2
Food and live animals	109	0,4	0,3
Beverages and tobacco	76	0,3	0,4
Animal and vegetable oils, fats and waxes	14		0,6

Source: EUROSTAT.

Trends in EU's Trade with Major Trading Partners

The Tables 6.4 & 6.5 indicate EU's trade, both exports and imports, with some of its major trading partners *vis-à-vis* India. The trends are shown for four years from 2002 to 2007. The Tables also indicate percentage of share in EU's trade with USA, Switzerland, China, Japan, Russia *vis-à-vis* India.

EU's Trade with Major Trading Partners

Table 6.4: EU's Exports

(million €)

	2007	% share	2004	% share	2003	% share	2002	% share
USA	261463	21.10	223912	24.3	220718	22.57	237080	24.0
Switzerland	92787	7.50	74960	7.79	71243	8.11	72636	8.07
China	71757	5.80	48039	5.0	40191	4.10	33822	3.42
Russia	89100	7.20	45664	4.74	37086	4.22	34275	3.81
Japan	43757	3.50	43067	4.5	40088	4.09	41507	4.20
India*	29481	2.40	17013	1.8	14235	1.45	12867	1.30

*India's rank is 14th
Source: EUROSTAT.

Table 6.5: EU's Imports

(million €)

	2007	% share	2004	% share	2003	% share	2002	% share
USA	181104	12.70	157443	15.3	151217	15.28	172690	17.57
China	231516	16.20	126737	12.3	95549	9.65	81504	8.29
Russia	143880	10.10	80539	7.8	67779	7.21	61908	6.57
Japan	78104	5.50	73536	7.2	66817	6.75	68114	6.93
Switzerland	76700	5.40	61409	5.9	58796	6.25	61411	6.52
India*	26262	1.80	16233	1.6	13354	1.34	12984	1.32

*India's rank is 13th
Source: Eurostat.

Trends in India's External Trade with Major Trading Partners

The Tables 6.6 and 6.7 indicate India's trade, both exports and imports, with some of its major trading partners *vis-à-vis* EU. The trends are shown for two years from 2003-04 to 2004-05 (April-November). The tables indicate both percentage changes and share in India's exports and imports with its trading partners.

EU's Views on the Doha Development Agenda Negotiations under the Auspices of the WTO

The successful outcome of the negotiations of the World Trade Organization's Doha Development Agenda (DDA) is an important step for bolstering economic growth, strengthening multilateralism and global governance, and sustainable development.

India's External Trade with Major Trading Partners (April-November)

Table 6.6: India's Exports (April-February)

(US$ million)

	2006-07 Export value of Goods	2005-06 Export Value of Goods	% Growth	% Share
EU	23,765.48	20,722.85	14.68	21.14
USA	16,916.26	15,569.19	8.65	15.05
China	7,254.63	5,781.90	25.47	6.45
Hong Kong	4,045.39	3,959.53	2.17	3.60
India's total Exports	51,981.76	45,673.47	53.14	46.24

(*Source:* CMIE).

Table 6.7: India's Imports

(US$ million)

	2006-07 Import Value of Goods	2005-06 Import Value of Goods	% Growth	% Share
EU	23,973.96	20,894.21	14.74	14.77
USA	9,228.93	7,038.71	31.12	5.69
China	15,668.08	9,649.63	62.37	9.65
Switzerland	7,981.22	5,831.43	36.87	4.92
Australia	6,241.06	4,461.80	39.88	3.84
Japan	4,036.74	3,179.76	26.95	2.49
Singapore	4,939.60	2,871.60	72.02	3.04
India's total Imports	72,069.59	53,927.14	283.95	44.4

Source: CMIE[30]; http://www.infodriveindia.com

A very substantial amount of work has been done since the negotiations were launched in Doha in November 2001 but EU believes that there is now a need to increase the pace of negotiations. In the European Union's opinion, the WTO members need, in the run-up to the Fifth Ministerial Conference in Cancun during 10-14 September 2003, to achieve real progress both in the market access areas and in the rule-making areas of the negotiations and to fulfill the development aspirations of the round.

The conclusion of the round by the end of 2004, the deadline agreed by all WTO members in Doha, remains a priority for the EU. The Fifth WTO Ministerial Conference held in Cancun where ministers took the necessary substantive decisions, provide the necessary political impetus to all the Doha Development Agenda in line with the concept of the Single Undertaking.

The EU believes that WTO members need to find convergence on the various DDA issues. The European Commission has been continuously holding detailed discussions on the agenda for Cancun with its key partners, including India.[31]

Key WTO Partners

India and the EU have historically played a critical role in creating new international structures, including the World Trade Organization (WTO). The WTO, which came into existence from January 1, 1995, has redrawn the contours of the international trading arena.

The WTO agreements relate to bringing about trade liberalization in traditional areas like trade in goods, agriculture and textiles as also new areas such as Trade Related Intellectual Property Rights (TRIPS), Trade Related Investment Measures (TRIMS) and General Agreement on Trade and Services (GATS). Lowering of tariffs and doing away with non-tariff barriers are some of the mechanisms through which greater multilateral trade liberalization is being attempted under the auspices of the WTO.

As the success of the multilateral trading framework rests on cooperation between countries, EU and India have been working together in a number of areas to bring about greater liberalization within the ambit of WTO. At the Doha Ministerial Meeting held in November 2001, the EU was instrumental in launching a new round of comprehensive multilateral trade negotiations to carry the process of trade liberalization further.

The various agreements signed at the conclusion of the Uruguay Round impose certain obligations on individual countries, including India, for compliance within an agreed time frame. Thus, there are ongoing negotiations, both at the bilateral level and at WTO, between India and EU in several areas concerning WTO compatibility of Indian trade and investment rules. The EU is also in the process of launching a comprehensive trade and investment development programme in India to further the process of cooperation and share technical expertise on various WTO and other related issues.[32]

Investment

The European Union has been the largest source of FDI inflows for India since the country began its journey on the path of economic reforms in 1991. The EU's share in India's FDI approvals during August 1991 to February 2007 is around 24 per cent. The investment approvals from EU have risen substantially in the last eleven years starting from US$ 78 million in 1991 to US$ 10.86 billion in 2007. During the period, actual FDI inflows from EU was to the tune of $4.09 billion, which comes to around 13.55 per cent of total FDI inflows into India ($30.17 billion). In contrast, the US share in total inflows is 10.37 per cent.

Table 6.8: Sector-wise FDI Inflows from EU

Sector	Number of FDI Approvals	Amount in US$ Million	%age of total Approved for EU
Fuel (Power & Oil Refinery)	183	4310.19	22.83
Telecommunications	156	2765.49	15.94
Transportation Industries	304	1512.53	8.13
Chemicals (other than fertilizers)	393	1129.87	5.69
Electrical Equipments (including computer software)	774	953.46	5.03
Total	1810	10,671.54	57.62

Source: SIA, GOI.

The sectoral break-up of investments from EU approved by the Government of India from August 1991 to May 2007 shows that the highest investment proposals have been in the Fuel

Sector (Power & Oil Refinery), which accounts for 22.83 per cent of the total FDI approved for EU. Telecommunications account for second place and Transportation Industries for the third place (Table 6.8). As far as technology transfer is concerned, 3734 technical collaborations have been approved for EU accounting for over 43.28 per cent of the total collaborations approved during August 1991 to May 2007. The highest technical collaboration has been in the Electrical Equipment (including computer software), followed by Industrial Machinery and Chemicals (Table 6.9).

Table 6.9: EU Technology Transfers to India

(Aug. 1991 to May, 2002)

Sector	No. of Technical Collaborations	%age of total
Electrical Equipment (including computer software)	496	14.81
Industrial Machinery	471	14.06
Chemicals (other than fertilizers)	409	12.21
Transportation Industry	259	7.73
Misc. Mechanical & Engg Industry	195	5.82[33]

India's regime for Foreign Direct Investment (FDI) has been considerably simplified and liberalized, however, important sectors still remain restricted to a certain extent for FDI (e.g. telecommunications, retail distribution, insurance, banking, aviation) or are banned (e.g. legal services).

In 2006 EU investment outflows to India amounted to €2.5 billion and represented 0.9 per cent of total FDI outflows from the EU. It grew to €10.9 billion in 2007. EU investment has mainly taken place in the power/energy, telecommunications and transport sectors.[34]

This flow of European cash into India surged more than fourfold last year, for surpassing European Union investment in China. It jumped to €10.9 billion (17 billion dollars) from 2.5 billion in 2006; which constitutes 24% of total FDI inflows (from August 1991-February 2007). India has also begun to invest in the EU in the recent years. Indian investment has also been growing steadily in UK, Germany and Italy.

However, there is clear scope for higher investment given the vast potential of the Indian market and the fact that India accounts for less than one per cent of total EU foreign direct investments.

Sectorally, the EU has a substantial financial stake in industrial machinery, transport, electrical goods and electronics, chemicals and consultancy. Since 1994, there has been a spurt in investments in the infrastructure and automotive sectors. There is an increasing interest shown by the European companies in the Indian food processing, horticulture and floriculture sectors. European companies also have a keen interest in the very vibrant Indian service sector, including IT, financial services, retail, and education.

India, thanks to the emergence of a number of multinational players at the global level, is now also emerging as a major investor itself, especially in areas where it has a core advantage such as IT and Biotech sectors. India's outward FDI stock has grown from $0.6 billion in 1996 to $5.1 billion in 2003, taking India to 14th place in terms of outward FDI stock among developing economies. According to recent reports, in the *City of London*, India has emerged as the second largest investor.

Joint Initiative for Trade and Service

The First EU-India Summit in June 2000 highlighted the need for making a joint effort to tap the potential for substantially enhancing trade and investment between India and the EU. In February 2001 the Eleventh EU Joint Commission encouraged industry to launch the "Joint Initiative to Enhance Trade and Investment". Under this "Joint Initiative" a group of European and Indian consulting companies (DMI and TAC in Europe, Ace Global in India) have carried out general as well as sector-specific studies, and, based on the results of the studies, developed a set of "Joint Recommendations" that both Indian and European business associations (CII and FICCI in India, UNICE in Europe) formally put to the political leadership.[35]

Business Contacts & Services

In this section, Indian SMEs can find pre-selected information for business on specific topics based on hyperlinks to websites at European and Member States level, such as standardization bodies and industrial property offices, EU "Single Market" Regulation, CE Marking & Directives, etc. This Internet service is to help SMEs to make the best use of the EU Internal Market potential.[36]

In 2007, the EU imported goods from India to the amount EUR 29.4 billion (mainly textiles/clothing, agricultural products and chemicals) and EU exports amounted to EUR 26.2 billion (mainly machinery and chemical products). Indian exports to the EU grew by 17 per cent in 2004 and EU exports to India increased by 16 per cent. Total trade in 2007 of over €55 billion is roughly balanced. EU accounts for 22 per cent of India's exports and 18 per cent of total imports. Among Europe's trade partners, however, India ranks as EU's 9th trading partner accounting for 2.4 per cent of EU exports and 1.8 per cent of imports, but its share has been increasing.

During April 2005-February 2006 Indian exports to EU amounted to US$ 22,315.02 millions which increased to US$ 25,721.55 millions. It registered a growth of 14.68 and 21.14 per cent respectively. While India imported goods from the EU to the tune of US$ 20,894.21 millions during April 2005 to February 2006 which rose to US$ 23,973.96 millions. The percentage growth was 14.74 for April 2005 to February 2006 and 14.77 for April 2006 to February 2007. Bilateral trade has steadily grown between 2001 and 2006 at over 10% on average and crossed €46 billion in 2006 (Indian exports €22.3 billion; Indian imports €24 billion).

It has grown impressively over the years, from €4.4 billion in 1980 to €40 billion in 2005. Trade with the EU represents more than 20 per cent of India's exports and imports and EU thus as a bloc is India's largest trading partner. The EU is also India's largest source of foreign direct investment. However, India accounts for just 1.8 per cent of total EU trade. India attracts only 0.3 per cent of the EU's worldwide investments.

During the Summit of 7th September 2005, the EU and India adopted a Joint Action Plan and agreed to take positive steps to further increase bilateral trade and economic cooperation and to tackle barriers to trade and investment. Specifically, they agreed to set up a High Level Trade Group to study and explore ways and means to deepen and widen their bilateral trade and investment relationship and agreed to cooperate on a number of other trade-related issues.

The High Level Trade Group reported to the Seventh EU-India Summit in Helsinki on 13 October 2006, that an expanded trade partnership be developed through the negotiation of a broad-based trade and investment agreement. The EU-India Summit endorsed the recommendations of the High Level Trade Group in agreeing that both sides move towards negotiations for such an agreement.

Goods and Services

The EU is India's largest trading partner and main source of foreign inward investment. The EU accounted for 22.6 per cent of India's exports and imports in 2007. India ranks as EU's 9th trading partner accounting for 2.4 per cent of EU exports and imports. In 2007, EU imports from India amounted to €23.75 billion (covering mainly textiles/clothing, agricultural products and chemicals) while EU exports to India amounted to €22.6 billion (covering mostly machinery and chemical products). During 2007 EU-India trade increased by 24.3 per cent and has increased with an annual average of 12.3 per cent between 2003 and 2007.

Given its developing country status, India's exports to the EU benefit from reduced tariffs under the EU Generalised System of Preferences. India is the largest beneficiary of this scheme with preferences covering imports of a value of €8 billion during 2005.

Bilateral trade in services has grown substantially in recent years and in 2004 India's exports of services to the EU amounted to €3.8 billion in 2004 (up from €3.0 billion in 2003), while the EU's exports to India amounted to €3.2 billion in 2004 (up from €2.7 billion in 2003). In 2007, the EU exported €9.0 billion of services to India while imports amounted to €6.6 billion. It means that the EU had a surplus of 2.4 billion in trade in services with India. India accounted for 1.7 per cent of total extra EU trade in services.

Negotiations for an India-EU broad based Trade and Investment Agreement were opened in Brussels on 28-29 June 2007. A second round of negotiations took place in New Delhi during the first week of October 2007. The third round of negotiations took place in Brussels from 6-12 December 2007. During the India-EU summit held on 30 November 2007, the two sides agreed to work towards early conclusion of the negotiations during 2008.

Tariffs and Non-tariff Barriers

Indian import tariffs have been substantially reduced, but still remain high by international standards. In addition to the Basic Customs Duty, various additional duties, taxes and charges apply resulting in a complex and non-transparent system.

Overall India's high tariff levels remain a genuine problem for European industry. Tariff reductions and in particular bindings on a much lower level are an important goal of the multilateral negotiations.

India also imposes a number of non-tariff barriers in the form of quantitative restrictions, import licensing, mandatory testing and certification for a large number of products, as well as complicated and lengthy customs procedures.

Trade Related Technical Assistance

Under the National Indicative Programme for India 2002-2003, the EU has in the Trade and Investment Development Programme earmarked €14 million to assist India in better integrating into the world economy and promoting bilateral trade. Specific projects aimed at helping India meet EU sanitary and phytosanitary requirements which deal with issues related to intellectual property rights and customs procedures, and facilitate investment in India. The EU also funds trade related projects under the Asia Trust Fund and the Asia Invest Programmes.[37]

DEVELOPMENT COOPERATION

The EU and its member states collectively make the biggest bilateral contribution to India's development programmes. In the 1990s, EU cooperation strategy focused on supporting the Indian authorities' own work in identified priority sectors such as primary education and healthcare, with strong emphasis on helping the poorest and most disadvantaged in society.

During the period 2007-13, the EU proposes to adopt a two-pronged approach to cooperation with India: on the one hand, to help India achieve its Millennium Development Goals by continuation of support in key social sectors (health & education) and, on the other, to implement the EU-India Partnership through an ambitious Action Plan which will support India's sector reform policies in favour of the poorest, promote dialogue in areas of mutual interest and enhance economic cooperation, all of which will help to generate wealth and employment in India.

The whole programme is supplemented by humanitarian assistance, in the event of disasters such as floods and drought, from the EU's Humanitarian Aid Office (ECHO) – for instance the terrible tsunami of 26 December 2004 and earthquake of 8 October 2005, to both of which ECHO responded with speed and efficiency.

At the same time, India is itself becoming an increasingly active player in an evolving development policy: it is recipient and donor—a user of developmental innovations and an exporter of concepts. India's position as an emerging bilateral donor under the "Indian Development Economic Assistance Scheme (IDEAS)" could pave the way for a fruitful EU-India dialogue on optimal implementation of development cooperation in third countries.

EC Cooperation

Development cooperation in the social sectors, and notably in health and education, is of the utmost importance if India is to achieve the Millennium Development Goals. Traditionally, the EC has supported India's own efforts to improve quality of life for the poorest and most disadvantaged members of society. Poverty alleviation has been the central objective in all projects. Since the mid-1990s, EC-India cooperation has been based on identified priority sectors for action: primary education and primary healthcare. This sectoral approach has been complemented by support for focused projects in fields such as rural development, irrigation, forestry, environmental rehabilitation and integrated watershed management. The current development cooperation is concentrated on sector support for elementary education and health and family welfare.

- The EC commitment since 1976 is of €2 billion. The current annual allocation is approximately € 80 million (€ 800 million when Member States included).

- Since 1995, India shifted the emphasis from individual projects to Sector Support Programmes in health (€240 million programme committed in 1996 and 2001) and basic education (€150 million committed in 1993, €200 million in 2000).
- The cooperation has moved from support to central government towards a comprehensive development partnership with two reform-minded Indian states.

The New Country Strategy Paper (2007-13) is focused on the social sectors and the implementation of the Action Plan.

Sector Policies and Programmes

Education: Education is a priority for EC-India cooperation and the EU's approach is to support the Government's own programmes, especially those that reduce disparities between genders, groups and religions and that favors the poorest and most disadvantaged.[38]

Sarva Shiksha Abhiyan: Building on the varied experience of European Commission (EC)—Indian collaboration under DPEP, the EC signed an agreement with the Government of India (GoI) in November 2001 to support the Sarva Shiksha Abhiyan (SSA) programme, the new national initiative for Universalisation of Elementary Education (UEE). Euro 200 million (Rs. 960 crore) has been committed for seven years of implementation.

The main objective of the EC grant is to reinforce the GoI's own efforts to universalize elementary education. EC funds will support the GoI to deepen and accelerate the process of reform in the Education Sector and to pave the way for new initiatives to provide education to the disadvantaged and the deprived, particularly girls.

In particular, these reforms and initiatives aim at enhancing quality of schooling at primary level (6-11 age) and upper primary level (11-14 age). The SSA programme seeks to carry forward the good experiences of DPEP in the areas of decentralized planning, community participation, pedagogical renewal, child friendly classrooms, etc. to cover the full elementary education cycle (6-14 age). The 93rd Constitution Amendment making

Universal Elementary Education a Fundamental Right, and with the EFA and Millennium Development Goals (MDG) for Education, provides the backdrop for concerted efforts by central and state governments to achieve the EFA goals.

Some of the objectives of SSA are to ensure that:

- All children enroll in school, of one kind or another, by 2003;
- All children complete five years of primary schooling by 2007;
- All children complete eight years of elementary schooling by 2010;
- Gaps between the schooling of girls and boys and between all social groups (e.g. scheduled caste and tribal children) by 2007 at the primary level and by 2010 at the elementary level are bridged; and
- Education of satisfactory quality is provided, with emphasis on education for life.

In December 2002, the EC commenced providing grant assistance to the GoI to implement the strategies of SSA, particularly in the deprived and disadvantaged pockets of India. The first tranche of €30 million was released in December 2002, based on an agreed pre-appraisal of the EC support to SSA. The EC grant to SSA is in the form of sectoral support, whereby the GoI will have the flexibility to deploy EC resources to implement its priorities. EC funds are to be released against outcomes and progress towards the goals and objectives of SSA. Building on the good experience of the donor consortium that supported DPEP, efforts will be made to develop a similar approach for external financing for SSA, whereby major donors act in concert to support and jointly monitor a program to improve elementary education with the GoI.[39]

District Primary Education Program (DPEP): In 1994, European Commision (EC) entered into an agreement for supporting the Indian Government's District Primary Education Programme (DPEP), with a grant of €150 million. This was the EC's first major initiative to provide sector development support to India to reform and improve primary education, with a focus on reducing disparities across social groups and across regions. The support to DPEP, which ended in December 2002, was the first round of an enduring collaboration in the education sector, beginning with primary education and is followed by a long-term commitment to universalising elementary education with the signing of a new agreement with the Government of India supporting Sarva Shiksha Abhiyan (SSA).

DPEP has been a target-oriented time bound programme aiming at overall improvement of the quality of primary education. In fact, it was DPEP's focus on the poorest and most deprived children, and emphasis on girl's education that catalysed the EC's decision to support the programme. Initiated in 42 districts with female literacy lower than the national average across 8 states, the DPEP eventually expanded to 275 districts in 18 states.

According to the findings of studies conducted within the programme and review missions, clear progress has been made in terms of increasing access and enrolment especially among deprived groups. Drop-out rates among children have been reduced and learning achievement studies have shown positive trends. The DPEP has contributed to decreasing differences in enrolment, drop-out and learning achievement among gender and social groups. The percentage of girls attending schools (6-10 years of age) in rural areas has increased from 55 per cent in 1992-93 to 75 per cent in 1998-99. For boys it increased from 75 per cent in 1992-93 to 83 per cent in 1998-99. An EC evaluation of its support to DPEP in the states of Madhya Pradesh and Chhattisgarh revealed that programme targets were mostly met. In Madhya Pradesh, the gross enrolment ratio increased from 72.65 per cent to 99.4 per cent during the programme period. The Education Guarantee Scheme model developed by the Government of Madhya Pradesh, by which the Government guarantees to provide a school and a trained local teacher, on the basis of community demand and joint contribution, is an acclaimed success story in taking primary schooling to the most remote locations of the state and has since been adopted as a national programme.

The qualitative impact is well illustrated in this excerpt from the "Study Hierarchies of Access":

> Classrooms were filled with young children eager to learn. The Education Guarantee Scheme and Alternate School's classrooms seem more democratic and in a perpetual state of flux...there was no furniture to restrict movement or establish authority. Girls and boys sit together in small circles...and teachers are literally on their feet, flitting from group to group and maintaining personal contact with the children....In the multigrade situation the teachers seemed to somehow handle the pressure of catering to children with different needs.... The children too were comfortable pursuing their tasks in consultation with each other as opposed to being monitored by the teacher. The children's ability to keep themselves engaged is a function of group dynamics created in the class whereby mixed groups of children with different abilities often provide the incentive and space for facilitating peer learning.... students took charge in assisting their peers in either solving a mathematical problem or teaching them to spell correctly. (Micro-study in Betul District, Madhya Pradesh)

The results of DPEP interventions and progress made so far are as follows:

- Over 86,850 new primary schools and 83,500 alternative schools opened. 39,500 new school buildings and 47,000 additional classrooms constructed;
- Over 153,000 additional teachers including para-teachers appointed to improve student-teacher ratio. 1.1 million teachers have been provided in-service training and grants and training provided to teachers to produce teaching learning materials for use in the classroom;
- Almost all the states have renewed or are in the process of renewing their textbooks for classes I—V through participatory process. Many states have also produced teacher handbooks and supplementary materials to help teachers to use the new textbooks effectively;
- Over 291,000 Village Education Committees, 143,000 School Management Committees and 196,000 Mother and Parent Teacher Associations formed and 3 million

community members trained in carrying out village/school planning and management and construction activities;

- Enrolments have increased by 2 million during 1995-2000 in eight states, with an annual compound growth rate of 5.5 per cent as against zero at the national level;
- Percentage of girls attending schools (6-10 years of age) in rural areas has increased from 55 per cent in 1992-93 to 75 per cent in 1998-1999. For boys it increased from 75 per cent in 1992-93 to 83 per cent in 1998-1999; and
- According to "Access and Retention Study" for 2002, enrolment in DPEP I states increased from 6.03 million in 1995-96 to 6.81 million in 2001-02. Percentage share of girls' enrolment to total enrolment increased from 45.6 per cent to 47.9 over the same period in these states.[40]

Education Guarantee Scheme (EGS)

On 20th August 1998, Madhya Pradesh declared that the State had completed the task of universalizing access to primary schooling. In less than two years it had provided schooling facilities in more than 30,000 habitations across the State. How was the State able to accomplish this in such a short period?

Acknowledging that the immediate challenge was to improve the outreach in remote habitations, a Lok Sampark Abhiyan (LSA)—People's Contact Campaign—was organised in 1996 in all districts of Madhya Pradesh. It revealed that only 70 per cent of habitations had access to schools within radius of 1 km and that 30 per cent of the children in 6 to 11years age group were out of school. Most of them had never been enrolled.

An alternative to formal schools was to be found, which could be implemented immediately, would be cost-effective and cover the large numbers. The Education Guarantee Scheme (EGS) was mooted in 1997 not only as a simple and practical strategy to universalize access to primary education but also as a means to evoke community ownership of the village school and processes of schooling. If a tribal area had 25 children (40 for non-tribal) and no access to a school within 1 km radius, the community could write to the administration through the village Panchayat demanding a school. The government for its part guaranteed that a school would be provided within 90 days of the demand. The community would identify an educated young people to be appointed as the teacher and provide a place to run the school. This guarantee was the beginning of a partnership between the community and the government based on mutual trust and sharing of responsibilities.

Keeping the equity issue in mind, the scheme by its very nature focuses on the disadvantaged groups. Almost 50 per cent of the EGS schools are in tribal areas and 70 per cent of the children enrolled belong to disadvantaged communities, 45 per cent of the children being girls. Most children are first generation learners, the main occupation of their families being agriculture, animal husbandry and labour.

By involving the community groups to carry out LSA on a regular basis, the importance of education of the children was highlighted, generating a tremendous peer pressure to persuade all parents to enroll their children. Taking schools to the door-step of the families facilitated the participation of girls. Appointment of local, and as far as possible, female teachers created confidence in the parents. So far 26,000 schools involving 1.2 million children and 28,000 trained teachers have been appointed across the state.[41]

Programme for Enrichment of School Level Education (PESLE)

This innovative project with a consortium of NGOs, collaborating under the umbrella of the Aga Khan Foundation was funded by the EC in 1999 with €11 million. The project aims to improve the quality of school level education in selected states of India by mainstreaming innovative small-scale experiments carried out by Indian Non-Governmental Organisations into the larger government and other systems, with a particular focus on marginalised and disadvantaged groups.

The project partners are aiming to develop and enhance "good school practice" in a variety of socio-economic-geographic settings to include the urban poor, working children, minority communities and children in poorly resourced government schools. These strategies and tools will be disseminated and mainstreamed in larger educational systems. The project is expected to generate a number of various approaches by which school quality can be improved.

The first external review of the project was carried out in November/December 2002, to review progress of the inception phase and to assess the quality of the consolidation phase plans and has reached positive conclusions about the relevance.

The review report commented that the approaches being developed in PESLE for quality education for disadvantaged communities are relevant as well as "extremely exciting and interesting. The opportunity to experiment with quality innovations and follow them into a wider constituency of learners and teachers is challenging but ultimately of great importance to the wider educational community in India".

The review has found that the partnership of NGOs is itself unusual and a welcome step in sharing and cooperating across diverse partners. PESLE has the potential to inform the development community of different and more cooperative ways of tackling the problems of poverty and educational disadvantage.[42]

Health

Support to Health and Family Welfare Sector Development: The EC-Supported Health and Family Welfare Sector Investment Programme (SIP) is being implemented since October 1998 with the aim of reforming the health care system in India focusing essentially on primary health care services, including first referral institutions, by involving the community. The SIP is an integral part of the Government of India's National Family Welfare Programme. Stressing a change management approach, the programme operates at all levels of the system—central, state and district—with emphasis on decentralization, community involvement in decision-making and capacity development of the health services providers. The duration of the programme is six years with a total EC contribution of €240 million (approx. Rs. 1150 crore).

Focusing on institutional development and attitudinal change, the programme is currently assisting over 50 districts in 24 states and several urban centers to enhance the quality of health care services for the disadvantaged populations including tribal. The decentralized management structure, set up in the programme, such as the Sector Reform Cells at the State level, integrated health and family welfare agencies at district level and autonomous management bodies at the facility level, is helping to improve the running of primary health centres and referral hospitals. A large number of health functionaries and rural people including women are being trained as part of awareness building. So far over 31 referral hospitals have been refurbished to provide services on a regular basis.

The programme is also supporting the improvement of existing government policies and procedures at national and state levels to facilitate the delivery of quality health care in the rural and semi-urban areas. Several policy reviews have been undertaken focusing on human resource management and rational use of infrastructure. With a view to involving the community and private sector, the programme is associated with over 40 NGOs and institutions as well as a number of Panchayati Raj Institutions, which are supporting activities at different levels. A part of the assistance to the Family Welfare sector, €40 million, is utilized to support the post-earthquake redevelopment of health service facilities in Gujarat. Nearly 100 temporary health facilities centres have already been established in the earthquake affected areas.

A number of nationally important interventions that include improving the logistics and distribution of drugs, social marketing of family planning devices and strengthening of financial and accounting services are being undertaken across the country. Apart from budgetary support to the central, state and district levels, the programme also provides technical assistance and resources for developing partnerships between India and European institutions and with civil society for implementing various reform initiatives. The scope of reform is immense. The EC support marks the beginning of much-needed qualitative improvements in the sector.

The program is in its fifth year of implementation and it continues to generate inspiration and interest in realizing the qualitative change that the sector aims to achieve.

Fight against HIV/AIDS: The EU supports the fight against the spread of HIV/AIDS in developing countries through a budgetary programme. The programme was started in 1987 and has since its inception supported interventions implemented by NGOs in over 90 developing countries.

In India the funded NGO projects include prevention, care and support, research on cost-effective prevention strategies, training programmes for medical professionals, and advocacy and legal support to people living with HIV/AIDS in their defence against discrimination.

Campaign against Drug Abuse: This budget line supports prevention and reduction of drug abuse and initiatives to evaluate the drug problem, prevent and combat drug abuse, provide training and help rehabilitation of addicted people.

The strategy focuses both on awareness raising to prevent drug abuse and on detoxification, rehabilitation and social reintegration of former drug addicts. Regional co-operation, including the exchange of experience and expertise is one of the main focuses of the EC interventions.

The EC has so far been the biggest donor in the Health sector. Based on the success of SIP, the World Bank, DFID, and various other donors are currently preparing a sector support programme for the Health Sector.[43]

Rural Development

Over the last ten years, the EC has financed 12 Rural Development and Natural Resources Management projects for a total of €240 million in the following fields: land reclamation; community forestry actions; irrigation and integrated watershed projects; agricultural production and marketing and horticulture development. Poverty alleviation has been the central objective of all the projects.

Besides the direct impact on livelihoods and food security and the marked improvement in environmental sector, the 12 EU projects have helped develop infrastructure and create vital extension and marketing linkages. This has allowed communities as a whole to play a greater role in shaping their own development.

One illustration of the success of EU-India cooperation projects is the restoration of the green cover of India's oldest mountain range, the Aravalli Hills, which act as a natural barrier between the Thar Desert and the fertile plains of eastern Rajasthan. In 9 years 38,050 hectares of common land were re-planted with trees, grass and vegetables, primarily by local women. The project has prevented further desertification of the Aravalli Hills, improved the living conditions of 825,000 people and improved the social status of local women.

Disaster Preparedness

The EC-India Disaster Preparedness Programme is a €10 million project with a four-year implementation period starting in January 2004. It is implemented through a Contribution Agreement between the EC and UNDP as part of the multi-donor programme of the Government of India for national disaster preparation and management. Its two main components aim at natural disaster risk management in four multi-hazard vulnerable states (Assam, Meghalaya, Sikkim, West Bengal), and at the reduction of earthquake vulnerability in 12 seismic-prone states.

Cooperation with NGOs

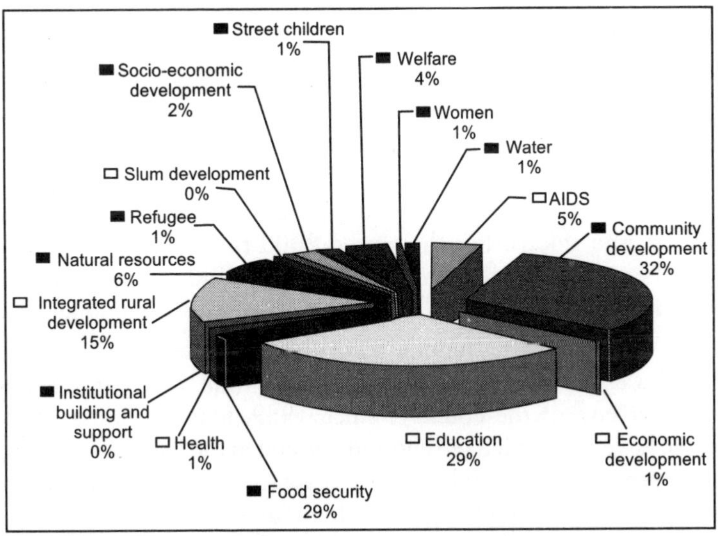

Figure 6.1: Distribution of Grants to Various Segments

There are lively civil society and NGOs in India that serve as counterbalance to the economic and political powers of the government and provide, therefore, an added dimension to the sense of democracy in the country. The EC Co-operation (through grants awarded following Calls for Proposals) has been quite successful in reaching out to the targeted community and in building bridges between European and Indian NGOs.

Humanitarian Aid

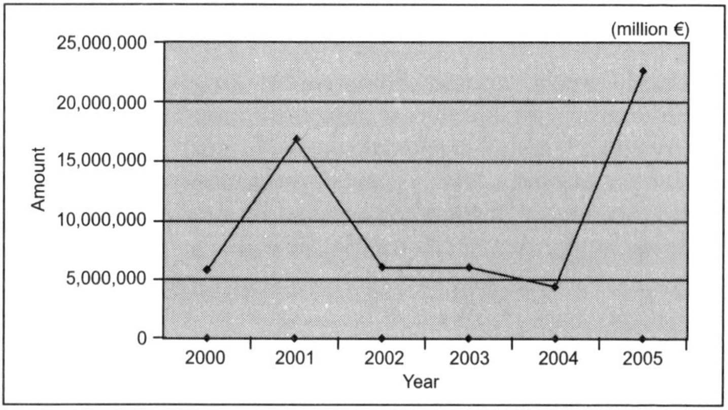

Figure 6.2: ECHO Budget-Humanitarian Aid 2000-2005

EU humanitarian assistance is channelled through the European Commission's Humanitarian Aid Office (ECHO). More than €61 million were allocated by ECHO budget during the period 2000 to 2004. In addition, €65 million from EU member states were channelled via ECHO during the same period. Where India is concerned, the main need is generally assistance following drought and floods. For the period 2000 to 2004, ECHO made a number of emergency interventions across India to help victims of floods and droughts, to a total value of €28.5 million.

In 2004, ECHO funded €3 million. Before the tsunami, ECHO's efforts were focused on meeting humanitarian needs at the other end of the country. Since 1989, tens of thousands of people have been killed or reported missing in the Kashmir conflict, and more than 350,000 have been displaced. The lack of security and widespread violence hinder humanitarian work and leave many people feeling isolated and vulnerable. The focus of ECHO's assistance was on providing protection, psycho-social support and primary healthcare to vulnerable groups and on raising awareness of the principles of international humanitarian law.

DG ECHO has funded projects addressing the needs of conflict-afflicted population in Jammu and Kashmir since 2002, amounting to €9 million so far. In 2007, the DG ECHO for the first time intervened in Chhattisgarh and the total assistance offered amounted €630,000. In Chhattisgarh, 20,000 poeple benefited from curative and preventive basic healthcare services and 7,500 internally displaced families benefited from improved water and sanitation. The DG ECHO approved a total of €11,000,000 in humanitarian aid for the flood victims (covering India and Bangladesh).

Funds were also allocated for victims of the exceptional monsoon floods that hit northeast India. ECHO funded medical supplies, shelter, food and basic essentials for the most vulnerable people affected by the floods.

Tsunami

The Indian Islands Andaman and Nicobar were close to the epicentre and consequently hit hard by the tsunami. The state of Tamil Nadu, and to a lesser extent Andhra Pradesh, Orissa and Kerala, also counted numerous victims, reaching more than 20,000 fatalities. Quickly, India refused international aid and requested that funds be directed to countries more in need. In addition, India helped those countries.

The EC has played a leading part in the international response to the tsunami. At the Jakarta Donors' Conference in January, the EC President pledged €123 million for humanitarian support and €350 million for longer-term reconstruction support. He also announced a series of flanking measures, such as trade concessions. For India, €10 million were committed for reconstruction of small boats, psychological support, water, and construction material for shelter.[44]

COOPERATION ON SCIENCE AND TECHNOLOGY

The EU-India Science & Technology (S&T) Cooperation Agreement was signed on 23 November 2001, at the second EU-India Summit in New Delhi by Mr. Pascal Lamy, Trade Commissioner for the European Commission and

Mr. Murli Manohar Joshi, the Indian Minister for Human Resource Development. The agreement is implemented by the Directorate-General for Research for the European Commission and by the Department of Science and Technology for the Government of India. Its aim is to facilitate cooperative research and development activities in science and technology fields of common interests for the community and India. It will allow participation of Indian scientists to all the Union's research activities and, reciprocally, will give access to European scientists in similar Indian programmes.

The agreement provides for:

- The participation of persons and legal entities, including the parties themselves, universities, research institutions, and other bodies or undertakings, in eachother's research projects;
- Pooling of research, training and development (RTD) projects already implemented according to the procedures applicable in the RTD programmes of each party;
- Exchange and sharing of equipment and materials;
- Exchange and provision of information and data;
- Visits and exchanges of scientists, engineers or other appropriate personnel for the purposes of participating in meetings, seminars, symposia, workshops and other research activities relevant to co-operation under this agreement;
- Exchange of information on practices, laws, regulations and programmes relevant to co-operation under the agreement; and
- Other activities as may be mutually determined by the Steering Committee in accordance with the applicable policies and programmes of the parties.

The first meeting of the Joint Steering Committee was held in March 2004 at which the modalities for implementation of the agreement were defined.[45]

First Steering Committee Meeting

The 1st Joint Steering Committee Meeting to operationalise the EU-India Science and Technology Cooperation Agreement took place in Brussels in March 2004 in which 5 topics were identified as priority areas for cooperation. They are, ICT, climate change and natural disasters, surface transport, nanotechnology and multifunctional materials, and health.

Keeping in mind the positive consequences on confidence building and networking that direct communication between the scientific communities, it was decided that workshops, co-organised by the Research Directorate General of the European Commission and the Department of Science and Technology of the Government of India in the priority areas mentioned above would be held to bring scientists together for an exchange of ideas and to serve as matchmaking events for future calls for proposals from the European Commission. These events would also showcase Indian expertise and incite European scientists to participate in Indian research projects.

Euro-India 2004 Co-operation Forum on the Information Society: The Euro-India 2004 Co-operation Forum took place in New Delhi during 24th to 26th March 2004. This was the fourth in a series of international co-operation events funded by the European Commission. It aimed at stimulating and spreading ICT innovations in business, culture, government, transport, and consumer and environmental protection. The event enabled ICT professionals, researchers, academics and public authorities from over 40 countries to showcase European projects, products and services, share ideas, expertise and project results, assess Indian demand for ICT goods and services and investigate co-operation prospects with potential partners.

EU-India Workshop on Climate Change and Natural Disasters: The University of Hyderabad from 6th to 10th September 2004 hosted the EU-India Workshop on Climate Change and Natural Disasters. The objective of the workshop was to present research activities in the areas of climate change and natural disasters and to jointly discuss these scientific areas with a view to identifying potential scientific topics for cooperation.

EU-India Workshop on Cooperation in Road Transport R&D: The Indian Institute of Science, Bangalore from 8th to 10th November 2004 hosted the EU-India Workshop on Cooperation in Road Transport R&D. The objectives of the workshop were to provide an exposure to the Indian scientific community of major EC funded projects in the domain, a presentation of the Indian research strengths and identifying new research areas where proposals with Indian partners could be submitted to future DG RTD calls.

EU-India Workshop on Nanotechnology and Functional Materials: The EU-India Workshop on Nanotechnology and Functional Materials was hosted by the S.N. Bose National Centre for Basic Sciences, Kolkata during 21st and 22nd March 2005. This area plays a significant role in the economic and technological growth in terms of new areas of activities as well as its role in health care applications. This Workshop was organized to have a direct interaction between the scientists and technologists working in this area in India as well as in the different economies of the European Union. The purpose of the interaction meeting was to generate awareness amongst the participating economies so that it can lead to project proposals in this area that can be submitted in the framework of FP6.

EU-India Workshop on Genomic and Biotechnology for Health: The EU-India Workshop on Genomic and Biotechnology for Health was hosted by the Institute for Genomics and Integrative Biology, New Delhi during 27th and 28th April 2005. The aim of the workshop was to present the forthcoming call of European Commission on Life Sciences, Genomic and Biotechnology for Health Thematic Priority Area, provide an overview of research being carried out in Europe and India in the domain and to formulate projects which could be submitted in response to the call for proposals.[46]

Second Steering Committee Meeting

The Second India-EU S&T Steering Committee Meeting took place in New Delhi on 29th April 2005, with the aim, among others, of reviewing the EC-India S&T actions taken during 2004-2005; recommending an EU-India S&T Action Plan for 2005-2006.

The review of the five Thematic EU-India Workshops held in India showed that the average participation in these workshops was 50 Indians and 8-12 Europeans. These Workshops allowed networking of scientists and the identification of topics of mutual interest for EU-India collaboration.

A Status Report on Indian Participation in European Commission funded projects showed that in the Sixth Framework Programme, till March 2005, 160 proposals involving 262 Indian participants had been submitted in response to calls for proposals from the European Commission. Of these 12 projects (2 in Information Technology; 2 in Life Sciences; 1 in Food Safety, 4 in Sustainable Development; 2 in international cooperation and 1 Marie Curie Fellowship) involving 16 Indian participants have been contracted for a total amount of €28,513,377.00, of which the share of the Indian participants is €885,624.00. It was agreed that during the period 2005-06, the following activities would be carried out:

Information Society Technologies

- Two preparatory meetings (one in India and one in Europe) to firm up collaborative research projects/actions involving European and Indian research entities in the domains of Information security covering cyber security framework, data and network tools, cyber forensics; language computing covering machine translation, text to speech, speech to text software across India-European languages; application dominant areas covering ICT applications in health, education and grass-roots governance; and
- Participation of Indian Scientific Team(s) to IST related European Technology Platforms Meetings & Actions (such as on Embedded Systems, Mobile & Wireless Communications, etc.) would be invited.

Genomic and Biotechnology for Health

- A European SMEs Meet on Disease Genomic in India for having transnational research wherein knowledge and methods derived from genomic are used for design and development of new safer and more effective drugs, new diagnostic tests and methods for early diagnosis and monitoring disease progression;
- An EU-India Meeting on "Systems Biology" in Europe for working out a Systems Biology Platform for understanding basic biological processes important for human health;

- An EU-India Workshop on Infectious Diseases (one in India and one in Europe) with focus on TB, HIV and Malaria; and
- A Preparatory Meeting for finalizing Research Training Network Project on Genome Information & Systems Biology involving European & Indian partners.

Nanotechnology & Functional Materials

- An Indian scientific mission to Europe in the domain of Nanolithography that could establish contacts and building intents for joint projects, accessing research facilities, advanced training;
- An EU-India workshop on Computational Materials Science;
- The European Commission would invite Indian participation in the international consultation on ethical aspects of nanotechnology that the Commission intends to organize; and
- The Indian side would invite European participation in international conferences on nanotechnology to be held in India (International Workshop on The Physics of Semiconductor Devices, organised by the National Physical Laboratory, New Delhi in December 2005; International Conference on Nano Science & Technology, organised by the Indian Institute of Technology, New Delhi in March 2006; and the International Conference on Nanostructured Materials NANO2006, organized by the Indian Institute of Science, Bangalore in August 2006).

Surface Transport Research and Development

- EU-India workshops in the domains of rail and maritime research and development;
- Establishment of linkages of Indian entities with the following European Technology Platforms: European Road Transport Research Advisory Council (ERTRAC); European Nanoelectronics Initiative Advisory Council (ENIAC); European Hydrogen and Fuel Cells Technology Platform (HFP); Embedded Systems (ARTEMIS); and Mobile & Wireless Communication (eMobility);

- Visit of an Indian scientific mission to Europe in Road Transport Research and Development, with the aim of projecting Indian R&D activity to European research institutions and industry as well as to create networks that could result in building intents for joint projects, and advanced training, through the establishment of a Research Training Network;
- European participation in Indian R&D projects such as hydrogen propulsion (combustion)and electronic control of hydrogen IC engine; tailor welded blanks and hydroforming of autocomponents, advanced electric hybrid vehicle technologies, fuel cell hybrids, technology for recycling automotive components, inspection and maintenance of vehicles, open standards for telematics platforms and e-toll collection.

High Energy Physics (Accelerator Science & Technology)

- An EU-India workshop in India on Accelerator Science and Technology (including on possible opportunities for Indian researchers for joining accelerator science research projects and accelerator facilities anticipated in Europe such as those at GSI Darmstadt, DESY Hamburg and CERN Geneva).

Aeronautics Research

- An EU-India workshop/Indian exploratory mission to Europe on aeronautics research and technology; and
- Establishment of linkages and possible Indian participation in meetings of the European Technology Platform—Advisory Council for Aeronautics Research in Europe (ACARE).

In addition, lateral entry of Indian research organisations, with Indian co-funding, would be encouraged in certain ongoing European Commission funded projects.[47]

Two Steering Committee Meetings have been held to establish the bases for this cooperation, the first in Brussels in March 2004 and the second in New Delhi in April 2005.

Indian participation in the European Commission funded research, however, dates back to the very beginning of the

Framework Programmes (the first one began in 1984), when the Central Pollution Control Board became the first Indian organisation to be funded by the Commission and carried out a project on Air Pollution Monitoring in Relation to Human Health in Metropolitan Cities of India. The project began on the 1st of January 1985 and lasted for 42 months.

Research in science and technology is the key to a better future and research lies at the heart of the European Union's strategy for becoming the world's most competitive and dynamic knowledge-based economy by the year 2010. To this end, the European Commission is responsible for a major international research framework program to generate new knowledge to bring about better coordination, improved complementarities of policies and programs of all the actors and of institutions involved in European research. The Commission's research investments focus on strategic priorities which produce a leverage effect and resources are directed to areas where European level action or cooperation can offer distinct advantages. The programme supports the development of lasting transnational networks involving academic research institutes and universities, manufacturing and service enterprises, SMEs, consumer groups and public authorities.

Within this overall context, international partnerships with countries outside the EU are an integral of Europe's ambitions, as research is increasingly becoming international and without boundaries. Therefore participation in European research is open to researchers from all over the world, very much including India.

Indian Participation has Steadily Increased

- Framework Program 2 (1987-1991): 14 projects with Indian partners;
- Framework Program 3 (1990-1994): 57 projects with Indian partner.[48]

Fourth Framework Program (FP4): During the Fourth Framework Program period 1994-1998, 33 projects with Indian partners, European Union RTD activities were carried out and the parallel Euratom Framework Program covering research and training activities were conducted in the nuclear sector.

The total budget for both EC and Euratom Framework Programs amounted to ECU 13, 215 million (EC: ECU 11,879 million, Euratom: ECU 1,336 million).[49]

Fifth Framework Program (FP5): During the Fifth Framework Program period, 1998-2002, priorities for the European Union's research, technological development and demonstration (RTD) activities in the 32 projects with Indian partners were set. These priorities have been selected on the basis of a set of common criteria reflecting the major concerns of increasing industrial competitiveness and the quality of life for European citizens.

The Fifth Framework Programme has two distinct parts: the European Community (EC) framework program covering research, technological development and demonstration activities; and the Euratom framework program covering research and training activities in the nuclear sector.

FP5 differs considerably from its predecessors. It has been conceived to help solve problems and to respond to the major socio-economic challenges facing Europe. To maximise its impact, it focuses on a limited number of research areas combining technological, industrial, economic, social and cultural aspects. Management procedures have also been streamlined with an emphasis on simplifying procedures and systematically involving key players in research.

Programs and Key Actions: A major innovation of the Fifth Framework Program is the concept of "Key actions". Implemented within the specific programmes, these flexible instruments are targeted at achieving solutions to topics of great concern in Europe. "Key actions" will mobilise the wide range of scientific and technological disciplines—both fundamental and applied—required to address a specific problem so as to overcome the barriers that exist, not only between disciplines but also between the programmes and the organisations concerned.

Rules: Modification to the rules covering participation and the dissemination of research results under the Fifth Framework Program were proposed by the Commission. Forming part of the FP5 legislative architecture, these rules will be implemented in a harmonised manner by the specific programs.

Budget: A budget of €13,700 million has been agreed for the implementation of the European Community section of FP5. Combined with the €1,260 million allocated to the Euratom program, this should bring the global budget for research during 1999-2002 to €14,960 million. (This represents an increase, in absolute terms, of 4.61 per cent compared to the Fourth Framework Program).[50]

It must be noted that in the 4th and 5th Framework Programs Indian organisations could take part only in the "International Cooperation" Program.

These projects cover a wide area of research including health, education and public awareness, food security, effluent treatments, bioinformatics and biotechnology, clean energy technology, quantum theory, etc. The project partners come from academic and research institutions, and other non-profit organisations. The most active participants in European Commission funded research have been the Tata Energy Research Institute (now The Energy and Resources Institute), New Delhi and the Indian Institute of Science, Bangalore.

Sixth Framework Program (FP6): The Sixth Framework Program (FP6) is the EU's most important program for research cooperation. With a total available budget of €17.5 billion over the five-year period from 2002 to 2006, FP6 is the financial instrument to make an integrated European Research Area a reality. While the main aim of FP6 is to improve the integration and coordination of European research, the Program also provides specific measures in support of international cooperation in Science and Technology.

International cooperation is considered a key aspect of FP6. As the European Commissioner for Research, Dr. Janez Potoènik has said: "As there is no alternative to the globalisation for the industry and the companies, there is none for the international cooperation. Most of the major scientific projects of today, such as the construction of the international space station and super particle accelerators need international cooperation. The same is true when meeting the challenges of global climate change and emerging disease." For the first time, FP6 offers funds for international partners in all areas of scientific research. Any legal entity—private or public—can participate in FP6 projects.

With the signing of the EU-India Science and Technology Cooperation Agreement, Indian researchers can participate as full partners in European Commission funded projects.[51]

Seventh Framework Program (FP7): On 6th April 2005 the European Commission adopted a proposal for a new EU programme for research. The proposal provides new impetus to increase Europe's growth and competitiveness, recognising that knowledge is Europe's greatest resource. The program places greater emphasis than in the past on research that is relevant to the needs of European industry, to help it compete internationally, and develop its role as a world leader in certain sectors. The program will also for the first time provide support for the best in European investigator-driven research, with the creation of a European Research Council. Focus will be on excellence throughout the program, a requirement if it is to play its role in developing Europe's global competitiveness. Another priority will be to make participation in the program simpler and easier, through measures addressing the procedures, plus a rationalisation of instruments. In spite of this new approach, there are many elements of continuity: in practice, for the majority of participants, the program itself will not change, but participation will become simpler.

Subtitled "Building the European research area of knowledge for growth", FP7 is designed to respond to the competitiveness and employment needs of the EU. The Commission proposes in particular to double the FP7 budget compared with FP6, raising to €73.2 billion over the period 2007-2013. According to the Commission proposal, FP7 will be organized in four specific programs.

Euro Cooperation: Where support will be given to the whole range of research activities carried out in transnational cooperation, from collaborative projects and networks to coordination of research programmes. International cooperation between the EU and third countries (including India) is an integral part of this action. Nine themes have been identified: (a) health; (b) food, agriculture and biotechnology; (c) information and communication technologies; (d) nanosciences, nanotechnologies, materials and new production processes; (e) energy; (f) environment (including climate change); (g) transport (including aeronautics); (h) socio-economic sciences and humanities; and (i) security and space.

Euro Ideas: Where an autonomous European Research Council will be created to support investigator-driven "frontier research" carried out by individual teams competing at the European level, in all scientific and technological fields, including engineering, socio-economic sciences and the humanities. Funding will be based purely on the scientific quality of the proposal.

Euro People: Where activities supporting training and career development of researchers, referred to as "Marie Curie" actions will be reinforced with a better focus on the key aspects of skills and career development and strengthened links with national systems.

Euro Capacities: Where key aspects of European research and innovation capacities will be supported: research infrastructures; research for the benefit of SMEs; regional research-driven clusters; unlocking the full research potential in the EU "convergence" regions; "Science and Society" issues; and, last but not least, activities to stimulate international RTD cooperation between the EU and third countries.

There is a strong element of continuity with the past in the proposed Seventh Framework Program. Projects undertaken by consortia of European partners will remain at the core of the programme, and the themes for these projects will remain more or less as now. The program will continue to develop the concept of a European Research Area. Funds will be used to develop and increase those elements of previous programmes that worked well: Marie Curie, SME actions, collaborative projects, Networks of Excellence. The aim of continuity will be strengthened through a programme that lasts 7 years (with the possibility of a mid-term review).

A key feature of FP7 will be a significant simplification of its operation. By focusing more on themes and less on instruments, the programme will be more flexible and adaptable to the needs of industry, as well as more straightforward for its participants.

The programme will have more focus than in the past on developing research that responds to the needs of European industry, through the work of Technology Platforms and the new "Joint Technology Initiatives". These will be projects in fields of major European public interest on subjects identified through dialogue with industry, in particular in the European Technology Platforms.

The programme will establish for the first time a "European Research Council", funding the best of European science, as assessed by peer review of European scientists.

International cooperation will no longer just be a separate part of the programme, but will be integrated into all four programmes, allowing projects to be carried out with international partners. In the same vein, the Science in Society action will have specific tasks, but the aim of anchoring science more closely in the needs and wants of European society will be considered in all parts of the programme.

Another new element will be the development of "regions of knowledge", bringing together research partners – such as universities, research centres, enterprises and regional authorities in a region to strengthen their research potential.

FP7 will also comprise a "Risk-Sharing Finance Facility" aimed at fostering private investment in research by improving access to European Investment Bank (EIB) loans for large European research actions. This mechanism will enable broader EIB lending to RTD actions.

The new proposal is based on a year-long process of consultations with interested parties. The approach proposed by the Commission in its communication of June 2004, which forms the basis for this proposal, have the strong backing of the scientific community.

In February 2005, an expert panel evaluated the previous framework programs and found that these programs had made a major contribution to the development of Europe's knowledge base and had had a positive effect on Europe's potential for innovation.

The Commission has also had numerous meetings with groups of scientists, scientific organisations and other umbrella bodies, at political or technical level, to discuss its ideas for the new programme and to involve the views of the wider community as much as possible.

Simplifying the administrative and financial rules and procedures of the Seventh Framework Program will be a decisive factor in its success. The Commission is proposing a series of measures to address issues relating to implementation at every level of the programme. These measures include:

- Rationalising the funding schemes—a new approach based on a simpler set of funding instruments;
- Using simpler, less bureaucratic languages, that is free of jargon and user-friendly;
- Reducing the number and size of documents;
- Reducing the number of request to participants and instituting a light submission procedure;
- Reducing a priori controls (i.e. controls before the project is approved);
- Increasing the autonomy of consortia;
- Streamlining the selection process; and
- Exploring new modes of funding and simplifying the cost-based funding system.

Even with the proposed increase in funds, the European research budget will represent less than 10 per cent of public spending on research and development within the European Union.

The reasons for proposing the increase in resources for the budget are several:

- The structure of the EU's budget should reflect the political priorities of the EU.
- Spending on research at EU level has a leverage effect on other sources of private and public funding. Each €1 of European money invested in research leads to an additional €1 of private investment.
- The political, economic and scientific context requires the development of a number of new actions that must be given sufficient funds if they are to fulfil their objectives.

- So far, a significant number of high quality proposals have to be rejected due to lack of available funds. An increase in resources at European level would give an added boost to a whole range of scientific activities which at European level have up to now been left aside.

Knowledge is Europe's best resource. Investing in knowledge is certainly the best way for the EU to foster economic growth, while at the same time ensuring social progress and environmental sustainability. Making the European Union a strong global partner has been set as a priority goal for the EU.

The EU's research policy, and the proposal for the new Framework Programme that will help implement it, play an important role in delivering these goals. Research is at the core of the EU's plan to stimulate growth and jobs: together with education and innovation, it is a key component of the "Knowledge Triangle". Europe must increase its research effort to 3 per cent of EU GDP and better exploit its capacities in this field, transforming scientific results into new products, processes and services, as part of its efforts to fulfil its goal of becoming the "most dynamic and competitive knowledge-based economy in the world".

Investment at European level, while remaining a small part of the total needed to achieve the 3 per cent target, can have a considerable effect. By increasing its investment in research, the European Union will set a clear example, to be followed by Member States and private investors. European level investment in research will be spent in areas that maximise the leverage effect on other types of investment.

Table 6.10: Details of FP7 Timetable

6th April 2005	Commission proposal
21st September 2005	Specific programme proposals
13th June 2006	Probable First reading at the European Parliament
July - December 2006	Final administrative stages in the co-decision process for adoption of FP7
December 2006	Launch of the first calls for proposals
February 2007	Conference to launch FP7[52]

COOPERATION ON COUNTER-TERRORISM

Terrorism is not a new phenomenon in Europe. Fight against terrorism is one of the greatest challenges faced by the EU today. In the United Kingdom, Ireland and Spain, it has caused 5,000 deaths in thirty years. It has become even more international in recent years. The bomb attacks in Madrid and London clearly demonstrate this point. Terrorism takes many forms and uses ever more sophisticated and deadly organizational techniques and operational methods. Bio-terrorism and chemical threats are all too real. Well-organised terrorist groups are receiving support from sympathizer networks in many countries, and have rear bases and sizeable financial resources.

In 1999, the EU Heads of State or Government initiated work on the basis of the Amsterdam Treaty, which strengthened the powers of the European Union in the fields of Justice and Home Affairs. The terrorist attacks perpetrated in the United States on 11 September 2001 threw the world into turmoil.[53]

The EU-India issued "Declaration against International Terrorism" on 23 November 2001 in New Delhi. Both EU and India affirm that international terrorism is a threat to peace and security. It constitutes a challenge to all States and the entire humanity and a grave violation of human rights. Given their tolerant character, open, democratic and multicultural societies are especially vulnerable to terrorist attacks. The struggle against terrorism is not against any community or faith.

All states have a responsibility to refrain from providing moral, material or diplomatic support to acts of terrorism, and prevent the use of their territory for sponsoring terrorist acts against other states. Both EU and India support the adoption on the basis of international law of decisive measures against all States, individuals, and entities, which render support, harbour, finance, instigate or train terrorists or promote terrorism. There can be no religious ethnic, ideological or any other justification of terrorism. EU and India also support the fight against international terrorism, wherever it occurs, regardless of its motives.

It is necessary that all States cooperate through all lawful means to prevent and suppress the financing of acts of terrorism in their territories.

EU and India reaffirm the central role of the United Nations in the efforts of the international community in the struggle against terrorism. They agree that such a struggle must be conducted in observance of human rights and the rule of law, which it aims to safeguard and strengthen.

They call for an early adoption of the draft Comprehensive Convention on International Terrorism and the Convention for the Suppression of Acts of Nuclear Terrorism. Adoption and implementation of these conventions as well as all other UN conventions would assist in strengthening the international legal basis for effectively combating the global menace of terrorism.[54]

EU Supports India's Fight against Terror

The European Union has condemned the attack on Parliament and pledged its support to India's fight against terrorism, which threatens democracy and human rights. "The European Parliament vehemently condemns the violent terrorist attack against the Indian Parliament. This attack was directed against the very institution that represents democracy and the rule of law," the 15-nation grouping said in a declaration. It deplored the loss of human lives and expressed "solidarity and support to the Republic of India in its fight against terrorism, which constitutes a threat to mutually shared values of democracy and respect for human rights". Indian diplomatic sources said the condemnation was an affirmation of the joint declaration against international terrorism adopted by the EU and India at their summit in New Delhi on November 23, 2001.[55]

EU's Action in Response to 11th September 2001

The European Union responded swiftly to the terrorist attacks of the 11th September 2001. Within days of the attacks on America, a series of concrete measures were tabled by the European Commission, which led to a Plan of Action adopted by special European Council on the 21st September.

Over the past year, the European Union has sustained its efforts as one of the leading partners in the global fight against terrorism. Implementing the Plan of Action, all EU efforts are guided by:

- Continued solidarity with the US;
- Determination in the fight against terrorism;
- Commitment to the security of all citizens in the EU;
- Efforts to tackle root causes of terrorism; and
- Contributions to better understanding between civilisations.

The EU has focused on those areas where it can complement the efforts made by individual Member States:

Transatlantic Cooperation: Europe-wide and transatlantic cooperation in the fight against international terrorism and cross-border organized crime has been stepped up, including on extradition, mutual legal assistance, migration and border control.

The EU adopted a European arrest warrant, a common definition of terrorism and a list of terrorist organisations. In addition, joint police investigation teams across the EU and a special Europol anti-terrorism unit have been created, as well as Eurojust, a co-ordinating body between Member States' law enforcement agencies.

EU Incorporates the Fight Against Terrorism: Diplomatic efforts, supported by the quick mobilization of trade and aid, have focused on Afghanistan, Pakistan, Iran, the Middle-East and the Euro-Mediterranean Partnership. The EU is the main international donor to Afghanistan, providing generous financial assistance to alleviate human suffering, to help integrate returning refugees and to support the Transitional Authority.

The EU has incorporated the fight against terrorism into all aspects of the EU's external relations. While implementing UN Security Council Resolution 1373, it went beyond UN sanctions and froze the assets of an important number of terrorist organisations. The EU has agreed joint law enforcement actions in the fight against terrorism with a great number of third countries throughout the year. At the same time the EU has encouraged dialogue to promote mutual understanding with other civilizations.

Air transport security has been improved with Europe-wide measures to prevent future terrorist attacks and the air transport industry has been supported. Economic and financial measures have been taken to dry up the sources of terrorist funding through intensified money laundering directives.

Emergency preparedness has been increased to protect public health and enhance civil protection in the event of terrorist attacks through the availability of medicinal treatment and the creation of a Monitoring and Information Centre providing for immediate response in the case of major emergencies 24 hours a day.

Police and Judicial Cooperation: By September 13, 2001, the Commission had tabled proposals for a European arrest warrant to supplant the current system of extradition between Member States and a common definition of terrorism and related penalties. The Council has formally adopted both proposals. They represent the first of many measures against all forms of cross-border organized crime, including terrorism.

Other measures, which include:

- Joint investigation teams of police and magistrates from throughout the EU;
- Routine exchange of information about terrorism between the Member States and Europol;
- The creation of a specialist anti-terrorist unit within Europol;
- The establishment of Eurojust, a co-ordination body composed of magistrates, prosecutors and police officers; and
- Political agreement of the Council on a framework directive on the mutual recognition between EU Member States judicial authorities on orders for the freezing of assets and the preservation of evidence.

Closer transatlantic cooperation:

- A co-operation agreement between Europol and the relevant US authorities was signed on 6 December 2001. A second agreement to allow the exchange of personal data is currently being negotiated;

- The EU is also engaged in talks with the United States to establish closer co-operation with Eurojust and the relevant US authorities;
- Efforts are underway to intensify cooperation in practical ways on border control and migration management;
- EU Justice Ministers agreed in April 2002 to begin negotiations with the US on closer cooperation on extradition and mutual legal assistance and negotiations are proceeding as planned; and
- Efforts are being made to strengthen co-operation between relevant law enforcement authorities in the US and in each of the EU Member States.

Global Fight against Terrorism

The EU has adopted the fight against terrorism as a priority policy objective. It has worked with the US to build a global coalition against terrorism, and to establish joint initiatives designed to defeat international terrorism. The fight against terrorism has been incorporated into all aspects of the Union's external relations.

Horizontal Actions

- EC external assistance programmes support the efforts of third countries to comply with UNSC Resolution 1373 on the fight against terrorism, and further consideration is being given to how further technical assistance could be made available.

Freeze of Terrorist Assets

- A regulation freezing funds and prohibiting provision of funds, assets, economic resources or financial services to terrorists were adopted in December 2001. Since 1999, over €100 million of terrorists' assets have been frozen throughout the EU.
- The events of September 11th demonstrated the need for political and cultural dialogue with those parts of the world where terrorism comes into being. The EU has supported dialogue to counter racial, religious and cultural prejudice. A Euro-Mediterranean Foundation is to be set up under the Barcelona Process. Firm commitments to

enhanced inter-cultural dialogue have been made at a meeting of EU Member States, Candidate Countries and the Organisation of the Islamic Conference in Istanbul during 12-13 February 2002.

Bilateral Relations with Third Countries and Regions

The European Union has redoubled its diplomatic efforts towards building an international coalition against terrorism:

- The EU is the main donor helping to rebuild Afghanistan through reconstruction and humanitarian assistance. At the Tokvo Donors' Conference in January 2002, the contributions of the European Commission and of individual EU Member States together, made Europe the most generous contributor. The EC alone has pledged €1 billion over the next five years; and
- In 2002 the EC provided €265 million instead of €200 million. The sum available for humanitarian assistance has been raised to €60 million from €25 million.

This money has not merely been committed, but is being deployed on the ground very swiftly. The EC is contributing more than any other donor to the operating costs of the new government (including salaries for police, nurses, doctors, teachers and civil servants). It is supporting 450 primary schools, and 200 clinics, and cleaning up five cities around the country to prevent diseases like cholera. It is also making a major contribution to the clearance of mines and the fight against poppy production.

Humanitarian Assistance

- The EU responded to Pakistan's changed position on the Taliban regime and its commitments to return to democratic rule, with increased financial assistance and a new cooperation agreement. A package of trade measures designed to significantly improve access for Pakistani exports to the EU has been approved. Furthermore, the Commission has mounted a major Election Observation Mission in the run up to the parliamentary elections on October 12, 2002 in order to assist this country in its difficult transition process towards restoration of full democracy;

- Negotiating directives for the Council has adopted a Trade and Co-operation Agreement with Iran. The EU calls on Iran to promote and protect human rights and fundamental freedoms, to sign, ratify and fully implement international instruments pertaining to the non-proliferation of arms and to join in the international fight against terrorism;
- The EU was already deeply involved in the search for peace and stability in the Middle-East long before the attacks of September 11, 2001, but those events have undoubtedly thrown into even sharper focus, the urgent need to tackle regional problems that can give rise to terrorism. The EU plays a crucial role in preserving the Palestinian Authority as a negotiating partner, by providing substantial financial assistance. The EU is also a key player in the "Quartet" (EU, US, UN and Russia) efforts to find a way forward in the Middle-East, and has prepared a "road-map" to guide actions on all sides towards the creation of a Palestinian State in 3 years' time; and
- Commitments to cooperate closely in the fight against terrorism have been included in or agreed alongside new Association Agreements between the EU, Algeria, Lebanon and Chile.

Concrete international commitments to fight against terrorism have been agreed upon with the United States, Russia, the 13 accession candidates, Norway, Iceland and Liechtenstein, Switzerland, Russia, Ukraine, Moldova and the western Balkan countries, the 12 partner countries of the Euro-Mediterranean Partnership, Israel, Canada, and India, as well as the Council of Europe. At the Ninth Ministerial Council of the Organisation for Security and Cooperation in Europe (OSCE), in December 2001, Ministers adopted a broad-ranging Action Plan on counter-terrorism measures.[56]

The fight against terrorism must entail daily action and is not only about making declarations, the European Commission

President, Romano Prodi, said on 30 November 2003, when asked about the role played by Pakistan in Jammu & Kashmir and Afghanistan. "We have always pressed Pakistan in the direction of active cooperation against terrorism. In spite of difficulties, progress has been made and we are really... pressing [the Pakistanis] to make further progress. It is clear that the fight against terrorism is not only a kind of declaration, but also daily, daily action... we know the difficulties... but it is in the interests of the countries [India and Pakistan] to cooperate in the common action against terrorism" he added.[57]

The Fourth Summit between India and the EU was held in New Delhi, India, on 29th November 2003. During the Summit, both sides agreed that terrorism is a global phenomenon that transcends border and region and can target any country. They expressed the belief that there can be no justification whatsoever for terrorism, and support the fight against international terrorism, wherever it occurs and regardless of its motives. Both EU and India called upon all states to fully implement their commitment under UNSC Resolution No. 1373 so as to ensure that their territories are not used for sponsoring terrorist activities against other states. As democracies founded on the rule of law, India and the EU remain committed to ensuring compatibility of counter-terrorism measures with universally accepted Human Rights standards and norms. Also called for progress towards the establishment of cooperation between Europol and Indian agencies.[58]

The Fifth Summit between the EU and India was held in The Hague, The Netherlands, on 8 November 2004. The EU was represented by the President of the European Council, Dutch Prime Minister Dr. Jan Peter Balkenende, the President of the European Commission, Dr. Romano Prodi, the Secretary-General/High Representative for Common Foreign and Security Policy Mr. Xavier Solana, the Commissioner in charge of Trade Relations, Mr. Pascal Lamy, and the Netherlands Minister for Foreign Affairs, Dr. Bernard Bot. India was represented by the Prime Minister, Dr. Manmohan Singh, the External Affairs Minister, Mr. Natwar Singh, and the Commerce and Industry Minister, Mr. Kamal Nath.

The leaders sent the following message:

- We unequivocally condemn all acts, methods and practices of terrorism and stress that solidarity and international cooperation are integral to combat terrorism.
- We emphasise that measures to combat terrorism should be comprehensive and sustained.
- We stress that further strengthening of cooperation in combatting terrorism is a priority area for the EU-India Action Plan for a Strategic Partnership. We will in particular seek to:
  - Deepen the international consensus and enhance international efforts to combat terrorism;
  - Reduce the access of terrorists to financial and other economic resources;
  - Protect the security of international transport and ensure effective systems of border control;
  - Address the issues which create an environment conducive to terrorism, including support for and recruitment into terrorism;
  - Explore ways to strengthen the counter-terrorism dialogue by covering, as appropriate, other security related issues.
- We will continue to support the work of the United Nations to ensure universal adherence to, and full implementation of, all UN Security Council Resolutions, UN Conventions on Terrorism and related Protocols, including promoting an agreement on the draft Comprehensive Convention on International Terrorism. The fight against terrorism must be carried out in full respect of human rights, fundamental freedoms and the rule of law.[59]

The European Council in December 2005 approved an analysis by the Presidency and the Counter-Terrorism Coordinator of the evaluation of national counter-terrorism arrangements. Good practices were highlighted and recommendations issued. In 2006 Member States reported to the Council on implementation of the recommendations. Many positive changes in Member States have been noted, including changes in legislation.

In its political dialogue with international partners the EU continued to promote the role of the UN in the fight against terrorism. In particular, the EU played a key role in supporting the adoption of the UN Counter-Terrorism Strategy which reflects the priorities of the EU's own strategy. Although progress on the UN Comprehensive Convention on International Terrorism remained blocked, the EU regards the conclusion of the Convention as a viable goal and remains committed to achieving consensus on that subject in the UN.

Cooperation between the EU and other important countries like the United States, Russia, Australia and other international partners has been extended further. A high-level political dialogue on counter-terrorism took place between the Counter-Terrorism Coordinator and the Indian authorities.

The Sixth EU-India consultations on terrorism took place in Brussels in December 2005. It was useful in taking forward cooperation between the EU and India in the fight against terrorism and organised crime. The EU Counter-Terrorism Coordinator visited New Delhi in October 2006 to establish contact with his Indian counterpart. Their talks were the occasion to explore how to take forward EU-India counter-terrorism cooperation.[60]

The EU-India summit in October confirmed the commitment of both sides to intensify their cooperation in this field. Following President Musharraf's visit to Brussels the Pakistani government indicated that it too would welcome a regular dialogue on counter-terrorism with the European Union. The Government of Egypt has presented a similar request.

In its dialogue with partners, bilaterally and multilaterally, the EU has continued to emphasize that the fight against terrorism must be conducted in full respect of the rule of law and human rights. On September 15 EU Foreign Ministers confirmed that the existence of secret detention facilities where detained persons are kept in a legal vacuum is not in conformity with international humanitarian law and international criminal law.

India and the European Union, held their Sixth Annual Summit on September 7, 2005 New Delhi. Prime Minister Tony Blair, President of the European Commission Jose Manuel Barroso, Secretary-General and High Representative Xavier Solana, EU External Relations Commissioner Ferrero-Waldner and EU Trade Commissioner Peter Mandelson represented the EU at the summit. During the summit the leaders of both EU and India agreed to intensify their cooperation in the fight against terrorism and signed a "framework agreement" on Indian participation in Galileo, though the signing of the formal agreement had to be deferred because of unresolved differences.[61]

On the question of terrorism, India came up with some "ambitious" suggestions, as Prime Minister Blair himself put it in his joint press conference with Prime Minister Dr. Manmohan Singh in Hyderabad House. Mr. Blair said: "The problem with terrorism is not just the people that commit the act of terrorism; it is those that support it, those that incite it, those that encourage it. I think we have got to take a very strong stand on behalf of the international community and say we condemn this and we condemn it utterly.... It is time we sent out a clear, unified message from the international community and said that it is no longer legitimate not merely in terms of committing acts of terrorism but in terms of supporting or inciting it."

He said this can be done by making sure that there is proper intelligence cooperation, that Europol and the Central Bureau of Investigation cooperate properly together and areas of practical cooperation like attacking sources of money laundering and financing of terrorism are effectively addressed. "The proposals from the Indian side are actually rightly ambitious in this regard. But these terrorists cross frontiers very easily and they do get access to funds as well as weapons and it is important that we are tackling every single aspect of this. So, I think that cooperation is important. But there is another area of cooperation as well which is also to talk about how we defeat the ideas and ideologies of these people," he added.

Prime Minister Dr. Manmohan Singh said, "The political declaration on the India-EU Strategic Partnership summed up the salient features of what the two wished to achieve together and added that at the top of the agenda was intensified political dialogue and cooperation for meeting common challenges and global threats, starting with terrorism. We have agreed that there is no place for terrorism in the civilized world and that we will work together towards fighting it. We have agreed on a detailed framework indicating how we will enhance our cooperation in this very important area.... We will also establish a security dialogue on global and regional security issues, disarmament and non-proliferation."[62]

On the fifth anniversary of the terrorist attacks in the United States, President Jose Manuel Barroso on behalf of the European Commission issued statement on 11 September 2006 in Brussels, which reads: "Five years have now passed since the terrible events of 11th September 2001. Today is a time to remember the victims and express our solidarity with those left behind by this and all other terrorist attacks. The EU response to the 11th September 2001 attacks in the United States was immediate with increased cooperation with the United States on the fight against terrorism. The European Commission will continue to deliver results through the EU Counter-Terrorism Strategy. More remains to be done such as fighting radicalization and recruitment. We need effective policies to prevent and detect the misuse of explosives, protect critical infrastructure and ensure transport security. Vice-President Frattini has written today to the US Secretary for Homeland Security and the US Attorney General to underline the continued commitment of the European Union to increased cooperation with the United States in this area. We are more determined than ever to tackle the causes, and the consequences of global terrorism. We have to tackle not just the methods used but also the ideas of those that wage this campaign. Ignorance and mistrust are essential to the terrorists' strategy. Our response must be to stand up for our values, namely respect for human rights, which are the surest guarantee of our future security."[63]

The Seventh EU-India Summit was held in Helsinki on 13 October 2006. The EU was represented by Mr. Matti Vanhanen, Prime Minister of Finland, in his capacity as President of the European Council, assisted by High Representative for Common Foreign and Security Policy, Dr. Xavier Solana, and by the President of the European Commission, Mr. Jose Manuel Barroso, European Commissioner for External Relations, Mrs. Benita Ferrero-Waldner and European Commissioner for Trade, Mr. Peter Mandelson, Mr. Erkki Tuomioja, Finnish Foreign Minister, and Mrs. Paula Lehtomäki, Finnish Minister for Foreign Trade and Development. The Republic of India was represented by Prime Minister Dr. Manmohan Singh, Mr. Kamal Nath, Minister for Commerce and Industry, Mr. Anand Sharma, Minister of State for External Affairs, and Mr. M.K. Narayanan, National Security Adviser.

The leaders sent the message on counter-terrorism:

- The EU and India stand united in facing the scourge of terrorism, which constitutes one of the most serious threats to international peace and security. The EU and India condemned terrorism in all its forms and manifestations, committed by whomever, wherever and for whatever purpose;
- The fight against terrorism can only succeed if it is sustained and comprehensive. The EU and India, therefore, attach great importance to counter-terrorism cooperation in the framework of the United Nations and share a commitment to universal ratification and full implementation of all international counter-terrorism conventions and related protocols; and
- The EU and India continue to work actively towards a swift finalisation of a Comprehensive Convention on International Terrorism at the UN.

They also welcomed the adoption of the first UN Counter-Terrorism Strategy by the General Assembly on 8 September 2006. The EU and India expressed their commitment to actively support implementation of the Strategy in all its dimensions. The leaders affirmed their commitment to combat terrorism with full respect of obligations under international law, in particular human rights law, refugee law and international humanitarian law. Both sides are committed to continuing their cooperation on counter-terrorism and look forward to holding their next regular consultations in 2006. Strengthening cooperation to combat terrorism continues to be one of the priority areas for the EU-India Strategic Partnership.[64]

The two EU-India summits held so far have stressed the importance of strengthening the UN's capacity to play its role in maintaining global peace and development. In this regard, EU and India have established a joint working group on counter-terrorism and to extend support to the Comprehensive Convention on International Terrorism.

The Eight EU-India annual summit took place on 30 November 2007 in New Delhi. The EU was represented by Jose Sócrates, Prime Minister of Portugal, in his capacity as President of the European Council and Jose Manuel Barroso, President of the European Commission. Prime Minister Dr. Manmohan Singh led the Indian side. The two sides discussed the various issues of mutual interest. It further strengthened the strategic relationship. A Joint statement and Joint Action Plan Implementation Report were issued at the summit. An Agreement for Scientific and Technological Cooperation was renewed and an MoU an Multi-Annual Indicative Programme 2007-2010 was signed between the two sides during the summit.

India and the EU reaffirmed their commitment to a rules-based multilateral trading system and stressed the need to intensify their bilateral trade relations. The successful and timely outcome of the Doha Development Agenda (DDA) multilateral trade negotiations remains the foremost trade policy priority of the two sides. Both sides are determined to work together to ensure the successful conclusion of the DDA negotiations through a comprehensive, balanced and ambitious result in all areas of negotiations. The leaders welcomed the progress achieved in the first few rounds of negotiations on the India-EU Trade and Investment Agreement and reaffirmed their commitment to further take it to a deeper level of trade relations. The leaders noted that bilateral trade and investment between India and the EU has been growing steadily which reflects the strengthening of bilateral economic ties.

EC Funds 15 New Security Research Projects to Combat Terrorism

During 2004-2006, the EC has been running a "Preparatory Action for Security Research (PASR)" funding scheme. This focuses on the development of a European security research agenda to bridge the gap between civil research supported by EC's Framework Programmes, and national and intergovernmental security research initiatives. The response to the PASR calls has been tremendous, with 165 proposals submitted to the 2006 call. With an overall budget of €15 million, the EC has announced that 15 proposals will be supported—eight technology projects and seven supporting activities. The eight technology projects cover the detection of explosives and biological agents, management tools for humanitarian and rescue operations, protection of drinking water network against chemical or biological terrorist attack, tracking system for identification of financial transactions linked to crime or terrorist activities, wireless communication network for emergency and security end-users. The seven supporting activities are complementary, covering some specific fields relating to the coordination of the security network, involvement of SMEs, human behaviour and standardisation. Given the success of the PASR, and in light of the increasing importance of security concerns, security research will be included in FP7, with a total budget of about €1.43 billion. As reported in the last edition of this newsletter, the European Security Research Advisory Board (ESRAB), which comprises of stakeholders to advise the EC on how FP7 research should contribute effectively to citizen's security—has recently published a report.[65]

COOPERATION ON CIVIL AVIATION

EU-India Aviation Summit

The First EU-India Aviation Summit was held on 22nd November 2006 in New Delhi. During the summit Shri Praful Patel, Minister for Civil Aviation and Mr. Jacques Barrot, Vice President, European Commission signed a "Joint Declaration" which laid the foundation for closer cooperation between the EU and India in a range of areas of civil aviation. "Given the strong growth and infrastructure challenges facing India's aviation sector, I am extremely pleased with the prospects of enhancing cooperation in civil aviation with India. The scope for cooperation is huge and will benefit both India and EU industry", said Vice-President Jacques Barrot in New Delhi. Both sides expressed happiness at the prospect of enhancing cooperation in civil aviation with each other.

India is one of the world's fastest growing aviation markets. During the first 10 months of 2006, domestic air passenger traffic in India increased by 50 per cent. Minister Patel and Vice-President Barrot have agreed on two important concrete steps forward in enhancing EU-India aviation relations in the future:

- As a first significant step, the two sides agreed to restore legal certainty to all the bilateral air services agreements between India and EU Member States. Therefore, it was agreed that a "horizontal agreement" would be finalized as a matter of priority. The aim of the "horizontal agreement" will be to amend certain provisions in the bilateral agreements thereby bringing these into conformity with Community law thus restoring legal certainty to these agreements and the operators flying under them.
- Secondly, building on the very successful results achieved under the 1999-2006 "EU-India Civil Aviation Co-operation Project" the two sides agreed to prepare a Joint Action Plan that will set out the key priorities for strengthening future technical and technological cooperation. This Joint Action Plan, which will also be finalized as a matter of priority, and a new technical cooperation programme that will start in 2007 will be important instruments in taking forward the wide range of areas of mutual interest of industry, regulators and the wider public of both sides, as identified during the aviation summit.

The Joint Action Plan will identify the main priority areas for future technical cooperation which will cover aviation safety including strengthening the cooperation with the European Air Safety Agency (EASA), security, airport infrastructure, air traffic management, environmental policy, economic regulation, training and industrial cooperation.

The Ministry of Civil Aviation of India and the European Commission jointly organized the first EU-India Aviation

Summit, which brought together more than 300 leading representatives of the Indian and the European Union aviation sectors representing public authorities, airlines, airports, aerospace industries and service providers.

The Aviation Summit demonstrated the growing importance of the EU-India relations in civil aviation and the excellent collaboration between EU and Indian industries. The EU-India air traffic has increased significantly in recent years. Since 1990, the number of seats available on scheduled non-stop flights between the EU and India has nearly tripled from 2.6 million to 7.4 million in 2006 (+180%). The Indian air transport market is among the world's fastest growing markets with an increase in air travel in the first ten months of 2006 approximately 50 per cent compared to the same period in 2005. The EU-India market is, therefore, of increasing strategic importance to both European and Indian carriers and industry in general.

The EU-India Aviation Summit was highly successful in bringing together all key stakeholders and in serving as a platform for identifying priority areas and ways forward in closer EU-India aviation cooperation for the future.

The Aviation Summit addressed a wide range of areas of mutual interest including notably:

- Aviation safety, security and environmental policies and scope for regulatory cooperation and convergence;
- Market growth and competition;
- Infrastructure needs and sustainable investment opportunities;
- Air traffic management and in this respect the potential for cooperation in the EU's Single European Sky Technology and Industrial programme, SESAR.

In 2004, India and the EU upgraded their already strong relationship into a strategic partnership. An agreed Joint Action Plan in which civil aviation plays a key role underpins this strategic partnership.

Since the adoption of the Joint Action Plan in September 2005, cooperation in the area of civil aviation has been given new impetus. In this context, three rounds of discussions have taken place on a "Horizontal Agreement" proposed by the European Commission and on the possibility of a new technical cooperation programme between India and the EU. It was agreed upon the need for finalization of a "Horizontal Agreement" on priority basis.

Building on the very successful results achieved under the 1999-2006 "EU-India Civil Aviation Co-operation Project", a Joint Action Plan for enhancing future technical and technological cooperation is under preparation. Both sides have agreed to finalise the Joint Action Plan on cooperation in the field of civil aviation on a priority basis. India welcomes the initiative taken by the European aerospace industry in ensuring continuity in certain areas of activities started under the EU-India Civil Aviation Co-operation Project."[66]

EVALUATION

Historically, India and the European Union have had strong ties since the early 1960s. But the relations took concrete shape when India was amongst the first developing countries to establish diplomatic relations with the then six-nation European Economic Community (EEC). As the EEC expanded from the six founding members to 25 in 2004, its relationship with India has also evolved and matured. The 1994 cooperation agreement between both sides gave a fresh impetus to bilateral relations. Together with the Joint Political Statement signed in 1993, it paved the way for annual ministerial meetings and a broad political dialogue.

The European Union (EU) is India's largest trading partner and the second largest source of approved foreign investment. A number of high level visits have been exchanged with the West Europe. India's trade with the countries of the region has grown and there has been a further strengthening of the investment and technology cooperation ties between India and Europe. The diversification and deepening of the economic linkages and continuing political dialogue between the two sides reflects a shared desire to pursue a closer relationship for mutual benefit. The First India-EU Summit in Lisbon in June 2000 marked a watershed in the evolution of this relationship. It highlighted the need for making a joint effort to tap the potential for substantially enhancing trade and investment. Since then there have been summit-level interactions. For India the Summit was a welcome opportunity to be recognized as a truly global player, receiving the same attention as other major partners of the EU. The Summit provided additional impetus to its policy of engaging India on all major issues of interest and concern. It was also a manifestation of the EU's will to engage India as a major player in an emerging multi-polar world and a milestone in EU-India relations. During this Summit the topics discussed covered the entire range of political, economic and global developmental and environmental issues between two democratic, responsible and influential partners on the world stage.

The Fifth EU-India Summit was held on 8 November 2004, in The Hague showed a strong determination to build a solid and broad strategic partnership. The meeting was held in a very friendly atmosphere and the dialogue was open and intense, with many areas of mutual agreement. Leaders officially endorsed the launching of a EU-India "Strategic Partnership". This "Partnership" as more than just the sum of its parts, it sees as a qualitative transformation in the way, which engages as equal partners and work together in partnership with the world at large.

The Sixth EU-India Summit in New Delhi on 7 September 2005 marked a step forward in bringing closer the two global leaders. The Strategic Partnership, issuing a Political Declaration and the decision to implement its dimensions through the adoption of a comprehensive Joint Action Plan, agreed at the summit has provided the momentum to make a decisive step forward, both in content and ambition. The two sides also signed a Framework Agreement paving the way for the Indian participation in the EU's global satellite navigation project, Galileo. It is an important milestone in EU-India relations and provides a clear road map for the coming years.

The Seventh EU-India Summit was held in Helsinki on 13 October 2006 with leaders from the EU and India. During the Summit discussion covered topics such as effective multilateralism, climate change, energy, counter-terrorism, and non-proliferation. A key outcome of the Summit was an agreement on the establishment of a high-level trade group to study and explore ways to deepen the relationship in trade and investment.

Leaders discussed progress since the last summit in 2005 in implementing the Joint Action Plan. Notably, there has been a strong increase in Erasmus Mundus student exchanges, more than double in the 2005-06 academic year.

The outcome of the two EU-India summits so far has stressed the importance of maintaining the momentum towards further trade liberalization and strengthening of the WTO, based on an agenda that adequately reflects the interest of all members of the multilateral trading system. Both sides also agreed that their bilateral cooperation on WTO matters should be put on a more solid and structured basis. The senior officials meet at least twice a year to hold regular, high-level dialogue covering all WTO matters, with a view to identifying common approaches that India and the EU could take on these matters.

Post-independent India until the beginning of the 1990s, followed a trade policy which was heavily influenced by the "Swadeshi" (self-sufficiency) mentality and the "licence raj" , a system of restrictions on production and imports. A second generation of reforms was initiated in 1999 to address issues related to lack of competitiveness, poor infrastructure and over regulation. India has set the ambitious target of an annual 8 per cent sustainable growth besides doubling the per capita income over 10 years.

The trade relationship between EU and India, today has gone beyond pure economic (trade and investment) interests. India-EU economic cooperation takes place through several horizontal programmes of the EU for Asia as well as India-specific programmes. With a view to promote business/industry collaboration, India-EU Partenariat has been organised in the past with the help of economic cooperation instruments of EU, e.g. Asia-Invest. The Partenariat took place in New Delhi in March 1999 bringing together 725 Indian and European companies. This event resulted in 110 agreements concluded between Indian and European SMEs.

India-EU economic relations are structured on the Agreement on Partnership and Development between India and the EU, which became effective from the beginning of 1994. There is an array of bilateral institutions, which derive their mandate from this Agreement and are used by both sides to engage in formal exchange of views and consultations on matters of bilateral interest. A Joint Commission headed by the Commerce Secretary on the Indian side and DG, External relations (Relex) on the EU side functions to facilitate bilateral exchange on important policy issues relating to trade and economic relations.

The cornerstone of European Union's link with India lies in its trade and investment relationship. The EU is India's largest trading and investment partner: the bilateral trade constitutes a quarter of India's total trade while the investment is around 14 per cent of India's total foreign direct investment inflows received during the period 1991 to May 2002. India and the EU have historically played a critical role in creating new international structures, including the World Trade Organization (WTO). The WTO, which came into existence from January 1, 1995, has redrawn the contours of the international trading arena. The WTO agreements relate to bringing about trade liberalization in traditional areas like trade in goods, agriculture and textiles as also new areas such as Trade Related Intellectual Property Rights (TRIPS), Trade Related Investment Measures (TRIMS) and services. Lowering of tariffs and doing away with non-tariff barriers are some of the mechanisms through which greater multilateral trade liberalization is being attempted under the auspices of the WTO.

As the success of the multilateral trading framework rests on cooperation between countries, EU and India have been working together in a number of areas to bring about greater liberalization within the ambit of WTO. At the Doha Ministerial Meeting held in November 2001, the EU was instrumental in launching a new round of comprehensive multilateral trade negotiations to carry the process of trade liberalization further.

The various agreements signed at the conclusion of the Uruguay Round impose certain obligations on individual countries, including India, for compliance within an agreed time frame. The EU is in the process of launching a comprehensive trade and investment development programme in India to further the process of cooperation and share technical expertise on various WTO and other related issues.

In the 1990s, EU cooperation strategy focused on supporting the Indian authorities' own work in identified priority sectors such as primary education and healthcare, with strong emphasis on helping the poorest and most disadvantaged in society. India is becoming an increasingly active player in an evolving development policy: it is recipient and donor, a user of developmental innovations and an exporter of concepts. India's position as an emerging bilateral donor under the "Indian Development Economic Assistance Scheme (IDEAS)" could pave the way for a fruitful EU-India dialogue on optimal implementation of development cooperation in third countries.

Development cooperation in the social sectors, and notably in health and education, is of the utmost importance if India is to achieve the Millennium Development Goals. Traditionally the EC has supported India's own efforts to improve quality of life for the poorest and most disadvantaged members of society. Poverty alleviation has been the central objective in all projects. Since the mid-1990s, EC-India cooperation has been based on identified priority sectors for action: primary education and primary healthcare. This sectoral approach has been complemented by support for focused projects in fields such as rural development, irrigation, forestry, environmental rehabilitation and integrated watershed management.

Education is a priority for EC-India cooperation and the EU's approach is to support the Government's own programmes, especially those that reduce disparities between genders, groups and religions and that favors the poorest and most disadvantaged.

Building on the varied experience of European Commission-India collaboration under DPEP, the EC signed an agreement with the Government of India (GoI) in November 2001 to support the Sarva Shiksha Abhiyan (SSA) programme, the new national initiative for Universalisation of Elementary Education (UEE). Euro 200 million (Rs. 960 crore) has been committed for seven years of implementation. The main objective of the EC grant is to reinforce the GoI's own efforts to universalize elementary education. EC funds will support the GoI to deepen and accelerate the process of reform in the education sector and to pave the way for new initiatives to provide education to the disadvantaged and the deprived, particularly girls.

The EC supported Health and Family Welfare Sector Investment Programme (SIP) is being implemented since October 1998 with the aim of reforming the health care system in India focusing essentially on primary health care services, including first referral institutions, by involving the community. The EU supports the fight against the spread of HIV/AIDS in developing countries through a budgetary programme.

The strategy focuses both on awareness rising to prevent drug abuse and on detoxification, rehabilitation and social reintegration of former drug addicts. Regional cooperation, including the exchange of experience and expertise is one of the main focuses of the EC interventions.

The EC has so far been the biggest donor in the health sector. Based on the success of SIP, the World Bank, DFID, and various other donors are currently preparing a sector support programme for the health sector.

Over the last ten years, the EC has financed 12 Rural Development and Natural Resources Management Projects for a total of €240 million in the following fields: land reclamation; community forestry actions; irrigation and integrated watershed projects; agricultural production and marketing and horticulture development. Poverty alleviation has been the central objective of all the projects.

The EC-India Disaster Preparedness Programme is a €10 million project with a four-year implementation period starting in January 2004.

The EU-India Science & Technology (S&T) Cooperation Agreement was signed on 23 November 2001, at the second EU-India Summit in New Delhi. The agreement is implemented by the Directorate-General for Research for the European Commission and by the Department of Science and Technology for the Government of India. Its aim is to facilitate cooperative research and development activities in science and technology fields of common interests for the community and India.

The EU-India issued "Declaration against International Terrorism" on 23 November 2001 in New Delhi. India and the European Union entered a new phase with both committing to jointly tackle terrorism and enhancing trade and investment. British Prime Minister Tony Blair and Indian Prime Minister Dr. Manmohan Singh launched a joint action plan in this regard at the Sixth India-EU Business Summit held in New Delhi. Both EU and India affirm that international terrorism is a threat to peace and security. It constitutes a challenge to all states and the entire humanity and a grave violation of human rights.

Given their tolerant character, open, democratic and multicultural societies are especially vulnerable to terrorist attacks. The struggle against terrorism is not against any community or faith. All states have a responsibility to refrain from providing moral, material or diplomatic support to acts of terrorism, and prevent the use of their territory for sponsoring terrorist acts against other states. Both EU and India support the adoption on the basis of international law of decisive measures against all states, individuals, and entities, which render support, harbor, finance, instigate or train terrorists or promote terrorism. There can be no religious, ethnic, ideological or any other justification of terrorism. EU and India also support the fight against international terrorism, wherever it occurs and regardless of its motives. EU and India reaffirm the central role of the United Nations in the efforts of the international community in the struggle against terrorism.

Besides that, it focused the importance of strengthening the UN's capacity to play its role in maintaining global peace and development. In this regard, both EU and India have established a Joint Working Group (JWG) on counter-terrorism and to extend support to the Comprehensive Convention on International Terrorism.

Since the adoption of the Joint Action Plan in September 2005, cooperation in the area of civil aviation has been given new impetus. In this context, three rounds of discussions have taken place on a "Horizontal Agreement" proposed by the European Commission and on the possibility of a new technical cooperation programme between India and the EU.

The Ministry of Civil Aviation of India and the European Commission jointly organized the first EU-India Aviation Summit, which brought together more than 300 leading representatives of the Indian and the European Union aviation sectors representing public authorities, airlines, airports, aerospace industries and service providers. The Aviation Summit demonstrated the growing importance of the EU-India relations in civil aviation and the excellent collaboration between EU and Indian industries. Building on the very successful results achieved under the 1999-2006 "EU-India Civil Aviation Cooperation Project", a Joint Action Plan for enhancing future technical and technological cooperation is under preparation. This Joint Action Plan and a new technical cooperation programme to be started in 2007 are important instruments in taking forward cooperation in the wide range of areas of mutual interest of industry, users, regulators and the wider public of both sides, as identified during the EU-India Aviation Summit.

The EU and India are more determined than ever before to broaden and deepen their cooperation. India-EU relations have grown exponentially from what used to be a "purely trade and business driven relationship" to one covering many other potential areas of mutual interest. The message is loud and clear. Both India and EU need to jointly work together to take their relationship to the next higher level of growth.

CHRONOLOGY OF EVENTS

1963: India establishes diplomatic relations with the European Economic Community (EEC).

1970: EC contributes EUR 147 million to Operation Flood Programme in the area of dairy development in India.

1971: EEC introduces general tariff preferences for 91 developing countries including India under the Generalized System of Preferences (GSP) scheme.

1973: India and the EEC sign Commercial Co-operation Agreement.

1976: EC contributes EUR 6 million, for drought-prone areas in U.P. and Gujarat, which marks the beginning of a regular Development Co-operation Programme with India.

1981: India and the EEC sign a five-year Commercial and Economic Co-operation Agreement (16 November).

1982: The Council of EEC Chamber of Commerce is set up.

1983: EC Delegation in India established at New Delhi.

1985: Commercial and Economic Co-operation Agreement is signed between the EEC and India.

1988: EC-India Joint Commission meeting held (March).

1988: Second meeting of EEC-India Industrial Co-operation Working Group held in New Delhi (March).

1988: Mr. Cheysson, member of the European Commission, visits India (24-25 March), meets Prime Minister Rajiv Gandhi, and confirms that the EC was committed to contributing to Phase III (1987-94) of the Operation Flood Programme. The aggregate total of the EC's aid to India comes to EUR 1000 million.

1988: Mr. M. Arunachalam, India's Minister of State for Industrial Development, visits the Commission (June).

1988: Mr. Dinesh Singh, India's Commerce Minister, visits the Commission (September).

1989: Euro-India Co-operation and Exchange Programme (EICEP) for exchange of faculty from management schools is launched.

1990: Mr. Inder Kumar Gujral, India's Minister for External Affairs, visits the Commission, new economic prospects opened up by the single market (March).

1990: EC-India Joint Committee meeting held in Brussels (May), India's Minister for Commerce, Mr. Arun Nehru, confirms India's commitment to strengthening the multilateral trading system.

1991: Following the assassination of Mr. Rajiv Gandhi the European Parliament condemns terrorism and political violence in India and salutes the governments determination to continue with the elections.

1991: Mr. Andriessen visits India, has talks with the Indian Prime Minister, Mr. P.V. Narasimha Rao, on the Uruguay Round and the textiles agreement.

1991: European Community Investment Partners (ECIP) scheme is launched in India to provide financing facility to promote EU-India joint ventures among small and medium-sized enterprises (SMEs) (November).

1992: Technical Office of the EC opened in Nepal (under the charge of the India Delegation).

1992: Fifth meeting between the EC Troika and India held in New Delhi, Mr. Matutes, member of the European Commission represents the Commission; participants welcome the sweeping economic reforms in India (March).

1992: Indian and European businessmen launch a joint initiative, Joint Business Forum (October).

1993: EC supports a major sectoral programme in Education (District Primary Education Programme DPEP) with a funding of EUR 150 million (15 June).

1993: Software Service Support and Education Centre Ltd. (3SE), set up in Bangalore, with the support of the EC, to promote EU-India joint ventures in Information Technology (November).

1993: EC and India sign Joint Political Statement, simultaneously, with the Co-operation Agreement on Partnership and Development (20 December).

1994: New GSP scheme for industrial products introduced (1 January).

1994: The EC Vice-President, Mr. Manuel Marin, visits India (27-29 March), meets the President of India, Dr. Shankar Dayal Sharma.

1994: The European Parliament adopts a resolution on economic and trade relations between India and the EC calling on India to continue its economic reforms.

1994: EU Troika meets the Indian Foreign Minister, Mr. Pranab Mukherjee, in Paris (6 April).

1994: Commission presents the EU's proactive policy towards Asia in a communication— "Towards a New Strategy for Asia" (13 July).

1994: EC-India Co-operation Agreement on Partnership and Development comes into force (1 August).

1994: Eighth meeting of EC-India Joint Committee held (10-11 October).

1994: Setting up of Technology Information Centre (TIC) in Delhi.

1994: Co-operation Agreement signed with Nepal (20 November).

1995: Vice-President of the European Commission, Sir Leon Brittan, visits India (December).

1996: Sir Leon Brittan, inaugurates the European Business Information Centre (EBIC), at Mumbai (January).

1996: Visit of the EU Troika, including Vice-President of European Commission, Mr. Manuel Marin (March).

1996: Co-operation Agreement with Nepal comes into force (1 June).

1996: Commission signs a new protocol on administrative cooperation, with the South Asian Association for Regional Co-operation (SAARC) (10 July).

1996: Commission adopts the communication on EU-India Enhanced Partnership (26 June); the Council approves the Communication (6 December).

1996: India Trade and Investment Forum held in Brussels, during 25 & 26 November, jointly chaired by the EC Vice-President, Mr. Manuel Marin and the Indian Minister of Commerce, Dr. B.B. Ramaiah.

1996: EU India Economic Cross-Cultural programme is launched (26 November).

1996: EC supports another major sectoral programme, in Health and Family Welfare sector with a funding of EUR 200 million.

1996: The Foreign Minister of Bhutan, Mr. Dawa Tsering, visits the Commission in Brussels (4-5 November).

1997: EC-India Joint Committee meeting held in New Delhi (May).

1997: EU-India Troika ministerial meeting held at Luxembourg (2 September). Indian side led by Ms. Kamla Sinha, Minister of State for External Affairs.

1997: Members of the European business community in India launch the Euro Club aimed at promoting business in and with India.

1998: EU-India Economic Cross-Cultural Programme elicits over 400 proposals; 28 projects selected for funding.

1998: Asia-Invest is launched to promote business and mutual understanding between Asia and the European Union (March).

1998: The EU Troika and the Commission take part in a meeting with representatives of the South Asian Association for Regional Co-operation (SAARC), on the sidelines of the UN General Assembly session, in New York (23 September).

1998: Annual ministerial level meeting between the EU Troika, Mr. Marin (for the Commission) and India's Minister of State for External Affairs, Ms. Vasundhara Raje takes place in New Delhi (November).

1998: Asia-Urbs is launched to promote cooperation between the municipal authorities in Asia and European Union.

1999: European Parliament endorses the Commission's Communication on "EU-India Enhanced Partnership" (12 March).

1999: "EU-India Partenariat" organized in New Delhi where more than 300 European small and medium-sized enterprises (SMEs) meet more than 400 India SMEs in one-to-one business meetings over two days (15-16 March).

1999: The Indian Minister for External Affairs, Mr. Jaswant Singh, visits Brussels and meets the EU Commissioner for External Relations, Mr. Chris Patten (September).

1999: The Indian Minister for External Affairs, Mr. Jaswant Singh, participates in EU-India ministerial meeting held in Helsinki where the proposal to launch an EU-India Round Table is formally adopted (December).

2000: The European Commissioner for Trade, Mr. Pascal Lamy, visits Mumbai and New Delhi (3-7 March) and meets the Indian Ministers for Trade and Commerce, Finance, Foreign

Affairs as well as business groups and the academia besides the Governor of the Reserve Bank of India in Mumbai.

2000: Mr. Pascal Lamy, Member of the European Commission responsible for trade, announces agreement on proposal for additional textile imports from India (May).

2000: The first-ever EU-India Summit held in Lisbon on 28 June. The Indian Prime Minister, Mr. Atal Bihari Vajpayee, travels to Lisbon along with a high-powered team including the Ministers for External Affairs, Finance, Trade and Commerce and Information Technology and meets the Prime Minister of Portugal, Mr. Antonio Gueterres, assisted by the Secretary General/High Representative for Common Foreign and Security Policy, Mr. Xavier Solana, and the President of the European Commission, Mr. Romano Prodi. The Portuguese Ministers for Foreign Affairs, Science and Technology and the Deputy Minister for Economy, and the European Commissioners for External Relations, Trade and Research also participated in the Summit. The Summit issued a Joint Declaration along with an Agenda for Action. The EU-India Civil Aviation Cooperation Agreement was signed.

2000: The European Union Film Festival held in New Delhi (6-13 October) and Calcutta (19-25 October). The Festival which had participation on the theme of "The City" with entries from all the 14 of the 15 EU Member States present in India was inaugurated by the Union Minister for Information and Broadcasting, Mrs. Sushma Swaraj, in New Delhi on 6 October.

2000: Continuing on the theme of the film festival ("The City"), the first-ever India-EU Conference, titled "Cities of Tomorrow: India-EU Meet on Sustainable Urban Development" was organized by the missions of the EU Member States and the EC Delegation in India, in collaboration with the New Delhi Municipal Council, School of Planning and Architecture, New Delhi and the Indian National Trust for Art and Cultural Heritage (INTACH) at Vigyan Bhawan, New Delhi (16-18 October). This joint initiative saw the participation of more than 20 European architects, urban planners and scholars with about 600 Indian participants including eminent architects and authorities. The Union Minister for Urban Development,

Mr. Jagmohan, inaugurated the meet and the Chief Minister of Delhi, Mrs. Sheila Dixit, chaired the Valedictory Session.

2001: The EU Commissioner for External Relations, Mr. Chris Patten, visits India (Jan. 25-30) and inaugurates the EU-India Round Table along with the Indian Minister for External Affairs, Mr. Jaswant Singh (Jan. 29). Mr. Patten also meets the Indian Minister for Finance, Mr. Yashwant Sinha, addresses the Indian parliamentarians and the business community and delivers the Jean Monnet lecture organised by the Jawaharlal Nehru University.

2001: On 26 January a devastating earthquake rocks Gujarat in which several thousand people are killed. The visiting Commissioner, Mr. Patten passes on a note of condolence from the President of the European Commission, Mr. Romano Prodi, to the Indian President, Mr. K.R. Narayanan. The ECHO announces an emergency humanitarian assistance of €3 million.

2001: Declaration by the Presidency on behalf of the European Union on the earthquake in India (29 January).

2001: Commission announces a further 10 million for humanitarian assistance for the victims of earthquake in India (01 February).

2001: The eleventh session of the EC-India Joint Commission, co-chaired by Mr. Prabir Sengupta, Commerce Secretary, Government of India and Mr. Guy Legras, Director-General for External Relations, European Commission, takes place in New Delhi (6 February 2001).

2001: The EU Commissioner for Agriculture, Mr. Franz Fischler visits India during April 16-18 and meets the Indian Minister for Agriculture, Mr. Nitish Kumar; Mr. Fischler also visits the Punjab Agricultural University at Ludhiana.

2001: Commission allocates 3.2 million for disaster prevention and preparedness programs in South Asia (26 July).

2001: The second meeting of the EU-India Round Table held in Brussels (16-17 July).

2001: Humanitarian response to the flooding in Orissa—Commission announces €2 million (27 July).

2001: EU-India Think Tank seminar held in Brussels (15-16 October).

2001: Second EU-India Summit held in New Delhi (23 November). The Prime Minister of Belgium, Mr. Guy Verhofstadt, and the President of European Commission, Mr. Romano Prodi, met the Indian leadership led by Prime Minister, Mr. Atal Bihari Vajpayee. The Summit issued a Joint Communique along with an Agenda for Action, and a Declaration against Terrorism. The EU-India Vision Statement on Information Technology and the EU-India Agreement on Science and Technology were highlights.

2002: European Commissioner for Enterprise and the Information Society, Mr. Erkki Liikanen visited India during 10-12 January. He participated in the CII Partnership Summit at Bangalore and also met with a number of key personalities both from the Government and the private sector.

2002: European Commissioner for Development and Humanitarian Aid, Poul Nielson paid an official visit to India from 28 January—2 February. During this visit he toured Madhya Pradesh and Gujarat, besides New Delhi, and took stock of EC supported development and humanitarian programmes in the region.

2002: Ninth European Union Film Festival was held in New Delhi during 5-12 March, followed by Chennai from 12-19 March and Kolkata from 22-31 March. All the 15 Member States of the EU participated in the film festival with films representing a wide variety of themes and cinematographic techniques.

2002: The meeting of the EU-India Sub-Commission on Trade was held in New Delhi on 9 April, 2002. Mr. S.N. Menon, Additional Secretary, Department of Commerce, Ministry of Commerce and Industry headed the Indian Delegation and the EU side was led by Mr. Robert Madelin, Director, DG Trade, European Commission.

2002: Mr. Chris Patten, the European Commissioner for External Relations visited New Delhi on 24 May 2002 and met his Indian counterpart, Mr. Jaswant Singh, Minister for External Affairs. Mr. Patten arrived in New Delhi during his visit to

Afghanistan and Pakistan. He also met Mr. Brajesh Mishra, the National Security Advisor and Mrs. Sonia Gandhi, Leader of the Opposition.

2002: The European Commission presented Country Strategy Paper 2002-2006 for India, which aims to chart out the course for development and economic cooperation between India and the European Commission for the period 2002-06. It is expected that the Budget Authority will make available some €225 million for the forthcoming five year period for EC development and economic cooperation.

2002: The President of the Party of European Socialists (PES) in the European Parliament, Mr. Enrique Baron, visited India during 30-01 October, along with a parliamentary delegation of his group. They met Indian Prime Minister, Mr. Atal Bihari Vajpayee and other Indian Ministers and Members of the Civil Society.

2002: The Third EU-India Summit was held in Copenhagen, Denmark on 10 October. The Prime Minister, Mr. Atal Bihari Vajpayee, assisted by Minister for External Affairs, Mr. Yashwant Sinha, and Minister for Disinvestment, Mr. Arun Shourie, represented India. The Prime Minister of Denmark, Mr. Anders Fogh Rasmussen, represented the EU in his capacity as President of the European Council assisted by the Secretary General/High Representative for CFSP, Mr. Xavier Solana, and the President of the European Commission, Mr. Romano Prodi. The Danish Minister for Foreign Affairs, Mr. Per Stig Moller, and the European Commissioner for External Relations, Mr. Christopher Patten, also participated in the Summit.

2003: EU Troika meets Indian Foreign Ministers in Athens (11 January).

2003: The Fifth EU-India Round Table held in Bangalore, India (8-10 March, 2002).

2003: EU Trade Commissioner Pascal Lamy visits India on 13-14 March to discuss bilateral trade issues as well as the World Trade Organisation's negotiations under the Doha Development Agenda with the Indian leaders.

2003: EU Cultural Weeks 2003 organised in New Delhi, Bangalore, Chennai, Kolkata, Mumbai and Chandigarh (22 November-04 December).

2003: The Fourth EU-India Summit between India and the EU was held in New Delhi, India on 29th November 2003. Prime Minister, Mr. Atal Bihari Vajpayee, represented India. External Affairs Minister Mr. Yashwant Sinha assisted him. The EU was represented by the Presidency of the European Council, Italian Minister of State for External Affairs, Mrs. Margherita Boniver, President of the European Commission, Mr. Romano Prodi, Secretary General/High Representative for Common Foreign and Security Policy Mr. Xavier Solana and the Commissioner for External Relations, Mr. Chris Patten.

2003: The Sixth meeting of the India-EU Round Table took place in Rome during 16-17 December.

2004: EU Trade Commissioner Pascal Lamy visits India on 19 January to enhance trade ties with the EU and to boost the WTO negotiations under the Doha Development Agenda.

2004: EU Commissioner for External Relations Chris Patten visits India on 16 February for a series of European Union (EU) Ministerial Troika (1) meetings. The Troika is led by the Irish Minister of Foreign Affairs, Brian Cowen, accompanied by the Dutch Minister for Foreign Affairs, Dr. Bernard R. Bot.

2004: Visit of Commissioner Erkki Liikanen for the Euro-India 2004 (March 2004).

2004: Commission Communication on "EU-India Strategic Partnership" of June 2004.

2004: The Fifth EU-India Summit was held in The Hague, The Netherlands, on 8 November 2004. The EU was represented by the President of the European Council, Dutch Prime Minister Dr. Jan Peter Balkenende, the President of the European Commission, Dr. Romano Prodi, the Secretary General/High Representative for Common Foreign and Security Policy Mr. Xavier Solana, the Commissioner in charge of Trade Relations, Mr. Pascal Lamy, and the Netherlands Minister for Foreign Affairs, Dr. Bernard Bot. India was represented by the Prime Minister, Dr. Manmohan Singh, the External Affairs Minister,

Mr. Natwar Singh, and the Commerce and Industry Minister, Mr. Kamal Nath.

2005: Visit of Trade Commissioner Peter Mandelson (January 2005).

2005: The Sixth EU-India Summit in New Delhi on 7 September 2005 marked a step forward in bringing closer the two global leaders, EU and India, with the political leadership issuing a Political Declaration along with a Joint Action Plan that spells out in detail the concrete steps both sides must take to transform the bilateral ties to a "Strategic Partnership". The British Prime Minister, Mr. Tony Blair, as the President of the EU Council, and the President of the European Commission, Mr. Jose Manuel Barroso and the High Representative for CFSP, Mr. Xavier Solana, led the European side while the Indian Prime Minister, Dr. Manmohan Singh, led his team. The European Commissioner for External Relations, Mrs. Benita Ferrero-Waldner and the Trade Commissioner, Mr. Peter Mandelson, participated along with the Indian Minister for External Affairs, Mr. Natwar Singh, and the Commerce and Industry Minister, Mr. Kamal Nath. The two sides signed a Framework Agreement paving the way for the Indian participation in the EU's global satellite navigation project, Galileo.

2006: EC Delegation puts up a EU Information Stall in "Kolkata Book Fair" and "New Delhi World Book Fair" (May).

2006: EU Film Festival 2006 in Delhi (3-10 March), Kolkata (17-24 March), Chennai (24-31 March) and Thiruvananthapuram (4-11 April).

2006: Asia-wide conference on AIDS, Malaria and Tuberculosis, New Delhi, (4-7 April).

EU-India Industrial Conference on Energy, 6 April, 2006, Delhi.

Visit of Mr. Andris Piebalgs, Member of the European Commission responsible for Energy (6-7 April).

Members of European Parliament visit to Punjab and Haryana from 15 April.

2006: EU-India Workshop on Infectious Diseases with focus on HIV/TB/Malaria in Bangalore (5-6 June).

2006: Celebration of Europe Day (9 May).

2006: EU Information Seminar for the Indian Media in Ahmedabad (4-5 August) and Guwahati (7-8 August).

2006: Visit of the President of the European Parliament, Mr. Josep Borrel Fontelles, to India (September-October 06).

Seventh EU-India Summit in Helsinki, Finland (13 October).

Humanitarian Aid: Commission allocates €4 million for victims of floods in India & Bangladesh (6 November 2006).

2007: Eighth India-EU annual summit (30 November).

2007: First India-EU Ministerial Science Conference in New Delhi.

2008: Ninth EU-India summit (29 September).

2009: EU-India sign joint declaration on multilingualism (23 official languages).

NOTES

1. Origins: EU-India Relations
http://ec.europa.eu/comm/external relations/india/intro/index.htm
2. *Ibid.*
3. *Ibid.*
4. Partners in Progress
http://www.delind.cec.eu.int/en/political dialogue/introduction.htm
5. India: Country Strategy Paper
http://www.delind.cec.eu.int/en/features/csp india.htm
6. EU-India Summits: Lisbon, June 28, 2000
http://ec.europa.eu/comm/external relations/india/intro/summ index.htm
7. Joint Declaration: 1st EU-India Summit
http://ec.europa.eu/comm/external relations/india/summit 06 00/joint declaration.htm
8. Civil Society Relationship
http://ec.europa.eu/comm/external relations/india/intro/political dial.htm
9. India-EU Round Table
http://ec.europa.eu/comm/external relations/india/intro/political dial.htm
10. Commissioner Chris Patten's visit to India, 25-29 January 2001
http://ec.europa.eu/comm/external relations/india/intro/political dial.htm
11. India-EU Round Table
http://ec.europa.eu/comm/external relations/india/intro/political dial.htm

12. Second EU-India Summit, New Delhi, 23 November 2001
http://ec.europa.eu/comm/external relations/india/sum11 01/index.htm

13. Third EU-India Summit, Copenhagen, 10 October 2002
http://ec.europa.eu/comm/external relations/india/sum10 02/index.htm

14. EU-India Business Summit
http://ec.europa.eu/comm/external relations/india/intro/political dial.htm#3

15. Fourth EU-India Summit, New Delhi, 29 November 2003 and Commissioner Patten's visit to India, 27-29 November 2003
http://ec.europa.eu/comm/external relations/india/intro/political dial.htm#3

16. Fifth EU-India Summit, The Hague, 8 November 2004
http://ec.europa.eu/comm/external relations/india/intro/political dial.htm#3

17. India-EU Strategic Partnership Joint Action Plan, 7 September 2005
http://www.europa-eu-un.org/articles/sv/article 5018 sv.htm

18. Sixth EU-India Summit, Delhi, 7 September 2005
http://ec.europa.eu/comm/external relations/india/sum09 05/index.htm

19. Seventh India-EU Summit
http://www.indembassybern.ch/pdf-download/India%20News%20Oct,%202006.pdf.

20. India's Trade and Economic Policy
http://ec.europa.eu/trade/issues/bilateral/countries/india/index en.htm

21. EU-India Joint Action Plan http://ec.europa.eu/comm/external relations/india/eco/index.htm

22. EU-India Economic Cross Cultural Programme (ECCP)
http://www.eudelindia.org/en/eco/eccp/eccp.htm

23. EU-India Small Projects Facility Programme (SPF)
http://www.eudelindia.org/en/eco/spf/spf.htm

24. EU-India Economic Cooperation
http://ec.europa.eu/comm/external relations/india/eco/index.htm

25. India's Trade Relations with European Union Countries
http://commerce.nic.in/annual2004-05/englishhtml/lesson-9.htm

26. India-European Union
http://meaindia.nic.in/onmouse/eu1.htm

27. Fifth India-EU Summit at The Hague

28. EU-India Business Dialogue
http://ec.europa.eu/enterprise/enterprise policy/business dialogues/india/eu india overview.htm

29. Third India-EU Business Summit, Plenary Session 3 Copenhagen, 9 October 2002.

30. EU-India Trade Relations
http://www.eudelindia.org/en/trade/trade.htm

31. EU's Views on the Doha Development Agenda Negotiations under the auspices of the WTO
http://www.eudelindia.org/en/trade/wto/index.htm

32. EU and India - Key WTO Partners
http://www.eudelindia.org/en/trade/key wto partners.htm

33. EU and India Investment
http://www.eudelindia.org/en/trade/investment.htm

34. Bilateral Trade Relations
http://ec.europa.eu/trade/issues/bilateral/countries/india/index en.htm

35. EU-India Joint Initiative for Trade and Service
http://www.eudelindia.org/en/trade/joint initiative.htm

36. Business Contacts & Services
http://www.eudelindia.org/en/trade/business contacts.htm

37. Bilateral Trade Relations
http://ec.europa.eu/trade/issues/bilateral/countries/india/index en.htm

38. EU and India Development Cooperation
http://ec.europa.eu/comm/external relations/india/intro/dev.htm

39. EU and India Development Cooperation: Education Sarva Shiksha Abhiyan
http://www.eudelindia.org/en/dev/education/ssa.htm

40. EU and India District Primary Education Programme (DPEP)
http://www.eudelindia.org/en/dev/education/dpep.htm

41. The Education Guarantee Scheme (EGS)
http://www.eudelindia.org/en/dev/education/egs.htm

42. Programme for Enrichment of School Level Education (PESLE)
http://www.eudelindia.org/en/dev/education/pesle.htm

43. Health: Support to Health and Family Welfare; Fight Against HIV/AIDS; Campaign Against Drug Abuse
http://www.eudelindia.org/en/dev/index.htm

44. Development Cooperation
http://ec.europa.eu/comm/external relations/india/intro/dev.htm

45. Science and Technology Agreement
http://ec.europa.eu/comm/external relations/india/intro/science.htm

46. EU-India Science and Technology Cooperation: First Steering Committee Meeting
http://www.eudelindia.org/en/stcoop/steering comm meeting first.htm

47. EU-India Science and Technology Cooperation: Second Steering Committee Meeting
http://www.eudelindia.org/en/stcoopsteering comm meeting second.htm

48. EU-India Cooperation in Science and Technology
http://www.eudelindia.org/en/stcoop/stcoop.htm

49. The Fourth RTD Framework Programme— 1994-1998
http://cordis.europa.eu/guidance/fp4 en.html
50 Fifth RTD Framework Programme
http://cordis.europa.eu/fp5/src/over.htm
51. Sixth Framework Programme (FP 6)—Introduction
http://www.eudelindia.org/en/stcoop/fp6 introduction.htm
52. The Seventh Framework Programme (FP7) 2007-2013: Building Knowledge Europe
http://www.eudelindia.org/en/stcoop/fp7 introduction.htm
53. The EU Fights against the Scourge of Terrorism
http://ec.europa.eu/justice home/fsj/terrorism/fsj terrorism intro en.htm
54. Declaration against International Terrorism, New Delhi, 23 November 2001
http://meaindia.nic.in/event/2001/11/23event01.htm#6
55. EU Vows Support for India's Fight against Terror (PTI 23-11-2003, New Delhi).
56. EU Action in Response to 11th September 2001: One Year After
http://ec.europa.eu/comm/external relations/110901/me02 187.htm
57. *The Hindu,* New Delhi, 30 November 2003.
58. Fourth India-EU Summit: Joint Press Statement 29/11/2003
http://meaindia.nic.in/declarestatement/2003/11/29js01.htm
59. Joint Press Statement for Fifth India-EU Summit
http://www.delind.cec.eu.int/en/political dialogue/summits/fifth/joint press statement.pdf.
60. EU-India Joint Action Plan: Implementation Report
http://pmindia.nic.in/visits/content.asp?id=140
61. EU-India Political Dialogue: Milestones
www.eudelindia.org/en/political dialogue/milestones.htm - 64k
62. "India-EU to Intensify Fight against Terror", *The Tribune,* Chandigarh, 7 September 2005.
63. 5th Anniversary of the Terrorist Attacks in the United States—Statement of President José Manuel Barroso on behalf of the European Commission, Brussels, 11 September 2006.
64. India-EU Joint Statement, October 13, 2006 Helsinki, Finland
http://pmindia.nic.in/visits/content.asp?id=139
65. PASR 2006: 15 New Security Research Projects to Combat Terrorism
http://europa.eu/rapid/pressReleasesAction.do?reference=MEMO/06/375&format=HTML&aged=0&language=EN&guiLanguage=en
66. India and the EU Agree to Strengthen Cooperation in Civil Aviation
http://pib.nic.in/release/rel print page.asp?relid=22238